Beyond
Treason

They were betrayed and abandoned by
their government

Reflections on the Cover-up of the June 1967 Israeli Attack on the USS Liberty an American Spy Ship

Our Middle East Foreign Policy
Quagmire

By

Robert J. Allen, J.D.

Liberty after the attack

Table of Contents

Copyright

Illustrations, Photos, Internet Links

The reader can use Google's search engine to look for more pictures related to the USS *Liberty*. Search for **Photos USS Liberty**.

The following Internet links will take the reader to various websites where documents, discussed herein, dealing the attack on the USS *Liberty* can be found. One link is supportive of the Israeli claim of mistake and another two are *Liberty* supported sites. Additionally, there is a link to the U.S. Department of State Office of the History where documents can be found. Finally, there is a link to the LBJ Library and U.S. Naval photo archive. Caveat: Internet website links maybe subject to change.

http://www.ussliberty.org

http://www.usslibertyinquiry.com

http://www.thelibertyincident.com

http://history.state.gov/historicaldocuments/johnson

http://www.lbjlibrary.org

http://www.history.navy.mil/photos/sh-usn/usnsh-l/agtr5.htm

http://www.nsa.gov/public_info/declass/index.shtml

Acknowledgements

I would like to acknowledge and thank those *Liberty* survivors and supporters who were so courteous to a stranger, answered questions and provided information pertaining to their saga and quest for justice. It was a true honor to be able to attend their 37th annual reunion.

Glossary and Acronyms

ACRP: Airborne Reconnaissance Program

AFSS: Air Force Security Service

AGTR: Auxiliary General Technical Research

CHOP: Slang for transferring command

CIA: Central Intelligence Agency

CINCEUR: Naval Commander in Chief Europe

CNO: Chief Naval Operations

COI: Court of Inquiry

COMINT: Communications Intelligence

CPA: Closest Point of Approach

CRITIC: High Speed Communication System

CTs: Communication Technicians

C-130: Air Force Electronic Surveillance Aircraft

DIA: Defense Intelligence Agency

DMZ: Demilitarized Zone

DTG: Date Time Group

EC-121: Navy US Electronic Surveillance Aircraft

ECM: Electronic Counter Measures

ELINT: Electronic Intelligence

FOIA: Freedom of Information Act

G-Group: Group within the NSA

GOI: Government of Israel

HUMINT: Human Intelligence

IDF: Israeli Defense Forces

JAG: Military Judge Advocate General

JCS: Joint Chiefs of Staff

JRC: Joint Reconnaissance Command

LVA: Liberty Veterans Association

MI5: British Internal Intelligence Service

MI-6: British Foreign Intelligence Service

MOSSAD: Israeli Intelligence Service

NCI: Naval Court of Inquiry

NFOIO: Naval Field Operational Intelligence Office

NSA: National Security Agency

NSG: Naval Security Group

PFIAB: President's Foreign Intelligence Advisory Board

PIM: Planned Intended Movement Report

PLO: Palestinian Liberation Organization

PTSS: Post Traumatic Stress Syndrome

SIGINT: Signal Intelligence

SIOP: Launch Procedure for Carrier Jets with Nukes

SITREP: Situation Report

TF-60: U.S. Naval Task Force 60

TPC: Technical Processing Center

TRS: Technical Research Ship

TRSSCOMM: Satellite Communication Dish on USS Liberty

UAR: United Arab Republic

UHF: Ultra High Radio Frequency

UNEF: United Nations Emergency Force

USN-855: Naval Security Group

USSR: Union Socialist Soviet Russia

VHF: Very High Radio Frequency

ZULU: Military Time Designation

Dedication

This work is dedicated to the victims of the 1967 Israeli attack on the USS *Liberty* and the U.S. cover-up, dead and living; and to those still seeking the truth. They are the real heroes in the struggle to preserve the *Rule of Law* not letting it become victim to politicians who lack the courage and understanding to know where the real strength of a democracy lies.

Author's Approach

This book is about a massive on-going government cover-up of the killing and wounding of American service personnel by a fledging ally. The consequence of which is that important government documents have either been destroyed or continue to be suppressed notwithstanding many Freedom of Information Act (FOIA) requests having been filed over the years—in short an apparent obstruction of justice. Issues of foreign policy and national security as well as being a matter of political cover for politicians complicate this matter.

The event being researched is the June 8, 1967 Israeli attack on the USS *Liberty*, an American intelligence gather ship off the coast of the Sinai in the Eastern Mediterranean during the Arab-Israeli Six-day War. While much time has elapsed since those events, the topic is still of interest as new information continues to dribble out. A number of authors have written about the Israeli attack on the USS *Liberty* and each has provided bits and pieces of the puzzle. Attention is directed toward those authors for nuances and those nuances are verified to the extent possible. The author's challenge is to ferret out facts pertaining to a public event that has provoked allegations of murder and war crimes.

In the course of events with the passage of time there have been efforts at misinformation and disinformation, in essence "an information war" with those claiming an intentional attack, and those contending the attack was a case of mistaken identity—a *friendly-fire* incident—something that can occur in the *fog-of-war*. Most importantly, the matter of the attack is a certainty, and who perpetrated it is a matter of certainty. The ship's crew

xiii

and families have suffered physically, psychologically, as well has having lost faith in their government who they feel has abandoned them.

Many of the important players of the time have since died, and some have refused to fully comment or discuss what happened on that fateful day on June 8, 1967 for various reasons including fear, loss of pension or other punishment (feasible or not), and even out of loyalty for their country and to an overriding sense of duty. In jest, one CT (communications technician) survivor, when I asked about the ship's mission, said he could tell me but then he would have to kill me. I never did get a straight answer. For those who have come forward with information they should be praised for their story is still incomplete.

Probably the most important issue is that certain questions have not been raised by the American public, the media, or the Congress of the United States—that beg asking. It is therefore the intent of this author to raise some of those questions even though the definitive answers continue to elude the many researchers. However, the questions themselves suggest the answer or possible answers and are an important process in its own right. Any good investigator needs to know how to raise the right questions—that is our purpose here. The investigative process should not be obstructed by intimidation or temerity. Several key questions are summarized here:

1. Was the attack the result of "mistaken identity" as claimed by the Israeli government, or was it an intentional act aimed at destroying the ship and crew?

2. Did the attack and killing of crewmembers constitute a prima facie case of war crimes including murder and assault?

3. Was the ship really a "neutral" ship, or did the U.S. government have an involvement in the Six-Day War on the side of Israel that had to be covered-up?

4. If there was a basis for alleging war crimes, and there was a U.S. cover-up, does the cover-up constitute a continuing obstruction of justice, conspiracy, or worse?

5. Did President Johnson fail in his duties as Commander-in-Chief, thereby abandoning and betraying the crew at a time when they were in harm's way?

6. Did the failure to render timely aid to the crew result in unnecessary deaths and suffering?

7. Was the USS *Liberty* setup for a "Gulf of Tonkin" like pretext to justify American intervention in the Six-day War on behalf of Israel to counter a Soviet threat?

8. Did the Congress of the United States participate in an on-going cover-up thereby failing in its constitution duty of over-sight?

The author is a retired 27-year law enforcement officer and retired attorney with training and experience in the development of investigative facts and evidence. At the outset, it is fair to say that the United States government has not officially conducted a complete forensic criminal investigation into the attack on the *Liberty* as it did in the USS *Cole* case. There was no effort to conduct interviews with participating Israeli military personnel; in fact, investigators were specifically denied this opportunity by representatives of the U.S. government. The handling of the *Liberty* and *Cole* incidents is an example of mirror-opposites.

Here we use the term "forensic" in the context of bolstering a case, position or argument before a court or before the public as in a debate.

For their part, the Israelis handled their investigation into the attack within their military system claiming there was "no prima facie evidence" of wrongdoing that would warrant formal charges, and in fact actually found fault with the U.S. government for not moving the ship from the area or at least advising Israel of its presence in the war zone. A prima facie standard is a very low standard by which to judge conduct in terms of whether it involves wrongdoing; simply put, it would be a slam-dunk case for any competent prosecutor to establish probable cause to believe that a crime or crimes had been committed. Here the tenor is "white-wash" to facilitate a political/military cover-up by the three governmental powers involved, the United States, Israel and USSR. Once the government decides to stone-wall, it takes enormous time and effort to overcome the withholding of information. The "System" seeks to protect itself and that usually means a cursory "internal affairs" review that is a clear-cut conflict of interest. There has been no congressional or judicial review of events within the civilian concept of free and open government—a failure of the concept of governmental "checks-and-balances".

Perhaps the best guide for the reader is to follow the idiom *res ipsa loquitor* or let the facts speak for themselves. Understanding the *Liberty* story is a key to understanding our strange and special relationship with the State of Israel, and our confusing Middle East foreign policy, or lack of a coherent policy. After years of supporting dictators in the Middle East, we are now witnessing historical events as these populations try to control their own political and economic destiny—the *Arab Spring* as it has become known. In essence, our policy of promoting "stability" via dictators rather than supporting human rights is failing—resulting in an embarrassment for the United States.

Clearly, a major objective of our foreign policy, rightly so, is to protect our oil interest as we are dependent on a Middle Eastern supply. The Mediterranean area and Africa, once tribal fiefdoms is now a collection of artificially created nations as a result of the U.S. and European powers controlling a partitioning and colonizing process over the last two centuries.

Our foreign policy is further subject to questioning regarding the matter of our handling Colonel Muammar Muhammad al Gaddafi of Libya. We came to an understanding with Gaddafi who was accused of terrorism, notwithstanding the fact that an intelligence agent from Libya was convicted of being responsible for the bombing of Pan Am flight 103 over Lockerbie, Scotland on Wednesday, December 21, 1988 with the loss of 270 individuals. Gaddafi never acknowledged any responsibility, however, Libya paid damages and subsequently, upon abandoning Libya's nuclear program, he was politically recognized by western powers with companies allowed to do business with that country. The intelligence agent, Abdelbaset al-Megrahi, was released for health reasons—he is now deceased. Now, during the recent uprising the claim has been made that Gaddafi, himself, had ordered the bombing. The media now reports that the U.N. is opening another investigation of Gaddafi. Based on current events he had been charged with crimes against humanity.[1] The point is that our government, for pragmatic reasons is willing to overlook terrorism and murder when it is in our apparent political and foreign policy interests. This example of Machiavellian pragmatism is not the first. As events unfolded, Gaddafi was removed from power and assassinated by his own people.

Wikipedia, the Internet encyclopedia site, offers a good summary of events dealing the Lockerbie bombing, refer to http://en.wikipedia.org/wiki/Pan_Am_Flight_103.

As a side note: At the time of the attack on the USS *Liberty* there were no ubiquitous personal computers or Internet to facilitate communication between *Liberty* survivors to keep them together as a cohesive group able to press their rights as Americans. However, in recent years information technology has made it possible to better research the issues. For example, various search engines such as Google make it easier to obtain information. Google Earth allows the researcher and reader to do a fly-over of the area of interest and to spot various features on the ground and measure distances. Finally, the technology even allows one to use Google to translate from one language to another and search foreign sites on the Internet. As an example, the Soviets played a major role in the Six-Day War drama and now documents in Russian and other languages can be instantaneously translated via your personal computer—a matter for personal research. Still, this does not penetrate the secret archives of the three government's active in this historical cover-up.   Try Googling the words *treason and USS Liberty*.

With you, the reader on board we will open the *Liberty Affair* as a research "cold case file"; after all, one would think that transparency in government is a good thing— the bureaucrats may disagree. The governments of the United States and Israel have effectively setup a firewall around the attack on the *Liberty*. Individuals with knowledge are dying off because of age, or are already deceased; and classified documents remain undisclosed while memories are fading. Additionally, the Navy Court of Inquiry was inept and ordered to participate in a cover-up; and crewmembers were ordered not to discuss details of the attack under threat of various penalties. Further, crewmembers, as military personnel, felt duty bound to their oath of allegiance to the country to follow orders. Perhaps, just as the Israelis felt duty bound, to follow their orders. Over the years there have developed important cracks in the so-called *wall-of-silence*. It was thought a lesson had been learned from the Nuremberg Trials, on the defeat of Nazi Germany, that following orders has its limit subject to a higher code and standard, that of the *Rule of Law* and the *Law of War*. Unfortunately, when it comes to the government, the rule is given lip service when other priorities come into play that conflict with it. Key individuals in high political office, in positions of command and control, claim "lack of memory" and the cover of "plausible deniability"—a euphemism for the end justifies the means.

Prologue

Legal Definition of Treason

The content of this book deals with a number of controversial issues and claims, in particular dealing with the actions of a former and now deceased President of the United States, Lyndon Baines Johnson, the 36th President of the United States.[2] There are inferences of treason and violation of his responsibilities as Commander-in-Chief involving the covering-up of alleged murder and war crimes committed against United States service personnel in the 1960s. An adjunct important and timely issue deals with the powers of the President and the extent to which he is entitled to the executive privilege and immunity from legal process. These issues are an undercurrent to the story of the Israeli attack on the USS *Liberty* and the subsequent, claimed cover-up. Consequently, some definitional references are in order.

It has not been often, thank goodness, that the country has had to confront the issue to treason. Most recently, allegations of aiding the enemy have emerged regarding the disclosure of so-called secret government documents as in the case of *WikiLeaks* and Julian Assange, who some are of the opinion should be charged under the 1917 Espionage Act.[3] Additionally, Army Pvt. Bradley Manning is now facing indictment or court-martial for aiding the enemy for his part in the disclosure of classified documents. He was arrested in May of 2010 while in Iraq on suspicion of passing classified documents to the whistleblower website, *WikiLeaks*.[4] Like the disclosure of the *Pentagon Papers* by Daniel Ellsberg during the Vietnam War, the government makes much noise with little coming of it, in part because of First Amendment rights. Now 40 years later the *Pentagon Papers* have been declassified.[5] Neither Manning nor Assange have been convicted as of yet, although Manning has been detained in a military prison. Some believe that the government is too quick to place a "top secret" label on documents and too slow to release them under the Freedom of Information Act. This latter point will be a problem confronting research into the attack and cover-up.

A case in point is the trial of Vice President Aaron Burr for treason in the early part of the 19th century, based on allegations put forth by President Thomas Jefferson. Burr was alleged to have coveted certain lands in the West. Chief Justice John Marshall held that there was no evidence to convict Burr in view of the fact that Jefferson refused to honor a subpoena for certain papers, claiming that the President alone had the right to decide what papers should be made available. Marshall held that Jefferson was indeed subject to the subpoena, supporting the contention that even the President is subject to the law. As will be noted, this issue will again arise during the Presidency of Richard Nixon, who was of the opinion that whatever the President did was not illegal. There is a tidbit of truth in the contention that "Power tends to corrupt, and absolute power corrupts absolutely. Great men are almost always bad men."[6]

The bottom line in the Burr trail was that the Constitution required the testimony of two witnesses to an "overt act", in Burr's case of waging war.

From a definitional standpoint, treason is an elusive term. According to the *Merriam Webster Dictionary*, it is fundamentally a betrayal of trust. The U.S. Constitution and case law provides a more definitive definition:

Definition of Treason: A breach of allegiance to one's government, usually committed through levying war against such government or by giving aid or comfort to the enemy. The offense of attempting by overt acts to overthrow the government of the state to which the offender owes allegiance; or of betraying the state into the hands of a foreign power. Treason consists of two elements: adherence to the enemy, and rendering him aid and comfort. Cramer v. U. S., U.S.N.Y., 325 U.S. 1, 65 S.Ct. 918, 9327 89 L.Ed. 1441. See 18 U.S.C.A. § 2381.

A person can be convicted of treason only on the testimony of two witnesses, or confession in open court. Art. III, Sec. 3, U.S. Constitution.

So, does the charge against Bradley Manning for "aiding the enemy" smack of definitional treason, chargeable as a felony punishable by death. It is a legal not emotional issue. The word "treason" can have several connotations, but the simplest to understand is that it connotes "a breach of trust". It is one thing to throw the term "treason" around without understanding its ramifications or limitations as applied in any particular setting. Simply put, from a legalistic standpoint the term may not apply in the broader context. This does not preclude other legal constraints from being applied to a particular set of circumstances, i.e., the application of the other criminal statutes.

The powers of the President of the United States have been a topic of constitutional discussion and debate since the country was formed. The extent and limitation on those powers is subject to interpretation in the context of various crises facing the country. In the aftermath of 9/11 President G. W. Bush took the country to war in Iraq under the falsehood that Iraq was a direct and imminent threat to the United States, because allegedly, Saddam Hussein possessed weapons of mass destruction—which subsequently were not to be found.

The contention has been made that Bush's actions in conjunction with Secretary of Defense Donald Rumsfeld, Vice President Cheney, National Security Advisor Rice, and Secretary of State Powell constituted a fraud on the citizens of the United States and that a pretext was developed to lead the country into a "preemptive war". An interesting book was published by a former U.S. Assistant Attorney laying out a probable cause basis for indicting the above individuals under Title 18, United States Code, and Section 371, which prohibits conspiracies to defraud the United States. The book *U.S. v. Bush* by Elizabeth de la Vega is a hypothetical argument paraphrased in the legal constraint of a legal indictment.[7] In short, the issue is whether or not the President's power is unrestricted or subject to various constitutional constraints including the Rule of Law. The author's objective was to present in a Grand Jury hearing format the issues and evidence to hold the President accountable for his actions or lack of action. Ultimately, the key question is whether the American people and Congress have the will to hold the executive accountable—a political as well as legal conundrum.

Elizabeth de la Vega is not the only legal writer to allege abuse of power against Bush. Vincent Bugliosi, a former Los Angeles prosecutor who prosecuted the Charles Manson case, has constructed a legal framework for the prosecution of G. W. Bush for murder.[8] In short, Bugliosi's position is that Bush lied to the country and led us to an unjust war where thousands were killed and this exceeded his authority under the law. He challenges the premise that the "King can do no wrong", a fundamental principle of English Law.

There is no doubt in Bugliosi's mind that even the President of the United States is not immune from the criminal law even while acting within the scope of his office. He agrees, however, that the President cannot be criminally prosecuted until he is out of office. Nevertheless, his actions while in office are subject to his being impeached under the Constitution.

The case against G. W. Bush and certain members of his administration is not hypothetical. Human Rights Watch as of July 2011 is calling for an investigation of Bush and his administration and accuses President Obama of not following through with his obligation under the Convention against Torture to investigate acts of torture and other ill-treatment of detainees. HRW notes the 107-page report, *Getting Away with Torture: The Bush Administration and Mistreatment of Detainees*, presents substantial information warranting criminal investigations of Bush and senior administration officials, including former Vice President Dick Cheney, Defense Secretary Donald Rumsfeld, and CIA Director George Tenet, for ordering practices such as "water-boarding," the use of secret CIA prisons, and the transfer of detainees to countries where they were tortured.[9] This program goes under the name of "extraordinary rendition".[10]

The term Rule of Law does not have a precise definition. Generally, it can be understood as a legal-political regime under which the law restrains the government by promoting certain liberties and creating order and predictability in how a government will conduct itself. In essence, it is a system of law that attempts to protect the rights of citizens from arbitrary and abusive use of government power. The concept will be severely tested to the extent that we are faced with being placed in a state of "perpetual war" against terrorism by our leaders.

Along this vain the issue of the President's power and grant of immunity was dealt with in the case of *United States v. Nixon*, 418 U.S. 683 (1974), which was not a hypothetical case. In this case, the argument centered on a subpoena for the production of documents requested by a Special Prosecutor. Held: The President's executive privilege is not absolute and must bend to Amendment 4 and Amendment 5 requirements of speedy and fair trials and of the ability of defendants to face their accusers. Courts are not required to proceed against the President as if the President was any other individual. Courts should review communications claimed to be privileged in camera (by the judge only in chambers).[11]

In the instance case of the Israeli attack on the USS *Liberty*, we will raise the issue of whether or not the Johnson administration, including the President himself, engaged in a conspiracy to obstruct justice, or worse, destroying evidence of crimes against United States military personnel. The key objective, like the hypothetical case against President Bush would be to have the Congress recognize the seriousness of the matter and hold long overdue hearings to find the underlying cause of the attack on the *Liberty*. Ultimately, the issue is not whether the technical term "treason" applies to the cover-up of the attack on the USS *Liberty*, but whether our service personnel were murdered and maimed while performing their duty on behalf of this country, the American citizens, and who bears responsibility. Did the President as Commander-in-chief adhere to his duty and oath of office?

A look at the map indicates why there has always been conflict here. This relatively small country constitutes a permanent crossroads of three continents. Thus it is subject to the strains and pulls of the world politics. In our time, oil, Soviet ambitions in the Middle East, the interests of the United States, Britain and France are far more responsible for maintaining the tension than the largely bogus pretext of Arab nationalism. If the Great Powers genuinely wanted peace, there would be no Arab-Israel conflict.

David Ben-Gurion, "Memoirs", 1970, World Publishing Co., page 68.

Introduction

The simple fact is that they admitted it. They had to after being caught red handed. The evidence did not sink to the bottom of the Mediterranean and there were witnesses.

The Israeli government admitted to the June 8, 1967 attack by Israeli Defense Forces on the American "spy" ship USS *Liberty*—the *Liberty* was a SIGINT or signals intelligence gathering ship.[12] In that attack, on an American ship in the Eastern Mediterranean, 34 military personnel including a civilian crewmember were killed, and 175 were wounded, with enough damage to the ship to end her useful service life. Among the 34 dead, 33 were naval personnel and one was a civilian employee of the National Security Agency—the NSA. The ship had a crew compliment of 290 officers and men including three civilian linguists. The number of wound has varied from 171 to 175 depending on the source. For years, the number wounded was reported as 171.

An April 9, 2012 e-mail response from former LVA President and survivor Gary Brummett now puts the number of wounded at 175. This number has changed a couple times in the last three months. Another survivor was recently found to have a couple small pieces of shrapnel in his back and will qualify for a Purple Heart. Elsewhere herein, I will use the number of 175 when referring to the number wounded.

A sterile diplomatic apology was made by the Government of Israel (GOI), without admitting culpability, and eventually, after some haggling compensation was paid to the families of the dead, and to the wounded for their injuries. The reported amount was 6.7 million dollars. Years later, during the presidency of Jimmie Carter, after more political pressure and haggling, the United States government received payment for the damage to the ship from the government of Israel in the reported sum of six million dollars. In view of the vast amounts of foreign aid provided to the State of Israel, one can speculate as to whom actually made these damage payments—was it the Unites States taxpayers?

In the aftermath of the attack by planes of the Israeli Air Force and motor torpedo boats of the Israeli Navy, some 40 plus years later, survivors continue to suffer a life time of trauma and the sense of abandonment by their government with no forum or remedies "apparently" available to redress the injustices suffered. For them justice is not measured in dollars. There is a lingering sense of betrayal by their then President and Commander-in-Chief, and the Congress of the United States. Subsequent presidents and congresses have perpetrated this injustice claiming no new evidence exists to warrant opening the matter for further investigation. It is no surprise that many of the crew suffer from posttraumatic stress syndrome; however, it is disconcerting to have the claim of PTSS used against them to undermine the survivors' credibility as witnesses—more on this later. After the passage of years as new information slowly emerges, the witnesses and victims to the event are now passing away due to age. Memories are fading and documents have become lost or destroyed—evidence of possible crimes committed at the governmental level.

To put matters into context, I had requested and received, a documentary video entitled *Loss of the Liberty*. With it, on USS Liberty Veterans Association stationary, was a personal comment by former LVA president, Phillip Tourney, noting: "No one should be allowed to get by with cold blooded murder not even Israel!"

Despite efforts by both the United States government and government of Israel to sweep the incident under the rug with the continuing cloak of official secrecy, the matter still lingers today, more actively than ever—after more than forty years. An open festering wound continues to exist in many quarters adversely affecting relationships between both countries—to some extent mitigated with the passage of time and the need to deal with real world crisis in the Middle East region. A simple question is do we spy on each other? Former U.S. government officials will claim that because of our special relationship with Israel that our national security has been undermined for political reasons at the presidential level.

The attack on the USS *Liberty* raises many questions, some answered, but more remain part of a continuing mystery. What was the ship doing so close to a war zone without an armed escort and adequate means of self-defense? What was the mission of the ship and crew, and was it really a *neutral* ship in international waters as claimed? Why was the ship attacked without efforts to adequately identify her and provide warning prior to the attack? It is claimed by surviving crewmembers that they had been under continuous air surveillance for hours prior to the attack. Why did the attack continue when identification became an issue? What is the hold that the government of Israel has on the government of the United States that would prevent a full and open hearing into the circumstances of the attack and the reasons for it? Did President Lyndon Baines Johnson breach his oath of office as President and Commander-in-Chief by his abandonment of the ship and crew by ordering the return of planes sent to her location for defensive cover? Did the recall of carrier planes sent to cover and aid the *Liberty* add to the death and wounded toll? Did his actions constitute treason or betrayal as alleged by some? Was President Johnson a victim of poor advice from his subordinates, perhaps some who had their own agenda? To these questions, add the question of whom in the Israel government hierarchy ordered the attack, and what was the reason or motive for such drastic action.

Did President Johnson, by his failure to hold Israel accountable commit an act of moral and political cowardice, and did the Congress of the United States fail in its constitutional "over-sight" responsibilities, again because of moral and political cowardice, or worse, being compromised by fear of the Jewish Lobby in this country? Could it be that Israel was in a position to blackmail the U.S. government and Johnson administration because of our covert involvement with Israeli intelligence leading up to the Six-Day War—to bring about a regime change in Egypt?

These are just a few of the questions that remain unresolved to this day with much conjecture, controversy and opinion. Shortly after the attack the U.S. media took a cursory look at the event, however the media's "investigative" efforts were ultimately pathetic with a short attention span in part due to the Vietnam War and other events, domestic and international. A number of authors over the years have touched on the subject, but mostly to a limited extent mentioning the attack on the *Liberty* briefly in the larger context of their work. Many documents pertaining to the Six-Day War and the attack on the USS *Liberty* remain classified to this day. What can be so damning in those documents that they cannot be declassified and made available · to the public? Notwithstanding many Freedom of Information Act requests, the conspiracy of silence and cover-up continues—why? Additionally, the Johnson Library seems to be slow in declassifying documents originating around the time of the Six-Day War, notwithstanding the claim that many have been released.

As we note the reaction today to the so-called WikiLeaks disclosures, government and the bureaucrats running the government are hypersensitive to the public they serve looking in on their workings. The claim would be that conducting government business would be hamstrung by inappropriate disclosures. There is a contention that the government classifies too much of its work, in a democracy, as being secret. Obviously, confidentiality is critical to the diplomacy process and legitimate national security interests. This problem of information leakage first became a major issue when Daniel Ellsberg released the *Pentagon Papers* in 1971 precipitating a constitutional First Amendment crisis. The contention between the government's need to maintain secrecy and the public's right to know remains in a delicate balance.

A small number of authors have delved into the matter of the attack on the *Liberty* in more depth coming from different perspectives. While the record of the attack in the archives of the United States government has been "sanitized" or destroyed, new information keeps coming to the surface filling in some of the gaps—the slow drip of time can be labor-some and frustrating. It is like working a gigantic puzzle with these authors providing a tidbit here and tidbit there, nevertheless, providing much less that a complete picture of what, why—we know by whom. In essence, the events surrounding the attack on the USS *Liberty* and the subsequent cover-up constitute on ongoing "cold-case" research file in this author's opinion because of the allegations of murder and war crimes that surround the event. There is no statute of limitations on murder. Truth-seekers will continue to chip-a-way at the stonewalling.

There is one caveat: A cold case file implies that a case has in fact been open for investigation. That is not the case with the attack on the *Liberty*. Notwithstanding the claim of certain persons that there have been many investigations, the Department of Navy has recently acknowledged that there never was an investigation "into the attack" by any governmental organization in the United States. "That investigation focused primarily on U.S. military communications problems prior to the attack and the heroic efforts of LIBERTY's crew in damage control during the aftermath of the attack."[13] There can be no clearer statement that there was "no investigation" into the actual attack.

A letter from Rear Admiral Merlin H. Staring (Ret.) and Rear Admiral Clarence A. Hill (Ret.), addressed to the Secretary of the Navy, The Honorable Gordon England, dated July 27, 2005, requested his support to generate a "full, fair, and objective United States Government investigation into the facts and records of the 8 June 1967 attack by Israel upon the USS LIBERTY (AGTR-5)." They cited a claim of war crimes against Israeli forces filed with the Secretary of the Army by the Liberty Veterans Association on June 8, 2005. Staring, a member of Admiral Thomas Moorer's independent commission looking into the attack, noted that the Navy's COI (Court of Inquiry) had an arbitrary period in which to complete its investigation of only seven days.[14] From a law enforcement investigative perspective, this would be a joke. Had the matter been turned over to the FBI to investigate, I am sure the result from an investigative perspective would have been different. Since the mid-1980s, the FBI has been involved in over 500 extraterritorial cases including the 1996 Khobar Towers bombing in Saudi Arabia in which 19 U.S. service members died; and the USS *Cole* attack investigation.[15] No law enforcement investigative agency has been allowed to get near to the *Liberty* case. While I will acknowledge that times have changed since the '60s, politics still control.

The U.S. Navy, in what some believe to be a blemish on its record, conducted a limited and cursory court of inquiry look into the matter. As noted above, that was totally incompetent and incomplete, with the presiding officer believing the attack was intentional—ordered to quickly complete the inquiry by Admiral John S. McCain, Jr., Commander-in-Chief, U.S. Naval Forces, Europe.[16] It would pale in comparison to the FBI investigation into the attack on the USS *Cole* by terrorists in the Gulf of Aden on October 12, 2000, wherein 17 sailors were killed, and 39 were wounded with extensive damage to the ship.[17] Then, the attack on the *Liberty* was not conducted by terrorists or an enemy state, but by a so-called ally— Israel. Years later the Naval Court of Inquiry would have its credibility undercut by its chief senior JAG advisor who would come forward in the fall of 2003 to allege a "cover-up" at the highest levels of our government.

Israeli investigations would be ordered, but would be just as deficient as the hastily called U.S. Naval Court of

Inquiry, except that Israel would push off blame onto the United States for not advising Israel of the vessel's presence in the area. A code of government ordered silence was imposed with the Rule of Law being thwarted. The investigations of both governments were primarily on the military side of government with no evidence of oversight by the civilian side of government—anathema of democracy. The stake of the military to insulate itself is a clear-cut conflict of interest.

As a challenge to the U.S. government's cover-up and credibility, a former member and chairman of the Joint Chiefs of Staff, Admiral Thomas H. Moorer,[18] would question the "special relationship" between the United States and the State of Israel and inferentially accuse the President of the United States of treason and undermining American interests and security in favor of Israel. It is astounding that high-ranking military personnel would make such strong statements against the political leadership of the country without resulting in major controversy and Congressional hearings. Recall when President Harry Truman fired General McArthur during the Korean War.[19] The relationship between the military and civilian side of government can be tenuous and contentious at times, but in our system of government the civilian leadership controls. An historical example of such contention was President Kennedy's refusal to order air-support for the failed CIA sponsored Bay-of-Pigs invasion of Cuba in April of 1961. The consequence was a rift between Kennedy and certain of his national security advisors, including some in the CIA, which prompted some to believe, began to sow the seeds for a presidential assassination.[20]

An independent commission headed by former and now deceased Admiral Moorer noted in its finding No. 12, the following as announced at Capitol Hill on October 22, 2003:[21]

> That a danger to our national security exists whenever our elected officials are willing to subordinate American interests to those of any foreign nation, and specifically are unwilling to challenge Israel's interest when they conflict with American interests; this policy, evidenced by the failure to defend the USS *Liberty* and the subsequent official cover-up of the Israeli attack, endangers the safety of Americans and the security of the United States.

The Congress of the United States in unprecedented fashion would refuse to look into the matter other than to look at the side issue of failed communications, with allegations being made that the continuing congresses over the years have been "bought and paid for" by the American Jewish Lobby and Israeli interests—a contention based on supposition. The general governmental guise or excuse for failing to release information or look into a controversial matter is that it would adversely affect our national security interests or adversely affect our relations with another country—the WikiLeaks syndrome that exaggerates the fall-out. This is a premise that should be subjected to continuing challenge to make sure that the underlying reasons are not "political-CYA"; with President Johnson not wanting to "embarrass an ally" or put himself on the bad side of the Israeli lobby in the United States. The exact quote attributed to President Johnson is illusive; however, one source seems to be an interview of three times LVA President Phillip F. Tourney reporting what Captain Joseph Tully of the USS *Saratoga* relayed to him. The quote is, "I don't give a [expletive] if that ship goes to the bottom and every sailor is lost. We will not embarrass our ally, Israel."[22] The context for the quote is the ordered recall of carrier planes dispatched to the *Liberty's* aid. President Johnson needed American Jewish support for his escalation of the Vietnam War and was not getting it. In addition, he needed Jewish funding and support for his reelection efforts.

Fortunately, notwithstanding pressure from the government, claims of duty and oaths of secrecy, along with threats of prosecution and other sanctions, one person did have the courage and tenacity to tell "his" story—that person being Jim Ennes, a survivor, and author of the *Assault on the Liberty*. Ennes's book, which came out in 1979 would detail the events of the attack, but at the same time cloud or leave out other details pertaining to the "true purpose" of the ship's mission. The ship's mission was something he may not have fully known about due to the compartmentalization of the ship's purpose for being in the area—that is, the so-called "need to know" game. Understanding the mission would help in understanding the Israeli motive for the attack.

Ennes's book would cause consternation within elements of the Israeli military establishment resulting in a subsequent IDF (Israeli Defense Force) History Department Report of the event specifically taking exception with the Ennes's book and many of his contentions. In various forums, allegations of anti-Semitism would be thrown around in typical fashion because of the criticism leveled at the State of Israel.

What would subsequently develop would amount to a second attack on the ship and crew in the form of a propaganda and disinformation war, a campaign that moved from the book venue with counter-views of the events to the new technology of the Internet. In a strange way, this conflict in the public forum would actually result in the development of new information shedding light on the events of the attack on June 8. This new information would actually fly in the face of statements from several presidents that there was "no new information" and therefore the reason they would not re-open the matter, notwithstanding requests over the years of *Liberty* survivors, supporters, and the Liberty Veterans Association.

This author, while tuned in to the events of the Vietnam War in front of the TV at dinnertime, developed a citizen's interest in the inconsistencies of our foreign policy. While serving as a police officer in a mid-size community certain events of the "sixties" would be impressed on my mind. Those events included the Bay-of-Pigs fiasco, the Cuban Missile Crisis, the assassinations of President Kennedy, Martin Luther King, Robert Kennedy and Malcolm X, but little pertaining to the Middle East conflicts; however, while serving in the Marine Corps in the late '50s there was scuttlebutt that we may have needed to ship-out due to a crisis in Lebanon. I had no separate recollection of the *Liberty* attack until recent years. On the other hand, I was aware and impressed by the efficiency of the July 1976 Entebbe raid by the Israeli IDF to save passengers who had been on a hijacked Air France plane; and by the dashing image of Moshe Dayan, eye-patch and all, as portrayed on TV news.[23]

The *Liberty* issue is very much a foreign policy matter in the context of our special relationship with the State of Israel, which, at the time, was a developing relationship almost stillborn because of the attack on the *Liberty*. As our State Department attempted to balance a policy between the Arabs and Israelis, did we find ourselves in over our heads in terms of naiveté? Did the Israelis play us as suckers? What was the agreement between the CIA

and Israeli Mossad that would have adverse consequ
for our country during at least two episodes ˅
American civilians and military personnel died in
numbers resulting from intelligence failures? The first
event being the October 1983 attack on the Marine
barracks in Beirut, Lebanon, and the other being the 9/11
Trade Center attacks in New York. Simply put, the U.S.
was at a disadvantage in the Middle East for gathering
HUMINT (human intelligence) because early on, there
was a protocol wherein we deferred to Israeli intelligence
to keep our CIA informed of events happening behind the
Iron Curtain. Reference can be made to the subsequent
9/11 Commission report dealing with our intelligence
failures.[24]

The failings of American intelligence were obvious to
others. Author Gordon Thomas, who has written
extensively about the intelligence industry, in his book
Secret Wars, points out that British master spy Sir John
McLeod Scarlett, head of MI-6, took particular note of
U.S. intelligence failing to provide policy makers with
"pre-emptive leverage" in dealing with major foreign
events.[25] One major CIA failure was to predict the
economic collapse of the Soviet Union.

My first awareness of the *Liberty* was in reading author
James Bamford's *Body of Secrets* detailing incidents of the
Cold War intelligence gathering activities of the super-
secret NSA or National Security Agency. His chapter
Blood dealt with the attack on the USS *Liberty* and left
me, as an American, "cold, angered and perplexed" by
what happened to the ship and crew. Bamford was an
investigative reporter for the ABC news department and is
one of the most knowledgeable persons in the area of
"signals" (SIGINT) or electronic intelligence gathering
methods and policies. He had written an earlier book

entitled the *Puzzle Palace* detailing the history and activities of the NSA.

The fact is that the USS *Liberty* was an NSA "asset" at the time of the attack. The attack was also an attack on that agency as well as an *act of war* against the United States, as would be alleged. There are indications that the Joint Chiefs of Staff wanted to retaliate for the attack on the *Liberty*, but were prevented from doing so. Complicating matters is the question of interagency compartmentalization where one department of the government does not know what the other is planning, or was really doing. The question is, whether or not the CIA in conjunction with the Israeli Mossad had a hidden agenda for the Middle East leading into the Six-Day War. Israel wanted a "green light" to attack Egypt from the Johnson administration—did Israel get it? Did we want Egyptian President Nasser over thrown? Was information kept from the President while a leading CIA master-spy was implementing a version of his own foreign policy without coordination with the White House and Secretary of State?

Several years would pass from the time of the reading Bamford's book until I would meet in him in person at the 37th reunion of the Liberty Veterans Association in Nebraska City Nebraska at the end of May, 2004. He is a slight, slender and balding man with a quiet but pleasant and easygoing mannerism—very approachable. Simply put, he gets credit for the courage to write about topics that many in government want kept in the dark, but obviously others would like more information available in the public forum believing that more not less government information and transparency is critical for a viable democracy.

In October of 2003 two events occurred, which would re-awaken my interest in the *Liberty*. The first had to do with a public news release on the steps of the Senate building in Washington DC. The Admiral Moorer Independent Commission released findings and conclusions pertaining to the attack on the USS *Liberty*—wherein, President Johnson was in effect, by inference, accused of treason and abandoning the *Liberty* crew—a serious breach of his constitutional duties as Commander-in-Chief of our Armed Forces, as well as putting American interests behind those of Israel. The second event was an affidavit and later a signed declaration from the former chief legal advisor (JAG) to the Naval Court of Inquiry alleging that President Johnson and former Secretary of Defense Robert S. McNamara ordered a cover-up of events surrounding the attack. The President, it is alleged, did not want to embarrass an ally.

Certainly, this was powerful stuff, but given limited play in the media. The media's lack of due diligence should not be a surprise since it was alleged that in the '50s and '60s the CIA had preempted many in the media during an operation called Mockingbird.[26]

Admiral Moorer, a former Chief of Naval Operations and the Chairman of the Joint Chiefs of Staff, would later pass away on February 5, 2004.

As I have indicated, there is "new evidence and information" pertaining to the attack, and there is now the allegations of implied treason and cover-up recently made. Are such drastic terms apropos or an overstatement? An inference or even an allegation of treason may fail from the standpoint of legal or constitutional nuances, but not from the standpoint of a "breach of trust" point of view.

C-SPAN ✓ or ✓ YouTube

The State Department conducted a conference on the Six-Day War and the attack on the USS *Liberty* in January of 2004 resulting in a release of documents pertaining to the Johnson administration handling of and involvement in the Middle East conflict pertaining to the events of the Arab-Israeli war in 1967.[27] Some new disclosures were made, but few opening up a true look at the *Liberty* attack and events that led to it. Much has yet to be disclosed.

The conference was not without controversy as one person with eyewitness knowledge was not included on the panel and that was Jim Ennes, one of the most informed individuals with knowledge of what happened on that ship because he was present. On the panel, dealing with the attack on the USS *Liberty* was James Bamford as noted above. Also, present was Michael Oren, author and Israeli apologist who supports the "mistaken-friendly fire" defense, and one A. Jay Cristol a federal bankruptcy judge from the 11th Judicial Circuit in Florida, whose book *The Liberty Incident* cause much new pain for survivors and families, yet affords some additional insights worth noting in due course.[28]

Cristol would make the *Liberty* a parallel career to his federal employment as a bankruptcy judge as he promoted his book *The Liberty Incident* and his website of the same name.[29] We will be referring to Judge Cristol herein.

Bamford would read the declaration of retired Captain Ward Boston JAGC, USN (Ret.) into the record that in essence, by reference, accused Cristol of being an Israeli agent.[30] Cristol in his book refuted the contentions of the crew and Ennes. In the audience were members of the *Liberty* crew and supporters who attempted to speak—however, the affair tended to degenerate into a shouting match with a great deal of emotion—understandably. The

xl

? fins?

forum was shown on CSPAN. The State Department would be accused of bias and the representative of the NSA History Department would claim that there "was no new information" in existence pertaining to the attack on the *Liberty*. This reference being to the release of certain communications between Israeli air-controllers and helicopters flying toward the *Liberty* "after the attack" as overheard by an electronic eavesdropping Navy EC-121 plane flying over the attack area at the same time.

The State Department was and is a major participant in the on-going cover-up even though it mediated the claims settlement process between the survivors and families and the Government of Israel; notwithstanding, Secretary of State Dean Rusk believed the attack to have been intentional. The claims settlement process was in the "best interests" of both governments not wanting the matter to get into the courts; nor did they want the matter to exacerbate public awareness as matters where pending in the United Nations critical to Israeli interests, namely that she not be made to surrender land gains made during the 1967 war.

Secretary of State Dean Rusk set forth the official position of the United States in a note to His Excellency the Ambassador of Israel. He stated, "…the Secretary of State wishes to make clear that the United States Government expects the Government of Israel also to take disciplinary measures which international law requires in the event of wrongful conduct by the military personnel of a State."[31] A *Liberty* supporter Internet website concludes that the Secretary of State of the U.S. puts his finger on the legal basis for dealing with the attack in terms of Articles 51 and 52 of the Geneva Convention.[32] The basis for the contention of a U.S. government cover-up can be found in those two articles and the United States Code that will be addressed later.

Without a doubt, the *Liberty* attack is a "cold case file" in every sense of those words, begging to be opened for a clean and honest review and investigation of events on that day in June 1967. The allegations are serious, murder and war crimes with subsequent cover-up and complicity by the United States government. Was the *Liberty* "setup" for a "Gulf of Tonkin" like fall—a pretext for the U.S. entering the war on the side of the Israelis? Did the Israelis warn our government to move the ship or it would be sunk? Was the United States government blackmailed into silence? If so, then by whom and what was the "threat" held over the government's head.

Certainly, these are serious questions that create an atmosphere of distrust, doubt and provide fodder for conspiracy theorists. The obvious reason for legitimate governmental secrecy is that it affects national security, however, what about the passage of time. Does national security completely trump a criminal investigation? What about the Rule of Law? Both countries like to claim the "moral high ground", but only to a limited extent where it conflicts with "political and national self interests" of the government and its politicians and bureaucrats. It would certainly be in the best interests of the peoples of both the United States and Israel to open the wound and let some light and air in on it to allow healing. Obviously, that is not in the interests of the "players" or "parties" still alive and subject to prosecution for serious crimes or embarrassment.

Israel's current U.S. ambassador and one of the strongest defenders of Israel, who wrote a book about the Six-Day War, Michael Oren, acknowledges the *Liberty* story hasn't receded into time.[33] In an article on the online version of the *Chicago Tribune,* he says that if anything "the accusations leveled against Israel have grown sharper with time." Oren is further quoted in the interview; that he "believed a formal investigation by the U.S., even 40 years later, would be useful if only because it would finally establish Israel's innocence."[34] His hope is certainly optimistic but probably off target based upon the U.S. government's behavior since the attack. As noted in the previously referenced letter from Captain Jane G. Dalton, Assistant JAG, the Navy plans no further investigation into the matter of the attack on the USS *Liberty*. Michael Oren is obviously entitled to his view. He is obviously well thought of by his government.

This author does not profess the ability to answer all of these many questions, but will attempt to put the attack into a new perspective for further research and discussion. Further, the author does not profess objectivity, but believes that an open and free discussion and look at the issues and facts creates the atmosphere for seeking the truth. The setting for this story and research is complicated by continuing enmity between Arabs and Israelis, specifically in the context of the Six-Day War and the June 5 Israeli preemptive attack on the Egyptian air force and airfields.

Egyptian President Nasser took steps threatening Israel including closing of the Straits of Tiran to Israeli shipping; The Soviets were plotting with Egypt and Syria; and the United States was interested in seeing a regime change in Egypt. The backdrop to the events of 1967 was years of Middle East intrigue and duplicity where the United States was both victim and perpetrator.

An effort to resolve questions is not helped by the fact that the crew of the *Liberty* has contentions among themselves as is common in many family settings. Not only do we have the relationship complications inherent with any officer and crew interaction, we also have the unique bifurcation of the ship's crews into the "General Service Crew" charged with the ship's operations, and

xliii

those of the Naval Security Group charge with the ship's secret mission—the "spooks". The operative rule is "need-to-know". This mix creates differing responses to the tragedy as will become clearer.

As noted above, it would be ludicrous to claim objectivity. Few who look into the *Liberty* story are. The methodology, since many witnesses are deceased or on in their years, or at a distance, is to look at documents, read what has been written, talk to crewmembers and generally use common sense with a little tenacity and apply what we call a "sense of justice" and the Rule of Law approach. There was no research budget as the topic is too big to attempt to break down the wall of secrecy without a concerted Freedom of Information Act lawsuit for non-compliance against the United States government. Whether that will ever happen, is an open and unresolved question. Various individuals including this author have made FOIA requests with limited success over the years.

One of the organizations best equipped to deal with FOIA obstruction by government is the National Security Archive Project at George Washington University in Washington D.C. As of yet they have not place the *Liberty* issue on their agenda.[35] I have personally raised the issue with a representative of the National Security Archive Project and received a reply from its director acknowledging it was not in their targeting sights. That is unfortunate because they have had many successes in prying government secrets loose.

The fact is that the United States government has not conducted a competent criminal investigation into the attack on the USS *Liberty* as it did in the USS *Cole* case. There have been no interviews and depositions taken from Israelis by the U.S. government. The Israelis handled their investigation internally within the military establishment claiming that there was no "prima facie"

xliv

evidence of wrongdoing that would warrant formal charges. The "prima facie" standard is one of the lowest standards by which to judge conduct in terms of whether it involves wrongdoing—simply put, it would normally be a "slam-dunk" case for any halfway competent prosecutor. The tenor is "white wash" for political, diplomatic and military reasons. Once the powers to be make such a sweeping decision it takes tremendous efforts to undo the cover-up. The "System" seeks to protect itself and this usually means a cursory "internal affairs" review that is a conflict of interest from word-go. There has been no judicial review of events within the framework of the civilian concept of free and open government.

The author's perspective is that of a twenty-seven year law enforcement career and as an attorney. The facts are that the attack did occur, the deaths and injuries did result, concerns about the ship's identity had been raised, and there had been a threat to sink the ship if not moved; and U.S. air cover and aid for the ship and crew was recalled.

The Liberty was the ugliest, strangest looking ship in the U.S. Navy. As a communications intelligence ship, it was sprouting every kind of antenna. It looked like a lobster with all those projections moving every which way.

Admiral Thomas H. Moorer, June 8, 1997.

Chapter 1

Operation Bravo-Crayon

Fig. 1, Picture of USS *Liberty.*

In June of 1967, James M. Ennes, Jr., was a lieutenant aboard the USS *Liberty*, he was an intelligence officer charged with keeping key electronic equipment operational and standing his turn at watch on the ship's bridge. Ennes had joined the Navy during the Korean War at seventeen years of age. He left the Navy and later

1

reenlisted with a commission in 1962, retiring from the Navy in 1978.

Ennes would be wounded early in the Israeli air attack on the ship and crew. He would be both victim and witness to one of the strangest events of the Cold War, events that are still the subject of continuing research and controversy that will not let this travesty rest.

Were it not for Ennes, there is a good chance that little would be known about the June 8, 1967 attack on the *Liberty* by Israeli Defense Forces, planes and torpedo boats—the IDF. His book *Assault on the Liberty* took ten years of his life to research and write. He has remained active in terms of his continued efforts to get the *Liberty* story out. The book when published caused some heartburn within the Israeli military establishment; and it was noted within the upper ranks of the National Security Agency, the result of which was a further clouding of the record by the government agencies. High-ranking military retirees claim that the naval record of the *Liberty* has intentionally been manipulated and warped. Ennes's efforts were "gutsy" in that the surviving crewmembers had been admonished not to discuss the events surrounding the attack.[36] While he is a witness to the attack, where there have been allegations of murder and war crimes, his book contains not only information from other witnesses, but key facts dealing with the attack. His writing reveals not only direct and circumstantial evidence, but also his continuing research further supplements the record. He was among the many survivors not called as witnesses before the Naval Court of Inquiry tasked to look into the attack.

Ennes's efforts were not without added consternation, as he would be accused of being anti-Semitic for

2

publishing a book adverse to Israeli interests. This was especially true since both the governments of the United States and Israeli wanted the matter forgotten and buried—in short covered-up. Both the governments of the United States and Israel have conducted a campaign of disinformation setting up a wall of secrecy around the event commencing on the very day of the attack continuing to the present. Crewmembers, subject to threats, intimidation and sanctions, were told they should not talk about the attack if asked by the media or to discuss it with family members. Fellow crewmember, Phillip F. Tourney, describes in detail the threats received from the admiral who would head up the Naval Court of Inquiry designated to look into the *Liberty* matter.[37]

In 1982, the Israeli Defense Forces History Department published a 45-page report it claimed to be the official Israeli version of events involving the attack on the *Liberty*.[38] Colonel Uri Algom, head of the IDF History Department, approved the report; authored by Lt. Col. Matti Greenberg, head of the Combat Research Branch. The report was prefaced with the following findings:

1. The tragic event of the attack on the American Intelligence ship "Liberty" (8 June 1967) became, over the years, an instrument in the hands of journalists and authors, with which to contend that Israel attacked the ship maliciously.

2. Recently, with the publication of the book, Assault on the Liberty, the American Congress appointed a committee, headed by Adlai Stevenson, for the purpose of

3

investigating the affair and publishing the results of the investigation.

3. Immediately upon learning of the appointment of the committee, it was decided that the History Department would research the affair and submit the official version of the State of Israel.

4. This research is based upon all the primary and secondary evidence available.

5. This article is the official version, written by Lt. Col. Matti Greenberg Head of the Combat Research Branch.

On a copy of the report in circulation, there is a hand written note on the cover page that the copy was presented to the U.S. Chief-of-Naval Operations when he visited Israel in 1982.

Subsequently, what would eventually become an information war would develop over the coming years that would involve responding books, TV documentaries, and the Internet World Wide Web domains and forums. Initially, Ennes's book garnered adverse criticism by some survivors who were afraid he would make money on the project to their detriment. They wanted to forget, having suffered trauma, they wanted to get on with their lives. Those who did not want to forget formed the LVA, the Liberty Veterans Association, whose primary objective was to seek a congressional investigation into what they perceived to be murder, assault and an ongoing governmental cover-up. The LVA was setup as a California non-profit corporation under Internal Revenue Code Section 501(c) (3), a tax-exempt veteran's organization made up of the surviving crewmembers of the USS *Liberty*.

The USS *Liberty* was officially designated as a United States Technical Research Ship, a euphemism, with the technical designation of AGTR-5 with the GTR-5 painted on the bow of the ship in tall white letters for all to see—who took the time to look.

The *Liberty* was in fact a "spy" ship, in a world of intelligence games competitively played for military, foreign policy and subtle political reasons. It is no surprise to know a country where such a ship would berth or be re-supplied would not necessarily want the controversy and attention associated with having a spy ship dock at her shores. The Navy's story was that the ship was involved in research into the electromagnetic phenomena, radio wave propagation and alike. As Ennes notes in his book, reporters would not be fooled and called her what she was—a spy-ship.

The ship was built for use as a World War II freighter. Oregon Shipbuilding Corporation of Portland, Oregon laid her keel on February 23, 1945. She was launched forty-two days later and was delivered to the Maritime Commission on May 4, 1945. Her name was *SS Simons Victory* chartered under general agency agreement by Coastwise (Pacific Far East) Line out of San Francisco for service during the closing months of the Second World War. She would later perform routine supply duty for States Marine Lines in both the Atlantic and Pacific oceans.[39]

During the Korean War, she served on supply duty with many ocean crossings to her credit. After the war in 1958, she ended up in the national reserve fleet in Puget

5

Sound at Olympia, Washington. She would be recalled to duty during the height of the Cold War in a new roll.

The intelligence community had plans for her and several other ships of her general description, in part, in response to the prowling Soviet trawlers off our shores and shadowing our fleets; it was determined that we would take a page from the Soviets and create our own SIGINT fleet of intelligence gathering ship platforms. When Frank Raven took over the newly formed G Group at the National Security Agency, he found a need for more efficient gathering of signals intelligence on a global basis.[40]

Raven wanted a "slow tub" that could mosey along a coastline slowly, taking its time while carrying out the secret mission. In all, nine ships with different configurations would be designated for this special duty. Initially, civilians operated the first ships as the operating crew; however, the Navy would staff the remainder of the ships in a dual configuration. That is, there would be the Navy crew operating the ship and another segment of Navy personnel from the Naval Security Group operating the "spook" or research department charged with gathering, analyzing and forwarding the work product of signals intelligence collection. They would proudly be referred to as "CTs" or communication technicians.

The Navy acquired the *SS Simons Victory* from the Maritime Commission in February of 1963. She was then delivered to Willamette Iron and Steel Corporation, Portland, Oregon for conversion to her new function. Ennes reports this was no small task as the job took twenty-two months at the cost of twenty million dollars—before the installation of specialized electronics for her new mission.

The ship had an overall length of 455 feet with a maximum speed of 18 knots. There were two complements of personnel based upon a "compartmentalized need-to-know" operational basis as noted above. The ship's operating crew consisted of nine officers and an enlisted complement of 151, while the intelligence operation required a crew of six officers and 128 enlisted personnel from the Naval Security Group.[41] The research crew would be augmented with one or more civilian linguists as needed.

The Navy used double talk to describe the ship's function and mission. Yet, as Ennes notes, those aware such as the merchants, bar girls and alike, knew the truth that the ship was an intelligence gathering ship. Loose talk could be expected during shore leave in the various bars where the sailors would relax and enjoy their respite from duty. To them the *Liberty* crew was known as "spooks". Of course, there was never an "official" confirmation of what the crew did. Importantly, as Ennes notes, "Even today, *Liberty* sailors are bound by stringent oaths of secrecy that severely restricts their freedom to discuss the ship's 'technical research' mission."[42]

Thirty-seven years after the attack as this author began researching the basis for this book, he had the occasion to bring the "mission" question up with Ennes, who offered a version that I thought was less than responsive. At the time, Ennes and this author were living in the Pacific Northwest on opposite sides of the state. It was and is this author's "feeling" that the crew is still holding back certain information as to the "true mission" of the ship during June, of 1967, during what is known as the Six-Day War. This is an unfortunate reality as it compounds the inability of one researching the attack to break down the wall of secrecy. It may simply be that compartmentalization of tasks successfully furthered the goal of secrecy—and many in the research crew were among the dead never to tell their story. Then again, these were men with strong pride in the job they were doing, still maintaining allegiance to country and the code of silence; notwithstanding, on occasion, bitterness shows through.

That bitterness and resentment is strongly felt even after all these years. In an interview for the October 2, 2007 article in the online edition of the *Chicago Tribune*, Bryce Lockwood freely expresses his feelings to the reporter. Lockwood, a Marine and Russian language linguist, awarded the Silver Star for his actions aboard the ship, directed his frustration at both Israel and our government; at Israel for failure to ID the ship before attacking it on the open sea, and for our government's failure to properly investigate the matter.[43]

On April 1, 1964, the *Liberty* was designated AGTR-5 as already noted. This means auxiliary non-combatant vessel of general or miscellaneous type assigned to technical research duty. She was re-commission on December 30, 1964 at Bremerton, Washington. Her first captain was Commander Daniel T. Wieland, Jr. He would relinquish command to Commander William L. McGonagle on April 25, 1966.

After sea-trials, she was assigned to Africa where she would crawl the coastline from Dakar to Cape Town, back-and-forth. Crew leave or liberty was in ports such as Monrovia, Luanda, Abidjan and occasionally Las Palmas. Ennes reports that for the most part duty aboard the *Liberty* was "unexciting". The crew, nevertheless, found ways to be entertained and amused to relieve monotony—what happens in port was better left in port. Sunbathing aboard ship in their lounge chairs was one way; another was to imbibe a little, stealthily aboard ship, sailors-will-be-sailors.

Jim Ennes reported that he transferred to the *Liberty* as a "career enhancing move" from the more mundane "staff function" aboard the Second Fleet flagship and heavy cruiser USS *Newport News*. He reported to duty on May 1, one day before leaving Norfolk May 2, 1967. He would be in charge of the ship's division of electronic maintenance technicians as part of the Naval Security Group.

Events developing in the Middle East were being "flagged" for operational elements of the United States Department of Defense. Concern had been developing for some time over the buildup of political and military tensions in the area. Both the Soviet Union and China, often in competition to each other, were beginning to find ways to exploit opportunities in the Middle East. By the end of the 1950s, Chinese Communist began to assert themselves in Iraq and Syria. Palestinian Liberation Organization (PLO) head, Ahmed al-Shukairy, the first head of the PLO, admitted to getting some Chinese aid. PLO personnel had been sent to Vietnam and China to observe communist guerilla activities and allegedly received Chinese arms.[44]

The Russians, remember that the Soviet Union was still viable entity, began to support succeeding radical Syrian governments with both economic and military aid, and had a stake from a prestige standpoint in not having those governments fail or be over-run. Russian personnel were based in Syria. The Russians were concerned that Israel could over-run Syria if it chose to do so, and began

9

to put pressure on Egypt to support Syria and to build their forces. Even to this day Syria is a proxy for the Russians with the Russians undercutting efforts in the UN to bring a halt to the Syrian uprisings of 2011-2012.

The U.S. government view was that Gamal Abdel Nasser, President of the United Arab Republic (UAR), was concerned about efforts of Saudi Arabia and Jordon to challenge his leadership of the Arab world. In January of 1967 Nasser further strained relations by the U.A.R. bombing of Najran in Saudi Arabia in late January 1967; and in Yemen, where the U.A.R. were fighting royalists' troops with a heavy Egyptian commitment of troops. Jordon, trying to avoid friction with Israel ordered a halt to Arab penetration into Israel by Palestinians.[45]

There were agitating "tank-tractor" clashes between the Syrians and Israel along their DMZ border, and there was an escalation on April 7, 1967 with a clash between Syrian MIGs and the Israeli air force, with six Syrian planes shot down. Escalations in Yemen allegedly included the U.A.R. use of poisonous gas on royalist troops on April 22.

In 1981, the NSA, National Security Agency, ordered an internal review of the attack on the *Liberty*, known as the *Gerhard Report* that is available on the NSA website.[46] It is reported therein that the NSA went on an "Alfa" readiness alert on May 14, 1967 when the U.A.R. placed its air force on alert and deployed naval units. This "Alfa" alert applied to all Middle East intelligence targets. This alert terminated three days later.

President Nasser began to take a series of steps that precipitated an atmosphere ripe for confrontation. On May 17, the First United Nations Emergency Force

(UNEF I), ceasefire line peace observers, were ordered to leave by Nasser who then ordered the deployment of Egyptian troops into the Sinai, risking a direct confrontation between Egypt and Israel. UNEF I was in place only on the Egyptian side of the border because of the 1956 Suez War. This was becoming déjà vu, much like what occurred in the 1956 Suez War, which was preemption on the part of Israel in conjunction with Britain and France to take control of the Suez Cannel.

Nasser further compounded Israeli concerns when on May 23 he ordered the blockading of the Straits of Tiran, at which time the NSA ordered a change from "Alfa" to ready condition "Bravo-Crayon" for all SIGINT communications in the Middle East.[47] Israel began a complete but quiet mobilization, and on May 30, Egypt and Jordan signed a five-year alliance, which in essence resulted in Israel being completely encircled.

Because of Israeli governmental dynamics, Prime Minister Levi Eshkol relinquished the dual role of Defense Minister to Moshe Dayan on June 1 as part of a unity government. On June 2 the United States and United Kingdom issued a joint statement to the effect that the Gulf of Aqaba was an international body of water to which all nations were entitled to free passage. Efforts by the Johnson administration to create an international coalition to break the Egyptian blockade failed to materialize. Nasser was crossing several Israeli "redlines" and creating a *casus belli* for war. Additionally, the administration was concerned with Nasser's anti-American rhetoric and his version of Arab nationalism.

The NSA decision to request the *Liberty's* deployment to the Mediterranean on May 23 was due to the raised

11

SIGINT alert from "Alfa" to "Bravo-Crayon". The *Gerhard Report* notes that this was only one of many actions taken to improve signals intelligence collection, processing and reporting in the critical weeks before the Six-Day War as the NSA action office, G6, began round-the-clock SIGINT operations out of Fort Meade.[48] This would be Frank Raven's G-Group.

The deployment consideration was based upon "customer needs" in the potential event that U.S. forces would somehow become deployed in the area due to hostilities. NSA's customer base included the President, the Defense Department, and CIA among others. Chapter II of the *Gerhard Report* remains substantially redacted as far as it pertains to "customer needs" and the technology. The report was initially marked "Top Secret Umbra" and was first released to the public in 2006 subsequent to an FOIA lawsuit. One small paragraph dealing with UHF and VHF communication intercepts was partially redacted. It noted that this type of intercept generally required a "line-of-sight" capability. The un-redacted portion did refer to the inclusion of airborne intercept platforms as being part of an overall intelligence gathering system. The advantage of ships was to be able to maintain longer time on station whereas airborne SIGINT/ELINT units had to be rotated over shorter periods.

The *Gerhard Report* contains a map showing the flight paths of US Navy EC-121 and USAF C-130 aircraft. These flights were increased from eight per month to one per day after the SIGINT readiness alert had been issued. These overhead flights will figure into the *Liberty* story in a very important way to be explained later. The EC-121 was a version of Lockheed's Super Constellation, the "Connie".

Fig. 2, EC-121 Aircraft.

http://www.vpnavy.com/vq2_aircraft.html.

It was noted that the U.S. SIGINT organization in the Middle East operated effectively with the use of ground stations and the overhead flights producing COMINT and ELINT, meeting customer needs pertaining to the U.A.R. and merchant shipping.[49] This reference to "merchant shipping" is a mystery, unless the reference is to Soviet supply ships and possible spy trawlers.

However, there were holes that the NSA had to consider—a sustained intercept capability was needed. The routine of five hours on station for operation of the EC-121s, and C-130s, was considered too short to be of material value. SIGINT planners considered issues of location and limitation of VHF/UHF line of sight problems. A ship borne collection capability was determined to be equal to 13 airborne collectors, and would operate off the shore of the U.A.R. They were more economical to operate and better able to respond to contingencies. The airborne collectors were not allowed to fly over land and their flight patterns were limited to flying over the Eastern Mediterranean. Airborne crews were concerned about being identified as an enemy aircraft depending on what direction they were flying, in the direction of Egypt or Israel as it would look on their radar screens. There is reason to believe that Israel did not want American over-flights for her own reasons that will become clear later.

The choice of ships for the mission was between the USNS *Private Jose F. Valdez* (T-AG 169) near Gibraltar and the *Liberty* in port at Abidjan on the Ivory Coast. The *Liberty* was chosen because of her 18-knot speed verses 8 knots for the *Valdez* and because of her multichannel VHF/UHF collection capability, which was better, and she was at the start of her deployment. As Ennes notes in his book they passed the *Valdez* when she was coming off station on her way home. A clarification is in order here regarding the *Valdez* and *Liberty*. *Valdez* had stopped in Rota, Spain ahead of the *Liberty* and off loaded data that was to be picked up by the *Liberty* when new linguist boarded to augment the onboard crew. This data had to do with electronic emitters such as radars and call signs that had been collected while the *Valdez* was in the Eastern Mediterranean.

On May 23, the Joint Chiefs of Staff Joint Reconnaissance Center had dispatched the *Liberty*, on her mission to the Mediterranean. As for the *Liberty's* modus operandi, reconnaissance operations came under the purview of the Joint Chiefs of Staff (J3), and the direction of a deputy director of reconnaissance. He was in charge of the Joint Reconnaissance Center. Mr. John Connell was the NSA representative to the JRC.[50] Initially the

14

ship was under the "operational control" of the Commander-in-Chief Atlantic. Technical control of the SIGINT operation was through the Director of the NSA in direct communication and coordination with the NSG, Naval Security Group, through its director. A collection assignment as stated by JCS guidelines would take into account technical factors determined by the NSA and safety factors as determined by military operational commanders. Therefore, there were at least three command levels involved with the command and control of this NSA asset, a confusing process to the ordinary civilian. One needs to understand the bifurcated command and control functions of management and operational control.

To clarify: The technical control of the SIGINT unit USN-855 was technically under the Director of the NSA, with management control of USN-855 being under the Director of the NSG. On the *Liberty*, this activity was physically located in the "research department" below decks, subject to access only with proper security clearances. It was a compartmentalized operation as already noted. Lieutenant Commander Dave E. Lewis was the commanding officer of the "research department" and his second in command was Lieutenant Maurice H. Bennett. Capt. McGonagle, the ship's captain, had clearance and would visit the department daily to receive briefings and review "special traffic" available there. On the *Liberty* there were three decks assigned to this operation. The lowest was for training and the fan room; the next was for R branch (collection) and O branch (communications). The top available deck was for T branch (other than Morris signals).

The *Liberty* had a distinct and unique configuration as a naval ship; she was unlike other ships in the sense she was loaded down with a wide assortment of antenna including Long-wire VLF/LF antenna, various ECM (electronic counter measures) antenna, 10' whip antenna, Discone omni-directional antenna, Monocone broadband omni-directional antenna, VHF-receive antenna, and 35' whip antenna. This list just applies to what was on or near the foremast of the ship. Typical of communication arrangements for the AGTR class ship, the *Liberty* had circuits for the ship's command in one location and those for its SIGINT detachment in a separate location. Command facilities included a "receive" terminal for fleet broadcasts, three circuits for on-line ship/shore radiotelephone and voice communications, and one additional order wire full-duplex circuit. This information is based on the *Gerhard Report*.

In a separate location, USN-855 had an on-line, full-duplex radiotelephone circuit, a secure one-channel moon-relay system known as the TRSSCOMM (technical research ship special communications system) that would involve bouncing a radio signal off the moon to NSA headquarters at Fort Mead, Maryland. This system was continually plagued with hydraulic problems. This was the type of equipment that Ennes and his crew were charged with maintaining. Of particular note is the full-duplex radiotelephone that would indicate the ship "may" have had direct communications with the NSA, subject to a relay process.

Ennes described the TRSSCOMM system as beaming a 10,000-watt microwave signal to the moon and bouncing it back from the moon to a receiving station at Cheltenham, Maryland. It worked when both stations could see the moon; however, the conditions were seldom satisfactory to where it was a dependable communication device.[51]

16

There was also a "receive-only" terminal for fleet broadcasts, and there were several off-line encryption devices.

Signal collection positions included one for direction finding, 17 for radiotelephone, 20 for manual Morris, 7 for automatic Morris, 7 for electronic countermeasures, 33 for non-Morris search and development, the latter for frequencies above and below 30 megahertz.

The ship had a major "antenna" footprint that was clearly distinguishable with 45 separate antennas that in essence made her an antenna farm. This point will become important in view of the Israeli claim of "mistaken identity" as we will later see.

Several communication functions are important from the standpoint of understanding the *Liberty's* mission and ability to detect a threat. First, did the ship have the ability to directly communication with the NSA; second, did the ship have the ability to communicate with a submarine; third, did the ship have the ability to pick up radar signals directed at her; and finally, did she pick up the communications from over-flying planes. Information on the technical functionality of these various devices is ambiguous. Later there will be a reference to the *Liberty* playing "radar tag" with over-flying Israeli planes on the day before the attack on her.

Not so visible was the ship's armament, which consisted of four .50 caliber machine guns, 2 front and two aft in gun-tubs, plus a browning automatic rifle and a number of small arms like .45 caliber automatic pistols. Clearly, the ship was not a "fighting ship" with the ability to defend her from attack; additionally, her slow speed made her a sitting duck.

On her fifth African cruise, the *Liberty* was at Abidjan, Ivory Coast at the end of May when she was ordered diverted to the Middle East by the JCS/JRC with approval of the Assistant Secretary of Defense. The ship was to be routed via Rota, Spain with the Commander-in-Chief Atlantic changing control to the Commander-in-Chief for Europe. The *Liberty* departed Abidjan at 0530Z on May 24, 1967.

Time and date group classifications will become important as we follow the *Liberty* to its new destination. For example, the date-time-group (DTG) of 240530Z May 1967 means 0530 Zulu or military time on May 24, 1967. Critical time-periods will become military in the Bravo zone, Sinai time, and Eastern Time in Washington DC. Estimated arrival time in Rota, Spain would be May 31, 1967. Once in Rota it came under the operational control of the U.S. Commander-in-Chief, Europe, General Lyman L. Lemnitzer who turned control over to the Commander-in-Chief, U.S. Navy for Europe, Admiral John S. McCain, Jr. This would be the father of Senator John McCain.[52] However, General Lemnitzer, Supreme NATO Commander from 1963 to 1969, wanted to be kept current on the SITREP (situation reports) reports and PIMs (planned intended movement reports) and any incidents.

Admiral McCain along with the NSA would get the various reports. *Liberty* was provided guideline instructions for moving into place and communications guidance. The ship would later come under control of the Sixth Fleet operating in the area of Crete. Repairs were being made to the TRSSCOMM system that had hydraulic problems as the *Liberty* entered the Mediterranean.

A controversial issue would be the additional crew picked up in Rota, Spain. According to the *Gerhard Report*, she took on board "six Arabic [redaction] linguists who would join USN-855 for expected work on U.A.R and [redaction] communications". The apparent controversy is that there was no known Hebrew linguist included in this group. References to redactions are to the blocked out sections of the *Gerhard Report*, information that has still not been disclosed notwithstanding the passage of time.

What is being hidden here after all this time? Try inserting in the redacted space words like "specialist" and "Israeli"—is that a possibility? "Special Arabic" linguists refer to those able to speak and understand Hebrew. Three of the Arab linguists were NSA civilians, Allen M. Blue, Donald L. Blalock and Robert L. Wilson. The remaining linguists were military personnel. As previously noted Bryce Lockwood was a Russian linguist. It appears that there were few Israeli linguists available during the lead-up to the Six-Day War. At least three will play important parts in the *Liberty* story.

It was not unusual to have civilian NSA members mixed in with the Naval NSG crew. They brought selected technical and linguistic capabilities. One reason for the mix could be the lack of sufficient personnel from one group or the other. Additional redactions to the *Gerhard Report* make it difficult to explore the assignments and instructions, leaving us to our own wits and ability to guess the ship's true mission. This author is not aware of clarifications being made by the surviving crewmembers.

To facilitate the planning for USN-855's collection mission, SIGINT managers had designated five

19

operational areas numbered west to east in the eastern Mediterranean near the coastline of the U.A.R., Israel, Lebanon, and Syria. Each measured about 50-by-50 miles. In proposing the five operational areas to the JCS, the Director, NSA had indicated his preference, based on wave propagation analysis of U.A.R. communications, for operational area three at 32:00-33:00N to 34:00E if operational and safety factors did not dictate otherwise. With territorial limits established by Middle East countries in mind, JCS subsequently directed the Commander-in-Chief Europe to deploy the *Liberty* to operational area three with the closest point of approach to Algeria, Libya, and the U.A.R. of 13 nautical miles during transit.

On arrival in operation area three, the CPA (closest point of approach) was to be 12.5 nautical miles to the U.A.R. and 6.5 nm to Israel. Admiral McCain directed the *Liberty* to comply with these instructions and she left Rota, Spain on June 2 at 1230Z heading through the Strait of Gibraltar on a course paralleling the North African coastline. During transit three Soviet destroyers were observed matching course and speed changes with the *Liberty* keeping a distance of 6,000 yards off her starboard quarter.[53]

In the meantime the NSA was arranging with the Air Force Security Service (AFSS), now the Electronic Security Command (effective 1981), for more expeditious processing of Navy's VQ-2 EC-121 and Air Force's C-130 intercepts, which had increased considerably from the now daily flights per the upgraded SIGINT alert. The intent was to create a technical processing center for the information acquired directly from the planes on return to base. Site locations are redacted in the *Gerhard Report*, however, it is noted that courier time for delivery of tapes to NSA was 72 hours. This would seem to be a long time in a war setting, however, emergency messages could be quickly transmitted.

Once the TPC (technical processing center) became operational on June 1, the linguists, divided into four operational shifts, processed the tapes as they were brought into the TPC compound from the aircraft, and the analysts/reporters produced their product contents with a minimum of delay as Critics, Spots electrigrams, or in the technical supplements to post-mission flight reports.

On May 29, in a message to USN-855, the Director, NSA had outlined the mission for the *Liberty* during its voyage to the eastern Mediterranean.

Commander-in-Chief Navy Europe advised the Commander, Sixth Fleet, Vice Admiral William I. Martin, on June 3, that *Liberty's* mission was to conduct an "extended independent surveillance operation in the eastern Mediterranean" and that Sixth Fleet might be called upon to provide logistic and other support.[54] Martin in essence was a conduit for JCS orders. Via a message, he had intended to board the *Liberty* on June 7 but war events over took the situation and the visit did not occur.

With the outbreak of the war imminent, the CINCEUR in a message to the Commander, Sixth Fleet and others took note of the movement of some 20 Soviet warships with supporting vessels and an estimated eight or 9 Soviet submarines into the eastern Mediterranean and Aegean. Operation Bravo-Crayon was specifically targeted on Soviet fleet activities. Admiral Martin was advised to keep his ships and aircraft at least 100 nautical miles away from the coasts of Lebanon, Syria, Israel and the U.A.R. and at least 25 nm away from Cyprus. These instructions did not apply to the *Liberty*.

The *Liberty* was to the south of Italy when the Six-Day War broke out on June 5, 1967. Consequently, the *Liberty* assumed a readiness condition and USN-855 began to keep abreast of events from NSA and field site SIGINT Readiness Crayon and other reports on the Middle East situation and, of course, from its own intercepts.

Understandably, the crew was apprehensive entering a war zone without escort. One was requested of Vice Admiral Martin but was turned down with the explanation that she, the *Liberty*, was a "neutral ship in international waters". The crew understood the need for general quarters drill, but allegedly took comfort in their non-combatant status, and as noted in the *Gerhard Report*, they were to be assured by the visibility of the American flag. The *Gerhard Report* notes that one USN-855 member recalled being told, "…if anything were to happen we were within ten minutes of air strike support and help. None of us were very worried…."

There was some concern within the NSA about *Liberty's* proximity to a war zone, and it was reported that NSA's Gene Sheck and Dick Harvey did ask the NSA liaison officer to the JCS/JRC, Mr. John Connell, on June 5 if any consideration was being given to a change in the *Liberty's* operational area. In a prior incident during the Cuban missile crisis, five years earlier, the USS *Oxford* had been pulled back from the Havana area. NSA's concern was for the technical collection arrangements, which would have to be adjusted if the *Liberty* was to be withdrawn. The NSA liaison officer discussed the matter

22

with the JRC's ship-movement officer and then advised Sheck and Harvey that no action was then under consideration.

On June 6, as she was passing between Libya and Crete, the *Liberty* reported to Sixth Fleet that its TRSSCOMM, which had malfunctioned, was back in operating order—at least temporarily. Advised that CINCEUR had not received PIMs, they provided date-time-group PIMs previously sent. USN-855's communications on 6 June to NSA was normal, and it was noted, "It was also in satisfactory communication with [redaction] in this period". It is worth noting this particular reference: "In satisfactory communication" with whom per the *Gerhard Report* at page 20. Is this a reference to the NSA, a submarine or who and what? An important element to the *Liberty* story begins to enter the picture.

In his book, Ennes makes note of being in the chart room and observing plots that included the *Valdez* that was returning home and another plot simply marked with "X". A mystery will surround this mark with Ennes making a mild inquiry and noting that it did not fall within his need-to-know criteria even though he was part of the intelligence group on the ship. Some speculation will cause him to think it might be a submarine tracking and below them.

On June 6, CINCEUR advised the Commander of the Sixth Fleet that at 0001Z 7 June 1967 the *Liberty* would come under, or be "chopped", to his control to facilitate area command and control and any possible requirements for protection during the Middle East hostilities. It was pointed out that *Liberty's* schedule might be revised for safety reasons "as dictated by the local situation."

23

Liberty acknowledged at 2036Z on the sixth. At the time, Captain McGonagle advised Commander Sixth Fleet that the ship was in "Readiness Condition Three-Modified" and reminded his superior of his self-defense limitations being only four .50-caliber machine guns and small arms.[55]

The issue of the "chop" date and Vice Admiral Martin's planned visit to the *Liberty* on June 7th might tend to lead to a conclusion that the war activities of the Israelis were "ahead" of sync with U.S. military commanders perceptions and actions—meaning they were caught off guard by the June 5th start of the war.

Three hours later the Commander Sixth Fleet cautioned *Liberty* by message to "maintain a high state of vigilance against attack or threat of attack" in view of the "unpredictability of U.A.R. actions." He directed the *Liberty* to report by flash precedence any threatening actions or "any diversion from schedule necessitated by external threat" and to submit "reports of contact with ships, aircraft, and submarines which are unidentified, of intelligence interest, or engaged in harassment." Admiral Martin instructed *Liberty* to copy the fleet broadcast and to use his fast carrier task force (TF-60) tactical circuits if necessary. Apparently, for one reason or another *Liberty* did not receive his message. This would be forbearer of several communication problems to plague the ship and the whole controversy surrounding the attack on the *Liberty* and its aftermath.

It would take some fifteen and one-half hours for the *Liberty's* position report of 0908Z of June 7 giving its position at 0800Z at 33-06N 28-54E to get to the Commander Sixth Fleet. *Liberty* was guarding the Naval Communications Station frequency at Asmara. On this

24

day, there were a number of actions under way to minimize the appearance of U.S. involvement in the Middle East hostilities and to change the *Liberty's* operational area.

JCS took note of allegations that U.S. personnel were in communication with Israel and were possibly providing military assistance. There was one Egyptian General, al-Ghul, who accused *Liberty* of jamming their radios.[56] Such allegations were coupled with earlier reports or claims that U.S. planes had assisted the Israelis in strikes on the Egyptians. JCS wanted assurance from Vice Admiral Martin that his aircraft had not violated the air space limitations as previously given; however, he did acknowledge communications with the American Embassy in Tel Aviv for testing purposes in case evacuation was necessary.

On the first day of the war, it was essentially over with the winner being the Israelis who had destroyed the Egyptian air force in early morning raids on June 5. Studying the successful Israeli drive into the U.A.R., the Director of NSA sought to move *Liberty* from area three to area two to the west. DIR/NSA sought the move at 2104Z via JCS/JRC; however, no action was taken on the NSA request even though the latter had reservations about the *Liberty's* safety.

Because of U.S. sensitivity regarding U.A.R. charges of complicity with Israel, and following a question from the U.S. Chief of Naval Operations about the wisdom of *Liberty's* assignment in the war zone, the JCS/JRC assessed the danger inherent in the *Liberty's* operations. Allegedly, the distance from the Sixth Fleet to *Liberty* was some 300 to 400 miles and taking into account the NSA's concern about mission degradation, JRC decided to accept the mission degradation. At the time of these deliberations, at 2300Z June 7, the *Liberty* had arrived on station in operational area three at Point Alfa.

In a message conveying the sense of urgency then developing with the Pentagon staff, JCS expressed concern in a message at 2230Z to Commander-in-Chief, Europe over the Middle East situation and stated that the JCS-directed operational area for the *Liberty* was "for guidance only" and could be "varied as local conditions dictated." The JCS instructions to the Commander-in-Chief Europe were to change the CPA to U.A.R. to 20 nm (nautical miles) and to Israel to 15 nm. This message would not reach the ship prior to the attack on her. The Department of Army Communications Center in error sent the message to the Naval Communications Station in the Pacific.

Subsequent discussions within the JCS/JRC resulted in a decision to pull her back to a 100 mile CPA, well away from hostilities. Why all this concern, when the Commander of the Sixth Fleet had decided she did not even need a destroyer escort? Something was obviously going on that perhaps the *Gerhard Report* did not want to disclose, or perhaps the authors did not know about.

Could it be that the U.S. government had received a threat from Israel to remove the ship or she would be sunk? This issue is at the heart of the *Liberty* controversy that we will look into in greater depth.

The *Gerhard Report* states that General Wheeler, Chairman of the Joint Chief of Staff was involved in the decisions as to the *Liberty's* position and proximity to a hostile shoreline. This point was made regarding the desire of General Earle Gilmore "Bus" Wheeler to support in any way the U.S. position taken at the UN in answer to U.A.R. charges of complicity.

U.S. Ambassador Arthur J. Goldberg had stated on the sixth to the UN Security Council that "All Sixth Fleet aircraft are and have been several hundred miles from the area of conflict."[57] Was his statement meant to include other elements of the U.S. military, such as a reconnaissance unit out of Germany? We will look at this controversial issue later.

Preparations were taking place on the carrier USS *America* for a press conference related to the U.A.R. charges of U.S. complicity with Israel in the prosecution of the war. Considering the Sixth Fleet's need to transmit other traffic of equal or higher precedence, Vice Admiral Martin's message to the *Liberty*, directing it not to approach the coast of the U.A.R., Syria or Israel closer than 100 nm, went out some four and one-half hours later, at 080917Z.

In the meantime, *Liberty* was on course, already in its operational area. Its position at 080800Z was within 30 nm of 31-45N 33-30E in area three. *Liberty* would never get the message to pull back. These communication snafus would become the subject of a congressional investigation, the only congressional investigation in the whole *Liberty* affair.

There is some question as to whether the *Liberty* actually got on station a day earlier than the June 9 scheduled arrival time. If that was the case, how do we explain sending a ship into harm's way for no apparent purpose; or to say it another way, to be late for the action it was intended to monitor. The Six-Day War did begin on June 5, 1967. In someone's plans, maybe it was not to start until June 15. Over the years, a great deal of controversy will arise because of the lack of available clarifying information; as a result, speculation and conspiracy theories will grow and nurture in front of the wall-of-silence. Did the Israelis jump-the-gun on a pre-arranged joint covert plan with the United States?

Once on station off Port Said in operational area three, USN-855 employed its collection positions primarily to develop U.A.R. [redaction] communications [redaction] according to the *Gerhard Report*. It then goes on to say the *Liberty* "had no specific assignment to intercept Israeli communications while it was in operational area three." It continues to say, "Omission of this tasking was, in part, owing to the lack of Hebrew linguists. But on the morning of 8 June its VHF search positions did produce three tapes of Israeli air traffic." The contents were later determined to be routine operational messages. The significance of this will become clear later.

Did the *Liberty* pickup Israeli air traffic pertaining to its targeting and identification on 8 June? Did these tapes survive the attack, or how did NSA otherwise get them. The *Gerhard Report* goes on to note that "as a by-product" of searching for U.A.R. communications in the Sinai, USN-855 also identified some 22 frequencies as Israeli, but again there was nothing relatable to the forthcoming attack.

The *Liberty* was capable of intercepting major Israeli communications, including Israeli Defense Force brigade and division level communications and movement orders, and the radar emissions and radio transmissions from aircraft that were flying in the war.[58]

28

Liberty's mission was to provide daily technical summaries for use by other collectors and NSA, enabling them to remain up to date on the *Liberty's* operation. Upon completion of its deployment, USN-855 was to send traffic and unprocessed tapes to NSA. In my mind there seems to be a lack of timeliness to this process with a war in progress.

Ennes in his book cites Frank Raven as the key person involved in the *Liberty's* assignment. Raven, who was in charge of G-Group at NSA, thought it was too dangerous to send the *Liberty* that close to shore, but he had to leave a meeting in which the matter was discussed, and since there was no further objection the project moved forward. Ennes notes that section head, John E. Morrison, Jr., an Air Force brigadier general finally agreed to the mission after asking a number of questions. Because the matter was urgent, he agreed to ask the Joint Chiefs of Staff to assume direct control of the ship.[59] It seems that it was unusual for the JCS to take control of a ship like the *Liberty*, whereas, in the *Gerhard Report* the process seemed a normal function for the JRC. Regardless, and with the preceding background in mind, the *Liberty's* Captain received the following message:[60]

> MAKE IMMEDIATE PREPARATIONS TO GET UNDERWAY. WHEN READY FOR SEA ASAP DEPART PORT ABIDJAN AND PROCEED BEST POSSIBLE SPEED TO ROTA SPAIN TO LOAD TECHNICAL SUPPORT MATERIAL AND SUPPLIES. WHEN READY FOR SEA PROCEED TO OPERATING AREA OFF PORT SAID. SPECIFIC AREAS WILL FOLLOW.

"I was seated in my office at the GHQ command post when I received a message that sounded odd: explosion had been reported in the El Arish area. By that time, El Arish was in our hands....I ordered the navy and air force to look into the matter..."

Chief of Staff Rabin, *Rabin Memoires*, page 108.

Chapter 2

Point Alfa

Sunrise on the morning of June 8, 1967 was 0443 AM local Sinai time.[61] *Liberty* had arrived on station at Point Alfa at coordinates 31-27.2N 34-00E at 0900 AM. This location was northwesterly of the Gaza Strip and Khan Yunis, and northeasterly of El Arish in the Sinai on the coast[62]. The distance was about 20 miles off shore from the Gaza. Ennes notes in his book that he takes to the bridge shortly after seven o'clock to find Ensign John Scott scanning the shoreline with binoculars and noting the "fabulous morning".[63] Scott was the ship's damage control officer who will later have his hands full and become one of the heroes involved in saving the ship. He advised Ennes that they now had ammunition at all four machine gun positions.

The men discussed having passed Port Said, Egypt, during the night, and noted the presence of shooting on shore with the night sky filled with smoke and fire. Scott briefs Ennes that shortly after sunrise they were picked up by an early morning reconnaissance flight. It would later be determined to be part of the Israeli coastal early warning system—the time was 0515. It was noted that the ship was circled three or 4 times by a "boxcar" type

30

plane, a Nord Noratlas 2501, that took off in the direction of Tel Aviv after the flyover. This would be the first of a number of over-flights during that morning and early afternoon. Ennes then relieved Scott at 0720.

The Nord Noratlas was an older two-engine plane supplied to the Israelis by the French that the French had used as a troop transport plane. It resembled a flying boxcar with twin tail rudders used by the Israelis as part of the coastal early warning system. As a help aid reminder for the reader, local time will be Sinai time, and Zulu time (Greenwich Mean Time) will be military time that is two hours ahead of local or Sinai time.[64]

Fig. 3, Israeli Nord Noratlas 2501.

http://www.oocities.org/capecanaveral/hangar/2848/noratlas.htm.

In the context of this flyover, a lingering question will be whether and to what extent the *Liberty* was picked up and monitored by Israeli coastal radar as she approached her operational target—point Alfa. Israel had several ways of knowing the ship was in the area, including a report that she played "radar-tag" with Israeli aircraft the evening of 7 June in route to Point Alfa. According to author Stephen Green, at around 10 PM as the ship was en-route to her assigned patrol area, "the ship's 'research department' detected jets—identified as Israeli by

31

Liberty's sophisticated radar-sensing equipment—circling the ship in the night distance".[65]   This is the first reference of the ship being subjected to Israeli surveillance. During this event, Green describes the jets as "homing their rockets in on the *Liberty*", and the small group in the ship's communications center used the ECM, electronic counter measure equipment, to "spoof" the jets by distorting the *Liberty's* radar signature.   Green attributes this information in his book to First Class Petty Officer Charles Rowley, who remembered that no one took this contact seriously, as the Israelis were "only playing games". Ennes reports that Rowley served as the ship's photographer.

Green alludes to the fact that Israelis may have been tipped off about the *Liberty's* mission because of close ties between the CIA and Israeli intelligence, specifically the Mossad who had been preplanning the Six-Day War. Based on surmised crew indifference, we will get a mixed picture of a crew concerned about entering a war zone; however, accustom to being left to themselves to slowly crawl a coastline—not to be bothered and somewhat oblivious to what was going on around them. Perhaps they were relying on the contention she was a neutral ship in international waters—a special status that would magically blanket the ship with a security shield. Their orders had been to report unusual activity including over-flights.

Stephen Green is one of the many authors who wrote about American and Israeli relations.   In 1984, he published *Taking Sides: America's Secret Relations with a Militant Israel.* Critics cite his support for the Arab side of the Arab-Israeli conflict as clouding his perspective.   Green claims that the U.S. Air Force supported the Israeli war effort in 1967 by providing four

RF-4C Phantom photoreconnaissance aircraft.[66] Recall in the previous chapter the contention and denial that we were aiding the Israelis. We will come across this claim again later. An editorial note by the State Department Office of the Historian notes that there is no evidence to support Green's reference to photo reconnaissance assistance being provided to the Israelis.[67]

It will become clear that the Israelis were well aware of the ship, and were anticipating the arrival of the ship in the area. A question arises as to whether or not someone had provided the Israelis a heads-up about the ship's mission as previously alluded to by Green. There is no hard evidence on this point, however, it appears that the Defense Department was warned to move the ship or she would be sunk.

Interestingly, in the spring of 2003 at Harvard University, Assistant Secretary of Defense for C3I, John P. Stenbit, is quoted in his paper as follows:[68]

> The Israelis called us up one day and said, "If you don't get that ship, the Liberty, out of this place we're going to sink it in twenty-four hours." We couldn't tell the ship to move when we got the data back because it was already under the water, because it took more than twenty-four hours for the data to wander in through the system and come out at the other end.

His reference to "it was already under water" is not clear because the ship did not sink. Perhaps he was referring to the fact that they were unable to get a warning message to the *Liberty* to pull back from the area—this is conjecture.

It is reported, again by Stephen Green, that "the Office of the U.S. Defense Attaché in Tel Aviv sent a startling message back to U.S. Army Communication Center in Washington by coded telegram: The IDF was planning to attack the *Liberty* if the ship continued to move closer to the Israel coast!"[69] Any warning or call back message did not arrive at the ship—a major communication snafu involving the JCS and NSA.[70]

Regarding the threat to sink the *Liberty*, a motive clue can be found in Chief of Staff, Yitzhak Rabin's *The Rabin Memories*. On June 5, "...we notified the American naval attaché in Israel that we intended to protect our shores from Egyptian naval attacks by employing a combination of naval and air units....We therefore asked that American ships be removed from the vicinity of the Israeli shore or that the Americans notify us of their precise location in the area near our coast."[71] Whether the request was phrased in stronger terms or interpreted to be a threat is unclear—it sounded like an ultimatum. Rabin was concerned about the *Liberty's* ability to monitor IDF signal networks by tracking messages transmitted between various headquarters.

Reviewing information found in the Israeli reports of the attack on the *Liberty* it is noted that this "Nord" flight had taken off from its base at 0410, and according to conflicting reports, the *Liberty* was determined to be a U.S. naval supply ship.[72] Another Israeli report would note the observation of a destroyer heading toward Gaza on a bearing of 120 decrees. It was the second report from the Nord that definitely changed the ID of the ship to that of a supply ship description.[73]

The *Liberty* was in readiness condition three modified with ammunition now placed at all four machine gun positions and men were on duty in battle dress in the two forward gun tubs or mounts. They were beginning to take on the apprehensive feeling of a crew entering a war zone.

Lieutenant Jim Ennes began his morning duty watch on the bridge at 0720Z or 0920 Sinai time noting how difficult it was to fix the ship's position along the nondescript coastline. *Liberty* was to go to Point Alfa and begin a slow crawl back to the west somewhat parallel to the coastline of the Sinai in the direction of Port Said. This course would lead to Point Bravo, fifteen miles ahead at 31-22.3N 33-42E. Ennes was able to spot the small desert town of El Arish and the town's minaret for a bearing and location fix. At Point Alfa, the *Liberty's* position would be approximately 16 miles from Khan Yunis, and 25 miles from El Arish. She would then change course to southwesterly toward Point Bravo and then northwesterly to Point Charlie, continuing this course unless ordered otherwise. Anyway, that was the plan and course for her signals intelligence-gathering mission, which required a line-of-sight range to the shoreline.

On the bridge with Ennes was a signalman, and quartermaster in charge of the men and responsible for keeping a notebook record, log, of watch conditions and orders given, including all course and speed changes. Also, present were a helmsman and engine-order telegrapher whose job was to relay orders to the engine room, and two lookouts. In an adjoining room was the radar operator. Ennes was the officer of the deck.

He took particular note that the ship's five-by-eight foot flag was fouled, entangled in lines as well as being dirty with soot and badly tattered. He ordered a new flag to be displayed. After a little discussion with Signalman Russell David, a new flag, his last one, was hoisted in place and flowing free and clear. The ship's executive officer Philip Armstrong alerted that there would be a General Quarters drill at noontime. Ennes checked the condition of the TRSSCOMM system, and was advised by Senior Chief Stan White, the electronics maintenance technician, that all was well and that it would be ready on schedule at 1400 hours for transmission. As noted by Ennes, the moon would be in a good position to talk to Cheltenham, Maryland—that is to bounce a signal off the moon. They could control any hydraulic leaks that remained an ongoing problem.

The Captain appeared on the bridge and reviewed the status of operations. He was advised of a small bomber type plane seen near the beach of El Arish and about the over-flight of the "boxcar" type plane. Now they were about 90 miles to the east of Port Said on a steady course of 253 degrees at five knots.

With today's technology, the reader can use *Google Earth* on his or her computer and actually overfly the area where the *Liberty* patrolled to get a better grasp of the locale, land and water terrain, and distances.

At 0850, there was another sighting of a plane passing the *Liberty's* stern. Ennes and Captain McGonagle watched the plane pass down the starboard side, then turn left and vanish in the direction of the Gaza strip. Clarification would show shortly before 0900 hours (local time), two delta-wing, single-engine jet aircraft orbiting the *Liberty* three times at 31-27N, 34-00E. The planes' altitude was estimated at 5,000 feet, at a distance of approximately two miles. *Liberty* was to notify the Commander, Sixth Fleet and others of this reconnaissance, stating that identification was unknown and that no amplifying report would be submitted—this time in compliance with orders. At the direction of the Captain, Ennes was to prepare a message of the sighting for higher authority, but being tied up with coastal piloting to maintain course he requested that Lieutenant Steve Toth the ship's navigator and intelligence officer draft the sighting message.[74]

A comment is in order here reference the "orbiting of the *Liberty*", which would indicate that the *Liberty* was subjected to reconnaissance. Some will claim that the over-flights were due to an Israeli operational traffic pattern that included the Sinai area and that the *Liberty* was not targeted or over-flown as many times as claimed by the crew. It might be questionable as to what a pilot could see at 5000 feet from a fast moving jet. From such a height, one can assume a good panorama view with the ability to see a ship's wake and direction.

Notwithstanding the fact that the crew and ship had entered proximity to a war zone, they were not to be denied their sunbathing time on blankets and lounge chairs. Ennes notes that while their "could" be a morale problem with such relaxed conditions, the Captain encouraged it and this was one reason the ship had good morale. Nevertheless, in view of the developing circumstances and the reconnaissance over-flights, one wonders if the ship and crew were at peak alert—that may have been the "modified" portion of readiness condition three. There were more plane sightings and the crew had to be called to a more alert status. Ennes

37

comments on the relaxed condition in more detail in his book.[75]

The quartermaster informed Ennes that the lookouts did not have binoculars. There were binoculars but not all look-outs had them—it appears that for whatever reason Lieutenant Toth collected them and stored them in the chart house—apparently his tidiness got the best of him as he was apparently concerned they would get banged up. This had not happened before—perhaps just a strange quirk or lapse.[76] Perhaps it was just a natural state of nervousness being so close to a war zone.

During an earlier sighting an Israeli pilot at first reported being fired on when attempting to ID the ship— later to be discounted when he was debriefed.[77] In his book, Ennes notes the time as just before 1000 local time, and describes the over-flying jets as French-built Dassault Mirage III fighter-bombers. France was Israel's main supplier of planes and weapons prior to the Six-Day War; however, President Charles de Gaulle would quickly impose an arms embargo on Israel prior to the war. Ennes notes that they were close enough to see clusters of rockets under the wings but could see no identifying markings. He states he checked the ship's flag condition and could see the pilots through his binoculars. It was his conclusion if he could see them that clearly; they could certainly see the ship's flag. They made three orbits and vanished. The sighting of rocket pods on the planes will raise an interesting issue to be referred to later.

Fig. 4, Israeli Mirage IIICJ.

http://www.jewishvirtuallibrary.org/jsource/Society_&_Culture/mirage.html

Obviously, with the war still going on, there was activity in the Israeli war rooms at the Kirya, in Tel Aviv, and at the Naval HQ, headquarters, at Stella Maris at Haifa.[78] The seeds of a controversy were being sowed. Once the *Liberty* had been spotted by the early morning flights, what did they do about it? There will be contentions that attempts had been made to contact the U.S. Embassy about the ship.[79] Chief of Staff Rabin, in his memoirs acknowledges we were advised to move our ships or to advise their position in the area. Author Michael Oren reports that Rabin conveyed his warning to the U.S. Naval Attaché, Commander Ernest Carl Castle and that any vessel sailing over 20 knots would be sunk.[80] At any rate, the *Liberty* was plotted on the Israeli Naval HQ plot chart.

Distracted by the plane sighting, the Captain inquired if Ennes had reduced the ship's speed from 15 to 5 knots—he followed through with the correction.

39

Interestingly, off duty personnel were still sunbathing themselves on blankets and lounge chairs.

The flying "boxcar" plane, the Nord, appeared again at 1030 and would return about every half hour or so.[81] Obviously, the Israelis were taking a real interest in the *Liberty*, but at a distance about three to five miles across the stern. No efforts were made to communicate with her. Ennes reports he again checked the condition of the flag and it was flying freely with the relative wind from dead ahead. The Captain felt that his ship was getting a good look over and that there would not be any mistakes in identification, which was of some limited comfort to him. At one point the Nord flew so close the rivets could be seen as she dipped down to about 200 feet from the water. The plane was so close that the engine vibrations reverberate off the ship's deck metal according to Ennes.

Strangely, toward the end of Ennes's watch, Steve Toth told him that the Captain had not yet released the sightings reports so they could be sent out.[82] This would not be the only report of erratic behavior on the part of the Captain—something out of character for him.

While the *Liberty* is doing her snail's pace crawl at five knots from Point Alfa to Point Bravo, with the surreal scene of sunbathing crewmembers, it is appropriate to recall that there is a shooting war going on less the 20 miles away in the Sinai.

At 1100 AM, while Israeli warships hunted for Egyptian submarines, the duty officer at IDF Naval Headquarters, Commander Avraham Lunz, concluded his shift. In accordance with "claimed procedures", he removed the green "neutral" marker representing the *Liberty* from the plot board contending that it was already

40

five hours old and no longer accurate. "As far as the navy was concerned, the *Liberty* had sailed away".[83] This position is not consistent with the continuing aerial surveillance, and coastal radar tracking. As for the issue of submarines, the Mediterranean was loaded with subs, many of them Soviet as we will later learn. It should be noted that after the first day of the war the Israelis controlled the skies but had unfinished business.

Lunz in his statement for the *Discovery Channel* television documentary, *Attack on the Liberty*, by Thames TV, referred to *Liberty* as an American type intelligence-gathering ship. He took off the battle control table the tower that represented this neutral American intelligence-gathering ship. He said he did not know the name of the ship but knew its function.[84]

On the fourth day of the war, Israeli forces were re-grouping along the border with Jordan in a defensive posture. Egyptian soldiers were in a rout and concerns about a massacre were rising, as Israelis were no longer able to provide for the large numbers of prisoners. Colonel Jackie Even, a tank commander, later testified, "I told myself, hold on, there's going to be a massacre here, with both sides shooting. Therefore, I ordered everyone, 'no killing soldiers'. Try to catch them and then let them go so that they'll spread the word that the Israelis won't kill them, just send them home."[85] There will be allegations that Israeli troops did kill Egyptian prisoners in a massacre. This will become one of the motive theories behind the attack on the USS *Liberty*, that it was an effort by a local commander to hide such an event. Author James Bamford notes this possible motive in his book *Body of Secrets* and the Chapter *Blood*.[86]

With Chief of Staff Rabin in control at the Kirya, it is unlikely that a local commander could or would have ordered an attack on the *Liberty*. The rationale for this position is, as Rabin notes in his memoirs, there was some thought the ship attacked was Russian. If valid, no lower rank commander would make a decision that would cause a confrontation between Israel and the Soviets—it would not make sense—Rabin would have been very upset. Israel was very concerned about bringing the Soviets into the war on behalf of her proxies.

Some 70 percent of the Egyptian armor had been defeated and now the urge was to rush toward the canal, notwithstanding Dayan's threat to court marshal any commander who pushed that far. Spectacular as the battles in the Sinai were, they were over shadowed by the millennial liberation of Jerusalem. "The Temple Mount is in our hands," General Gavish purportedly bemoaned to his officers, "We've lost the glory." Some of that glory could now be regained, however, along the banks of the Suez Canal.[87]

"The Israeli government never set goals for the war," recalled Rehavam Ze'evi, the deputy operations chief. "The objectives rose from the bottom up, from the military to the political echelon. Only after the war did the government draws circles around our accomplishments and declare that these were its original goals. However, in one theater the government would stand firm to exercise control, and it would be the Cabinet and not the army that would decide when and where to strike Syria".[88]

Because of constant shelling and harassment over time by the Syrians along their border with Israel, there was a popular thirst to teach them a lesson and strike into the

Golan hills. Rabin as Chief of Staff would have to confront the Israeli Northern Commander, David Elazar, and hold him and his forces back from an all out assault. Rabin ordered a halt to the invasion of Syria around 1000 hours Sinai time on June 8, this would be a controversial act.[89] The question will arise, did his desist order have anything to do with the presence of the *Liberty* in the area. Would the Johnson administration approve or disapprove of an invasion of Syria? What would the Russians do if their proxy was attacked? After all, the Soviets were pressuring both Syria and Egypt to stand up against the Israelis as America's proxy in the Middle East. These were strategic not mere tactical field operational issues to be pondered at the highest echelons in the Israeli military and government.

An underlying question would be how close we were to a major escalation and confrontation between the world's two super-powers. This will be discussed later as a nuclear-armed Russian submarine will have targeted Tel Aviv. Further, the 744 Bomb Squadron at Beale AFB in California will have its B-52s with nuclear cruise missiles on "alert" and sitting at the launch point on the runway at 1100 local time and 0500 Washington time— 0200 California time.[90] Were we heading for a nuclear confrontation more dangerous than the Cuban missile crisis of 1962? Not two, but three nuclear-armed parties were involved in conflict, with the inclusion of Israel because of its stealth Dimona nuclear project. The Soviets had placed TU-95 Bears on alert in the southern Crimea. Did Israel in fact have one or more nuclear weapons at the time of the Six-Day War? These issues certainly had to be under consideration by the U.S. government even though preoccupied with an ongoing war in Vietnam.

At 1130 the *Liberty* arrived at Point Bravo and executed a right turn to a new course of 283 decrees, heading toward Point Charlie At 31.31N 33.00E. The mission required that the ship reverse course every ten hours retracing the same three-point pattern until further orders.

There had been a small plane or bomber flying back and forth along the coastline by El Arish; suddenly Ennes noticed that a huge explosion rocked the town of El Arish sending up a lot of smoke. The plane was no longer visible. He notified the Captain. At noon, with thick smoke all along the coastline, Lieutenant Lloyd Painter was ready to assume the watch. Ennes updated him on the explosion, the surveillance by the jets and flying boxcar—the Nord, and the coordinates for Point Charlie.

Around 1120 some Israeli activity was developing at Naval HQ. Israeli Motor Torpedo Boat Division 914 consisting of three boats, T-203, T-204, and T-206 was instructed to sail from Ashdod to patrol the coast from Ashdod to Ashkelon. The division Commander, Moshe Oren, not to be confused with Michael Oren the author, was on the command boat T-204. Udi Erell, the son of Israeli Rear Admiral Shlomo Erell, was on one of the boats. Years later in an interview for the BBC TV documentary, *Dead in the Water*, he would state that the boats were in the harbor when the boat siren sounded and everyone had to get onboard to head out. The reason for the alert was not immediately made known to the MTB crews.

Coincidently, around the same time at 1124 local time, an interesting thing developed. There was a report from an Israeli command post that El Arish was being bombarded from the sea. Reference is made to the first post attack Israeli report dealing with the attack conducted by a Colonel Ram Ron dated June 16, 1967.[91] The flying boxcar plane, the Nord, appeared again over the *Liberty* at 1126 hours. At 1127, the IDF General Headquarters at the Kirya in Tel Aviv gets the report of shelling from the Southern Command.[92] All of this was within minutes of the explosion at El Arish. Ennes's report of the explosion was around noontime.[93] Now the Israeli Supreme Command perks its ears up and the Southern Command reports that the shelling did not reach the coast. While there may be some time discrepancies, the consensus as to timing of these events is not really disputed in either the Israeli or the *Liberty* camps. The question is what did they mean and what is stirring afoot?

At 1145 the shelling reports were passed to Fleet Control Operations Center to Commander Lunz and Captain Rahav, that since they had the attention of Supreme Command, they should be taken seriously. Recall Lunz went off shift at 1100 and the *Liberty* plot marker was removed. The Head of Naval Operations now ordered the torpedo boats to explore in area of El Arish. However, the division commander, Moshe Oren, was not told about the shelling or what to look for.[94]

Meanwhile, George Golden, the ship's engineer, reports at 1145, "I have a lounge chair, most of us do have; while lying on my back sunbathing, I noticed a plane flying over. I dozed off, and approximately 25 minutes or so later on, I woke up and saw a plane circling again coming from the port beam, crossing the ship."[95] The GHQ (General Headquarters) Tel Aviv receives a second report of ship activity off El Arish.

To summarize, we have a large explosion at El Arish, then there are reports of shelling from the sea that does not land on the coast. The Israeli Supreme Command now takes note of what is developing. During this process, we have multiple over-flights of Israeli aircraft who one would expect would be reporting on what the ship below, the *Liberty*, was doing. Recall the *Gerhard Report* notes that while *Liberty* had no specific assignment to intercept Israeli communications while in area three, nevertheless, her VHF search positions produced three tapes of Israeli air traffic. It was later determined that the content was "routine operational messages".[96] These tapes were a by-product of searching for U.A.R. communications in the Sinai, while incidentally, USN-855, identified some 22 Israeli frequencies. We do not know what happened to these tapes or how they happened to be transported or transmitted to the NSA. The question is, over what time frame these tapes covered. The NSA will claim there were no U.S. intercepts dealing with the actual attack. We will get into the issue of intercepted communications later as they will become an important part of the *Liberty* story. The Israeli radar tag with the *Liberty* on the evening of the seventh should have been recorded electronically in some format—but nothing has become known.

The Israeli contention will be that contact and the location of the *Liberty* had not been updated for five hours and her marker was removed from the navigation plot table at Stella Maris, Naval HQ, at Haifa by Lunz going off duty. All of this is very important because it will begin to form the basis for the Israeli claim of mistaken identity in its subsequent attack on the *Liberty*. The effort here is an attempt to overlay facts from the

46

different perspectives of the ship, crew and the Israeli command structure.

At 1200, the motor torpedo boats are told to steer to a point 20 miles North of El Arish. This would be the approximately position of the USS *Liberty*. Remember the armament configuration of the *Liberty*—four .50-Calibre machine guns in tub mounts. These would not be able to bombard or even fire on the coastline—certainly; they would not be the cause of the shelling claim or the explosion. At 1205, we have a conflicting piece of information from the *Ram Ron Report*. It would be the first Israeli inquiry into the attack on the *Liberty*, apparently ordered by Israeli Chief of Staff, Rabin. Captain Rahav at Naval HQ orders the shelling report checked with orders for the MTBs to get ready to sail.[97] Previously, we noted they were directed to patrol between Ashdod and Ashkelon. Of course, in reporting war events confusion will exist. The fact is the Israelis will contend that both MTBs and attacking aircraft were dispatched at 1205.[98]

Michael Oren in his book *Six Days of War* will report that at 1125 the explosion in the area of El Arish was actually the result of a blast at an ammunition dump. Further, he notes that the Israeli observers noted two vessels offshore and concluded that the Egyptians were shelling them from the sea. It is contended that such a bombardment had indeed taken place the previous day, according to both Israeli and Egyptian reports.[99]

Author Michael Oren goes on to note that while the *Liberty* had made a course change toward Port Said, in the "Pit" at the Kirya, reports of the shelling "unsettled Rabin", who had been warned of a possible Egyptian amphibious landing near Gaza. He reiterated the standing order to sink any unidentified ships in the war area, but also advised caution as Soviet vessels were reportedly operating nearby. Rabin's concerns reinforce the point that no local commander would on his own order a strike on the *Liberty*. Later we will learn later that it was the Russians who were actively considering a landing force.

Author Isabella Ginor will report that the Israelis were tracking as many as 43 Soviet ships. Remarkably, Oren goes on to say, "Since no fighter planes were available, the navy was asked to intercede, with the assumption that air cover would be provided later."[100] The lack of available planes would seem to conflict with observations by the *Liberty* crewmembers of multiple over-flights; also remember the Arab air forces had been destroyed during the first day of the war on June 5.

As a side note, Michael Oren, a strong defender of the Israeli version of events and promoter of the "friendly fire" theory of the attack on the *Liberty* will become Israel's ambassador to the United States in 2010.

In summary, first, Rabin is the person, as Chief of Staff, who made the initial threat to sink the *Liberty* if she were not moved from the area. Lunz had removed the plot marker because of no updates of her position per claimed protocols. *Liberty* reports multiple reconnaissance over-flights. *Liberty* makes no mention of other ships in her area. Later Israeli reports will refute that no planes were available; rather they were dispatched at the same time as the motor torpedo boats as noted above. Was the stage was being manipulated and set for carrying out the "threat"? Was the El Arish ammo-dump explosion a pretext for justifying what would later happen to the *Liberty*? Israel's IDF was in control of the El Arish area.

Michael Oren notes: "More than half an hour passed without any response from naval headquarters in Haifa. The general staff finally issued a rebuke: 'the coast is being shelled and you—the navy—have done nothing.'"[101] Captain Izzy Rahav, who had replaced Lunz according to Oren, in the operations room, needed no more prodding. He dispatched the three torpedo boats of the 914 squadron, code named *Pagoda*, to find the enemy vessel responsible for the bombardment and destroy it. The time was 1205 PM.

Rabin in his memoirs noted that he was seated in his office when he got an odd message about explosions in the El Arish area. He noted that Israel had already secured the area and he thought that Egyptians could be coming in from the sea. **He ordered planes and the navy to deal with it**. The Admiral of the Navy, Shlomo Erell, had left the Naval Headquarters to go down to the docks leaving Rahav in charge—more on this point later.

Rabin, in charge of operations, seems to be calling all these shots. After all, he is in charge of all military operations under Moshe Dayan, the Minister of Defense. A diagram of the Israeli command structure dealing with the attack on the *Liberty* can be found on the Internet, a copy of which is posted here:

http://www.thelibertyincident.com/command.html.

Rabin had ordered the attack on Syria stopped at 1000 Sinai time. What were his concerns? Oren indicated Rabin's fear was of an Egyptian amphibious landing near

Gaza and of Soviet ships in the area. Were these various factors playing on his mind and to what end?

For one thing, we know there was a substantial Soviet armada within the region along with a number of submarines. Note the following from an English version of *Pravda*:[102]

> The Soviet submarine K-172 under the command of Nikolay Shashkov armed with missiles and nuclear warheads was at the very same moment in the Bay of Sidre. The submarine received instructions to surface and deliver a blow against the Israeli coast if the Americans landed troops on Syrian shores. The submarine had eight nuclear missiles onboard. However, as we know the Israeli coast means the whole state of Israel stretched along the sea. Israel would have been completely destroyed if such blows were delivered by the Soviet submarine.

The Bay of Sidre is off central Libya. The Israeli coastal defense strategy calls for the IAF to shoulder a big responsibility, while the Navy's role is less defined. In fact, for years the Navy has been trying to define its place in the scheme of things. It is possible that the planes tracking the *Liberty* were also looking for Contact "X" or Egyptian and Soviet submarines. To say that the focus was on Egyptian submarines or an Egyptian amphibious landing would seem to be a misnomer considering the destruction of the Arab air forces and the defeat of Arab forces in the Sinai.

Therefore, on the personal level, the pressure was on Rabin as he was faced with some serious decisions to make as Chief of Staff. The popular position within the military and populous was to attack Syria and teach her a lesson, yet he had to look at what the Soviets would do if its main proxy in the area were attacked. The USS *Liberty* was caught in the middle of the dilemma; with the U.S. government being perceived by the Israelis as less than fully committed to "their agenda"—they needed an insurance policy to counter the Soviets. Was the *Liberty* it?

While Rabin was the operational commander of the military, the question is where was Dayan, the Minister of Defense? Rabin reports that on June 7 Dayan ordered Jerusalem's Old City to be occupied as quickly as possible. "The most coveted target". He notes that at 7 AM that morning, Dayan had entered the war room and he himself issued the order. Dayan was actively in control of operations establishing strategic objectives.

Did the Israelis have a legitimate concern about a potential Soviet threat? Dr. Isabella Ginor, a researcher into the history of the Six-Day War, contends that arrangements were made for Soviet Arabic interpreters stationed in Egypt to be informed that they would be posted to ships of the Black Sea Fleet now cruising off Israel's shore. "One of the interpreters...said he knew for sure that we would be attached to a 'desant' (Russian meaning descent, or landing) force that would be landing in Haifa [Israel's main commercial harbor and naval base] or slightly northward." The interpreters were to handle liaison with Israel's Arab population, "who were longing for us."[103]

She further notes that the Israelis appeared to be more concerned about the threat by the Soviet Fleet than the Americans were. The Israeli military's representative told the U.S. defense attaché on May 25: "We are very

51

anxious to know what [the] Soviet fleet in [the] East Mediterranean is doing...."[104]

Most interestingly, Ginor notes, "There were minor incidents between Soviet ships and Israel patrol craft which fortunately ended peacefully."[105] How are we to interpret Rabin's threat to sink ships? Did this threat only apply to Egyptian and U.S. ships? It would appear that the treatment of the USS *Liberty* should be construed in terms of the Israelis concern about the presence of so many Soviet vessels—the attack threat was limited and defined—Israel was not about to attack a Russian ship.

Indeed, Rabin had a lot on his mind and was concerned: "...I had led the country into war under the most difficult circumstances." Reports were that preceding the start of the war he was on the verge of a nervous breakdown and pulled himself together just in time. This information had been kept from the public until years later.[106] His relationship with Minister of Defense Moshe Dayan was tenuous at best. As Chief of Staff, Rabin had to be the "detail" person, while Dayan could set the strategic and tactical policy. If Dayan said, "do this", then it was Rabin's duty to find a way to get it done. The relationship between Dayan and Rabin is both dynamic and problematic—a power struggle?

Notwithstanding the claim of a possible breakdown by Rabin, he was more aggressive than Dayan was, especially when it came to Syria. There are two issues to be played out in our *Liberty* saga: First, bowing to U.S. pressure, Israel declined to tell the world how advanced it nuclear weapons program was, and second, that Rabin with Prime Minister Eshkol's backing wanted war against Syria and was doing his best to bring it about. "Three days later Rabin chimed in, giving four different

52

interviews to four different newspapers in which he said that more IDF operations might be necessary to change the regime in Damascus and make Syria stop supporting the PLO."[107] The contention is Shimon Peres wanted to have a nuclear demonstration to head off the war; and the desire for regime change in Syria will constitute a prime motivator for Israeli actions—an apparent dichotomy.[108] What are we to make of the claim that the U.S. wanted the Israeli nuclear program kept quiet?

For a current illustration as to how the Israelis perceive the Chief of Staff's role in a crisis, note the current investigation into the Chief of Staff's handling of the Gaza relief flotilla controversy.[109] Once the Chief of Staff becomes engaged, the burden falls on his shoulders—he is held accountable, or so it would appear.

Getting back to activity on the *Liberty*, the General Quarters drill alarm sounded at 1310. It was to require a practiced response to a gas attack. As noted by Ennes, it was due to an erroneous report of gas usage ashore. By this time, the message ordering *Liberty* to pull away from the coast should have been received, but it was lost in the communications fiasco. The General Quarters Drill secured at 1348. Ennes reports the Captain as saying, "It's good that we have sunbathers on deck. It helps to show that we're peaceful."[110] The Captain complemented the crew on the drill and cautioned them to be alert as there was a war going out there.

At 1317, MTB Division 914 was advised by Naval HQ of the shelling report in the area of El Arish. Moshe Oren, the MTB commander was told to listen to air-sea-liaison channels 86 and 186, and that planes would be dispatched, "after they detected the ship".[111]

Then at 1341, the motor torpedo boats pick up their target 20 miles NW of El Arish.[112] The torpedo boats pick up the *Liberty* on their Kelvin-Hughes war surplus radar at extreme range.

As the *Liberty* crew was wrapping up after the GQ drill, a bridge telephone talker, still winding up his cable but not unplugged advised the Captain of three high-speed aircraft, sixteen miles away, and approaching the ship from 082 decrees—the general direction of Tel Aviv, the Israeli capital. Then combat control corrected the report, advising that "the contacts are fading; they appear to be weather."[113] Combat control then revised again and noted that three high-speed surface craft were approaching the ship from the same bearing as the aircraft, at 35 knots.

Lieutenant Lloyd Painter called to the Captain, "Captain, you gotta look at this! I never saw anything move so fast."[114] Ennes, the Captain, Jim O'Connor, and the XO, Philip Armstrong, including the ship's photographer with camera were on the bridge. Ennes said he was the first to spot the single delta-wing Mirage jet about 45 degrees above the water, paralleling their course in the pattern that had become routine. Ennes raced for a fix mounted telescope, while O'Connor searched the sky with his binoculars.

Painter in his testimony before the Naval Court of Inquiry would state that as the Captain watched the planes, he noted they were probably going to attack, and ordered Painter to alert the forward gun mounts. He testified he was unable to contact them and saw two of the kids blown to bits. Things were happening so quickly, and then he saw the quartermaster standing next to him hit, apparently from flying porthole glass, when

54

the attacking planes strafed the bridge area. Running as fast as he could to his general quarters station he came across the ship's postal clerk lying there cut in half from the strafing—to die in spite of efforts to resuscitate him. He returned to the bridge to find the Captain wounded and lying on a stretcher. The counsel for the court asked if he saw the national ensign flying, and Painter said he did. When pressed as to whether he saw the ensign flying in the morning and after the torpedo attack, he said he saw it both before and after the torpedo attack.[115]

From the evening before until now there had been 11 over-flights noted. Had the ambush been set and the trap been tripped? Below is a map of the area.

Fig. 5, Map of Area Showing Al Arish.

LIBERTY IS A CLEARLY MARKED UNITED
STATES SHIP IN INTERNATIONAL WATERS, NOT
A PARTICIPANT IN THE CONFLICT AND NOT A
REASONABLE SUBJECT FOR ATTACK BY ANY
NATION.

June 6, 1967
reply from Vice Admiral Martin.

Chapter 3

A Neutral Ship in International Waters

The crew of the *Liberty* was just securing from it general quarters practice drill when the Captain remarked, "It's good that we have sunbathers on deck, it helps to show that we're peaceful." Over the ship's general announcing system he complimented the men on the drill and cautioned them that they were in a war zone to emphasize the dangerous situation they were in— pointing to the fires in the area of El Arish. He noted that local forces knew the *Liberty* was in the area.[116] Did they—and what "local forces" was he referring to? The Israelis had secured the El Arish area on the 2nd day of the war—6 June.

The Captain's position on the sunbathers contrasts with his request to Vice Admiral Martin for a destroyer escort. When there was no order pulling the *Liberty* back from her closest proximity to the coastline, the Captain had appealed to Vice Admiral Martin, drafting a request that a destroyer be sent to remain within five miles of the ship to serve both as an armed escort and as an auxiliary communication center.

This reference to the requested destroyer escort being an "auxiliary communication center" raises an interesting point. Was *Liberty* assigned to be the primary communication link for a submersed submarine marked as the mysterious "X" that Ennes observed on the *Liberty's* plot table. This is speculation as submerged subs at the time had limited communication capabilities. Perhaps the *Liberty* could have served as a communication link between it and key government agencies charged with monitoring events in the Eastern Mediterranean. One method of communication could have involved an acoustical link.[117]

The Captain had established a "modified condition readiness three", which he defined in a memorandum to key personnel on the bridge:[118]

> Effective immediately, two men will be stationed on the forecastle as additional lookouts/gun crews...Lookouts and forecastle gun mount personnel are to man mounts and defend the ship in the event of surprise air/surface attack while regular General Quarter's teams are being assembled. . . Any unidentified surface contact approaching the ship on a collision or near collision course at a speed of 25 knots or more is to be considered acting in a hostile manner and Condition of Readiness One is to be set immediately...Any unidentified air contact approaching the ship on an apparent strafing/bombing/torpedo attack is to be considered hostile. . . It is better to set general quarters in doubtful cases than to be taken by surprise and be unable to fight the ship. Take immediate action as may be required by the situation, then advise me of what steps have been taken.

Ennes reports that on June 6th we received Admiral Martin's reply to our request for an armed escort: "LIBERTY IS A CLEARLY MARKED UNITED STATES SHIP IN INTERNATIONAL WATERS, NOT A PARTICIPANT IN THE CONFLICT AND NOT A REASONABLE SUBJECT FOR ATTACK BY ANY NATION." In the unlikely event of an inadvertent attack, he promised, jet fighters from the Sixth Fleet carrier forces could be overhead in less than ten minutes. Besides, he concluded, every commanding officer has authority to withdraw from danger. Request for escort denied!

Around 1350 Sinai time, the bridge phone talker advised that the Combat Control Center was alerting them to three high-speed aircraft sixteen miles away and approaching the ship from 082 degrees, the general direction of Tel Aviv and the Israeli coastline. Actually, this direction was in line with Ashdod on the Israeli coast. Tel Aviv is further north. Next, the radar operator advised that three high-speed surface vessels were moving toward the *Liberty* on the same bearing at 35 knots.

While technically off duty, Ennes was still present on the bridge with the Captain, Jim O'Connor, and Philip Armstrong the ship's executive officer. The ship's photographer, Petty Officer Rowley, who brought a camera with him, joined them.

The Captain had testified before the Court of Inquiry that it was not possible to see identifying insignia on the over-flying aircraft. Ennes reports that he was the first to spot a single delta-wing Mirage fighter jet about 45 degrees off the water and paralleling the ship in a manner that had become routine with the recon flights of the

59

previous hours. Several sailors had gathered to observe the planes. As Ennes used the ship's telescope, Rowley called, "Mr. Ennes, he's not there. He's up ahead".

Confusion and chaos began to reign. Ennes states that Jim O'Connor spotted bright flashes under the wings of the French built jet in time to dive down a ladder.[119] He was struck in midair, severely wounded by rocket fragments before he crashed onto the deck below. Ennes related that he seemed to be the only one left standing as the jet disappeared astern of them. Around him, scattered about carelessly, men squirmed helplessly, like wounded animals—wide-eyed, terrified, not understanding what happened.[120] The Captain testified before the Court of Inquiry that while observing the planes he did not believe them to be in "a hostile attitude". He heard a loud explosion on the Port side and upon checking found 55-gallon fuel drums burning "furiously". He witnessed personnel being blown around off their feet and he grabbed the engine order annunciator and "rang up all ahead flank".

The Captain testified he ordered Lt. Bennett to notify the Chief Naval Operations of the attack via Hi-com and to request assistance—that attacked by unidentified aircraft. McGonagle will testify to six to eight strafing attacks with planes criss-crossing the ship. He grabbed a camera from the bridge safe and took pictures of the attacking planes in order to identify them, as well as the motor torpedo boats and helicopter later flying to the ship. The Captain testified he turned the film over the USS *America* for later disposition. He testified he noticed a burning sensation and oozing blood on his trouser and some minor pain but could keep walking.

Then a second plane moved on them as Ennes noted that his khaki uniform was bright red from two dozen rocket fragments buried in his flesh. He reports that his left leg was broken above the knee and hung from his hip like a great beanbag. Ennes, struck in the first attack would find cover until aid would come to him. Ennes notes that he was able to find brief refuge in the ship's doctor, Dr. Kiepfer's, stateroom. Concerned with the broken bone in his leg cutting an artery, he mused as to who might be attacking them. He states in his book that they knew the Arab air forces were crippled; however, the Arabs blamed the United States for their problems and falsely charged that American carrier-based aircraft had assisted Israel. Michael Oren in his book on the *Six Days of War* notes an Egyptian General blamed the *Liberty* for jamming their radios and making their retreat all the more difficult. He thought to himself, it would certainly be difficult to accept Israel as the attacking party.

Lieutenant Ennes, along with the rest of the crew now became both witnesses and victims to one of the most tragic and unusual naval engagements in history. He would take on the additional role as investigative-reporter of the events, spending years talking with survivors and reconstructing the events of June 8, in preparation to later publishing his book. In the meantime, he witnessed the rockets penetrating the steel of the ship "like fire-breathing creatures." With the passage of years, information on the attack would dribble out to supplement the observations of Ennes and the ship's crewmembers.

Yiftah Spector was a young Israeli pilot and was the flight leader of *Kursa* (Couch), a flight of two French built Mirage IIICJs. He had the USS *Liberty* in his plane's gun sight. Without warning or making an identification run, as contended he did, he let loose with his cannons wreaking havoc below on the decks of the *Liberty*. He will claim to have made identification runs as noted below in his words.[121]

"I did not fire on the Liberty as a human target. I was sent to attack a sailing vessel. This ship was on an escape route from the El Arish area, which at that same moment had heavy smoke rising from it," Spector said. "It was thought to be an Egyptian vessel. This ship positively did not have any symbol or flag that I could see. What I was concerned with was that it was not one of ours. I looked for the symbol of our navy, which was a large white cross on its deck," he told the *Jerusalem Post*. "This was not there, so it wasn't one of ours".

While Spector will later claim he made two identifying runs, the *Liberty* crew disputes this. Ennes would state in his book that he felt the surge of heat and thought somehow the ship was doing the firing—his mind asked, "We're shooting!" "Why are we shooting?" He reports that the air filled with hot metal as a geometric pattern of orange flashes opened holes in the heavy deck plating. An explosion tossed our gunners high into the air—spinning, broken, like rag dolls. He finally realized that "they" were being pounded with a deadly barrage of aircraft cannon and rocket fire.[122]

Fig. 6, Alleged gun-sight photo of Liberty.

Spector would deny he was armed with rockets, and years later would reflect on what has grown into a major controversy involving whether or not the *Liberty* was flying the American flag. The IAF (Israeli Air Force) indicated the only photos taken of the ship were from Spector's gun cameras, which automatically switched on whenever he fired.

"I was told on the radio that it was an Egyptian ship off the Gaza coast. Hit it. The luck of the ship was that I was armed only with light ammunition [30mm] against aircraft. If I had had a bomb it would be sitting on the bottom today like the Titanic. I promise you," Spector said. "The crew should be thankful for their luck" [that I was on an air-

63

to-air mission and did not have any bombs]. "It is a pity we attacked. I'm sorry for poor Capt. (William Loren) McGonagle, who was wounded in the leg and the other guys who were killed and wounded."

As a side note, James Scott, author of *The Attack on the Liberty* wrote that Spector declined his request for an interview, but did invite him and his dad for coffee at his home in the Tel Aviv suburbs. At the time of this visit, Spector was a 66-year-old retired Brigadier General. James Scott is the son of then Ensign John Scott who was on the bridge of the ship and was relieved by Ennes on the morning of June 8. Their meeting with Spector concluded with a handshake and Spector saying he was sorry.[123] This face-to-face meeting took place in the fall of 2007 during the Scotts' visit to Israel.

As noted, Spector's statement conflicts with the memory of the *Liberty* survivors, and other evidence. Suffice to say that the survivors are rankled by his apparent arrogant tone regarding their "luck". Spector: "They must understand that a mistake was made here. The fool is one who wanders about in the dark in dangerous places, so they should not come with any complaints." Later Spector would concede to author A. Jay Cristol that he did have a couple of air-to-air missiles—rockets. Cristol would note in his book, *The Liberty Incident* that *Kursa's* flight leader recalled this on June 10, 1992, twenty-five years and two days after the event that he was armed with missiles.[124] He and his wingman made three strafing runs and exhausted their ammunition by about 1404 local time to return to their base.[125] An Internet search indicates that the Mirage IIICJ was the first Israeli plane to carry air-to-air missiles. Plane hobbyist report that the Mirage IIIC was armed

64

with twin 30 mm DEFA revolver-type cannons fitted in the belly with gun ports under the air intakes. Modifications resulted in as many as five stores of pylons able to carry Sidewinder air-to-air missiles. Later to be replaced by the French missile, Matra Magic. [126]

It would indeed be ironic if in fact the Israeli planes attacking the *Liberty* were armed with U.S. supplied missiles. The R.550 Magic was a short-range missile designed in 1968 by the French company Matra to compete with the American AIM-9 Sidewinder. [127] If this dating is correct, then the missiles used could have been American Sidewinders. While Israel exploited whatever assistance it could get, America did not become a major arms supplier to Israel until after the Six-Day War. France, a major Israeli arms supplier, had implemented an arms embargo at the time of this war. Prior to the war the U.S. was not ready to become Israel's major weapons supplier, notwithstanding the Sidewinder issue. In a memorandum from General Wheeler, Chairman of the JCS, dealing with the matter of arms for Israel, it was Wheeler's contention that the balance between the Arabs and Israel would be upset if the U.S. provided arms as requested. It was the JCS position not to provide arms other than the Hawk missiles already provided under the Kennedy administration. [128]

The Israelis, rightfully, are proud to broadcast their successes in the intelligence arena, when appropriate for their public relation purposes. One story deals with the efforts to obtain the Soviet's most sophisticated jet, the MIG-21. After covert coordination on the intelligence level, an Iraqi pilot defected to Israel on August 16, 1966. Escorted by Mirage jets the pilot landed at Hatzor airbase. Americans were amazed at the Israeli coup and wanted to get their hands on the plane to learn all about it. The Israeli response was, "...not so fast! First, we will test it ourselves, then you will provide us with information about the SA-2 missiles, and supply us with 'Sidewinder' missiles, and then we will talk". The Israelis reported that a person named Joe Jordan, who was an American test pilot of the F-111, started testing the MIG-21. America eventually got the plane and Israel got the information on the SA-2 Soviet missile and began receiving Sidewinder missiles.[129] This is not to say that the missiles used on the *Liberty* were in fact American absent more information. However, it is plausible that Spector did not want to acknowledge using missiles because of how sensitive the issue might have been. To this author's recall, there was no discussion on *Liberty* forums dealing with the possibility that American supplied missiles hit the *Liberty*.

Other nations including the Swiss adapted the Sidewinder to their version of the Mirage. The Sidewinder went into service in the late '50s.[130] A second source has been found who says that Israel did in fact use the Sidewinder in 1967. "The Sidewinder's first combat use was in October 1958, when Taiwanese in F-86s launched them against Chinese MiG-17s, claiming as many as 14 shot down in one day. AIM-9s scored most of the air-to-air kills made by US Navy and Air Force aircraft in the Vietnam War, <u>and by the Israeli Air Force in the 1967</u> [underline by this author] and 1973 wars in the Middle East."[131] A third source is a book by Norman Polmar, *The Naval Institute guide to the ships and aircraft of the U.S. fleet*, on page 514 he attributes many Israeli kills during the 1967 and 1973 wars to the Sidewinder.[132] For another reference to Israel receiving the Sidewinder note an article on U.S. Israeli arms trade.[133]

Notwithstanding this information, it appears inconclusive as to when the Israeli IAF began using the Sidewinder. Another issue with the AIM-9 Sidewinder is that it was not useful on close to ground targets until later modified to include this capability.[134] Again, the dating of the Sidewinder is subject to questioning in terms of being adapted to IAF use; however, Cristol in his book is specific when he says *Kursa* leader used air-to-air missiles on the *Liberty* after first denying he had missiles. On the intelligence level, the Israelis are good at bartering; it goes to the heart of the "special relationship". They make an intelligence coup and we want in on it.

Cristol in his book did not identify *Kursa* flight leader by name. However, Michael Oren does in his book *Six Days of War*. He most likely identified one of the Israeli pilots prior to Spector's interview with the *Jerusalem Post*.[135]

Spector reportedly left the IAF after refusing to fly against the Palestinians. In October 2003, the first Israeli pilot to reach the ship broke his 36-year silence on the attack during his interview with the *Jerusalem Post*. Brig-Gen. Yiftah Spector was a triple ace, who shot down 15 enemy aircraft and took part in the 1981 raid on the Iraqi Osiris nuclear reactor.[136] The *Jerusalem Post* obtained a recording of Spector's radio transmission in which he says: "I can't identify it, but in any case it is a military ship".[137]

The *Liberty* will be confused with an Egyptian ship referred to as the *El Quseir,* a horse transport and supply ship—a major controversy. The *El Quseir* is much smaller than the *Liberty*, less than half her size, did not have the antenna array, or hull numbering, and appears to have spent the entire Six-Day War in port at Alexandria.[138] Michael Oren in his book dealing with the Six-Day War states that Spector made an identifying pass at 3,000 feet and reports "He saw 'a military vessel, battleship gray with four gun mounts with its bow pointed toward Port Said…[and] one mast and one smokestack.'" He reports Spector concluded that this was a "Z", or Hunt-class destroyer and he requested additional jets loaded with iron bombs.[139] A "Z" Hunt-class destroyer would certainly not be confused with the *El Quseir* or the *Liberty*. This discussion and conjecture defies logic when one looks at the vessels notwithstanding issues of distance and other visual obstacles such as smoke.

Actual Proportions
All images to scale

USS Liberty
455 feet in length, 10,680 tons displacement

Egyptian "Z" or "Hunt" class destroyer
326 feet in length, 2,575 tons displacement

El Quiser ("El-Kasir")
275 feet in length, 2,750 tons displacement

Fig. 7, Comparative photos.

Source:
http://www.usslibertyinquiry.com/arguments/american/elquseir.html.

69

Spector claimed he fired 30mm armor piercing rounds that led the Americans to believe they had been under rocket attack. His first pass ignited a fire, which caused the ship to billow black smoke that Spector thought was a ruse to conceal the ship. "I'm sorry for the mistake," he said. "Years later my mates dropped flowers on the site where the ship was attacked."

Over the next hour and seven minutes the *Liberty* will be under sustained attack by multiple Mirage and Mystère, French built, jet planes beginning at 1356 Sinai time. Kursa leader is authorized to attack, followed by motor torpedo boats firing several torpedoes at the ship, with one striking her below the waterline in the area of the research department almost sinking the ship.[140]

Because of the air attack 9 crew members will be killed with many wounded. The torpedo boat attack will run up the total killed to 34 of the *Liberty's* crew, dead on the scene, and 175 wounded out of a total crew of 290 members including officers and the NSG 855 department. The NSG contingent included three civilians. Israel will claim the attack was a case of mistaken identity and the United States government would, in a highly controversial move, for convenience sake accept the apology of the Israeli government, notwithstanding many U.S. government leaders holding the belief that the attack had to be intentional. Reluctantly, Israel would eventually pay reparations for the dead and injured in the amount of $6.7 million dollars; and years later, another $6 million, during the Carter administration, for the loss of the ship. Here we will attempt to find a better understanding of what actually transpired that 8th day of June 1967.

From the outside looking in during my research into the attack on the USS *Liberty*, it became clear that for any researcher a big problem would be "data overload", in short too much information, much of which is unverified with more remaining classified. Some "volunteers" have done extensive studies of the trajectory of rounds fired at the ship and the flight pattern of the planes among other technical issues. For example, in a war crimes complaint filed with the U.S. Department of Defense, it is alleged that the air attack, which lasted approximately 25 minutes, resulted in unmarked Israeli aircraft dropping napalm canisters, firing 30mm cannons and rockets, causing 821 holes in the ship with more than 100 being rocket-size hits. It will be further alleged that there were 30 or more sorties by a minimum of 12 attacking jets which were alleged to have jammed all five of the *Liberty's* emergency radio channels.

Fig. 8, showing rocket and cannon damage to bridge.

The longer the *Liberty* controversy traverses time, the more complex these issue will become because of the lack of "connectors or linkage" and timeline confusion. Uncertainty and speculation breeds conspiracy theories. This would be a problem in any complex investigation. Information and communication technologies of today can help to mitigate the problem. To my knowledge, while there have been ad hoc analysis of various issues, there has been no official forensic investigation. Nevertheless, much is not disputed. The essence is mistaken identify verses an intentionally planned and executed attack. The problem is that the attack did not succeed in sinking the ship and evidence.

It is the author's opinion that as we look into the air and torpedo boat attack on the *Liberty* we should take advantage of the passage of time to over-lay information from various sources that have developed over the years. This approach may be a source of agitation for those on either side of the "mistaken identity/intentional attack" view of the *Liberty* story. As in any investigation, all sources are equally creditable until shown to be otherwise; and, if "disinformation" enters the review process, it must be put into context to be discounted. For example, several authors will pick up the claim that Soviet TU-95 Bear long range bombers were based in Egypt, and while handed over to the Egyptians, Soviet pilots were suspected of still being in control of the aircraft at the start of the war. There is no evidence supporting this contention that this model plane was based in Egypt. This claim apparently started with Jim

73

Ennes who stated monitoring the TU-95s were part of the *Liberty's* mission.

One of the most controversial sources of information as far as *Liberty* survivors are concerned comes from the research work of one A. Jay Cristol who published his book *The Liberty Incident* in 2002. Cristol has been previously referred to. In Appendix 2 of his book, he discloses the content of alleged Israeli Air Force audiotapes of the air attack and the motor torpedo boat attack that he was granted access to during visits to the Israeli embassy in Miami, Florida where he resides, more on Cristol later. It should be noted now that *Liberty* researchers have not had access to either the Israeli tapes or the intercept tapes of the actual attack that were alleged to have been collected for the NSA by the EC-121. In a disputed context, the NSA denies there were intercepts of the actual attack. The NSA will subsequently release transcripts of Israeli helicopters flying toward the wounded *Liberty* that were intercepted and recorded <u>after the attack</u>.

There will be communication between *Kursa* flight and the motor torpedo boats that are fast approaching *Liberty's* location. *Kursa* flight, with Spector as the leader and his wingman will be followed seconds later by *Royal* flight consisting of two French, Dassault built, Super-Mystères armed with napalm canisters.

Fig. 9, Photo of Super-Mystère:

Source:
http://www.jewishvirtuallibrary.org/jsource/History/Mystère.html.

A few minutes earlier, motor torpedo boat division 914 reports the target [*Liberty*] at a range of 17 miles and doing an impossible speed of 28 knots. *Liberty's* maximum speed was 18 knots and she was doing 5 knots during her traverse from Point Alfa to Point Bravo along the coast when attacked. A controversy will arise over the reading of the obsolete radar on board the Israeli MTBs. The IDF Navy HQ War Log will show that the MTB Division 914 requests air assistance and the planes are "dispatched". The MTB Division is instructed to turn to aircraft frequencies. *Kursa* flight is to be vectored towards the target's reported position with the instructions: "If it's a warship, then blast it."[141] Amazingly, the Israeli aircraft and motor torpedo boats are vectoring on the same trajectory toward the *Liberty* as previously noted—082 decrees from the Israeli coastline, from Ashdod and most likely Hatzor airbase.

Sometime around 1990 the Israeli government through the IDF released what was purported to be tapes of the Israeli air-controllers talking to attacking pilots and the motor torpedo boats. The tapes and transcripts will become another highly controversial issue, and the

75

question will be whether they are real or have been doctored. This author will address the controversy surrounding the Israeli audiotapes in more detail in a following chapter dealing with the air attack.

Key players in this drama will include Israeli Chief of Staff, Yitzhak Rabin, who was in the "Pit" at the Kirya in Tel Aviv during the attack on the *Liberty*. There is going to be contention between the two camps as to what actually occurred and how various events should be interpreted. In short, A Jay Cristol will contend that this was a "naval" situation controlled by Naval HQ at the Stella Maris in Haifa and that Captain Issy Rehav was in charge as the tactical commander, and that the order to attack "if it's a warship" was his decision. This issue probably gets to the crux of the matter, however, the record needs to be developed further. Was he put in a position of being "left holding the bag"? The Israeli admiral in charge of the navy had left HQ for the docks during this critical decision time.

The *Liberty's* log at 1351 reflects a radar contact of three surface craft approaching at 32,000 yards and this information relayed to the bridge as previously noted. The report included possible aircraft passing over the surface ships. This may indicated that the dispatch of planes and motor torpedo boats was nearly simultaneous; although the Israeli contention is that, the MTBs were to call for air assistance because of the target's speed. Recall that Israeli planes were scarce at this time due to assignments; notwithstanding, numerous surveillance over-flights were made of the *Liberty*.

Ennes will later note that the ship's radar was disabled and that Radar man Charles J. Cocnavitch left his post to operate a nearby gun mount.[142] Further, Ennes notes the

76

motor whaleboat, on the *Liberty*, was burning from a napalm hit.[143] Three 55-gallon drums of fuel are set a fire creating black smoke. Spector referred in his prior statement to this smoke. It was not intended to conceal the ship; rather it is the result of being hit by attacking planes. Ennes notes the effort to begin destruction of code related materials in the research department area.[144] They had weighted bags to contain secret materials to be thrown overboard to sink to the bottom of the Mediterranean.

As the captain previously noted, he felt it was known the ship was in the area. With all the prior air reconnaissance, it is hard to understand how the Israelis could not know the *Liberty* was in the Eastern Mediterranean. One of the controversial contentions will be that while the *Liberty* was identified earlier in the day, at Naval Headquarters, her plot marker on their tracking map had been removed by a person named Commander Avraham Lunz, allegedly because of the lack of a position update when he went off shift at 1100 Sinai time.

This begs the question because Israel was capable of monitoring the many ships of both the Sixth Fleet and the Soviets who had seventy some ships in the area as noted by Yitzhak Rabin in his memories.

Further, when one studies the Israeli air controller recordings, it will be clear that the *Liberty* was under surveillance via the Israeli coastal early warning radar system and that with the many over-flights they never did lose track of her during June 8. In fact, over-flights continued past 1100 when Lunz pulled the plot marker. There will be a contention that the Israeli pilots and MTB crews had been ordered to attack the ship, and they ignored or did not want to know it was American.

77

From the Naval Court of Inquiry Record: [O'Malley] "Yes sir. I had the con on the 12 to 1600 watch. From 1220 to 1230 is when an Israeli twin-engine plane, well we didn't know it was Israeli, just a twin-engine plane very similar to a flying boxcar, circled us once in a long elliptical circle and they drew near. We found out on questioning, after they went away, Mr. ENNIS said the plane had come out almost periodically every 20 to 40 minutes, and would make one pass in a high circle and head back to land".

Notwithstanding the issue of the ship's identity being in question, the attack proceeds. *Kursa* flight makes its three runs and *Royal* flight follows up within seconds. There will be some confusion among the crew as to how many planes were involved and how many attack sorties were made on the ship. A *sortie* is counted as one attack by one plane; a single plane can make several sorties. There will be a contention that the planes had no markings on them; however, in a special report by the online *Chicago Tribune* dated October 2, 2007, entitled *New Revelations in Attack on American Spy Ship*, the article's author reports that Theodore Arfsten, a quartermaster, remembered watching a Jewish officer cry when he saw the blue Star of David on the planes' fuselages. Jewish crewmembers on an American ship could be expected as acknowledged by Rabin in his memoires, who noted they were included in the casualties. On the other hand, would one expect to have an American flying an Israeli plane attacking an American naval ship?

Some information suggests that one or more of the attacking pilots may have been American according to author Anthony Pearson. Anthony Pearson was one of the first journalists to report on the *Liberty* story in depth with his book *Conspiracy of Silence the Attack on the USS Liberty.*[145]

Pearson, who had been researching his *Liberty* story for *Penthouse* magazine, producing two articles in 1976; he published his book in 1978. In the magazine article, he states that there were two Americans involved in the attack on the *Liberty*. In the book version he reports that he traveled to Tel Aviv and reported in to the Israeli military censor's office requesting information on the *Liberty*. While he was advised there wasn't much information, an attractive female in the IDF uniform appeared at this hotel room to hand him a package on the *Liberty*, which was not much of anything other than a summary of the June 11, 1967 Israeli Court of Inquiry report. This may have been the *Ram Ron Report* referred to in a previous chapter. The report put the blame on the *Liberty* for acting furtively. Pearson claims that the girl named Ruthy and he went for a drink at the Hilton hotel. The girl was interested in the fact that Pearson was doing his research for *Penthouse* magazine. She allegedly was interested in becoming a photographic model and their conversation continued. While Pearson was suspicious of her desire to help him with his research, he nevertheless continued to seek her help in locating sources.

She provided him with information about a man who flew an American made Phantom jet and was about to return to the U.S. Ruthy showed up at a meeting with Pearson bringing this pilot. The pilot claimed he was a U.S. citizen from Baltimore who fought in Vietnam and when he got out of the military, he moved to Israel to be with his parents who had immigrated to Israel in 1959. He joined the Israeli Air Force as a pilot instructor and when the war broke out, he led a squadron of Dassault

Mirages on a strike against Egyptian fighter-bases west of the Suez Canal. This pilot claimed he flew the mission against the USS *Liberty*. This person told Pearson that he was told there was an enemy ship off El Arish and that it was some Russian electronic spy ship. His story included the fact that contact was made with the Sixth Fleet advising there were no U.S. ships within 600 miles of the Gaza coast. He said three pilots flew the mission in three Mirages. One was another Vietnam vet and the third was a native born Israeli. The contention that the target was some kind of Russian spy ship negates the contention of the *Liberty* being mistaken for an Egyptian horse transport ship.

Pearson continues to relate the conversation that U.S. Navy markings were clear and that they sought reconfirmation of the order to act and the order was to aim for the antennae and radar tracking gear. The pilot felt it was an American ship and asked Pearson what he would have done once he had orders and a double confirmation to the effect that the ship was not what it appeared to be. The pilot told Pearson his parents were so upset that an American ship was targeted that they admonished their son that the Germans were "merely following orders" (referring to the Second World War). The conversation concluded with his statement that he was not proud of what he had done.[146] Notwithstanding this type of information, as I recall during my visit with Jim Ennes, he discounted Pearson's credibility, although speculation has swirled within *Liberty* circles that one or more Americans did fly against the ship as Israeli pilots.

Unfortunately, Pearson did not provide documentation in his book and he has been long dead. We do not know who the Israeli pilot from Baltimore was nor do we know who Ruthy was. Pearson speculated that she could have been a PR person for the IDF or a Mossad agent. At any rate, Pearson's story adds more controversy to the *Liberty* story. Pearson was writing for *Penthouse* because it was one of the few forums available to him for such a story. The regular media after a cursory look at the attack lost interest.

Ennes in a June 1993 article for *Washington Report on Middle East Affairs* reports the following: Fifteen years after the attack, an Israeli pilot approached *Liberty* survivors and then held extensive interviews with former Congressman Paul N. (Pete) McCloskey about his role.[147] According to this senior Israeli lead pilot, he recognized the *Liberty* as American immediately, so informed his headquarters, and told to ignore the American flag and continue his attack. He refused to do so and returned to base where he was arrested.

Later, a dual-citizen Israeli major, told survivors that he was in an Israeli war room where he heard that pilot's radio report. The attacking pilots and everyone in the Israeli war room knew that they were attacking an American ship, the major said. He recanted the statement only after he received threatening phone calls from Israel.

Radio monitors in the U.S. Embassy in Lebanon also heard the pilot's protests. Then U.S. Ambassador to Lebanon Dwight Porter has confirmed this. Porter told his story to syndicated columnists Rowland Evans and Robert Novak and offered to submit to further questioning by authorities. Unfortunately, no one in the U.S. government had any interest in hearing these first-person accounts of Israeli treachery.[148]

Ennes reports that in the pilothouse, Quartermaster Floyd Pollard stretched to swing a heavy steel battle plate over the vulnerable glass porthole. A rocket, and with it the porthole, exploded in front of him to transform his face and upper torso into a bloody mess. Painter helped him to relative safety near the quartermaster's log table before leaving the bridge to report to his battle station.

On the port side, just below the bridge, a fire erupted from ruptured fifty-five gallon drums of fuel. Lieutenant Commander Armstrong the ship's XO (Executive Officer) bounded toward the fire yelling, "Hit 'em! Slug the sons of bitches!" he must have been saying as he fought to reach the quick-release handle that would drop the flaming and still half-full containers into the sea. A lone rocket suddenly dissolved the bones of both of his legs.[149] Armstrong would eventual die of his wounds, despite the heroic efforts of the ship's doctor, Dr. Richard F. Kiepfer. The ship's doctor would be awarded the Silver Star for his going on deck to rescue the injured while being subjected to "murderous" torpedo boat machine gun fire—this per the war crimes complaint that we will address in a separate chapter.

Ennes reports that while the first plane emptied the gun mounts, the second plane through extraordinary luck or marksmanship, disabled nearly every radio antenna on the ship, temporarily preventing the call for help. Following up the faster Mirage jets were the slower Dassault Mystère jets carrying dreaded napalm—jellied gasoline. The Mystère pilots rocketed the ship from a distance and then dropped their napalm canisters.

The Israeli pilots including Spector noted the lack of anti-aircraft fire. If the *Liberty* were a true warship, she would have had the capability of defending herself with the traditional anti-aircraft armaments that a warship would be expected to have. She could not defend herself;

she was a "neutral ship in international waters", with air cover promised to be minutes away!

SHIP UNDER REPEATED AIR ATTACK WITH TWO
OR MORE A/C MAKING COORDINATED
STRAFING, ROCKET, AND INCENDIARY RUNS
OVER SHIP. (8 killed 75 wounded including Captain).
THROUGHOUT TOPSIDE AREA FROM SHRAPNEL
AND SHOCK OF EXPLODING ROCKETS.

Liberty's Log.

Chapter 4

"RockStar…"

With the ship under attack, she was frantically trying
to get out a call for help. Radioman Chief Wayne L.
Smith: At 1158Z is when we started to call any station,
this is *ROCKSTAR*. We passed a Zulu precedence to this
message. At 1200Z, *ROCKSTAR* was called by
Schematic saying, "…you are garbled…say again". We
repeated three times to them that we were under attack at
1358 local time.[150] At the same time, the motor torpedo
boats are asked by Israeli Naval HQ if they can see the
planes and the response is we can hear them. The *Liberty*
log records a single aircraft sighted approaching the ship
from 135 degrees relative at 5 to 6 miles distance at an
altitude of approximately 7000 feet. The aircraft passed
down the track of the ship.[151] *Schematic* was the code
name for the Sixth Fleet aircraft carrier USS *Saratoga*.

Hatzor is an Israeli air force base located in central
Israel near kibbutz Hatzor. It is southeast of Ashdod.
The Royal Air Force initially constructed this base in
1945 during the British Mandate of Palestine, named for
the nearby Palestinian village as RAF Qastina. During
the War of Independence, the base was evacuated by the

British and taken over by Haganah forces.[152] The attacking planes are believed to have come from this base.

Author and Israeli supporter, A. Jay Cristol, notes that Chief Air Controller, Colonel Shmuel Kislev was sitting two chairs from General Motti Hod, the commander of the Israeli air force, in the "Pit" at the Kirya. Depending on the author, we get into a conflict as to the exact location of the key players. Israeli historian, Michael Oren, reports that Minister of Defense Moshe Dayan was away visiting Hebron, while General Hod was at a briefing; however, as a matter of certainty, Oren notes that Chief of Staff Rabin was in fact in the "Pit" taking personal command of the situation including the dispatch of helicopters after the attack to locate survivors.[153] The helicopter dispatch will present its own issues. Rabin is the highest-ranking Israeli with his fingerprints directly on the *Liberty* attack, because of his command position as noted above.

Royal flight consists of two Super-Mystère B2 jets armed with 30mm guns and two canisters of napalm and two 216 US gallon drop tanks. Mystères attacked the ship broadside.[154] As for the question whether the ship's guns fired at planes, the *Kursa* flight leader, Spector, says there was no anti-aircraft fire—this allegedly surprised him. Of course the *Liberty* did not have anti-aircraft guns other that the four .50 caliber machine guns, which could have provided some limited air defense.

A troublesome scenario was set in play wherein the objective of the attacking Israelis was to sink the ship—would this result in the premeditated murder of the crew—as alleged. *Res Ipsa Loquitor* is an idiom for "let the facts speak for themselves". As we will see, whether she was "American" had been raised by L.K who was in the command post, and was ignored. We will meet L.K. later. According to author Anthony Pearson's interview with the Israeli pilot from Baltimore, twice confirmation was sought prior to attacking the ship because of identity issues.

Even to this day, those with Israeli associations strongly deny the attack was intentional. In a February 19, 2010 visit to the Victor Ostrovsky's Fine Arts Gallery in the Scottsdale, Arizona Old Town district, Victor denied that those he knew would do such a thing to an American ship. Ostrovsky was the author of two controversial books on the Mossad of which he had been a former member. He offered no particular insights into how the matter could be an issue of mistaken identity— our conversation was very brief. Strangely, he briefly alluded to JFK, President Kennedy, perhaps to see if I wanted to pursue that "conspiracy". One would understand the context better by reading his two books dealing the Mossad.

In his book *By Way of Deception*, Ostrovsky describes the Mossad as being very interested in the Kennedy assassination promoting the theory that it was a Mafiosa hit actually aimed at Texas governor John Connally, wherein Lee Harvey Oswald was simply a dupe. Allegedly, the motive for the attack was that the mob wanted to muscle into the oil business. Ostrovsky describes the Mossad re-enacting the shooting and finding that it was impossible for Oswald to do what he was alleged.[155]

Ostrovsky was recently cited in an article by writer Alison Weir dealing with a claim that in an online, January 3rd, 2012, article by the owner-publisher of the

Atlanta Jewish Times a reference was made "suggesting that Israel might someday need to 'order a hit' on the president of the United States." Does this sound outlandish? The reference to Ostrovsky is that he gave details that in 1991 an Israeli undercover team planned to assassinate a U.S. president. The intended victim was George Herbert Walker Bush. Ostrovsky provided details on this claim three years later in his 1994 book, *The Other Side of Deception: A Rogue Agent Exposes the Mossad's Secret Agenda.*[156] Alison Weir reports that the publisher, admonished by others in the Jewish community, subsequently resigned.[157] The alleged plot against Bush obviously did not go forward.

The point is that the American public has no idea what goes on in the underworld of intelligence agency plotting and machinations. Covert activities are the hidden part of the government iceberg that goes mostly unchecked and is anathema to democracy—often resulting in *blowback*. Since the Six-Day War was an intelligence driven event, the question is was the attack on the *Liberty* an example of such blowback.

"Blowback" is a CIA term first used in March 1954 in a recently declassified report on the 1953 operation to overthrow the government of Mohammed Mossadegh in Iran.[158] Perhaps the most disastrous blowback was 9/11 that emanated from our failed policy in Pakistan and Afghanistan when we abandoned the Mujahidin we had supported to get the Russians out of Afghanistan in the 1980s, one of the reasons we had to go back into that region. For more on this area of interest that included the Unocal battle for oil pipelines read the *Taliban* by Ahmed Rashid and his chapter 13.[159]

After the above brief digression and getting back to the attack on the *Liberty*: The problem we have appears to be the old conundrum of "following orders" in a wartime setting without question—but questions were raised. It is definitely possible that the order was carried out with remorse and subsequent regret as expressed by *Kursa* flight leader, Spector, and the pilot allegedly interviewed by author Anthony Pearson. Air controller Kislev claims in an interview for Thames TV that he was upset over the thought the ship could be "American" and he threw down his headset.[160]

The fifth standoff message, 080917Z, from COMSIXTHFLT to *Liberty* ordering a 100-mile pullback arrived at Army DCS Relay Station Asmara. This message was sent by mistake to NCS Greece instead of NCS Asmara at 1415. Message failures will be the only issue investigated by Congress and the Naval Court of Inquiry.[161]

The carrier USS *Saratoga* was heading 90°/17 knots and was close to rendezvousing with the carrier USS *America*, TG60.1 and TG60.2 were about to merge into Task Force 60 (TF60). The air wing commander from *Saratoga* was aboard *America* for a press conference. *America* was conducting a SIOP (Single Integrated Operational Plan) load and launch drill for the tactical delivery of nuclear weapons. Only A-1 and A-4 aircraft in the Sixth Fleet were configured to carry nuclear weapons. The concept was an "over the shoulder delivery." The aircraft would pull up at a 45° angle before reaching the target and pitched the weapon towards the target just prior to executing a *half-Cuban-eight* maneuver in an effort to get away from the blast. The SIOP exercise was a highly regimented, very complex

88

load and launch exercise conducted under severe security, thus tying up the flight deck for a prolonged period.

Captain McGonagle: "While I observed this aircraft, I did not see it approach the ship directly in a hostile attitude." Some in the crew considered his testimony before the Naval Court of Inquiry (NCI) as less than assertive. "Within a couple of minutes, a loud explosion was heard that appeared to me to come from the port side of the ship. I immediately ordered the general alarm to be sounded, and this was done. (...LT BENNETT, to report to CNO via the hicom that *LIBERTY* was under attack by unidentified jet aircraft and that immediate assistance was required)."[162]

Some timeline items worth noting are as follows:

1358: Attack starts.

1400: Chief Smith: "I immediately picked up the hicom transmitter which was on UIC 32, auxiliary radio. We started to transmit with it. No station heard us, and five minutes or so later the transmitter was reported to have blown out."

1401: The MTBs were ordered to continue toward the ship fast.

1402: *Royal* flight is given permission to attack the ship. *Liberty* would start calling for help at 1358. There is a report of the *Liberty's* radios being jammed.[163]

1402: The MTBs are finally getting close enough to the ship to see the smoke from the explosions.

89

1404: *Kursa* flight had used up its ammunition, and was ready to leave the target while *Royal* flight attacks. *Royal* misses with the napalm.

1405: *Liberty* sounds the general alarm for fire.[164] The engine room is given the "all ahead flanks" alarm. *Liberty* LOG: SHIP UNDER REPEATED AIR ATTACK WITH TWO OR MORE A/C MAKING COORDINATED STRAFING, ROCKET, AND INCENDIARY RUNS OVER SHIP. (8 killed 75 wounded including Captain). THROUGHOUT TOPSIDE AREA FROM SHRAPNEL AND SHOCK OF EXPLODING ROCKETS.

1408: Chief Smith: "We called at 1208Z *Schematic* (the *Saratoga)* and repeated three times that we were under attack. Immediately after 1208Z, still in the same minute, they rogered the message."

The attack will continue even though there have been repeated questions about the identity of the ship. If there ever was an issue regarding mistaken identity, it no longer provides cover for the Israelis and the IDF. From a legal standpoint, the Israelis had both "actual knowledge" and "constructive knowledge" that the ship was a U.S. naval ship. This has ramifications for issues of both criminal and civil liability. To make it simple, further investigation was required to determine, in the case of the *Liberty*, the identity of the ship's nationality.[165]

The issue of actual and constructive knowledge is a legal construct that attaches liability for a course of action. For example, for a person in authority to say "American" and then to ignore the warning is at a minimum "constructive knowledge" of identity that

90

warrants an effort to establish identity before committing to a course of action. For various reasons already mentioned, the Israelis also had "actual knowledge" of the ship's presence in the area—she was under continual air and radar surveillance.

With the conclusion of the air attack the air force controllers were still in control of the overall situation as certain NSA transcripts will attest with two Israeli helicopters being guided toward the ship—for what purpose? This was developing at 1413 per IAF audio tapes. At 1417, the IAF reports men jumping over the side of the ship—this did not take place. However, MTB Division 914 <u>is ordered not to attack</u> as possible misidentification has occurred, and there might be a need to render help.[166] Nevertheless, the torpedo boat attack continued with deadly results.

In view of the possibility of Israelis' attack being an error, the Captain yelled to machine gun mount 51 to hold fire. He had previously ordered the gunners to fire at the torpedo boats. His order to hold fire apparently went unheard and Mt. 51 fired a short burst about 1431—well into the attack. The reconstructed *Liberty* log reports one round shot off. The Israeli flag is then spotted on one MTB. Gun Mount 53 opened with "effective fire" on the center of the MTBs. Then the MTBs began strafing the starboard side. The crew could not get to Mt. 53 because of fire and smoke. Ensign Lucas was ordered around portside to stop Mt. 53. Simultaneously, the CO passed word to standby for torpedo attack. Lucas reported no one was in Mt. 53; apparently, rounds were cooking off from fire and heat.

Captain McGonagle's statement to the Naval Court of Inquiry:[167]

It was not possible to read the signals from the center torpedo boat because of the intermittent blocking of view by smoke and flames. At this time, I yelled to machine gun 51 to tell him to hold fire. I realized that there was a possibility of the aircraft having been Israeli and the attack had been conducted in error. I wanted to hold fire to see if we could read the signal from the torpedo boat and perhaps avoid additional damage and personnel injuries. The man on machine gun 51 fired a short burst at the boats before he was able to understand what I was attempting to have him do. Instantly, on machine gun 51 opening fire machine gun 53 began firing at the center boat. From the starboard wing of the bridge, 03 level, I observed that the fire from machine gun 53 was extremely effective and blanketed the area and the center torpedo boat. It was not possible to get to mount 53 from the starboard wing of the bridge. I sent Mr. LUCAS around the port side of the bridge, around to the skylights, to see if he could tell QUINTERO, whom I believed to be the gunner on Machine gun 53, to hold fire until we were able to clarify the situation. He reported back in a few minutes in effect that he saw no one at mount 53. As far as the torpedo boats are concerned, I am sure that they felt that they were under fire from USS LIBERTY.

There have been references to the Captain's behavior coming into question, and one of the items may well have related to his testimony about the center MTB coming under fire that was "extremely effective" when there was no one alive in the gun tub to be shooting—apparently rounds had "cooked off". The tenor of his testimony seems to be apologetic toward Israel and suggestive of a possible mistake in identity not withstanding a sustained air attack that killed and wounded a number of his men. It is safe to say that one would expect the ship and crew to defend the ship and themselves under any circumstances. Interestingly, the Captain, in his testimony, acknowledged life rafts being placed in the water; however, he made no mention of the rafts being machine gunned by the torpedo boats.

Ennes notes in a supplement to his book that Captain McGonagle's testimony before the NCI was at odds with the recollections of the crew. He would only acknowledge that "his crew" believed the attack to have been deliberate. Prior to his death of lung cancer on March 3, 1999, he acknowledged that the attack was not a "pure case of mistaken identity", and wanted both governments to release details as to why the ship was attacked.[168]

Lieutenant Junior Grade Lloyd C. Painter would testify after the Captain on this point. He was the officer of the deck on the 1200 to 1600 watch. He had this to say about the disposition of the ship's rafts referring to Damage Control:[169]

> At this time, the DC central passed the word to prepare to abandon ship. We then filed out to our life rafts which were no longer with us because they had been strafed and most of them were burned, so we knocked most of them over the side. At this time the torpedo boats, three of them, that had torpedoed us, were laying off, waiting for us to sink, I believe. Anyway, they didn't come near us at this time.

The issue of the rafts being "strafed" is important. In a later chapter, we will look at the war crimes complaint filed by the LVA with the Pentagon, wherein it is alleged that the motor torpedo boats strafed the rafts, and that this action was part of the basis for alleging that war crimes had been committed against the crew.

The Captain testifies that at 1426 or 1427 torpedoes were launched with one crossing the stern of the ship by 25 yards. A torpedo is spotted missing the ship by seventy-five feet; then the ship's general announcing system came alive to warn: "Stand by for torpedo attack, starboard side."[170] Lieutenant George Golden, the ship's engineer, ordered: "Evacuate the engine rooms!" The standby for torpedo warning was also heard in the "spook" department.

Chief Smith: About 1217Z, we called *schematic* again saying, "Be advised that we have been hit by torpedo, listing about 9 degrees, request immediate assistance". Times may vary from person to person based upon their recall.

This time appears to be an error on the part of Chief Smith. A. Jay Cristol reports that at 1436 the MTB division said the identification of ship as the *El Quseir* was definite. Further, he reports that Rahav gave final approval for the attack at 1430.[171] The actual time the torpedo hit was approximately 1435 local time and 1235Z, this per the reconstructed log. Remember the DTG rule regarding time. There is a two-hour difference between military and local Sinai time.

Ennes reports Petty Officer Joseph C. Lentini, working in the crypto area had his leg grazed by a bullet with his shoe filling with blood. As Lieutenant

94

Commander Dave Lewis was about to put a battle dressing on Lentini, he froze with a focused look at the exterior bulkhead of the coordination center—the torpedo had struck lifting the ship up causing a huge hole with water rushing in. For many, death was instantaneous while sitting at their duty stations. Burnt paint chips and deafening blast from the Italian-made torpedo temporarily blinded Lewis.[172] Twenty-five men died from torpedo and strafing attack. The crew will be commended for its damage control efforts.

Fig. 10, Torpedo hole in starboard side of ship.

95

Marine Staff Sergeant and Russian linguist, Bryce Lockwood found a person pinned underwater, freed him and pushed him up through the deck hatch that would soon be battened down, reopened and closed again, trapping some below in the research compartments.[173] The immediate need was to save the ship and prevent the greater loss of life. Throughout the attack, the Captain remained on the bridge with the dead and wounded around him. He himself had been wounded in the air attack, but insisted on staying on the bridge—in charge of his ship. He would receive the Medal of Honor during an unusual ceremony at the Naval Yard in Washington DC—not at the White House from the President, as is the custom. The medal citation excluded any reference to Israel as having attacked the ship. This governmental conduct would add to feeling of victimization by the survivors.

The ship lifted up and inclined to about 12 degrees. She did not roll over and finally settled with a starboard list. Her steering was out as were the boilers and she had to be steered from a stern position manually with directional orders from the bridge. Fears were that the ship could run aground without steering control. Still there was no help from the Sixth Fleet planes. The "prepare to abandon ship" order was given. "Disable the main engines, and scuttle the ship", was heard by Golden over the sound-powered telephone from the bridge.[174] The abandon ship order was to become a controversy in its own right—had it actually been given.

As previously noted, the ship's rafts were heaved over the side of the ship to be used by the crew, when suddenly the motor torpedo boats making parallel runs along the ship began firing at the empty life rafts.

Lieutenant Lloyd Painter was witness to this event.[175] Three time LVA president and *Liberty* survivor, Phillip F. Tourney, supports Painter's testimony and witness to the damage done to the ship's life rafts. He believes that the President of the Naval Court of Inquiry, Admiral Kidd, did not want him to testify about the strafing of the rafts by the MTBs, consequently, he was sent on sudden leave to Rome after having arrived in port with the ship for damages assessment and repair.[176]

Certainly, the torpedo boats were within eyesight of the *Liberty* at the time of the machine-gunning of the rafts. One *Liberty* survivor would report that he had eyeball contact with a torpedo boat gunner. The following picture was taken from the *Liberty*.

Fig. 11, Israeli MTB seen from USS *Liberty*.

97

As the torpedo boats faded in the distance, helicopters approached the *Liberty*: "Stand by to repel boarders!" barked the announcing system, while runners spread through the ship yelling "helicopters" "stand by to repel boarders!" Ennes reports that two Hornet assault helicopters, each loaded with armed men in battle dress approached the ship. He reports a sailor yelled, "They've come to finish us off." Ennes reports the helicopters did not try to land and made no effort to communicate with the ship. They bore the "blue or black Star of David" on a white circular field, and were marked H4 and H8. These helicopters were French-made Aerospatiale SA321 Super Frelon (Hornet) helicopters designed for assault and anti-submarine operations.[177]

Israel ordered 12 helicopters in 1965 to provide the IAF with a heavy lift transport capability. The close ties between Israel and France in the mid 1960s made the choice of a French helicopter inevitable and in early 1965, an IAF delegation of air and ground crews left for France to study the new aircraft.[178]

Fig. 12, Photo Super Frelon helicopter.

Source:
http://www.jewishvirtuallibrary.org/jsource/Society_&_Culture/sfrel
on.html.

Sixth Fleet planes will be launched and recalled—twice! One COMSIXTHFLT message at 081305Z promises, "Sending aircraft to cover you." This was 55 minutes after *Liberty's* first call for help. Ennes says he and crew were aware of an earlier message saying help is on the way at 1220Z.[179] It is reported that the voice of Secretary of Defense, Robert McNamara was heard saying "Tell Sixth Fleet to get those aircraft back immediately," he barked, "and give me a status report."

Fig. 13, Secretary of Defense Robert McNamara, LBJ Library.

J.Q. "Tony" Hart, according to an online *Chicago Tribune* article on the *Liberty*, was a chief petty officer assigned to a U.S. Navy relay station in Morocco that handled message traffic between Washington DC and the Sixth Fleet, verifies the call from McNamara. He was able to listen in on the call between the Secretary of Defense and Rear Admiral Lawrence Geis, commander of the *America's* battle group, and heard McNamara order the recall of planes.[180]

When Geis objected noting that the *Liberty* was under attack and needed help, Hart is quoted as saying that McNamara retorted saying, "President [Lyndon] Johnson is not going to war or embarrass an American ally over a few sailors." When later question about the *Liberty*, McNamara then 91, told the *Tribune,* he had "absolutely no recollection of what I did that day, except that "I have a memory that I didn't know at the time what was going on."[181]

Ennes in his book on page 77 and 78 discusses the call from McNamara overheard by Hart. He noted that a few minutes after the McNamara call, the Chief of Naval Operation (CNO) came on the air and he bellowed: "You get those fucking airplanes back on the deck, and you get them back *now!*" During all this activity, the reporters on board the carrier were oblivious of what was going on with the *Liberty* and plane recall.

Captain Joseph Tully, USN, the former Commanding Officer of the USS *Saratoga* will attend the LVA's 28th anniversary reunion in San Diego, California, and give a speech to the survivors and supporters. He noted that the *Saratoga* as part of the Sixth Fleet carrier strike force was near the Greek Island of Crete. The force included the Flag Ship *Little Rock*, a cruiser, with Vice Admiral William I. Martin; the USS *America*, a new carrier on its first Mediterranean cruise, commanded by Captain Don Engen, with Rear Admiral Larry Geis, embarked as Commander of Carrier Division Four. Additionally, there were about a dozen escorting destroyers.

Vice Admiral Martin, the senior officer was conducting various maneuvers. Tully related that in an unusual manner, the *Saratoga's* communication officer personally delivered a message to him on the bridge. The message was in plain text, not encrypted, from the USS *Liberty*: Any or all U.S. ships or stations, "*Liberty* is under attack by unknown enemy air and surface units. Request assistance." The communication officer confirmed that he had authenticated the message.

Tully stated that the *Saratoga*, and he thought the *America*, was also in a state of readiness to "launch at least nine aircraft of various types loaded with 500 pound all-purpose bombs and ready machine guns, steam to the catapults, aircraft spotted to launch and pilots standing by."

A check with the navigation officer (now Rear Admiral Max K. Morris, USN retired) revealed that "we" were only 15 to 20 minutes from the *Liberty* and could be of immediate assistance. "I personally called Vice Admiral Martin via our primary tactical radio circuit, read him our *Liberty* message and added, 'Unless otherwise directed, I plan to launch my Ready Strike Group in support of *Liberty*.'"

Cpt. Tully

Tully said Martin voice approved his intention and directed *America* to launch her Ready Strike Group also. *Saratoga* launched, and while the planes were still in sight, he noted that *America* did not launch. Rear Admiral Geis on *America* ordered the recall of the aircraft with instructions not to jettison the 500-pound bombs. Planes were routed to a NATO ammo depot in Crete.

Vice Admiral Martin ordered another strike sortie in support of the *Liberty* at about 1500, which was accomplished, to be recalled, with loaded planes again being rerouted for off-loading. Note the following message:[182]

Telegram From the Commander of the Sixth Fleet (Martin) to the Commander in Chief, European Command (Lemnitzer)
June 8, 1967, 1320Z.
081320Z. SITREP 06001. Attack on *Liberty*.
SITREP One.
1. At 081252Z USS *Liberty* reported under attack at posit 31.23N 33.25E, was hit by torpedo and was listing badly. Attack forces hereby declared hostile by

102

COMSIXTHFLTIAW
CINCUSNAVEURINST P03120.5B. *Liberty*
message authenticated.
2. Have directed TF 60 to proceed toward
scene. Task Force 60 present posit 34.22N
24.28E.
3. Have directed *America* to launch four
armed A4's and *Saratoga* to launch four armed
A1's with fighter cover to defend USS *Liberty*.
Pilots directed to remain clear of land. Tankers
also will launch, will relieve on station.
4. ETA first ACFT on scene one hour and 30
minutes after launch. Estimate launch at
1345Z.

A reading of this message would say it was unrealistic to promise air cover to the *Liberty* within a matter of minutes if called for assistance. The *America* with two destroyers would not arrive until the next morning, after the damage was done, to assist the *Liberty*. Admiral Martin's caution that planes would be able to support the *Liberty* if needed did not materialize. Was this failure to provide air cover in a timely manner result in more *Liberty* casualties?

The *Saratoga* would later make a routine visit to Athens where Captain John Dick who knew nothing of the *Liberty* attack relieved Tully. The Sixth Fleet Strike Force had remained together for two more days and split up. The events of the Six-Day War were winding down. Tully was reassigned to the Bureau of Naval Personnel in Washington. He did not learn the details about the *Liberty* until he obtained a copy of Ennes's book.

Tully summarized by noting that Rear Admiral Kidd was directed to conduct a classified inspection of communications in the Mediterranean area; but he did not think Kidd was knowledgeable in intelligence matters. Kidd did not interview him and he noted while they were classmates at the Naval Academy, they were not friendly. He noted that Rear Admiral Geis died not long after the incident and that Vice Admiral Martin suffered a cerebral stroke and could not be a witness. He further claims that he and Captain Engen had not been interviewed about the *Liberty* affair.

He concluded his address to the LVA by noting that the *Liberty* was the only incident of major damage to a U.S. ship since the sinking of the USS *Main* in Havana Harbor in 1898, [183] prior to the Spanish American War that had not been investigated by the U.S. Congress—this must tell something. [184]

In a February 12, 1990 interview on radio station WOJB in Wisconsin, host Don Brooks, questioned Tully about the plane recall ordered by Secretary of Defense McNamara. Tully: "An order issued, from either, Vice Admiral Martin or Rear Admiral Geis to be ready to launch in 90 minutes. I went back and said, hell, I can launch right now." Someone wanted *America* to participate in the launch. Therefore, ninety minutes later there was a second launch and a second call back when the planes were still within sight of the carrier. Tully could not recall if it was Martin or Geis who ordered the recall.

Secretary of Defense, now deceased, Robert McNamara, when questioned about the *Liberty* said he could not recall events of that day as noted above—he consistently took the "I don't know excuse". Could the planes have provided air cover in time to prevent further casualties is a key question? The *Saratoga* "rogered" the call for help at 1208Z, 1408 local time; meantime, the

104

motor torpedo boat attack continues and the *Liberty* is hit by the Israeli torpedo around 1235Z and 1435 local time. The carrier planes would have had approximately 25 minutes to get to the *Liberty* prior to the torpedo hit. Had the launch continued, it is conceivable that the Israeli's command and control would have noted the launch, and more could have been done to stop the torpedo attack, thus saving lives and preventing more casualties. The President of the United States, the Commander-in-chief, and Secretary of Defense in essence abandoned the *Liberty* and her crew—[McNamara retorted saying, "President [Lyndon] Johnson is not going to war or embarrass an American ally over a few sailors."] The cover-up begins.

Here and elsewhere in this book there will be references to President Johnson saying, "he would not embarrass an ally", or something similar, in the context of having the carrier planes recalled from going to the aid of the *Liberty*. There are two sources for this quote, first "Tony" Hart as noted above, and Lt. Commander Dave Lewis relating what Admiral Geis told him in confidence based up Geis talking directly to President Johnson going over McNamara's head challenging the order to recall. Lewis divulged his conversation with Geis after Geis had passed away. After some consideration on my part, I believe this issue is important enough to include the whole reference to the plane recall:[185]

> Lieutenant Commander David E. Lewis, USS Liberty's chief intelligence officer (who was severely wounded in the attack) has reported a conversation with Admiral Lawrence R. Geis, the Sixth Fleet carrier division commander, who visited Lewis after he had been medically evacuated by helicopter to the aircraft carrier

USS America. According to Lewis, "He (Admiral Geis) said that he wanted somebody to know that we weren't forgotten" attempts HAD been made to come to our assistance. He said that he had launched a flight of aircraft to come to our assistance, and he had then called Washington. Secretary McNamara came on the line and ordered the recall of the aircraft, which he did. Concurrently he said that since he suspected that they were afraid that there might have been nuclear weapons on board, he reconfigured another flight of aircraft - strictly conventional weaponry - and re-launched it. After the second launch, he again called Washington to let them know what was going on. Again, Secretary McNamara ordered the aircraft recalled. Not understanding why, he requested confirmation of the order; and the next higher in command came on to confirm that "President Johnson...with the instructions that the aircraft were to be returned, that he would not have his allies embarrassed, he didn't care who was killed or what was done to the ship "words" to that effect. With that, Admiral Geis swore me to secrecy for his lifetime. I had been silent up until I found out from Admiral Moorer that Admiral Geis had passed away" [transcript from NBC's Liberty Story, aired on national television 1/27/92]. This statement by Commander Lewis has recently been corroborated by Tony Hart, a Navy communications technician stationed at the U.S. Navy Base in Morocco in June, 1967. Mr. Hart connected the telephone conversation between Secretary McNamara and Admiral Geis and stayed on the line to keep them connected. Hart has been recorded as saying that he overheard Admiral Geis refusing

106

McNamara's order to recall the Sixth Fleet rescue aircraft while the ship was under attack. Mr. Hart reported that McNamara responded, "we are not going to war over a bunch of dead sailors."

On another point that needs to be clarified is the contention that the JCS wanted to retaliate against the Israeli port of Haifa for the attack on *Liberty*. There is an ambiguity as to whether the dispatch of the carrier planes was related to the JCS strike position, and how far any JCS retaliation plan progressed, if at all, before being countermanded.

Yigal, you have a ship at 26. [Twenty-six is a site designation.] Take *Kursa* over there. If it's a warship, then blast it.

Shmuel Kislev, chief Israeli air controller at the Kirya.

Chapter 5

The Air Attack

There is general agreement as to the timing of the air attack on the *Liberty* as being 1358 Sinai time.

Sometime around the late 1980s, the Israeli government through the IDF released what was purported to be tapes of the Israeli air-controllers talking to attacking pilots and the motor torpedo boats. The tapes were initially used as background in the Thames TV production, *Attack on the Liberty*.[186]

The tapes and transcripts will become another highly controversial issue, however, a critical component to understanding how the attack was set up and executed. Those in the *Liberty* camp question there authenticity. Whether they are real or doctored, or portions have been edited out is an ongoing question. The atmospherics because of the attack is a tepid lack of trust in the GOI and U.S. government, and tendencies are to believe the worst. Notwithstanding the controversy, it is this author's opinion that the tapes are helpful evidence regarding the question of whether the attack was a case of mistaken identity, or an intentional attack to sink the ship or put her out of commission. Regardless, the range of culpability runs from negligence, to recklessness, to outright criminal conduct.

Israeli historian, Dr. Ahron Bregman, in his book *A History of Israel* notes that he also was able to listen to the tapes. He states that a key to understanding the events of the attack "lies in the recordings of conversations, over the radio system, between Israeli pilots—attacking the ship—and the air control tower in Tel Aviv." He states "What then follows is extraordinary and, indeed, highly suspicious, and seems to indicate a possible cover-up by the Israelis..."[187]

Federal bankruptcy judge, and author, A. Jay Cristol is known to have had access to the Israeli tapes. He reports that during the 1967 war, the Israeli Air Force headquarters at the Kirya recorded the radio communications between Israeli pilots on UHF frequencies. They made audiotape recordings of telephone conversations between the chief air-controller, a Colonel Shmuel Kislev who was at the IAF HQ, and other controllers at Israeli Air Control Central, Air Control South and Air Control North. Cristol integrates this information into one continuous transcript adding bracketed explanatory comments. He notes that "unrelated subject matter" has been omitted—a subjective position to say the least. His decision to exclude "any information" can be suspect on his part and could suggest an author's bias. It is my intention to keep the transcripts as presented in Appendix 2 of Cristol's book, *The Liberty Incident.*[188] They may be difficult reading, but certainly clarify what was happening from their viewpoint. This author will provide some additional information and editorial comment, dividing the process into chapters dealing with the air attack and torpedo attack.

Certain *Liberty* supports and researchers will contend that these transcripts are a fraud; however, we are going to take a different approach and review "all information" regardless of the source as should be done in any investigation. If you are dealing with a rape, robbery or homicide you look at all sources of information, excluding nothing. Anything less would be investigative incompetence. In the meantime, we should consider the proffered evidence for what it is, "statements against interest", an exception to the Hearsay Rule of evidence law, and as such, should be given a presumptive credence and probative value.

I mention this reference to the rules of evidence law because Judge Cristol in his book cites the Hearsay Rule to denigrate and impeach the witness contentions of the *Liberty* crew as being second and third-hand hearsay and therefore their witness to events on June 8 is colored and biased.

Cristol notes that a female voice in Hebrew inserts the time of day and he claims the sequence is accurate to the second. The setting is June 8, 1967 the fourth day of the Six-Day War, a Thursday. The *Liberty* is in the eastern Mediterranean at Point Alfa and headed toward Point Bravo off the coast of Gaza and El Arish in the Sinai.

Regardless of one's preformed opinions on the matter, it is clear that the Israelis committed a considerable amount of resource and time to the attack. This would be self-evident from reading the full transcripts. There is no reported similar incident during the Six-Day War that has drawn as much attention and analysis as the attack on the USS *Liberty*.

As background information, in addition to the *Liberty* the NSA had aircraft in the air doing COMINT/ELINT reconnaissance flights gathering signals intelligence information. One plane is a U.S. Navy EC-121 that we previously referred to. A question will be what information is the plane and crew gathering from their listening processes? Cristol surmises that any NSA information should be "identical" to the IAF tapes and transcripts. The trouble seems to be that the NSA claims there were no tapes of intercepted communications pertaining to the air and torpedo boat attacks; this claim goes to the heart of the *Liberty* controversy. Is the U.S. government lying? The lack of U.S. transcripts is disputed as will be noted. Did someone in the U.S. government order the destruction of evidence of a possible crime? Has there been an obstruction of justice? NSA transcripts from the EC-121 will begin after the attack is over as Israeli helicopters are flying toward the wounded ship.

Again, Cristol notes that he first obtained access to the IAF transcripts and translations on June 18th and 19th, 1990; and had the opportunity to listen to the tapes on those days together with two Hebrew linguists, one a native-born Israeli and the other an American qualified in Hebrew, and six of the original air controllers involved in the attack. Certainly, this was an extraordinary grant of access to otherwise secret information—it clearly connotes an objective. The Israeli transcripts have been put into the public domain as representatives of the *Jerusalem Post* were also allowed to listen to certain portions of the transcripts in 2004. To this author's knowledge, representatives of the *Liberty* survivors have never had access to these transcripts other than via the above sources, nor to my knowledge has a formal request been made of the Israeli government. They are an obvious effort to present the Israeli viewpoint.

Cristol further notes that "In September 2001, the Israel Air Force provided access to the tapes of the air controller's telephone conversations (commencing at 1342 Sinai time) and pilots' transmissions on the attack channel frequency (commencing at 1329 Sinai time), as well as a transcription of the air controllers' telephone conversations. An additional listening session for Cristol took place on September 7, 2001, which included three Hebrew linguists, two native-born Israelis and one American." It is believed Cristol obtained access to this information at the Israeli Embassy in Miami, Florida.

Key players in the Israeli tape scenario are the air controllers: *Homeland* call sign of the air controllers; Kislev: Shmuel Kislev, chief air controller at the Kirya; Giora: Deputy chief air controller at the Kirya; Robert: Chief air controller at Air Control Central, twenty-five miles south of Tel Aviv; Shimon: Deputy chief air controller at Air Control Central; Menachem: Chief air controller at Air Control South, near the Sinai border; Yigal: Deputy chief air controller at Air Control South; and, L. K., a weapons system officer. L.K. will be identified as previously noted in the prior chapter.

Aircraft will include: *Kursa:* Two Mirage IIICJs that made the initial air attack run; *Royal:* Two Super-Mystères that made the second air attack run; *Menorah:* Flight of four Mirage IIICJs, armed with five-hundred-pound iron bombs; *Nixon:* Flight of two Mystères loaded with five-hundred-pound iron bombs; *Chalon:* One Mirage IIICJ; and, *Ofot:* helicopters, referred to as *Ofot* 1, *Ofot 2,* etc.

Watercraft includes *Pagoda:* Motor Torpedo Boat Division 914, consisting of MTBs 203, 204, and 206 and led by Lieutenant Commander Moshe Oren. MTB 206, *Migdal*, is the only MTB with a working UHF radio.

Cristol refers to certain communications-taking place on an attack frequency beginning at 1329 Sinai time. He does not provide that information in his book, but for the sake of this exercise, we will start the clock at 1030 Sinai time with the following information inserted into the transcript timeline as comments from various sources.

As background information, between 1030 and the time that the Israeli tape timeline starts the following occurs: Over-flights continue and the *Liberty* crew cannot determine the identity of the planes as there appears to be no markings. Whether or not there were markings on the planes is an open question. Some reported observations put the planes at too high an altitude or distance from the ship. One report has a Jewish crewmember breaking into tears upon seeing the Israeli symbol on one of the planes. The *Liberty* is removed from the plot table at Naval Headquarters by Commander Avraham Lunz at 1100 his shift change, because information on the ship has apparently not been updated per protocol. Additionally, in his book, Cristol reports that at 1100 Rear Admiral Shlomo Erell has left Naval HQ. At 1100, the second in command of the navy, Captain Issy Rahav, assumed tactical command when Erell left Stella Maris on Mount Carmel to go down to the port of Haifa. Not only did Lunz order removal of the plot marker, but also he did not inform Captain Rahav of his action when Rahav took command.[189]

Admiral Erell's role in these events is important in that he may have objected to the attack on the *Liberty* as

113

being outright murder. The CIA had received raw intelligence from a source not disclosed that Minister of Defense Dayan ordered the attack, and that an admiral ordered it stopped. It would appear that the admiral had to be Erell when he later returned to Naval HQ. No other Israeli admirals are identified in the context of the *Liberty* saga or the Six-Day War. A copy of that Central Intelligence Agency memorandum in circulation follows.

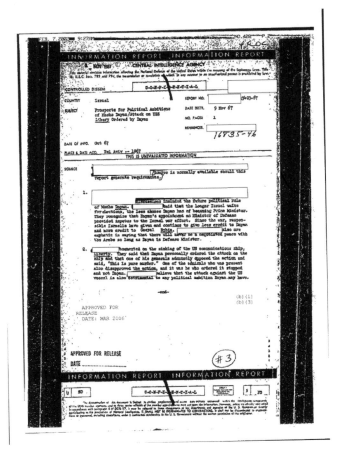

Israeli MTB Division 914 consisting of three boats sails from Ashdod to patrol from Ashdod to Ashkelon on the Israeli coast. As previously noted the boats are designated as T-203, T-204, and T-206 with the division commander, Moshe Oren, on board boat T-204. One of these boats had Admiral Erell's son on board, Udi Erell.

At around 1124, a report from an Israeli command post and the air force informs that El Arish is being bombarded from the sea. Ennes reports having seen explosions in the area of El Arish. Michael Oren, the Israeli historian will claim that the explosions were from an ammunition dump explosion. At this time, El Arish is under the control of Israeli forces. At 1126, surveillance aircraft return every 30 minutes and still no markings are observed. In the following transcript all times are Sinai times, and comments are those of this author, bracketed information is from author A. Jay Cristol's transcripts as appears in Appendix 2 of his book. The Israeli transcripts begin as follows with a reference to "Unknown", not a forthright way to start a disclosure process.

Start Transcript

1343

UNKNOWN: Navy received a report that two miles at sea, off El Arish, there is something that's pounding El Arish. Their torpedo boats are going towards there.

GIORA: I heard. I took helicopters from El Arish. I spoke with him. He went out to have a look and says he doesn't see a thing.

UNKNOWN: There's contact with the field but not with the city. [El Arish airport is located inland several miles south of the city of El Arish. At this time the airport was in Israeli control.]

KISLEV: Yigal, have *Chalon* take a look.

YIGAL: *Chalon.*

KISLEV: Clear.

SHIMON: Robert, have him take a look. He's circling the same area.

KISLEV: Can you see him, Shimon?

116

north along the coast." This refers to an event on June 7.

1344

SHIMON: Yeah. Sure, Yigal, can you see route 4? Have you informed him of 20,000 feet of altitude?

UNKNOWN: Do you have Tiyeh 39 10? [Tiyeh is phonetic for tet, the ninth letter of the Hebrew alphabet. The numbers are grid coordinates.]

UNKNOWN: Tiyeh 39 10, one moment.

1345

KURSA: We're switching to military power. Affirmative, northern direction. [*Kursa* has just been given a vector to a target.]

KURSA: Fuel okay, 3,000 [liters].

1349

YIGAL: Robert, where is *Menorah* now?

1350

KISLEV: Forget about *Menorah*. Yigal, you have a ship at 26. [Twenty-six is a site designation.] Take *Kursa* over there. If it's a warship, then blast it.

[At this point, the air force has a request from the navy to assist the chase of the vessel and, on urging from General Hod, via Commander Pinchas Pinchasy, has obtained authority from Captain Issy Rehav, who has tactical command of the navy at headquarters at Stella Maris, Haifa, to attack the ship, "if it's a warship." Attack is

117

conditionally authorized by Kislev at 1350 subject to *Kursa* identifying the ship as a warship.]

YIGAL: Clear.

> **Author's Comment:** At 1351, while on course 283T, three small surface contacts at a range of 32,200 and bearing 082T were picked up on the *Liberty's* radar. At 1353, the radar reported possible aircraft passing over the surface contacts.

1351

UNKNOWN: Wait a minute, Kislev. The navy says that there are two [sic; there were three] torpedo boats of ours in the area called *Pagoda*. They are on frequency 186.

[A minute later the navy warns of its own boats in the area. There appears to be more concern for preventing the aircraft from attacking the Israeli Navy than for further identification of the target, which has been identified as enemy under existing Israel Navy Rules of Engagement (ROE). The Israel Navy ROE are quite similar to the U.S. Navy ROE for 1967.]

KISLEV: If it's a warship, you can throw [attack]. There are two torpedo boats of ours. They want to know. They want [the pilots] to see them or call them on 86. Robert, do you have *Royal*? [Kislev knows that *Royal* has already taken off from an air base in the north.]

ROBERT: *Royal*?

SHIMON: He's at Hava 16 10 [Hava is phonetic for het, the eighth letter of the Hebrew alphabet. Again, grid coordinates.] That's track 15.

KISLEV: Robert, take *Royal* along the coast so that if *Kursa* identifies, he can go in. [Kislev positions *Royal* to prepare to follow *Kursa* on the attack.]

ROBERT: Okay.

KISLEV: Menachem, how much fuel does *Kursa* have?

MENACHEM: He's got a lot. A minute ago he had 3,000 [liters].

1352

KURSA: What is the range? Seven turns. 040 degrees. Roger. [*Kursa* asks the distance to the target. Confirms a slight right turn to point at the target.] I'll stay on 19 and 9 [two radio frequencies, or channels.] How do you call the torpedo boats? *Pagoda*? *Kursa* 9 and 3.

1353

KURSA: *Homeland*, keep on directing me to the place.

HOMELAND: 045[°], 20 miles. Ah, can you see them at the moment?

> **Author's Comment:** Again, the suggestion is that the *Liberty* is under coastal radar surveillance and the planes are vectored to the target—the *Liberty*. In his book, Dr. Bregman in part covers some of the exchanges between controllers and pilots. He refers to a question that is very clearly heard over the tapes and is aired in the control room in Tel Aviv: "What is it? An American [ship]?"[191]

1354

KURSA: Affirmative, it looks longer by eyesight.

1354

L. K.: What is that? Americans?

[No one had any data on the location for Americans. Without hard data, the subject was not pursued further. Following the tragedy, L. K. was called before the examining judge and testified in the second Israeli investigation. On October 1, 2001, this author [Cristol] obtained the declassification of L.K.'s testimony on July 4, 1967, before the examining judge. The following is his sworn response to a question asking why he mentioned Americans:

> I was on duty and I was on the [communications] line K.M.NK. (Weapons Systems Officer).... It is clear to me that I threw in [i.e., posed] the question—a shout which is written [in the transcript?]. It does not relate to the conversation that was conducted on the line at that same moment. Since at the time the conversation was about an attack on missile bases.
> In relation to this there are two possibilities:
> It is possible that this question was asked during a conversation with Lieut. [--] of his [probably a typo for "my"] unit with whom I spoke about the ship that purportedly was shelling El Arish, and the Air Force was about to attack it jointly with the Navy. I at that time expressed an opinion that we had taken only one action, that is to say, we had ascertained it was not an Israeli ship, and we did this through the naval representatives who were sitting with us.
> The hour was approximately 1350.

120

I was not the officer who would have been able to decide on an attack, but it was my duty to be as a passive party on the line in order to absorb information that might have helped, but like any officer I wanted to help, and therefore I wanted to suppose to the ears of [i.e., alert] those [officers] who were managing the war to a possibility-supposition that it was an American ship. That was only my supposition, since it was my assessment that it was not [an] Egyptian [ship], for they would not dispatch a solitary ship to our coast, and therefore I thought there was such a possibility.

All those who were connected on this line were able to hear me. Of course, all of them were overcome by this and they began to ask [questions] and then I did not want to delay the attack on the ship [because] they said it was shelling El Arish. And since the supposition was not based on data but on an assessment—supposition--therefore I did not want to delay the thing. Therefore I immediately retracted. Today I understand that had I persisted in my supposition, it would have been possible to prevent the tragedy. I did not know about the existence of an American ship in the morning.]

Author's Comment: L.K. raises the possibility that the target is an American ship. Michael Oren in his book *Six Days of War* at page 265 identified L.K. as Lazar Karni, an IAF air controller whose job was to listen to ground-to-air communications and make occasional suggestions. He did his job and was ignored. The following becomes critical from Dr. Bregman's view point because of the importance of voice inflections. Note L.K.

says the Air Force was to attack "jointly" with the Navy.

SHIMON: What Americans?

KISLEV: Robert, what did you say?

[No one answers.]

UNKNOWN: I'm putting Squadron (*Palga*) 116 on alert. [Squadron 116 is a reference to *Nixon* Flight.]

KISLEV: Okay.

KISLEV: Does he see more torpedo boats north of him?

1355

KISLEV: Menachem, if there are three torpedo boats, it's a possibility that they are ours. [Note that Kislev now has the correct number of torpedo boats" three rather than two, as stated incorrectly above at 1351, four minutes earner.]

SHIMON: Pay attention, *Kursa*.

1355

KURSA: *Pagoda* from *Kursa*. Are you *Migdal*? [Because *Migdal*, MTB 206, possesses the only functional UHF radio in *Pagoda*, MTB Division 914, *Kursa* must relay communication to Division Commander Moshe Oren, aboard MTB 204, through *Migdal*.]

MIGDAL: Affirmative.

KURSA: Are you attacking some ship now?

MIGDAL: We're on our way to one.

KURSA: Okay. .. I'll come and give you a hand. Where are you?

KURSA: *Migdal* from *Kursa*, are you three? [*Kursa* sees the three MTBs and asks if they are a formation of three.]

KURSA: There's no need. Bring yourselves up some. 10-15 kilometers from the boat. Is it in the direction of your (garbled) home?

KURSA: I see you on a right turn. Why are you turning? It's not in that direction.

MIGDAL: Okay, all right. Affirmative. . . . Affirmative.

1356

MIGDAL: *Kursa*, can you identify the target? [At 1356, *Kursa* was authorized to attack the ship "if it's a warship."]

KURSA: Can you identify his target, *Migdal*? [The MTBs and the aircraft are each asking the other to identify the ship.]

KURSA: She's running from you in the direction of El Arish, excuse me, Port Said. What is it? What is it? A destroyer? A patrol boat? What is it?

MIGDAL: *Kursa*, can you manage to identify it?

KURSA: I can't identify it, but in any case it's a military ship.

MIGDAL: Okay, what is it?

KURSA: It has one mast and one smokestack.

MIGDAL: Roger.

123

KURSA: It has one mast up front.

1356

SHIMON: Menachem, *Kursa* is calling you.

SHIMON: He says he is starting strafing them.

MENACHEM: I told him that if it's a warship, he can start to attack. That was the last command.

> **Author's Comment:** Menachem is the chief air controller at Air Control South, near the Sinai border. Note that *Kursa* flight cannot identify the ship but is still ordered to attack.

KISLEV: Menachem.

MENACHEM: Does he have authorization to attack?

KISLEV: He does. If this is a warship, then yes. *Royal* is to be turned there.

MENACHEM: Okay.

KISLEV: Send *Royal* over there with bombs [ptzatzot-Hebrew for bombs]. [Kislev believes at this point that *Royal* has iron bombs.]

ROBERT: On what frequency are you attacking?
SHIMON: She's running away from them. [At this point Shimon apparently sees the ship on his radar.]

> **Author's Comment:** Here we have an actual confirmation that "the ship" is seen on coastal radar. Note the *Liberty's* top speed is 18 knots, but she is only doing 5 knots on her course to Point Bravo. Dr. Bregman, in his book, notes that Colonel Kislev, in an

124

impatient voice is heard over the tapes saying: "I have already said: If this is a warship...to attack."[192] Dr. Bregman has dealt with these tapes in the context of voice inflection, which is very important, as anyone would know in terms of knowing intent and demeanor. Voice inflection can denote intent or the lack thereof.

KISLEV: Menachem, after he attacks have him explain to *Royal* how to find her.

SHIMON: She's running fast.

KISLEV: Okay, attack.

SHIMON: Robert, have *Royal* call us on 19. [At this time *Royal* is on another channel (frequency). *Royal* is arguing with his controller about the fact that he is carrying napalm, not iron bombs.]

ROBERT: *Royal* to you on 19.

1357

SHIMON: Just a minute, Kislev, we see the ship. [Shimon sees the ship on his radar scope.]

SHIMON: That's one hell of a ship. [Shimon commenting on the radar signature of the ship.]

ROBERT: Menachem, I'm passing (code words for *Royal* Flight) to you on 19. *Royal*. El Arish at 20,000.

KISLEV: Menachem, have them tell us if there is Nun Mem [the Hebrew letters for NM, representing *nagid metosim*, meaning antiaircraft fire].

1358

KURSA...

> **Author's Comment:** At 1358, Chief Smith
> on the *Liberty* is calling for help: "Any
> station, this is Rockstar, we are under attack".
> The *Liberty* is not equipped with anti-aircraft
> guns.

1358

KISLEV: Menachem, nu? [An idiom, "So what is happening?"]

MENACHEM: We're asking him. She's not shooting back.

KISLEV: Not shooting? Give me 19. [Kislev is puzzled by the report that the ship is not shooting at the attacking aircraft.]

1359

KURSA: We've hit her a lot. . . . But maybe she is doing it on purpose [putting out smoke], I don't know. Oil is spilling out into the water. I'm in eye contact. Great, wonderful. She's burning. She's burning.

ROYAL: What ship, *Kursa*?

1359

MENACHEM: Did you hear? He's hit her a lot. There's a lot of black smoke. There's an oil leak into the water. [This was more likely a gasoline leak from the fuel cell that was near the motor whale boat located on the deck of *Liberty*.] He's continuing.

KISLEV: Was there any Nun Mem on him?

126

MENACHEM: She's burning. The warship is burning.

1400

ROYAL: [Apparently we miss a transmission from *Kursa* to *Royal* where *Kursa* asks *Royal* the traditional "How do you hear me?" *Royal* responds with "5X5," the traditional aviator's idiomatic response "I hear you perfectly."] 5X5, eye contact with the target. [*Royal* sees *Liberty*.] Eye contact with *Kursa*. [*Royal* sees *Kursa* flight attacking the target.] *Royal* requests 15,000 feet. [At 1357 *Royal* was at EL Arish at 20,000 feet and wants to come down to set up for attack.]

KURSA: Okay, *Kursa* is coming in . . . you a bit further in. I'll go in the direction . . . Okay? [*Kursa* seems to be telling *Royal* he is going in on another run and also talking to his wingman.]

KURSA WING: . . . I think she is putting out smoke on purpose, it's coming out of the chimney. Okay, I'm finished too. . . . [*Kursa* exhausts its ammunition on the third pass and pulls off at about 1401.]

1400

MENACHEM: Shmulik [a diminutive for Shmuel, Kislev's first name], she's burning. [Menachem is obviously excited.] The minute *Kursa* is finished, we're sending in *Royal*.

KISLEV: Right. Sink her.

> **Author's Comment:** Notwithstanding various questions as to the ship's identity the order still is "Sink her".

MENACHEM: Sink her. Okay.

1401

KURSA: The ship is really burning. There is a large fire and a lot of black smoke.

1401

KURSA: *Royal*, your altitude? We're at 5,000 feet.

ROYAL: You're east, right?

KURSA: We're south of the ship.

ROYAL: . . . [Apparently *Royal*'s transmission was blocked by some one's transmission. It was probably an inquiry of whether *Kursa* was clear of the target, as the answer from *Kursa* is "Affirmative."]

1401

KISLEV: Menachem.

MENACHEM: We're sending in *Royal*.

KISLEV: Okay.

1401:52

ROBERT: . . . This ship?

KISLEV: Menachem, if *Royal* has napalm, it will make things easier.

1402

KURSA: Affirmative.

ROYAL: Not ours?

128

ROYAL: *Homeland*, can you hear? Call Homeland on 19. Ask if it's allowed to go in.

ROYAL: *Homeland* from *Royal*. Is it permitted to go in?

ROYAL: I understand, do not go in. Fine, we're circling above the ship at 15,000 feet. Tell him the navy will be arriving before us, I can see.

KURSA: 5 and 3. I've got him. [*Kursa* is apparently relaying to control for *Royal*.]

ROYAL: Does *Royal* have permission?

KURSA: Affirmative, you have permission *Royal*.

1402

SHIMON: Menachem, *Royal* is calling you.

MENACHEM: He got off the line.

1402:11

SHIMON: Kislev, there is doubt about the identification.

[Note, about 19 seconds have elapsed since Robert came on the loop at 1401:52. At this point, the lack of return antiaircraft fire and some questions from naval headquarters at Haifa, possibly received by the naval liaison officer with Robert, as a result of communication with Haifa, raised some doubts.]

KISLEV: If there is a doubt, then don't attack. [Again Kislev, the skilled professional, does not take over the tactical situation at the scene but puts a restriction on the attacking aircraft.]

129

SHIMON: Don't attack, Menachem. Robert, pay attention. There is doubt as to the identification.

KISLEV: What does that mean? [Kislev, ever vigilant, wants an explanation. He is asking Robert, who has a naval liaison officer, Yoshua Barnai, at his side.]

ROBERT: Okay, you may attack. [Apparently he has resolved the identification issue either with the naval liaison officer or through him to naval headquarters at Stella Maris, Haifa.]

KISLEV: You may attack.

> **Author's Comment:** Again, notwithstanding identity questions, the attack is pushed. Someone is giving an overriding command.

1402:32

ROYAL: Sausages, in the middle and up . . . in one pass. Two together. [*Royal* Flight Leader tells his wingman to drop both of the napalm canisters on the first run.] We'll come in from the rear. Watch out for the masts. Don't hit the masts, careful of the masts. I'll come in from her left, you come behind me.

SHIMON: Next formation--get a briefing on what took place.

ROBERT: Authorized to sink. [This comes from the naval liaison with Robert.]

KISLEV: You can sink it.

SHIMON: *Royal* started chatting.

ROBERT: One eight [most likely referring to sector coordinates], that is not the ship. Wait a minute.

KISLEV: Menachem, is he blasting (*dofek*) her?

MENACHEM: He's going low with napalm.

UNKNOWN: No, Robert, it is not worthwhile.

> **Author's Comment:** "UNKNOWN" jumps in and gives the order to stop the attack, but it continues with UNKNOWN still participating. Note the time of 1402:32.

KISLEV: You don't need any more for the ship. Enough.

MENACHEM: There's no need. Our forces are there. So is the navy.

SHIMON: It's worth it just for insurance.

KISLEV: But napalm went there. [Kislev apparently does not understand the effect of napalm against a ship. It may have some value in the suppression of anti-aircraft fire. Here there was no antiaircraft fire.]

UNKNOWN: What can napalm do [to a ship]?

> **Author's Comment:** Again, notwithstanding the identification issue the attack proceeds. This time they are using napalm with one canister missing the ship and the other causing some fires. "UNKNOWN" asks, "What can napalm do?" Clearly, there is someone in the command center who is involved but lacks some military knowledge. The author is raising the question as to whether this could be Rabin, the Chief of Staff, who has involved

himself in the attack. It certainly would not be general Hod who should know what napalm could do. *Liberty's* log reflects a notation at 1403 of a large explosion on the port side. This would be the gasoline drums.[193] At 1404 *Kursa* flight leaves and *Royal* attacks. Cristol in his book acknowledges that each plane in *Kursa* flight made three strafing runs.[194] At 1405, *Liberty* sounds the general fire alarm.

1404

ROYAL: . . . on the right side of the stern. . .

ROYAL WING: You've missed by an undershot. [Referring to the napalm.]

ROYAL: . . . a deep gash. . .

1405

KISLEV: What is *Kursa* reporting? Was there any Nun Mem?

MENACHEM: I passed him to 33 and asked for a report.

KISLEV: Robert, ask *Kursa* if there was any Nun Mem. [Kislev is still concerned about the lack of antiaircraft fire.]

ROBERT: Kislev, the navy asks not to sink her completely; they want to get close and have a look.

> **Author's Comment:** Now the Navy has reservations and wants a closer look. Between 1405 and 1410 the *Liberty* was under repeated air attack. The attacks were made in a criss-cross fashion over the ship with each attack

132

coming at approximately 45 second to one minute intervals. The attacks caused three major fires topside covering large areas of the ship with flames and smoke. Was the Navy's reservation caused by Admiral Erell's return to Naval HQ? Upon being briefed, he countermanded the attack order previously given and his order was transmitted by radio to the MTB division commander on board MTB 204. Commander Oren would claim he never received the countermanded order, however, there is evidence the order was received by the CIC officer on MTB 204. It is not known if the order was received before or after the torpedoes were launched and in the water.

SHIMON: Have them rescue the people with the torpedo boats to help.

ROBERT: Okay, finish with this formation. The torpedoes are coming up to them.

1406

KISLEV: Robert, what does *Kursa* say?

ROBERT: I'm telling you already. "This is easier than MiGs."

KISLEV: What's the situation now?

1407

ROYAL: Fine, pull up.

ROYAL: . . . I'm behind you. Careful of her antennas.

1407

UNKNOWN: I don't know. Number Two [*Royal* Wing] hit [with a napalm bomb] . . . and now he's strafing.

1408

ROYAL: *Homeland* from *Royal*, how do you hear me? She has some kind of marking, P30 and something.

1408

KISLEV: Robert, take 116 flight out there, too. [*Nixon* flight-An attack by this flight with iron bombs would very likely have sunk the *Liberty* in the next seven or eight minutes.]

ROBERT: Okay.

MENACHEM: Her marking. . . [cut off by Kislev]

KISLEV: Yes, I heard. We're checking.

SHIMON: Robert, take 116 flight to . . .

1409

ROYAL: *Homeland*, if you had a two-ship formation with bombs, in ten minutes before the navy arrives, it will be a *mitzvah*. Otherwise the navy is on its way here. [*Mitzvah*, a good or worthwhile deed. The old competition between navy and air force rears its head.]

1409

SHIMON: Before the navy arrives, it will be a mitzvah. [Shimon wants the target for the air force, with the navy left out.]

KISLEV: Take 116 flight in the meanwhile. Who is checking this? [Kislev is still concentrating on identification, while Shimon is enraptured at the prospect of beating the navy to the target.]

SHIMON: *Royal* reported that it will be a mitzvah, before the navy comes.

KISLEV: Look for a flag if they can see one. Have *Royal* look. See if they can identify with a flag. [*Liberty's* flag was shot from the halyard on the first pass by *Kursa*. It is about ten minutes later, and the second flag has not yet been hoisted.]

> **Author's Comment:** Note Spector in *Kursa* flight made no mention of a flag even though

he years later said he did not see one. Now for the first time *Royal* is being asked to look for a flag. Also, note the attitude of "competition" between the controllers, Air Force and Navy. FOLLOWING RECEIVED FROM ROCKSTAR I AM UNDER ATTACK MY POSIT 31 23N 33 25E. I HAVE BEEN HIT. REQUEST IMMED ASSISTANCE. Since all broadcast messages received from *Liberty* were on a non-secure voice circuit, transmitted repeats by other commands are sent unclassified.[197]

1410

ROYAL: (unintelligible)

ROYAL: Twelve o'clock... look higher. Now left, slowly, slowly. . . a bit faster so it will stay external, okay?

1410

ROBERT: Kislev, They're [the navy] asking us here [at the Radar Air Control Central where Robert sits with Yoshua Barani] not to do anything else about her. They want to take her. I want to receive an answer.

> **Author's Comment:** Robert at the radar control center is saying that the Navy wants a shot at the ship. Below the MTBs are advised the planes are on their final run and leaving it to the torpedo boats to finish the attack with the planes failing to have sunk her. Reference is now made to the *Liberty's* hull markings. Israeli author Michael Oren identifies one of the Mystère pilots as a Captain Yossi Zuk.[198]

KISLEV: No, no. They're [the navy]... .

136

1411

ROBERT: Menachem, is *Royal* leaving?

MENACHEM: Wait a minute, he's reporting something.

KISLEV: Okay, attack, Menachem. [Apparently Kislev is about to send in *Nixon* flight.]

1411

ROYAL: *Homeland* from *Royal*, do you read me? Pay attention, this ship's markings are Charlie Tango Romeo 5. Pay attention, *Homeland*, Charlie. . .

> **Author's Comment:** At 1411 the MTB Division is advised that the planes are on their final run and now the boats are to attack. [IDF History Department/MTB Division 914 War Log.] *Royal* Flight reports: "*Homeland* from *Royal*, do you read me? Pay attention, this ships markings are Charlie Tango Romeo 5. Pay attention, *Homeland*, Charlie Tango Romeo 5. There is no flag on her!" [IAF audio tapes.][199] MTBs are told it was a destroyer, and told to attack. Kislev says leave her and thinks American.

1412

... Tango Romeo 5. There is no flag on her! She looks like a minesweeper with that marking. Roger, I'm leaving her. I'm staying around one more minute. [*Royal* misread GTR-5 as CTR-5. At this point, both he and control are alerted to the fact that she is not marked like an Arab ship.]

1412

ROBERT: Menachem, has *Royal* come out? [Robert is making sure that it is clear for 116 Flight to go in.]

MENACHEM: Not yet.

ROBERT: What height? What height is *Royal* reaching [descending to]?

MENACHEM: Charlie Senator Romeo. [Menachem relays even more incorrect markings: CSR-5.]

KISLEV: Leave her! [There is a dramatic change in the tone of Kislev's voice. Kislev knows that Egyptian ships are marked in Arabic script. English or roman letters are not used and, ironically, Arabic numbers are not used. Approximately sixty seconds before, Kislev had authorized *Nixon* Flight to attack, and now he cancels the air operation with the terse "Leave her."]

ROBERT: Leave her? What ship is this?

KISLEV: Leave her! Menachem, report the approximate damage. *Nixon* Flight to her [original] mission.

> **Author's Comment:** Kislev calls the planes off.

1413

ROYAL: *Homeland*, 5X5 [advising control that he hears perfectly], there's external fire on her, a lot of hits on her upper parts. People are jumping into the water. [This was not correct. No one jumped into the water; life rafts were thrown into the water, and this maybe is what *Royal* saw.] She's not shooting at all. She has hardly any armaments on her. She's going full steam toward the north.

1413

KISLEV: Shimon, Robert, we're sending two helicopters to them. [Kislev moves to a rescue mode.]

ROBERT: Okay, clear. I'm sending helicopters.

> **Author's Comment:** Note the reference to two helicopters, which are Super Frelons for troop transport or anti-submarine warfare. Some members of the *Liberty* crew will claim they are full of armed troops. Of particular importance is the fact that Dr. Bregman notes at 1414 a pilot can be heard over the tapes asking: "What state [does the ship belong to]? He states that Kislev responds "Probably American", and the pilot says "What?" Kislev responses again, "Probably American". Dr. Bregman remarks that while there has been a "positive identification as American", 12 minutes later the torpedo boats attack and put the *Liberty* out of action almost sinking her.[200]
> The Israeli contention will be that they tried to call the Navy off but failed. The reader should note that there is no reference in Cristol's Israeli transcripts for the time of 1414 as described by Dr. Bregman. Is this an example of Cristol taking some license with how much information he included in his Appendix 2 transcripts? In the preface to these transcripts, Cristol was precise to say they were accurate within seconds. Again, voice inflection is important in terms of understanding simple print transcripts. Access to the actual audio tapes is the critical evidence. IAF senior air controller Colonel Kislev orders *Royal* Flight "Leave her." The air attack is over. MTB Division 914 reports it sees aircraft have left.

[IAF audio tapes/Navy HQ War Log.] The
IDF History Report at p. 15 indicates the
planes left the area at 1416.

MENACHEM: Kislev, what country? [Menachem has
become concerned.]

KISLEV: Possibly American.

1415

SHIMON: Kislev, maybe you know which countries are
around here. If it's possible to take them, they are taking
care of it. [Shimon still believes that the ship is Egyptian.
He is concerned about rescue operations if the seamen are
Egyptian.

1417

ROBERT: There is no contact yet with *Menorah*. He's
around the canal at low altitude. I don't have any contact
with him yet. [The war goes on. *Menorah* Flight must be
monitored and controlled.]

1419

ROYAL: I'm in the direction. . .

1419

KISLEV: Robert, do you have contact with *Ofot* 1 and 2?

ROBERT: Okay, Tm trying. None yet.

SHIMON: Kislev, I have *Ofot* 2 in Taiman Field.
[Taiman is an air base in the south near Beer Sheba.]

ROBERT: Okay, I'm trying. None yet.

SHIMON: Kislev, I have [*Ofot*] 2 in Taiman Field.

KISLEV: Not him.

1425

KISLEV: Robert, Two [*Ofot*, a Super Frelon 807] is in Taiman Field?

SHIMON: Yes, with the Minister of Defense.

SHIMON: Frelon from Air Force Base 8 [Tel Nof, located south of Tel Aviv] is ready to leave for the ship. Shall I send him out? Operations notified Base [censored].

KISLEV: Okay.

1429

KISLEV: Robert, is there any contact with the Super Frelons?

SHIMON: Yes.

1434

ROBERT: Kislev, it's an Egyptian supply boat. My "admiral" is next to me. I'm touching him. [Robert is referring to the naval liaison officer Yoshua Barnai. Robert is elated. The navy MTBs on the scene had identified the ship as Egyptian.]

KISLEV: Is that true or not? [Kislev is extremely excited, but still the same precise professional.] Where did he get it [the positive identification] from?

ROBERT: The helicopter went away from there. That is what he [Yoshua Barnai] says.

KISLEV: If so, then have the helicopter get out of there. [Kislev has become concerned about the safety of the helicopter that was sent to rescue Americans and is near the ship now identified as Egyptian.]

ROBERT: The torpedo boat is taking care of it. It's an Egyptian supply ship. They're torpedoing it now.

End of transcripts. Refer to next chapter

There are two items of importance reference the above transcripts: First, it is noted that at 1413 above two helicopters are dispatched to the *Liberty*. As we will later see, the NSA has released its own transcripts as picked up by the EC-121 dealing with voice communications from the helicopter pilots, the torpedo boats and the controllers. These intercepts are recorded as occurring between 1229Z and 1328Z (1429 and 1528 Sinai time) on June 8. The question is how do they synchronize with the Cristol Israeli transcripts? We will cover this point in the next chapter dealing with the torpedoing of the *Liberty*.

The next item of significance is the reference at 1425 Sinai time by Shimon to the Minister of Defense, Moshe Dayan being placed at "Taiman" Field with *Oft* 2 a Super Frelon helicopter. At 1425, there is a reference to Super Frelon 807; this is the first reference to an aircraft call sign. This is noteworthy because at 1429 the Navy EC-121 intercepts will begin dealing with the flight of 2 Super Frelon helicopters, 810 and 815, vectored toward the wounded *Liberty*. The NSA saying there were no tapes of the actual attack released these intercepts.

The lack of intercepts dealing with the actual air and torpedo boat attacks goes to the heart of whether or not there was a conspiracy to cover-up, whether or not the attack was intentional, and whether or not evidence was destroyed—more on this later.

The reference to Taiman Field near Beer Sheva is actually believed to be a training field privately owned and operated for over 25 years by Captain Eli Peretz of Ayit Aviation the current operator.[201] Taiman Field is now referred to as Sde Teyman Airport. Author Cristol uses the word Taiman, which when "Googled" turns up no relevant reference. The Southern Command used the field during the Six-Day War.[202] The airbase is approximately 55 to 60 miles from the area of El Arish where the *Liberty* was attacked off shore. It is about 4.7 miles northwest of Beer Sheva along highway 25. The question of how Minister of Defense Moshe Dayan's location at the time of the attack plays into all this will be addressed later.[203]

At 1419, MTB Division 914 Commander Oren orders the torpedo attack according to the IDF History Department and the MTB division's log. The IAF command at the Kirya tells the Naval Command at Stella Maris there is doubt about the target's identification, and Naval HQ tells Division 914 not to attack. There is a conflict on the command boat as to whether to attack or not to attack. The issue is since the torpedo boats are on the surface of the water and within attack range, what are they seeing in terms of identifying the target? Rather what did they fail to see?

Because of the **ordered recall** of aircraft from the carriers *America* and *Saratoga*, no help will arrive to assist the *Liberty* and crew. Consequently, more American service members will be killed or wounded. In fact, the politicians in Washington left the whole crew and ship in jeopardy.

1404 to 1410 *Liberty's* Log [reconstructed]: Ship under repeated air attack with two or more unidentified aircraft making coordinated strafing, rocket and incendiary runs over the ship. Three major fires are burning topside covering large areas of the ship with flames and heavy smoke. A total of eight officers and men were killed outright or died from injuries received during the air attack, one officer killed on 04 level, one man killed at machine gun 52, one died of wounds received on the main deck starboard side and two died of wounds received on the 01 level portside. Approximately seventy-five were wounded, including the Commanding Officer, throughout topside areas from shrapnel and shock of exploding rockets.

Moshe Oren will claim he did not get Rabin's order to hold back. The order appeared in T-204's logbook. Historian Michael Oren would later claim while he never received the order, he paused at 6000 meters and scrutinized the ship. In spite of smoke, he could see the vessel was not the destroyer that had presumably shelled El Arish, but most likely a freighter that had either serviced that destroyer or evacuated enemy soldiers from the beach. He claims he consulted his intelligence manual, and found that the ship's silhouette resembled that of the Egyptian supply ship (horse transport), *El Quseir*.

Michael Oren, *Six Days of War*, page 267.

Chapter 6

Torpedoed

Based upon our reading of the Israeli transcripts in the previous chapter, several items immediately gain our interest. First, Cristol does not identity who "UNKNOWN" is, even though it is obvious that he is in a command position in the Kirya calling the shots. We have raised the question as to whether or not it could be Chief of Staff Rabin. This is important because it puts top Israeli commanders in the middle of the attack on the *Liberty*. The four top leaders we are concerned about who could have ordered the attack, objected to the attack, or ordered the attack to cease are IDF Chief of Staff, Yitzhak Rabin, General of the Air Force, "Motti" Hod, Minister of Defense Moshe Dayan and Rear Admiral Shlomo Erell, head of the Navy, or the Israeli Prime Minister, Levi Eshkol.

Early speculation after the attack by U.S. government politicians was that they had no idea who may have ordered the attack; however, the thought was it was some lower level commander, for example, the commander in the Sinai.

It is clear as to who is in charge and giving orders. The current Israeli ambassador to the U.S., and historian, Michael Oren points to Rabin. Oren's book published in 2002 puts Chief of Staff Rabin in the "pit" at the Kirya. He demands to know what is being done about shelling from the sea.[204] The fact is there was no shelling. There is a tentative report that the Egyptians shelled the coast on June 7. Ennes reported seeing a small plane flying near El Arish and seeing explosions. Apparently, an ammunition dump exploded. Was this a cover story for setting up the attack on the *Liberty*? One item does become clear, and that is the *Liberty* was tracked by coastal radar in addition to numerous over-flights that *Liberty* survivors claim were conducted to monitor the ship. The transcripts show that IAF General Hod was sitting next to Kislev in the Kirya. Author A. Jay Cristol confirms this, that he is sitting two chairs from Kislev.[205]

The reader might be thinking if the Israelis had such a hard time keeping track of the *Liberty*, what was she doing with regard to all the Soviet ships in the area.

Michael Oren in his book confirms that Rabin was in the "Pit" fearing the ship they were attacking was Russian. Rabin in his memoirs notes: "Our forces had attacked a Soviet spy vessel...Are we facing massive Soviet intervention in the fighting?"[206] Rabin goes on to note how the Soviet navy had been reinforced beginning on May 15. He notes relief on hearing that it was an American ship, with the expression of regret and notification to the American embassy. The problem we have here is that the Israeli transcripts give no hint of the "target" ship being suspected as Soviet, only as the

146

Egyptian horse transport ship. Certainly, it would have been malfeasance for the IDF to attack a Soviet ship, even by mistake, considering the Supreme Command's concern about Soviet intervention on behalf of Syria—the Soviets were the wild card in the Six-Day War.

Rabin further notes: "The frightful prospect of a violent Soviet reprisal had disappeared." Perhaps the whole *Liberty* saga can best summed up in that sentence—one must ponder that. What exactly caused the Soviet threat to dissipate?

Michael Oren states that Dayan is away visiting Hebron and General Hod is en route from a briefing, noting, "The Chief of Staff took personal command of the situation."[207] The Chief of Staff is the key military operational leader serving under the Minister of Defense. Dayan made certain key decisions, some of which Rabin did not agree with and said so in his memoirs.

The issue of who on the Israeli side was in command is important. Michael Oren is straightforward on this point; however, Israeli apologist A. J. Cristol seems to be trying to hide this in his book as he inserts the "UNKNOWN" persona into his version of the Israeli transcripts, while contending they were accurate. Cristol makes limited mention of Rabin in his book.

Recall that at 1100 Avraham Lunz removed the *Liberty* plot marker at his shift change because there had been no position update. At 1120 MTB Division 914, *Pagoda,* is ordered to sail out of Ashdod. At 1127, IDF GHQ Tel Aviv gets the Southern Command report of shelling of El Arish from the sea. The head of operations wanted the report verified to see if Israeli naval ships were in the area.[208] Admiral Erell had left Naval HQ for

147

the port at Haifa with his second in command Captain Issy Rehav left in charge. Rehav gave the order "If it is a warship" attack it. Why Erell left HQ for the port at this particular time is unclear. He had a son on one of the torpedo boats, and perhaps he did not want to be a party to the attack order—this is a supposition on my part, but it would certainly be a human reaction. If he left HQ under such circumstances, then it would be a matter of passing "the buck" down the ranks because his second in command, Captain Issy Rehav was left on the "hot-seat". Rehav would resign from the Navy even though he was next in line to become the commander of the navy. Cristol notes the following:[209]

> Ambassador Evron told this author that the issue of punishment had often been discussed between him and Itzhak Rabin, who on numerous occasions had said to Evron that it was unfortunate that there had been no formal punishment of some military person involved, because people in the United States interpreted the lack of punishment of a lower-ranking person as an indication of a cover-up at a higher level.

Cristol in his book, Chapter 11, *Did Dayan Order it*, places Dayan sitting with troops having lunch at Et Zion Bloc on the road to Hebron at 1335 per the photo on page 146 of his book. However, the transcripts put the Minister of Defense at Taiman field (Teyman Field) at 1425 with Super Frelon helicopter 807, or *Oft* 2. This reference to the Minister of Defense will have another importance that we will discuss in the chapter on the NSA intercepts. It was the Southern Command located in the Sinai that raised the alarm about shelling from the sea. Dayan was in direct contact with the Southern

Command in this period. Certainly, by the second day of the war the IDF was in control of the Sinai in the El Arish area.

The issue of how long the planes were on target and how many actually participated in the attack is a matter of interest only and has little to do with the why and motive of the attack. On Internet forums there has been a lot of discussion as to whether attacking forces jammed the *Liberty's* communication system, and if so, how did they do it. There had been reports of a buzz saw sound. Certainly striking the antenna system would target the communication system on the ship. As an example of forum discussion, one of the *Liberty's* supporters did some math on the subject and noted: [210]

> One of the most controversial aspects of the attack on *Liberty* has been how long the air phase lasted. The Israelis say about 14 minutes; the *Liberty* crew says approximately 25. I thought I'd make an attempt to resolve the issue. The attacking planes came in 4 flights, *Kursal*--2 Mirage lllc, *Menorah*--4 Mirage lllc, *Royal*--2 Super Mystère, *Nixon*--2 Mystère. 10 aircraft total. The main armament for each was two 30mm cannon with 125 rounds apiece. A likely scenario would have the planes beginning their strafing runs about 2,000ft out from *Liberty*. At 350 mph this would have given the pilots some 3 seconds of firing time. A 1G turn at 350 mph has a 1.5 mile radius. It would take nearly 1.5 minutes to bring the plane back to *Liberty*. The cannons on the jets had a firing rate of 1,200 rpm or so. This would give each plane two 3 second bursts or 2 firing passes at *Liberty*. Total 3 minutes to complete. Multiply that by

the 10 planes and we have 30 minutes. It's obvious the Israelis emptied their ammunition trays, validating the claim made by *Liberty's* crew.

A former U.S. Air Force "top-gun" would also analyze the attack noting that the first planes flew by the ship identifying it as their assign target, then turned back to attack from low altitude hitting the forward gun tubs, showing a level attack exactly as described by the crew. He would note it was not as described in A. Jay Cristol's book.[211]

The ship had 821 plus bullet and rocket holes in its superstructure. Let us continue with the review of the Israeli transcripts as we move into the motor torpedo boat phase of the attack. First, author Michael Oren notes that Rabin orders two helicopters to check for survivors who the pilots said had jumped overboard. These are two Super Frelons with armed troops on board as contended by some of the *Liberty* crewmembers.

At 1435, per the *Liberty* log, TORPEDO HIT STARBOARD SIDE AMIDSHIP. TWENTYSIX MEN DIED AS A RESULT OF THE TORPEDO HIT AND MTB STRAFING FIRE. The ship lost electrical power.[212]

Israeli transcript continues

1435

ROBERT: Where are the helicopters you sent?

KISLEV: The helicopters are back.

ROBERT: Tell them to go away.

150

KISLEV: Just a minute. Robert, get the guys out of there. [The air force tries to conduct rescue operations in the midst of the naval attack.]

KISLEV: Just a minute, Robert, for. . .

SHIMON: I'm keeping them aside; I just want to see.

KISLEV: On the side until he will identify.

ROBERT: Have him stay on the side, they're putting torpedoes into it. You can get the guys out later.

MENACHEM: Kislev, Air Force Commander is arriving in ten minutes. I've informed him and told him to bring the helicopters because we have torpedo boats in the area. He said okay.

SHIMON: What's the call sign of the torpedo boats?

UNKNOWN: *Pagoda.*

> **Author's Comment:** If the air controllers are talking about rescue, they are also intent on having a torpedo put into the ship. Reference to these two helicopters, Super Frelons, by *Liberty* survivors is that they were filled with armed soldiers and it appeared they were going to finish them off. This was the conclusion of Commander Dave Lewis one of the wounded survivors.[213] Obviously, this was speculation under adverse circumstances as no shots were fired. Did General Hod leave the Kirya to go to Air Control South near the Sinai? "UNKNOWN" says the torpedo boats call sign is *Pagoda*, so again it appears we are talking about two separate individuals in a command position.

151

1436

ROBERT: The air force has no identification problems. I won't have anyone telling me again that the air force has any identification problem. [Robert became incensed at the suggestion that the air force might have any problem with identification.]

MENACHEM: Now, listen, I've also told the Air Force Commander that this ship was finally identified as Egyptian. I told him we're transferring the helicopters. We're not sending them, because we have torpedo boats. We'll keep them aside, to pull the survivors out of the sea. They're putting another torpedo into her. Just in case. I hope this torpedo will hit. [Menachem's understanding of the events at sea is inaccurate. A single torpedo attack was made. Five torpedoes were launched. One torpedo, the last launched from the last boat, T-203, hit the ship at about 1435.]

> **Author's Comment:** Note below where Robert says the torpedo hit and the time was recorded as 1437. Read what Menachem had to say if there was any doubt about the intent to sink the ship. Of five torpedoes that were launched only one hit the ship. The helicopters had been held back until after the torpedo attack and are now allowed to check for survivors. Also, note that the Air Force Commander agrees with holding the helicopters back until the torpedo attack is finished. A major contention is that the air controllers were unable to get word of the identification of the ship to the Navy, so how does the Air Force Commander, now in the Sinai, figure into this equation knowing he is holding back the helicopters until the

torpedoing of the ship. Menachem then says the Commander is not in the picture and does not know what is going on.

1437

ROBERT: The torpedo hit.

1438

ROBERT: You can send in the helicopter in order to get the people out of the water. Tell the helicopters they are not Americans, they're Egyptians. [The navy has now convinced the air force that the ship is Egyptian.]

SHIMON: Who'll guard the guys in the helicopters?

ROBERT: I hope there are more people in the helicopters. [Robert expressed concern for security and hoped there are more than just the pilot and copilot on the helicopters.]

SHIMON: I think it is better the torpedo boats should take them. They should sit on the torpedo boats who'll put them ashore.

ROBERT: I told the Air Force Commander we're not sending the helicopters because we have torpedo boats; he said fine.

1439

MENACHEM: If there is a helicopter nearby, have him start getting them out of the water and take them to El Arish. Air Force Commander is not in the picture and doesn't know what's going on, but I don't have time to run over and tell them the whole story.

ROBERT: Just tell me what to do with the helicopter.

SHIMON: . . . said get the people out of the water.

ROBERT: You can pick them up and hit them over the head. [Robert's solution to the rescue of the Egyptians.]

UNKNOWN: Robert, did you hear my theory? Just when the navy saw we're getting them off, they began shouting.

1440

ROBERT: Kislev shouted "Americans." [It was Kislev at 1414.]

UNKNOWN: How many helicopters are on their way?

SHIMON: Super Frelon. [Not responsive; the question was how many, not what kind.]

MENACHEM: Giora, they went to EI Arish to tell them that Egyptian sailors are arriving, from the sea. From a boat they sank.

KISLEV: I said so. Have the helicopters take them out slowly, slowly. And inform EI Arish.

MENACHEM: Robert, I don't think they managed to sink her.

ROBERT: They took her apart. (garbled)

> **Author's Comment:** Immediately above and below we have confusion among the air controllers and whoever is in control, "UNKNOWN". They think the ship was sunk but then learn it was not. At 1456, there is still confusion about identity. This is almost an hour after the initial air attack.

1451

ROBERT: There is another ship. Can you see her? [Robert probably sees the image of the *Liberty* on his radar screen and identifies it as another ship because he believes that the *Liberty* was sunk.]

> **Author's Comment:** Robert is at Air Control Central 25 miles south of Tel Aviv as he monitors the ship on his radar.

1454

ROBERT: Shimon, does Yami have contact with the helicopter? The identification is not clear yet.

1456

KISLEV: Robert, what do you say about the identification?

ROBERT: The navy says that even though they sent a torpedo, there is a part which is unclear. Soon I'll ask what language these guys talk, then we'll know for sure. [The controllers are still unsure of the identification of the ship 19 minutes after the torpedo attack.]

KISLEV: Have they taken them [the survivors] out yet?

ROBERT: I have no idea.

KISLEV: What about the Super Frelon?

ROBERT: Immediately.

1457

SHIMON: The Super Frelon has no contact with the torpedo boats. Can he go in alone and get them out?

155

KISLEV: Can he see people in the water? [There are none to see. At this point, with the Super Frelon hovering nearby and the torpedo boats lying nearby; the *Liberty* survivors are bracing for another attack and have no idea that the operations are now devoted to rescue.]

SHIMON: He's getting closer.

1501

KISLEV: Shimon, what about the Super Frelon?

SHIMON: He is 12 miles from them now. He has eye contact with the ship. He's asking for relays in the air. Between him and the torpedo boats, it's being taken care of.

1504

SHIMON: Kislev, first, Giora said before that if they're Arabs, take them to El Arish. They're not Arabs.

KISLEV: Take them to Lod. [Lod was Israel's international airport, later renamed in honor of Ben-Gurion.]

ROBERT: Is there any identification yet?

SHIMON: None yet.

MENACHEM: Is it American after all?

SHIMON: That's still not clear, Menachem.

MENACHEM: Why did they blast a torpedo?

SHIMON: They [the navy] probably can't read English.

1505

KISLEV: Shimon, well, what about the helicopters?

SHIMON: He's still three miles away. He's going to start. He's above them, and he'll give a report any minute now.

1509

KISLEV: It's not clear what's happening here. I don't understand.

1510

SHIMON: Kislev, there are no people. He sees boats [probably the life rafts] but no people.

KISLEV: The navy also reports that there are no people. He sees boats but no people

SHIMON: They have three more torpedo boats around... He's coming in low in order to see better. The Mirage pilot [sic; it was the Super Mystère pilot, *Royal* Flight Leader] reported people jumping.

KISLEV: Robert, have the helicopters come home. Both of them, and without picking anyone up.

ROBERT: Okay.

1512

SHIMON: Kislev, there is an American flag on board.

> **Author's Comment:** We now have tentative confirmation of an American flag after numerous references to the possibility that the ship is American. *Liberty* survivors will claim the MTBs machine-gunned the deployed life rafts.

157

KISLEV: Sure or not sure?

SHIMON: He'll check again. He reported it. He'll check a second time.

KISLEV: Have him get a good look at the flag.

1513

KISLEV: S, nu?

SHIMON: Here, he's reporting in a second.

1514

SHIMON: Kislev, it's an American flag. People keep hiding every time he flies over.

KISLEV: I understand. Okay, come home.

1515

KISLEV: Shimon, do you have contact with the helicopter in Sinai?

> **Author's Comment:** This may be a reference to the Minister of Defense's Super Frelon helicopter that was at Taiman field earlier. It seems the efforts are to either advise him, or coordinate with him, or both.[214]

SHIMON: None.

1516

KISLEV: Shimon, doesn't the Super Frelon have gas?

SHIMON: He reported that he's short.

KISLEV: One of them should go to EI Arish.

SHIMON: Okay.

KISLEV: One to EI Arish and the other home. Is there QL there?

SHIMON: Nothing.

> **Author's Comment:** According to the *Liberty's* log, power was restored to the bridge, but the rudder did not respond so steering had to be accomplished by using the aft steering control position. *Liberty* will have suffered the most casualties and dead because of the torpedo hit. What will develop will become an even greater mystery when planes are launched from the Sixth Fleet carriers to assist her and then be recalled, allegedly by the Secretary of Defense McNamara and the President himself. *Liberty* would not receive U.S. aid until the next morning.

1519

KISLEV: Shimon, try to find the helicopter in the Sinai.

1604

SHIMON: Kislev, the ship hasn't sunk yet. She's getting farther and farther away. She's going north. [North would have been out to sea and away from the coast.]

1605-1724

No transmissions relating to the *Liberty* during this time period.

Author's Comment: Damage control time for the Israelis: Amazingly, for 1 hour and 19 minutes there is no communication traffic recorded dealing with the attack or alleged rescue effort. Or author Cristol has deleted it from "his" transcript. The ship was not sunk and the Sixth Fleet has been alerted with a potential for a confrontation with the Israelis. Kislev asks Shimon to find the helicopter in the Sinai; it is believed according to prior reference, that is the Minister of Defense, Dayan. Below at 1742 "UNKNOWN" refers to the Air Force Commander, General Hod, and a phone conversation with Shimon. The U.S. Naval Attaché, Commander Castle is called at 1614 by the Israelis and notified of the attack. By 1713, the MTBs disappear out of sight and at 1615; two unidentified jets approach from the starboard and reconnoiter from a distance.

1725

ROBERT: Is there contact with the helicopter? I returned the second helicopter too. Answer, you're the only one left.

1742

SHIMON: 36 Super Frelon searching for the damaged ship. What shall he do? Should he save the people?

UNKNOWN: Shimon, the Air Force Commander [General Hod] wants you. Is someone answering there?

UNKNOWN: Answering, yes.

1743

SHIMON: Wait a minute, I'm picking up the phone.

1751

KISLEV: I'm not sure. He's bringing the American ambassador over there. [In fact it was Commander E. E. Castle, the U.S. Naval Attaché from the embassy in Tel Aviv, and the assistant Naval Attaché, Lynn Blasch.]

SHIMON: Is he afraid they'll open fire on him?

1819

SHIMON: They're going home.

KISLEV: In the area, I understand.

SHIMON: Kislev, the Super Frelon asks what to do with the ship.

KISLEV: He landed there. He has to try and land it on the ship.

1820

KISLEV: Shimon, tell him not to take any people because of flight safety.

SHIMON: Okay.

1821

SHIMON: He asks, if there are wounded on board, if he can take them?

KISLEV: If his passenger wants it, yes.

SHIMON: So I'll tell him according to the considerations of his passenger.

KISLEV: Okay.

> **Author's Comment:** A third helicopter has
> flown toward the wounded *Liberty* with
> Commander Castle on board. The United
> States now officially knows that it was the
> Israelis who attacked the ship. Captain
> McGonagle will wave this helicopter off with
> Commander Castle dropping a note on his
> calling card asking if there are casualties. At
> this point there might be a question of why the
> Captain didn't request medical assistance for
> the wounded. It is believed that this helicopter
> is *oft2* or Frelon 807 that was used by Dayan.

1834

KISLEV: Shimon, what about this *Ofot*?

SHIMON: *Ofot* 2? He's got a lot. Forty miles by sea to
the ship.

1840

SHIMON: Kislev, he's very close to the ship, he'll try to
let him [Commander E. E. Castle] down soon.

KISLEV: Is he trying to land?

SHIMON: He is close and is starting to organize above
her.

1857

SHIMON: Kislev, the ship didn't want to stop. The
passenger didn't manage to persuade her. They threw a
note. They said in return that there...is
no...(unintelligible) [believed to be "casualties." This

was in error. There were many dead and many more wounded.]

KISLEV: Okay, the helicopter is coming back.

2130

The tape continues to 2130. There are no other transmissions relating to the *Liberty*.

Transcript ends

We have this continuing question about identity and resolving the issue in favor of continuing the attack. What is so dangerous about this particular ship if it is suspected of being an Egyptian horse transport ship? Would the Israelis risk attacking a Soviet ship? Why spend so much time and resource on it. How many other ships were attacked during the Six-Day War that was actually won on the first day of the war? The contention is that earlier in the day Israel depth charged a suspected submarine off its coast; however, its nationality was unknown. Certainly, they were alert to what was happening on her coast. June 6, the Egyptians in turn sent two destroyers with some escorting vessels against Elat, 1 submarine against Haifa, and 1 submarine against Ashdod. The task force in the Red Sea never made it to Elat, turning back after its presence had been detected by the IAF—a wise decision, some would say. The submarines were located by Israeli sonar, attacked with depth charges, and forced to retreat without having achieved anything in particular.[215]

If there had been a serious investigation of the attack on the *Liberty*, the transcripts discussed in this and the prior chapter would form a solid basis upon which to take depositions that would certainly undercut the contention of mistaken identity. If mistaken identity were still the issue then culpability would deal with negligence and recklessness in the context of manslaughter.

Again, there are questions about whether or not a flag had been seen. It appears that professionals are caught in a conflict between upper command with the order and their sense of what is right. They will continue to "follow orders". Kislev will later claim that he was "fighting mad" and threw down his headset on learning "American".

The *Liberty* had sent out a call for help that had been acknowledged. Planes were twice dispatched from the Sixth Fleet carriers but are called back. No help will get to the *Liberty* until the morning of the ninth.

The air force is told to get out of there as Robert asks, "Leave her! What ship is this?" It is apparent that elements of the command and control were not briefed on the attack and the order was treated as a "routine" matter in the context of the shelling of El Arish, which was used by the Supreme Command as a ruse for implementing the order to the attack and sink the *Liberty* under existing rules of engagement. In which case there would have to be a contention that the ship, the *Liberty*, was moving faster than she was capable—knowing she was only doing about 5 knots when the attack started with 18 knots being her maximum speed.

At 1413, Chief Air Controller Kislev now concedes that the ship may be "American". If there had been a question of mistaken identity as a viable defense it is now lost as, the attack will continue with the appearance on the scene of the three motor torpedo boats in Division 914, *Pagoda*, under the command of Moshe Oren. Dr.

164

Bregman who has a copy of the Israeli tapes places emphasis on the voice inflection of those talking and notes Kislev saying it is "probably American". Certainly, at a minimum, the Israelis had "constructive notice" if not actual notice that the ship was American.

At 1419, MTB Division 914 Commander, Moshe Oren, orders the torpedo attack.[216] The MTB Division War Log states 1419 for the order. IAF Command at Kirya tells Naval Command at Stella Maris there is doubt about the target's identification. Stella Maris orders MTB Division 914 not to attack. Navy Admiral, Erell, returns to the Stella Maris command post, having departed earlier to visit Haifa harbor.[217] *Saratoga* receives *Liberty's* voice message on hi-com stating she was under attack, her position and request for assistance.[218] The Israelis have to have known that help has been called for because transmissions are in the clear.

At 1450, Admiral Martin transmitted directly to *America* ordering her to launch four armed A-4s and provide fighter cover and tankers, which were to proceed to 31-23N 33-25E to defend the *Liberty*. He also transmitted directly to *Saratoga* to launch four armed A-1s ASAP same mission.[219] The next day Admiral Martin sent the following message to CTF60, Admiral Geis: "In the rush of getting the flight off to protect *Liberty*, I went direct to your carriers bypassing you. The action was inadvertent and I apologize [sic] for it." At 1454, *Saratoga* transmitted that *Liberty* has broadcast she has been hit by torpedo, is listing badly, and requires immediate assistance. Time of receipt of this message was not recorded.[220] The *Liberty* lost communication ability until 1555

At 1511, the National Military Command Center (NMCC) in the Pentagon received a phone message from USCINCEUR in Stuttgart, Germany with first word of the attack.[221] Ennes reported that word of the attack reached President Johnson in the White House "about two hours after it all began." He noted that Pentagon officials had been aware of the situation for nearly forty minutes when National Security Advisor Walt Rostow telephoned the President to tell him a U.S. ship was in trouble.[222] Johnson ordered an emergency meeting to be held in the White House Situation Room, and fearing that the Soviet Union was involved, he summoned our ambassador to the U.S.S.R., Llewellyn Thompson, who was in Washington. Unruffled, the President went about his ordinary business while he waited for his advisors to assemble.[223] The National Security Agency is notified of the attack by telephone from the NMCC.[224]

Fig. 14, National Security Council Meeting of June 7, 1967, LBJ Library.

Clockwise from left: Clark Clifford, Walt Rostow, Sec. Henry Fowler, Vice President Hubert Humphrey, Gov. Farris Bryant, Leonard Marks,

Amb. Llewellyn Thompson, Richard Helms, ?, ?, Nicholas Katzenbach, Sec. Dean Rusk, President Lyndon B. Johnson (far right), Sec. Robert McNamara, Cyrus Vance, Gen. Earle Wheeler, McGeorge Bundy.

Commander Ernest Castle, our military attaché in Tel Aviv, will get a helicopter ride to the ship but not land on her because the *Liberty's* Captain waves him off. President Johnson will advise Soviet Premiere Kosygin that he is sending planes to investigate the *Liberty's* situation—planes that did not show up.

Israel apologizes. The 744th Bomb Squadron at Beale Air Force base in California is taken off alert status. President Johnson arrives at the Situation Room at 1106 Washington time. At 1110, Washington time Ambassador Barbour cables to keep things quiet for fear the Arabs will think there is collusion between the U.S. and Israel.

Admiral Geis transmitted the text of Admiral Martin's 1450 message to *America* and *Saratoga* adding "ASAP" and "Defense of *Liberty* means exactly that."[225] At 1316Z (1516 Sinai time), the Commander, Task Force 60, reiterated the order to the *America* and the *Saratoga*, adding, **"Defense of USS *Liberty* means exactly that. Destroy or drive off any attackers who are clearly making attacks on *Liberty*. Remain over international waters. Defend yourself if attacked."** [Emphasis is mine]. The launch of planes order is rescinded. A direct military confrontation with Israel is avoided! More American service members are killed and wounded.

The Commander in Chief, European Command, notified the National Military Command Center by telephone that the *Liberty* was under attack, hit by a torpedo, and was listing to starboard.[226]

Moshe Oren will claim he did not get Rabin's order to hold back. The order appeared in T-204's logbook. Oren would later claim while he never received the order, he paused at 6000 meters and scrutinized the ship. As previously noted, in spite of smoke, he could see the vessel was not the destroyer that had presumably shelled El Arish, but most likely a freighter that had either serviced that destroyer or evacuated enemy soldiers from the beach. He claims he consulted his intelligence manual, and found that the ship's silhouette resembled that of the Egyptian supply ship (horse transport), *El Quseir*. It is claimed the other MTB captains reached the same conclusion independently. Moreover, when he tried to signal the ship, asking for its identity, he received no explicit response. Oren ordered his squadron into battle formation.

Five torpedoes were fired with one hitting the ship. According to the IDF History Report, the MTBs began their coordinated attack at 1443 with MTB T-206 firing two torpedoes from 1000 yards then 550 yards with no recorded hits.[227] A minute later, T-203 fires two torpedoes from 2000 yards, with one going off target and the second hitting the ship on the starboard side under the waterline. Finally, T-204 fired one torpedo with no sighting of its course. The MTBs then move to the other side of ship for a closer in attack and note the GTR lettering on the side of the ship, and the Division Commander orders the cessation of all fire at 1447.[228] The Division Commander claims that only after moving closer to the ship did he see a small flag and a code flag with the ship's name on it. Obviously, the crew was

168

lucky that more than one torpedo did not strike its target. With one torpedo fired from 550 yards, one would think the ship could have been identified as something other than an Egyptian horse transports ship.

The ship will go into damage control mode and tasked to recover any sensitive documents that might have leaked from the hole in the side of the ship. JCS will authorize the use of force. JCS will want to bomb the naval base at Haifa where attacking MTBs came from. Author Richard Deacon notes on page 182 of his book: "At first the US Chiefs of Staff were goaded into proposing a 'quick, retaliatory air strike on the Israeli naval base which launched the attack'". However, wiser heads prevailed and this was stopped before there could be disastrous consequences. Deacon had footnoted a reference to *CIA: the Myth and the Madness* by Patrick J. McGarvey, a former CIA agent. McGarvey on page 17 of his book claims to have witnessed the JCS proposal.

McGarvey noted that with the North Korean attack on the *Pueblo* a year after the attack on the *Liberty*, the JCS again recommended an air strike. In both cases, the political administration in power exercised restraint.

At 1129 Washington time, JCS cancels the use of force authorization. Thus, it would seem that the JCS order to attack was not related to the attempted dispatch of carrier planes. At 1130, the Pentagon gets ready to issue its first press release. Meanwhile, the war between the Arabs and Israelis continues. Dayan will authorize the attack on Syria at 0400 on the morning of June 9, 1967—a complete change of mind with Rabin concurring.

1435 *Liberty* Log [reconstructed]:   Torpedo hit starboard side amidships. Twenty-five men died because of the torpedo hit and MTB strafing fire. Torpedo hit in vicinity of the research quarters station.   This and adjacent spaces were flooded instantly and most personnel in these spaces died of either the blast or drowning.

In an audio tape interview, he recalled being a young Navy Ensign and he recalled hearing a "code 1" yelled over the intercom system of the plane coming from the "tent". The plane immediately entered into a high-speed dive to clear the area. He thought that the Russian or Egyptian planes were coming to kill them.

Charles B.
Tiffany, navigator on the EC-121.

Chapter 7

The NSA Intercept Mystery

The key to understanding whether the attack on the *Liberty* was intentional and subsequently covered-up, is to look at the issue of the missing NSA intercept tapes, allegedly obtained by the EC-121 flying over the Eastern Mediterranean during the attack on the *Liberty* at 1358 Sinai time.

After a careful reading and examination of Judge Ahron Jay Cristol's Israeli transcripts discussed in Chapters 5 and 6, in the context of total available information, there is strong probable cause to believe that the attack on the USS *Liberty* was intentional and covered up.[229] Covered up by whom?" The answer is by both the Johnson administration and the Israeli military establishment—a cover-up that continues to this day. In the transcripts there were numerous opportunities to reconsider the target's nationality and identity, something that is required pursuant to the Law of War; nevertheless, there was a persistent, almost frantic, push to attack and sink the ship—the USS *Liberty*.

The handling of the attack by the U.S. government will clearly mark a split between the political and military components of our government, something that happens-from-time-to-time without lasting adverse consequences—or so it appears.

The *Liberty* was not the only National Security Agency asset in the Eastern Mediterranean during the Six-Day War on that deadly June 8 date in 1967. There were two ELINT and SIGINT airborne collectors, an Air Force C-130 and a Navy EC-121. The NSA *Gerhard Report* notes: "The major part of the U.S. VHF/UHF collection came from Navy EC-121 and Air Force C-130 flights out of Athens on intercept missions largely specified by NSA."[230] Author James Bamford reports that there were at least three Hebrew linguists assigned to the Athens post.[231] The C-130 flew some eight sorties a month in the Eastern Mediterranean prior to May 23 as part of the U.S. Airborne Collection Reconnaissance Program (ACRP). The EC-121 was also flying about eight sorties a month in the same general area for both COMINT and ELINT purposes that are for the collection of communications and electronic signals.

The initial NSA SIGINT Readiness Alert Alfa was for a broad general collection purpose, whereas, condition Bravo-Crayon was stepped-up to include the *Liberty* because of certain Soviet threats prior to the war. The *Gerhard Report* notes that after May 23rd the C-130 flew daily flights for NSA specified intercept missions and the same held true for the EC-121 daily flights—after the start of the war the EC-121 flights were twice a day in direct support of the Sixth Fleet. At the NSA's suggestion, the Navy rescheduled the flights so that they would complement each other with the C-130 flying

172

morning hours beginning at 0300Z, and the EC-121 departing at 0800Z. The *Gerhard Report, Attack on a SIGINT Carrier, U.S.S. Liberty* still contains numerous redactions preventing full disclosure of key information.

A map included in the *Gerhard Report* shows the EC-121 flying a course over the Mediterranean parallel to the coast of Israel on a line from North of Lebanon southwesterly to just shortly south of Tel Aviv and back and forth. The C-130 flew a course parallel to the United Arab Republic in a direction from southeasterly to northwesterly and back and forth. These flights were clearly over water and not over land avoiding any penetration of sovereign territory. Nevertheless, the flights were not without danger and pilots and crew experienced a continuing concern about efforts to shoot them down.

Charles B. Tiffany was the navigator on the EC-121 on June 8, and while he did not have clearance to know what was going in the "tent" secure area of the plane controlled by the NSA and Naval Security Group communication technicians (CTs), he had specific memories of that day in 1967. In an audio tape interview, he recalled being a young Navy Ensign and hearing a "code 1" yelled over the intercom system of the plane coming from the "tent". The plane immediately entered into a high-speed dive to clear the area. He thought that Russian or Egyptian planes were coming to kill them. He later learned that the "tent" had been monitoring the Israelis on UHF and the threat had come from the Israeli air controllers talking to pilots to "clear the air".[232]

What is interesting about Tiffany's "code 1" comment, is that there was a report floating around that the IDF Air Force Chief of Intelligence, had made threats to attack planes or ships as a result of prior incidents where U.S. Navy aircraft had "accidentally" penetrated Israeli control zones.[233] His counterpart, Lt. Col. Bloch, advised the U.S. Naval Attaché in Tel Aviv, Commander Castle, that such comments were facetiously made. Without elaborating at this time, it is sufficient to note that the Israelis were concern about over flights of Israel's secret nuclear weapons reactor at Dimona—rightly, so, as they thought Nasser might seek to bomb the facility. Contrary to Bloch's contention, the shoot-down threats were not idle threats. The Dimona site was a crown jewel guarded by U.S. Hawk missile batteries ready to shoot at any invasion of the critical air space. The Kennedy administration made the Hawk missiles available to Israel—a controversial reversal of policy opposing Israel's nuclear program—thus one of the first U.S. arms deals favoring Israel.

A word about the reports from U.S. Defense Attaché Castle who was located at our embassy in Israel: The documents on the State Department's Office of Historian website contain mostly generalized speculation with little verifiable facts. The Department of Defense National Military Command Center seven-page document from Castle is not posted on the State Department website. It is easy to see how people in Washington DC jumped to conclusions or "directed" the tenor of any future investigation towards a "tragic accident" conclusion. By way of example, note the following:[234]

Document 276. Telegram From the Defense Attaché Office in Israel to the Defense Intelligence Agency[1]
Tel Aviv, June 13, 1967, 0835Z.
0884. Ref DIAAP–5 7657 June 67.[2]

174

1. Have queried our primary source who says impossible at this time to go back to the secondary. Secondary source is not, in fact, a witting supplier of info but rather a knowledgeable person whose conversations occasionally reveal useful info. To ask direct questions would put him on guard and dry up the source.

2. Primary source states from context of original conversation he believes strong probability the reference transmissions took place prior to 080600Z.

3. Further information received from Embassy officer who spoke to young IDF Navy officer. The Navy officer claims he was aboard one of attacking MTBs. MTB saw a ship under air attack with smoke issuing from sides. Thought they saw guns on bow. They joined in attack and after torpedo launch at about one mile close to short distance at which time they saw US flag which had been obscured by smoke. Officer says CO of his MTB extremely remorseful and concerned.

4. From data available here ALUSNA reconstructs probable but not certain series of events.

A. IDF aircraft reported ship and identified her as US.

B. IDFAFHQ may or may not have broadcast info to all units, but probably uninformed aircraft returning from strike in Egypt with unused rounds attacked *Liberty*.

C. MTB's saw aircraft attack and presumed *Liberty* to be Egyptian ship. Therefore they eagerly raced into action without waiting to identify our ship.

5. Coordinated with Embassy.

Footnote No. 2 referenced above, after the date heading, refers to a possible informant from Israel Aircraft Industries that seems to go nowhere in terms of a follow-up investigation. U.S. personnel were not allowed to follow-up with the Israelis. In addition, the referenced document seems to have been lost. An understanding of the role played by IAI as an Israeli defense supplier would make the potential informant creditable, but subject to jeopardy.

> [2] Not found; it apparently requested additional information concerning telegram 0854 from USDAO Tel Aviv, June 10, which reported that an Israel Aircraft Industries official had told a U.S. Air Force representative that on the morning of June 8, he had heard transmissions on Israeli Air Force air-to-ground control frequencies of an aircraft that had sighted a ship and had identified it as having a U.S. flag.

Reference the above important information about the flag being seen, a close look at Castle's communication to the NMCC shows the 7-page document divided into 3 of 3 pages and 4 of 4 pages. On page 2 of the second group appears to be the reference to the informant in paragraph 13, which according to Castle is subject to "limited addressees" including the CNO and DIA.

U-2 over-flights of Dimona in the Negev desert had been made in the '50s and early '60s during construction of the site. On February 21, 1973, Israeli F-4 Phantom II fighter jets had shot down a Libyan airliner for violating Israeli airspace over the Sinai Peninsula. Of the 113 on the regularly scheduled flight between Tripoli and Cairo, only five survived including the co-pilot. Bad weather was blamed for the plane being off course.[235] More will

176

follow on Dimona, and Israel's shoot-down of one of its own that encroached on the site. Tiffany's concern was well placed, notwithstanding that contention that the U.S. and Israel were friendly toward each other.

Michael Prostinak, a Hebrew linguist on the EC-121 flights, positioned in the "tent" was quoted to say that these flights lasted for eight hours duration.[236] This would put the plane in the air at the time of the attack on the ship. The flights took off at 1000 Sinai time (0800Z), and eight hours would clearly put it in the air during the attack on the *Liberty*.

To emphasize the danger as being very real, a North Korean MIG-17 shot down an EC-121 flight on April 15, 1969 while on a reconnaissance mission over the Sea of Japan. All 31 Americans on board were killed when the plane crashed 90 nautical miles off the North Korean coast—another chapter in the long saga of "Cold War" heroes. The Nixon administration elected not to retaliate; but after a brief naval demonstration, it resumed flights within a week avoiding further confrontation.[237] Here we are dealing not with a belligerent state but with a fledging ally.

The essential key question is whether those flights on June 8, 1967 intercepted any information that would shed a light on what happened to the *Liberty*. This will become the NSA intercept mystery that has a direct bearing on whether the attack was covered-up, and whether or not evidence of a crime was destroyed pursuant to a conspiracy to obstruct justice. Did the NSA obtain intercept communications that showed that the Israelis saw an "American flag" on the ship their planes and torpedo boats were attacking and ignored it?

177

Three individuals are key players in this mystery. One is a supervisory communications technician and Hebrew linguist on the board the EC-121 along with another Hebrew linguist who brought the communication traffic to his supervisor's attention, and a third Hebrew linguist at NSA headquarters who will state he translated tapes received from the EC-121, but which excluded intercepts of the attack itself.

James Bamford, in his book *Body of Secrets*, and the Chapter *Blood* identified Navy Chief Petty Officer Marvin E. Nowicki as being a Hebrew and Russian linguist on board the EC-121 flight on June 8.[238] Nowicki was in charge of six ELINT specialists that included two Hebrew linguists and two Arabic linguists. The Israelis used mostly UHF while the Arabs used VHF frequencies. The EC-121 had the "Big Look" to get and trace radar signals.[239] Bamford has written several books dealing with the NSA and is considered an expert on the subject. He is a former ABC investigative reporter. I met him briefly at the LVA annual meeting in Nebraska City, Nebraska in 2004.

Bamford quotes Nowicki as being advised: "Hey, Chief. I've got really odd activity," Prostinak called out as he hit the record button. "They mentioned an American flag."[240] Israeli aircraft were completing an attack on some object.[241] Clearly, the reference is to an attack by Israeli aircraft; then, the Hebrew linguist called again that there was different activity that involved surface craft and more references to the flag. It is particularly important at this point to reference a transition from air attack to surface craft attack.[242] The two Hebrew linguists had never heard anything similar and will later verify that the COMINT, voice traffic, dealt with the attack on the *Liberty*.

It now appears that Michael Prostinak was the other linguist as noted in a book by author James Scott. Prostinak was not identified in Bamford's book or that of A. Jay Cristol, who referred to a linguist who did not want to be indentified; however, Prostinak is also mentioned in Michael Oren's book, by name on page 268.

Prostinak confirms and backs up Nowicki and their take-off from Athens on the morning of June 8 for an eight-hour flight. The U.S. Air Force Security Service in conjunction with the NSA had established an intelligence-processing hub at the Athens international airport. Prostinak noted that one of the operations of the hub was to review the intercepts and notify the communication technicians like him as to what to watch for such as call signs, unit identities, and frequencies to monitor and watch for. Note in the Cristol Israeli transcripts the lack of "call-signs" other than a very limited usage such as the term *Pagoda* for the MTB division name. In addition, there was the *Migdal*, MTB 206, reference that it had the only working UHF radio among the three boats. The only other call sign used in the Israeli transcripts is a bracketed reference to helicopter 807, *Oft2*, being at Taiman Field in the Sinai on page 218 of Appendix 2 in Cristol's book. In the author's opinion, having been familiar with call signs in police work, the lack of call signs is significant, and therefore, a less than accurate translation. In the Israeli transcripts, names are dubbed in for call signs.

Collector planes had limited on-site time due to fuel limitations; the *Liberty* did not have that limitation so plane operations had to be staggered, and as previously

179

noted the flights increase to two a day. Prostinak says that the C-130 flights took off at 5 AM and they took off five hours later. Prostinak supports the flight plan as reported in the *Gerhard Report* previously cited even though times might be off depending on whether one is using military or local time. Their job was to intercept air, ground communications, and record them if they had potential intelligence value. James Scott, in his book, reports that Prostinak described how there was a flurry of activity in Hebrew that made it difficult for him to ascertain whether he was listening to aircraft or ground forces. At any rate, as Nowicki had noted, Prostinak called out "Hey, Chief....They mentioned an American flag".[243]

Nowicki will cause some controversy in later years since he will claim that what he heard convinces him that the attack was a case of mistaken identity. While Nowicki and Prostinak will reach different conclusions, the important point is that they both agree to the fact that intercepts were made of the whole attack. Nowicki will send a letter to Mr. James Bamforth (sic), care of Washington, DC, dated March 3, 2000. Nowicki's letter, which was an addendum exhibit to A. Jay Cristol's FOIA lawsuit, is posted on Cristol's website. Nowicki also sent a letter to the Wall Street Journal dated Wednesday, May 16, 2001, page A-23 noting his opinion and the existence of intercept tapes. The letter to Bamford is included here because it clarifies the issues:[244]

> Dear Jim:
> As a follow-up to our e-mail and telephone exchanges, I am enclosing sensitive information about U.S. intelligence collection techniques that I engaged in during a career in the U.S. Navy spanning over 20 years. Like

you, I am interested in preserving certain historical events surrounding SIGINT collection. I believe it is important that future generations understand and appreciate the efforts of the Cold War warriors.

In this correspondence, I am concentrating on a single event that involved the USS Liberty in June 1967. As you know, Jim Ennes and members of the Liberty crew are on record stating the ship was deliberately attacked by the Israelis. I think otherwise. I have first-hand information, which I am sharing with you. I was present on that day, along with members of an aircrew in a COMFAIRAIRRECONRON TWO (VQ-2) EC 121M aircraft flying some 15,000 feet above the incident. As I recall, we recorded most, if not all, of the attack. Further, our intercepts, never before made public, showed the attack to be an accident on the part of the Israelis.

To support my claim, I am forwarding four enclosures of information. My story is over 30 years old but there are certain events that are imbedded in my memory, including a scary night flight into the battle zone and the attack on the Liberty. Enclosure (1) begins with a narrative entitled, "Assault on the Liberty: The untold story from SIGINT." Enclosure (2) provides a postscript to the attack in the years that followed. Enclosure (3) gives my views of additional evidence of a mistaken attack by the Israelis, contradicting Jim Ennes in his book. Enclosure (4) discusses Ennes's cover-up conundrum, asks who was ultimately responsible, and why the presence of our VQ mission was never revealed.

181

In addition, I am enclosing personal information about my 24-year career in the US Navy and Naval Security Group. I am doing this for the purpose of helping you see how I might assist you with other aspects of your historical account of SIGINT. You may, for example, be interested in stories how we hunted Soviet TU95 Bears in the Atlantic and searched for SA-2 sites in southern Algeria during flights into the Sahara. A chronology of my duty stations and professional experience is found in Enclosure (5).

Finally, on a cautionary note I would appreciate it if you would cull any information that crosses the bar of national security, in addition to the names of colleagues cited herein. I do not have permission to use their names. If you have any questions or need clarification, please do not hesitate to contact me. Thank you and good luck with your book.

Sincerely,

Marvin E. Nowicki, Ph.D.

On July 2, 2003, in unprecedented fashion, the ultra secret National Security Agency (NSA) released important formerly secret transcripts and recordings of Israeli air controllers, and helicopters, flying toward the *Liberty*. This release was pursuant to a Freedom of Information Action (FOIA) lawsuit filed by A. Jay Cristol in Federal District Court for the Southern District of Florida.[245] Cristol appeared in the case "pro se", meaning he represented himself as plaintiff. He was appealing an administrative denial of his FOIA request for certain information in the possession of the NSA. U.S. Attorneys represented the government from the Department of Justice, along with an assistant general counsel from the Civil Litigation and Administrative Law department of the NSA. The period he was looking at was 1100Z (1300 Sinai time) and 1300Z (1500 Sinai time), obviously on June 8, 1967. A few portions of Cristol's petition are summarized as follows because of the verifying information contained therein:

2. Specifically, Plaintiff filed a request with the NSA pursuant to FOIA by letter dated April 26, 2001, a copy of which is attached as Exhibit "A". Plaintiff's request sought access to tapes, recordings, or other electronic or paper recordings of surveillance of common voice radio transmissions made or intercepted on June 8, 1967 by the U.S.S. Liberty, the U.S.S. Amberjack, and a U.S. EC-121 aircraft during a deployment in the Eastern Mediterranean. Importantly, Plaintiff did not seek the disclosure of information pertaining to the type of equipment used in or the manner of making the documented transmissions. Rather, Plaintiff's requests were exclusively limited to identifying and reviewing transmissions that either have already been disclosed to the public through the open radio and/or materials that demonstrate the existence of such transmissions - neither of which are exempt from disclosure.

11. Plaintiff will address each requested item in a separate count. As follows:

COUNT III - FOIA request for tapes, recordings, or other electronic or paper records of surveillance of VHF/UHF or high frequency voice radio transmissions made or intercepted on June 8, 1967, between 1100Z (1300 Sinai time) and 1300Z (1500 Sinai time) at or near El Arish on the Sinai

183

Peninsula, Eastern Mediterranean by any EC-121 aircraft (probably assigned to VQ-2 detachment stationed at Athens, Greece, under control of FAIRECONRON TWO).

COUNT III - 27. The NSA has admitted in its recently partially declassified document, United States Cryptologic History - "Attack on a SIGINT Collector, the U.S.S. Liberty (S-CCO)" of 1981 and referred to as National Archives Document Number SRH-256, that on June 8, 1967 it operated EC-121 aircraft from Athens, Greece which aircraft flew in a pattern which placed them at or about 60 nautical miles from the scene of the attack on the USS Liberty at or about 1400 Sinai time on June 8, 1967.

28. The Navy EC-121 aircraft that flew the mission on June 8, 1967 was Bureau #135757 and its navigator was Charles B. Tiffany. It was on an IQS mission and the flight lasted 8.4 hours.

29. The NSA operated a SIGINT surveillance compartment aboard said aircraft which was commonly referred to as the tent.

30. The senior enlisted navy person in charge of the tent was Chief Petty Officer Marvin E. Nowicki.

31. Chief Nowicki was a Hebrew linguist, referred to in 1967 as a "special Arabic" linguist.

32. A second Hebrew linguist (who does not wish his name disclosed but whose name is

known to the NSA) was monitoring Hebrew language voice transmissions in the "tent" on June 8, 1967 and he alerted Chief Nowicki to certain transmissions he found of interest. Both Chief Nowicki and the second Hebrew linguist heard the transmissions and recorded same.

33. Thereafter Chief Nowicki and the second Hebrew linguist listened to the tapes on the ground at Athens airport.

34. The tapes were communications of Israeli pilots and ground controllers during and after the attack on the USS Liberty at or after 1400 Sinai time on June 8, 1967.

35. The tapes were transmitted to NSA headquarters in Fort Meade, MD where they were studied, transcribed and translated by a third Hebrew linguist who became well versed in their content and who briefed Marshal Carter, the then director of the NSA, on the contents of the tapes.

36. CPO Marvin E. Nowicki remained in the Navy, advanced to commissioned officer status and worked at the NSA on the Israeli and Near-East desks from 1968 to 1971 in "G" group under Frank Raven including work in G643.

37. CPO Marvin E. Nowicki, later Lieutenant Marvin E. Nowicki and now Dr. Marvin E. Nowicki has publically confirmed the foregoing in an email letter to one James Bamford, a copy of which is attached as Exhibit "H".

185

38. The tapes were last seen by Dr. Nowicki at NSA headquarters in the spaces of G643/the Israeli military section of NSA.

39. The third Hebrew linguist (who also does not want his name disclosed but who is known to NSA) has confirmed to Plaintiff the existence of the tapes at NSA, Fort Meade, MD and his examination and translation of the tapes in the late 1960's.

40. The collection of the materials on these tapes was overt intelligence collection. The platform used for collection, EC-121-135757 was in international airspace. The transmissions were broadcast in the open and were not encrypted. The equipment used to receive and record the transmissions was a radio receiver and a tape recorder.
41. The transmissions may have been located by use of a frequency scanner but Plaintiff does not seek any disclosure of data relating to equipment used, i.e. scanner, radio receiver or recorder.

48. The Israel Air Force released transcripts and translations of the transmissions to Thames TV in 1987.

49. The Israel Air Force also released access to the tapes, transcriptions and tapes to Plaintiff in 1991 and in 2001.

50. Plaintiff has published annotated translations of the tapes in his book "The Liberty Incident" as Appendix 2.

51. Prior to publication of Appendix 2, Plaintiff communicated with Dr. Nowicki (NSA Hebrew linguist #1) and NSA Hebrew linguist #3 about the contents of the tapes. Their descriptions of the contents of the tapes were essentially the same as the contents of the Israeli Air Force tapes which they had neither previously seen nor heard.

The government's answer to Cristol's petition was pretty much boilerplate. However, on July 2, 2003, the NSA declassified, and released to the Plaintiff via overnight courier, allegedly, all of the actual recordings and English translations (including summaries of those translations) held by the NSA that relate to the USS *Liberty* incident—we are lead to believe that these are the only tapes and transcripts. This contradicts the contentions of the three linguists as set out in Cristol's lawsuit, Nowicki, Michael Prostinak, and linguist No.3. Cristol indentifies a Richard Hickman as linguist No. 3 located at the NSA.[246] In item No. 51 from his lawsuit, Cristol notes he communicated with "...linguist #3 about the contents of the tapes. Their descriptions of the contents of the tapes were essentially the same as the contents of the Israeli Air Force tapes..." This is a significant factor to be acknowledged reference research into the *Liberty* matter.

Of particular interest in Cristol's lawsuit are the time references as noted in item No. 34 above, the tapes pertained to communications with pilots and air controllers; and in item No. 38, where the tapes were last seen by Nowicki in the Israeli Military Section of the NSA, specifically G643. Subsequent to the lawsuit actually getting into court, the NSA settled the matter with Cristol by releasing transcripts of intercepted

187

communications between Israeli helicopter pilots, air controllers and the motor torpedo boats beginning at 1429 Sinai time or 1229Z. Just 4 minutes prior, in the so-called Israeli transcripts reported in Appendix 2 of Cristol's book, is a reference to the Israeli Minster of Defense, Moshe Dayan, at Taiman Field (Teyman Field) with Super Frelon helicopter *Oft-2* (Super Frelon 807) per the following Israeli excerpt:

> **1425** KISLEV: Robert, Two [*Ofot*, a Super Frelon 807] is in Taiman Field?
> SHIMON: Yes, with the Minister of Defense.
> SHIMON: Frelon from Air Force Base 8 [Tel Nof, located south of Tel Aviv] is ready to leave for the ship. Shall I send him out? Operations notified Base [censored].
> KISLEV: Okay.

This is rather cryptic in terms of what it means. Since the Israelis put the transcripts out into the public forum, why would they want to play games by referring to an "UNKNOWN" and now censoring part of the transcript? What are they trying to hide, or was it Cristol's decision to obscure who UNKNOWN is?

Did NSA intentionally delete intercept information prior to 1429 (1229Z) stating it had no information on the air attack, because of the reference to the Israeli Defense Minister? Dayan, in the Sinai was in close proximity to the Southern Command where the shelling claim originated. This could have put Dayan in the middle of things discounting the possibility it was lower ranked commander who ordered the attack on the *Liberty*. Alternatively, were the tapes ordered confiscated at the direction of President Johnson?

Both Nowicki and Prostinak say intercept tapes were collected and sent to the NSA; and Nowicki says they were in a specific location at NSA. The linguist at the NSA allegedly supports Cristol's contention. We will learn more about linguist No. 3 and his work shortly.

In a 2007 online *Chicago Tribune* article, Michael Prostinak is quoted as saying that more than three recordings were made that day.[247] He said at least one tape was missing that had to do with the attack on the *Liberty,* "...We knew that something was being attacked...during the attack was when mention of the American flag was made." The plane's navigator, Charles Tiffany, has verified the excitement reference the UHF traffic. Prostinak said they were unaware of the *Liberty's* presence 15000 feet below. After listening to recordings released by the NSA, Prostinak found that two tapes were missing.

He said one tape; designated A1104/A-02 begins at 2:29 p.m. local time (1429), just before a torpedo hit the *Liberty.* The contention is that the torpedoing took place at 1435 Sinai time. Prostinak said a preceding tape; A1104/A-01 was missing. This tape most likely would have recorded the actual attack according to Prostinak. Both Nowicki and Prostinak make specific reference to the missing tapes. Prostinak said a tape preceding one made at 3:07 p.m. by other linguists on board is also missing. He stated that when they landed at Athens all tapes were rushed to the NSA facility where Hebrew linguists waited and where the tapes were taken from them. The article reports another linguist, unidentified, said there were as many as "five or six" tapes recording the attack on the ship.

189

One of the mysteries surrounding the *Liberty* attack deals with the issue of what linguist specialties were on aboard the ship. Some are quick to say there were no Hebrew linguist, only Arabic and Russian with the caveat that there was at least one with "special Arabic" abilities, and that he appears to have been the only civilian killed on board the ship, named Allen Blue. He was apparently able to understand Hebrew. The NSA was short on Hebrew linguists, so they were not specifically excluded from the mission; although considering the circumstances, it would be strange to go into a war zone without the ability to understand the spoken languages of the area and of the participants in the conflict.

On the NSA FOIA website dealing with disclosures on the *Liberty* attack, there is a document dealing with an "oral history" (OH) interview for a Richard Hickman. Hickman describes that he was formerly on board the *Valdez* when it was returning home and passing the *Liberty*. He separated from the *Valdes* and flew home. He was a Hebrew linguist in the Naval Security Group, and was going to be assigned to the *Liberty* as she headed to the Mediterranean, but because he was a "short-timer", the assignment was not made. Instead, he was assigned to NSA headquarters as a linguist transcribing EC-121 tapes. Judge Cristol identifies and confirms the third Hebrew linguist as Richard W. Hickman on his website where there is a link to his oral history interview document for downloading.[248]

Yitzhak Rabin, the IDF Chief of Staff, in his *The Rabin Memoires* was of the belief that Hebrew linguists were included among the American Jews serving on board, some of whom were killed or wounded. He noted, "The vessel's task was to monitor the IDF's signals networks for a rapid follow-up of events on the battlefield by tracking messages transmitted between the various headquarters."[249] While the U.S. government claims by implication we were not eavesdropping on Israel, Rabin says it did happen. It is a silly comment that we do not spy on each other—how naïve. How about the U-2 flights over Israel's nuclear facility at Dimona previously noted?

Getting back to Mr. Hickman's oral history interview, the OHs are like a deposition in that they are a semi-formal inquiry pursuant to one's government duties. They are not under oath. Oral history projects are to facilitate research and develop information. Hickman had his interview on April 30, 1980, and NSA representatives told Richard Hickman his statements would stay secret, however, that did not remain true because of FOIA disclosure requests dealing with the *Liberty* attack. One of the four interviewers was Bill Gerhard, author of the *Gerhard Report*. The oral histories provided information for the final *Gerhard Report*. Hickman was assigned to NSA in G6 group—the Israeli desk. He states he was friends with Al Blue killed in the torpedo attack. In response to the question whether he had anything to do with the *Liberty*, he responded:

> My only real involvement with the LIBERTY incident was transcribing the intercept that VQ-2 *picked* up after the *incident* had actually happened, the attack itself, had happened. There were rescue helicopters that--Israeli helicopters— that had gone to the scene and they intercepted the comets of those helicopters and that tape was sent back to NSA for transcription and I transcribed that tape. The transcripts are available and are a part of the history, but that was really my only involvement.

191

An interesting thing occurs when Gerhard asks the following question that is a "leading question" on the issue of identification. Hickman is forthright in acknowledging his bias toward Israel: [Gerhard's name is misspelled in the Hickman OH].

> GERHART: (5G) the transcripts (1G) tend to show that the Israelis were confused as to the nationality.
> HICKMAN: That's right, that's right, and that is my only real access to information as to what was available, other than the readings of course but from the SIGINT picture that I witnessed, I would tend to say that the Israelis did not know that they had attacked a U.S. vessel and naturally that is up for grabs as to what other people think what happened. But granted that's my evidence that was available to me at the time, and that's probably a little bit of bias and prejudice on my part. I was partial to the Israelis as a nation having learned the Hebrew language. And you know, sort of learned to know the Israelis for what they were and what they were up against. But I just don't feel that they would have done that if they knew. But the SIGINT picture in my mind shows that they didn't know. They were confused as to whether they spoke Arabic or English, where to take them. They asked if they were flagged, whether there were bodies in the water? You know, things of that nature.

Hickman's answer above sounds honest and straightforward. He was mistaken on one point and that was that VQ-2 Naval Squadron and the EC-121 did not fly out of Rota, Spain as he stated; it flew out of Athens as Michael Prostinak has stated, although the home base

192

may have been Rota. Actually, Spain was the home base and Athens was a forward base during the Six-Day War.

Hickman went on to say, he knew the linguist picked up by the *Liberty* at Rota, Spain; Al Blue, Bob Wilson and Don Blalock and they were Arabic linguists. The only Hebrew linguist on the ship was a Navy Chief named Baker, and his knowledge of Hebrew was suspect because he had not been working with it. Ennes does not mention a Chief Baker in his book, nor was he listed among the dead. The NSA's Bob Farley questions Hickman:

> FARLEY: Dick, was the make-up of the component, the Security Group component aboard the VALDEZ similar to the LIBERTY? Do you have any thoughts on that?
> HICKMAN: The VALDEZ was more of a civilian ship than was the LIBERTY. And the entire crew was civilian on the VALDEZ the Security Group part of the ship was all Security Group personnel. I think there was a lot less idea of actually what we were doing onboard that ship than if I was on board the LIBERTY. The LIBERTY was more of a naval vessel than was the VALDEZ.

In 2003, the NSA released transcripts of the helicopters, and a summary of the EC-121 intercept communications as relates to those helicopters. In that summary was a translator's note that says:

> (TR-Note: It is believed that Thorn made an error and wanted to call 815. The call sign 185 however has been used by an Israeli jet aircraft (either a Mirage or a Mystère). It is of course possible that Thorn had previously

been in contact with 185, but if this was the case there are no COMINT reflections of this activity.)

"…there are no COMINT reflections of this activity". The translator was Richard Hickman per his statement in his OH. Was there an effort to cover-up or selective memory lapses? How did the translator know that call sign 185 was an Israeli fighter jet? His interview clearly, but ambiguously, states the helicopter references were the only communications. This does not jive with what both Nowicki and Prostinak contend; and Cristol in his FOIA lawsuit, represents linguist No 3 as telling him. In fairness to Hickman, he may have only been given a segment of the EC-121 intercepts and he may have known how Israeli planes were designated with call signs from his tour on the *Valdez*. This does not explain the reference to a particular call sign. The absence of call signs in Cristol's Israeli transcripts is puzzling since Cristol claims them to be accurate transcriptions.

As a side note, Hickman's oral history interview was taken in 1980, a number of years after the attack. The OH project may have been prompted by the publication of the Ennes's book on the attack, which came out a couple of years prior.

Whether Hickman was only given the helicopter intercepts or had access to all the intercepts is important. Prostinak referred to at least three tapes. If Hickman recognized call sign 185 was a plane, either Mirage or Mystère, it means he had some knowledge of call sign specifics. Is it possible he knew the call sign because he actually had access to the attack portion of the intercepts? In the above transcriber quote, the reference is to MTB *Thorn* as trying to talk to 185, possibly transposing the

194

call sign from helicopter 815. Cristol in the Israeli transcripts notes that *Migdal* has the only UHF radio. He does not list a *Thorn* among the MTBs.

According to Cristol, the Division 914 MTBs were named after birds of prey: 203, named *Aya;* 204, named *Daya;* and 206, named *Tahmas.* These names do not match the NSA intercept summary document allegedly prepared by Hickman. The MTBs used the call sign names *Thorn, Crisis* and *Pagoda.* In the lead comments to his transcripts, Cristol refers to 206 as *Migdal.* It is the only boat with the working UHF radio as previously noted. Therefore, in two contexts MTB 206 is called both *Thorn* and *Migdal.* Admittedly, this is confusing for the reader while the problem could be a translation issue.

Cristol in his book provides the following information on the MTBs: "The boats were built in France and were powered by two Napier Deltic diesel engines and capable of forty-two knots, according to *Jane's Fighting Ships.* They carried a nominal crew of fifteen and were armed with one 40-mm cannon facing aft; one 20-mm cannon on the bow, and two .50-caliber machine guns, one on each wing. They carried two German aerial 19-inch torpedoes mounted on launchers or throwers, often referred to as torpedo tubes. They were not torpedo tubes in the classic sense but rather a throwing device that pushed the torpedo over the side and away from the boat. The boats were equipped with old U.S. World War II-surplus Kelvin-Hughes radar, but only one boat had true motion radar. They also had UHF radios that had been installed about a week earlier. Only Boat 206's UHF radio was operable."

The NSA EC-121 transcripts start at 1428 Sinai time (1228Z) just 3 minutes after the reference to the Israeli

Minister of Defense, Dayan, at Taiman Field, (Teyman Field), in the Israeli transcripts. Is this a coincidence or done purposely to withhold information that might implicate the Minister of Defense in the attack on the *Liberty*? He was to become the prime suspect in the minds of some. The torpedo is reported as hitting the ship at 1435 Sinai time, with reports varying by minutes. Having established the context for the intercept dilemma, what was happening on the *Liberty* when the Super Frelons arrived? It is important to keep the time factors straight.

Jim Ennes in his book reported that the *Liberty's* announcing system barked, "Stand by to repel boarders!"[250] At approximately 1308Z (1508 Sinai time), two Israeli Super Frelon helicopters loaded with armed troops appeared on the scene and began to hover and circle the ship. These helicopters are the ones referred to in Cristol's Israeli transcripts, as noted in the previous chapter that were allegedly sent to render aid. The reference to *Ofot* as a designator for the Israeli helicopters does not jive with the released NSA intercepts. They are simply referred to as 810 and 815.

Were these helicopters, allegedly with armed troops onboard, sent to finish off the *Liberty* crew as some survivors speculated, or were they dispatched to assist in a rescue? If the helicopters were loaded with armed troops, where were the survivors going to fit in onboard? Both the NSA and Israeli transcripts talk about rescue. The helicopters are sent toward the ship and then recalled, with a certain cryptic tone.

Hickman in his OH says he and Nowicki attended language school together. [Nowicki's name is redacted from the OH]. At any rate to get a feel for the difference

196

between the NSA transcripts and those released by the Israelis, we need to review a file that was downloaded from the NSA website several years ago by this author. By the way, any person can go to the NSA website and download the various documents.[251] At the time of the initial release, there were three additional ".pdf" documents released dealing with helicopters 810 and 815, the Super Frelons. With various redactions, they look like translator's worksheets. While these documents contained many redactions, the summary file has fewer redactions. The NSA translator summary of the aftermath of the attack was addressed from the Director of the NSA to the White House and had a date of June 22, 1967. It was originally marked secret and was entitled "Sigint Readiness Bravo 'Crayon' Report Nr. 2149" dealing with the aftermath of the Israeli attack on the USS *Liberty* on June 8th 1967.

The translation is based on Israeli plain language VHF/UHF voice communications intercepted between 1229Z (1429 Sinai time) and 1328Z (1528 Sinai time); and it is stated that the intercepts deal only with the aftermath of the jet aircraft and motor torpedo attacks on the *Liberty*. The document flatly states, "There are no COMINT reflections of the actual attack itself". The torpedo attack starts at 1429 and one can assume that there should have been intercepted communications dealing with that part of the attack. References to *Thorn* and *Pagoda* are not reflected in the NSA intercepts until 1304Z or 1504 Sinai time—strange.

Recall in the prior two chapters that the Israeli transcripts as published in Cristol's book in Appendix 2 identifies the participating planes by a name designator such as *Kursa*, two helicopters as *Ofot* 1 and 2, and the torpedo boats by numbers 203, 204 and 206 designated as

197

Pagoda (MTB Division 914). Air controllers are referred to by their names. The NSA transcripts use the same numbers for the MTBs but add call names *Thorn*, *Pagoda* and *Crisis*. While confusing, *Pagoda* is the code name for the group of three torpedo boats—the division. The air controller at Hatzor is designated as *Tribune*; and there is a reference to *Jewel* most likely located at Haifa, Naval HQ, but not otherwise identified. It is safe to say that the Israeli transcripts dealing with the helicopters do not completely jive with those released by the NSA. Cristol had claimed that they would be identical.

On page 218 of Appendix 2 to Cristol's book, there is a bracketed reference to *Ofot*, a Super Frelon 807 at Taiman field (with the Minister of Defense). Again, 807 is the only call sign used to reference the planes and helicopters, other than 810 and 815. There seems to be some "apparent confusion" as to the identity of Super Frelon 807. In the Israeli transcripts at 1419 and 1425, the helicopter at Taiman Field, 807, is also referred to *Ofot* 2. It was not one of the two flying towards the damaged ship. Per the Israeli transcripts (1834 to 1857 Sinai time) *Ofot* 2 was used to transport Commander Earnest Castle to the *Liberty*. The helicopter crew was most likely in earlier communication with the Minister of Defense, Dayan at 1425 per the transcripts. Circumstantially, this would mean that Dayan knew the attack was taking place and allowed his pilot and helicopter to be used to ferry Castle to the ship.

To put this in a time context, at 1231Z (1431 Sinai time) the *Liberty* log reports that the MTBS are machine gunning the ship; and this is followed up by the actual torpedo attack. So, again, is it realistic to believe that there were no intercepts of the motor torpedo boats

198

attacking the ship? Nevertheless, per the Israeli transcripts, the helicopters are dispatched:

> At 1413 LT [local time], 1213 Z, IAF HQ (Kislev tells Simon and Robert) reports two helicopters are going to be sent out to the ship. [IAF audiotapes.] See Cristol's Appendix 2 to his book, page 218. Cristol and the Israelis claim they are to look for survivors.

The report of men jumping into the sea from the USS *Liberty* is bogus. I have asked both the Liberty Veterans Association attorney and James Ennes if there was any truth to that issue—the answer is no. Further, it is clear from the transcripts that Israeli Command and Control structure quickly moved into a "crisis management and damage control mode"—otherwise known as "CYA", around the above point in time. There was no reported controller traffic for an hour and nineteen minutes between 1605 and 1724 per Cristol's Israeli transcripts on page 222 of Appendix 2 in his book. Are we to assume all the action went into a state of suspended animation for this period?

The first NSA time reference to the Super Frelon helicopters is 1229Z (1429 Sinai time) above Ashdod, on the Israeli coast. Note the following from the NSA transcripts:

> 1231Z, [Tribune] TO 815: PAY ATTENTION: HERE IS A WAR-SHIP THERE WHICH WE ATTACKED. THE MEN JUMPED INTO THE WATER FROM IT. YOU WILL TRY TO RESCUE THEM. I UNDERSTAND IT WAS HIT AND UNABLE TO FIRE.

199

At 1232Z, the Controller, [Tribune] advises 815 that he has "Visual ((radar)) contact with you". This same reference to "radar" is noted again at around 1238 to 1240Z. The range reference notes that it appears the ship was 50 miles away from the helicopters.

The above does not appear in the Israeli transcripts and the ship is torpedoed around 1435. Robert says "Have him stay on the side, they're putting torpedoes into it. You can get the guys out later." Robert is referring to having the helicopters "stay on the side", while the ship is torpedoed. Even though the helicopters are apparently sent to rescue survivors, they are told to hold off until the ship is torpedoed. Do they not expect casualties to result from the torpedo attack? It is as if they are adlibbing a script on the go.

Based upon the above transcript and checking for the word radar in the Israeli tapes, it is possible that it was Robert or Shimon who was in fact *Tribune* at Air Control Central at Hatzor Airbase south of Tel Aviv. We do not find the word *Tribune* anywhere in the Israeli transcripts. Further, in the Israeli transcripts there is no entry for 1231Z or 1431 local time. There is no entry for 1232Z or 1432 local time. The dialogue for 1238 does not match up either. Cristol had said that the NSA transcripts should match up with the Israeli transcripts—they do not.

1234Z, [Tribune] TO 815: AT THE MOMENT IT IS STRAIGHT AHEAD AT A RANGE OF ABOUT 50-MILES. PAY ATTENTION: THIS SHIP IS NOW IDENTIFIED AS EGYPTIAN. YOU CAN RETURN HOME.
1238Z, [Tribune] TO 810: MEANWHILE, YOU WILL CONTINUE ON HEADING OF

250 FROM ASHDOD. YOU WILL HEAD
TOWARD THE SHIP.
1239Z, [Tribune] TO 810 AND 815: They are
both directed to the ship and told the ship is
listing.

Again, the above NSA transcript does not jive with the
Israeli one. If the helicopters were on a rescue mission,
why were they told to return home just because the ship
was "claimed" to have been identified as "Egyptian"?
This is clearly the time when damage control begins in
earnest. The order to return home is then reversed. If the
two transcripts do not match up it is possible that not all
channels were recorded or disclosed with the Israeli
transcripts. There could be a translation problem, or the
conclusion could be both sides are withholding
information.

The key question is what happened to the tapes and
transcripts referred to by Nowicki and Prostinak? Some
helpful information has become available over recent
years that shed some light on this question.

Three individuals have come forward including
California immigration attorney James Ronald Gotcher,
who on June 8, 1967 was a Sergeant in the United States
Air Force, assigned to the 6924th Security Squadron at Da
Nang, Republic of Vietnam. In a declaration dated
September 2, 2003, he stated he was in a position to note
a CRITIC message, informing us that USS *Liberty* was
under attack by Israeli aircraft. Shortly thereafter, they
began receiving rough translations of the Israeli air to air
and air to ground communications.[252] Mr. Gotcher was
the advocate for both the LVA and individual survivors.
He makes no bones about his bias.

He further stated that the next day they received final translations of the intercepts and there were virtually no difference between versions. Gotcher stated, "While I have a clear recollection of reading transcripts of conversations between pilots and controllers, I do not recall ever reading anything similar to the transcripts recently released by the National Security Agency concerning Israeli helicopter pilots. It was clear from the explicit statements made by both the aircraft crews and the controllers that the aircraft were flying a planned mission to find and sink USS *Liberty*."

He said his understanding of what he read led him to conclude that the Israeli pilots were making every effort possible to sink USS *Liberty* and were very frustrated by their inability to do so. Approximately ten days to two weeks later, they received an internal NSA report, summarizing the Agency's findings. The report stated, in no uncertain terms, that the attack was planned in advance and deliberately executed. The mission was to sink USS *Liberty*. A few days after the report arrived, another message came through directing the document control officer to gather and destroy all copies of both the rough and final intercept translations, as well as the subsequently issued report.

He further stated, "After the destruction of those documents, he saw nothing further on this subject. He has read the translated transcripts, released by the Israeli government, which purport to be actual transcripts of the air to ground communications between the controllers and the attacking aircraft. He knows this document to be a fabrication because he read the actual intercepts and they were nothing like this. It is not possible that the differences could be due to different translations being used."

The second person to come forward was Stephen Forslund who submitted a statement that he was a former Air Force intelligence analyst. His statement, which is not dated nor signed, is available online.[253] In his statement, he noted; "For many years I have periodically been reminded of those days in June 1967 that had such an impact on me as a young man. It has been frustrating that, for all that time, I have had to stifle the shout I wanted to make over the injustice that was committed."

"I finally feel the overwhelming compulsion to say something about what I witnessed. I do so with fear and discomfort because of the oath of secrecy we all took and the uncertainty over the legality of speaking out. What motivates me to speak is the fact that nothing I can add will harm our nation or compromise our intelligence sources at this late date. I can be written off as a liar or 'conspiracy weirdo' or prosecuted if they want to admit that what I say is true."

He further states in his declaration, "Much discussion has gone on about what the NSA archives hold about the *Liberty* attack. The latest I read, stated that the only and final "tapes" that the NSA has released show that helicopters sent by Israel to the site of the attack on the *Liberty*, after the attack, were unaware of her nationality. Much importance is put on this issue by different factions in this debate. Parties state that these are the only tapes of intercepts that exist. That may very well be true, now. Nothing I can say will change anyone's mind but I have to state, for my own peace of mind, what I witnessed as an all source intelligence analyst for the U.S. Air Force during the 6 day war."

He states there were other intercepts, and he and many others like him, read transcripts of the air-to-air and air-to-ground communications of the fighters who attacked the USS *Liberty*. "We read these in real time during the day the attack occurred. These intercepts were preceded by many others we read that week that started with the opening attack by Israel in the war and included intercepts of messages between the USA and Israel in which our government stated their knowledge of the Israeli's pre-emptive attack that began the war and warned Israel to cease their activities."

On the day of the attack on the *Liberty*, he said he read yellow teletype sheets that spewed from the machines in front of me all day. "We obtained our input from a variety of sources including the NSA. The teletypes were raw translations of intercepts of Israeli air-to-air and air-to-ground communications between jet aircraft and their ground controller. I read page after page of these transcripts that day as it went on and on. The transcripts made specific reference to the efforts to direct the jets to the target which was identified as American numerous times by the ground controller. Upon arrival, the aircraft specifically identified the target and mentioned the American flag she was flying. There were frequent operational transmissions from the pilots to the ground base describing the strafing runs. The ground control began asking about the status of the target and whether it was sinking. They stressed that the target must be sunk and leave no trace. The pilots stated they had made several runs and the target was still floating. The ground control station re-iterated that it was urgent that the target be sunk, leaving no trace. There was a detectable level of frustration evident in the transmissions over the fact that the aircraft were unable to accomplish the mission quickly and totally."

He further states: "The aircraft eventually broke off and we received no further transcripts of the event. I have since learned in later descriptions of the attack that torpedo boats attacked the *Liberty* also. I saw neither intercepts nor analyses that addressed that attack. An hour or two later I was discussing the event with a team member and he stated they had received, during the time frame of the attack, an intercept of a U.S. State Department message to Israel stating that the United States had full evidence of what had occurred in the attack on the *Liberty* and strongly warning Israel to cease activities immediately."

Forslund became aware of the attack on the ship when watching the evening news and read about it in the newspaper the next day.

"I read these discussions debating whether Israel intentionally attacked the USS *Liberty* and what their motivation would have been for a deliberate attack. I can't debate their motivation. But, I will carry the memory of those transcripts with me until I die. We all lost our virginity that day."

The third person was Harold Max Cobbs who directed his statement, in letter format, addressed to Jim Ennes dated April 13, 2004, which is posted online. He stated: [254]

> I was a 20-year-old CTM3 when. I arrived in Morocco, July of 1967. I was young and new to the NSG world. While performing my duties on base, I was a witness to the collection and order to destroy ALL traffic regarding the attack on the USS *Liberty*. Not wanting to believe what I had just seen and

hard, I made the comment to comm officer, Lieutenant Rogers, "That's just not right!" Upon making the above comment I received a severe lecture regarding the following of direct orders. I did not have the understanding at the time, being young and new to the NSA, the implication of the "order" given. The order was to collect all traffic and put it in the mulcher. After the material had been mulched, it was taken out back and dried. This was not enough. It was then incinerated in the oil furnace. I followed my orders as directed and went on with my duties.

In May of 1967 I received orders to NCS Sidi Yahia and on to the U.S.S. *Liberty*. I was in "crypto" school at the time of the attack. I realized that when I heard about what had just happened to my fellow Navy brothers, that given a slight change in orders or timing, I too could have lost my life on that fateful day in 1967.

He further stated, "Something has to be done to bring the deliberate government cover-up to the attention of the American people, force a REAL independent investigation, and give some solace and justice to the survivors and families of the dead."

Anyone can draw his or her own conclusions. Has our government been caught in the process of destroying evidence of possible crimes against U.S. service personnel and this ship? The administration chose to suppress information rather than risk severely damaging the relations with the State of Israel over an act of war. At the time, Moshe Dayan became the prime suspect for issuing the order to attack the ship. Even the Thames TV production people, who per Cristol had a copy of the

Israeli tapes, were pointing at Dayan and asking the "key question". The rest of the unreleased NSA transcripts would have been devastating to the State of Israel from a public relations and historical perspective. While, for their reasons, Israel released their version of the attack tapes to Dr. Bregman, Thames TV, and Judge Cristol; it is obvious from reading Cristol's inserted comments that his mission was pure and simply "misdirection" and still is. The NSA helicopter transcripts had not been released when Cristol published his book.

One other fact that Cristol notes is that the only Admiral the Navy had was Shlomo Erell. Analysis of the transcripts also puts him in the middle of the *Liberty* attack. As for Cristol's contention that everyone, including Thames TV, is wrong on Dayan, he points out that Dayan's political career was not harmed. Certainly, Dayan is an Israeli hero; however, his record must stand on its merits. All I can say to the Judge is read your own book! Look at page 218, at 1425 Local time. This is 4 minutes before the portion of the NSA EC-121 intercepts kick in. Are we to believe that the EC-121 suddenly turned its receivers and tape recorders on at precisely this point in time and action? Hickman did say in his OH that there was a certain amount of skill or luck in picking up intercepts. One had to be paying attention and be on the right frequency—apparently Prostinak was.

At 1420 Local Time, Navy Chief, Admiral Erell, returns to the Stella Maris command post, having departed earlier as noted to visit Haifa harbor.[255] At this point, the author would ask if Admiral Erell ever went by the code name *Jewel*. This person is referenced as being at Haifa, but is not otherwise identified in the released portion of the NSA helicopter transcripts.

What is the clandestine reference to "getting the helicopter out of there? Is this a reference to Super Frelon 807 (*Ofot* 2) with the Minister of Defense? At any rate, Admiral Erell has a real crisis and mess on his hands; did he order an end to the attack?

Nevertheless, analysis of the transcripts clearly shows the following: 1) Israeli Command and Control was clearly tracking the *Liberty* via a coastal radar and air early warning system. 2) The air controllers and helicopters were being choreographed in a crisis management and damage control mode. 3) The claim by motor torpedo boats that the "target" (the *Liberty*), was fleeing on a course of 283 toward Port Said at speeds of 28 to 30 knots is bogus, and at a minimum grossly incompetent. 4) The NSA, for purposes of their FOIA release made a "cut" between 1425 and 1429, releasing only the latter portion of the intercepts from the EC-121. The portions not released had to do with Minister of Defense Moshe Dayan as noted above.

The above information, with other developing evidence, notwithstanding the missing NSA intercept segments of the attack itself, clearly show that the air and sea attack was command and control coordinated on a "need-to-know" basis. It is only when command and control enters into a "crisis and damage control mode", that other elements are necessarily brought into the crisis where the "scripting" is necessary and the cover-up begins. Simply, the **"threat to the sink the *Liberty* if not moved"** was made good, except the plan failed. The Sixth Fleet had been alerted and advised it was sending "air-cover" with authorization to use all necessary force—**this force would have engaged U.S. Naval aircraft in a deadly force conflict with the IDF air and sea forces**

Of critical importance, is the fact that President Johnson wanted specific information from his Special National Security Committee headed by McGeorge Bundy, as Executive Secretary, that included **"a special study on strafing & torpedoing of USS *Liberty*--pilot conversations, etc.--everything we can get--NSA, etc."** CIA Director Helms was to provide this information; a CIA memorandum resulted that was less that assertive.[256] The question is, did President Johnson get the information he wanted, and if not, why not? Was there an effort by certain key staff members, such as Walt Rostow, to give the President "political-cover" by withholding key information—in essence "deniability"? Historians will have to come to their own conclusions. On this point, former CIA Director, Richard Helms, noted that the purpose of the 303 Committee, referred to elsewhere herein, was to give the President "deniability". A comment: The desire to provide a president with political-cover or deniability is not a defense to a charge of obstruction of justice.

The State Department conference on the Six-Day War and the *Liberty* held Monday, 1/12/2004, left the author with the clear impression that NSA has more to cough up. That more is the missing portions of the NSA intercepts that bless him, Judge Cristol, in his suit, claimed he wanted. Judge Cristol should have pursued his FOIA lawsuit fully. The NSA since has added more disclosures to its FOIA website, but still nothing about the missing transcripts. If Cristol had pursued his lawsuit to trial, it might have coughed up the sought after documents subject to an *in camera* review by the Court in which case the government might have asserted a national security interest exemption from disclosure. That would created an admission that they existed.

Two final points to keep in mind as the reader posits this matter: First, on certain pilot dialogue transcripts, the Israeli attacking pilots use the phrase **"watch out for her antenna"** referring to a caution to a fellow pilot in his dive attack and pull up.[257] This certainly indicates the attacking pilots knew the ship's purpose, configuration, and vulnerability. See Ennes, *Assault on the Liberty,* as pertains to the efforts to call for help and damage to the ship's antennas and electronics. Commander Dave Lewis had stated that his people had to string long wire to serve as an antenna to get the call for assistance out. Amazingly, the previously referenced CIA memorandum seems to say that the Egyptian horse transport ship, *El Quseir,* could have been confused with the *Liberty.*

President Johnson had also tasked his foreign intelligence advisor, Clark Clifford, to look into the matter of the attack on the *Liberty*. There is one reference to an excised segment of the Clark Clifford's report, dated 6/18/1967, to the President pertaining to the attack on the *Liberty* making the following observations: [258]

> The attack was executed with complete surprise, remarkable efficiency, devastating accuracy and deeply tragic results.
> [The Israelis claim]: The Liberty acted with lack of care by approaching excessively close to shore in an area which was a scene of war, without advising the Israeli authorities of its presence and without identifying itself elaborately. The Liberty tried to hide its presence and its identity both before it was discovered and after having been attacked.
> [Our findings of Fact]: At all times prior to, during, and following the attack, the Liberty

was in international waters where she had every right to be. As a noncombatant neutral vessel she maintained the impartial attitude of neutrality at all times prior to the attack.

i. (2) [---- excised ----] received information from a reliable and sensitive Israeli source reporting that he had listened to IDF air-to-ground transmissions on the morning of June 8 indicating Israeli aircraft sighting of a vessel flying the U.S. flag;

[Conclusions]: The unprovoked attack on the Liberty constitutes a flagrant act of gross negligence for which the Israeli Government should be held completely responsible, and the Israeli military personnel involved should be punished.

While Clark is critical of the Israeli action, his overall report finds "gross negligence" and nothing more serious but he expects punishment. Referenced the excised portion, it could refer to Commander Castle's report reference the person from Israeli Aircraft Industries and sighting the American flag. This is consistent with the reporting from the EC-121 intercepts as discussed above. The Clark report undercuts the NSA position that there were no COMINTS, intercepts, of the actual attack stated in the "summary aftermath" report submitted to the White House by the Director of the NSA, allegedly, Hickman's work-product. Perhaps the NSA lost the "chain of custody" of the tapes at the request of the President via Bundy and Helms.

U.S. State Department history document 236 dated 6/9/67, dealing with notes of a special committee to the National Security Council, indicates that Clifford recommended a harsh line be taken against the Israelis for the attack, that they be treated as if the Arabs or USSR attacked the ship:[259]

> Clifford: My concern is that we're not tough enough. Handle as if Arabs or USSR had done it. Manner egregious. Inconceivable that it was accident. 3 strafing passes, 3 torpedo boats.

Further, State Department history documents 258 6/10/67, and 284 6/13/67 involved Johnson's special assistant Walt Rostow and CIA Director Helms in dealing with the intercepts and all details surrounding the attack.[260]

> A covering memorandum from Helms to the President states that it was the "special study" he had requested the previous evening. Helms' notes of the June 12 meeting of the NSC Special Committee indicate that the President requested a "special study on strafing & torpedoing of USS *Liberty*—pilot conversations, etc.—everything we can get—NSA, etc."
> Rostow sent a preliminary version of this report to the President at 12:45 p.m. on June 13 with a covering memorandum calling it "CIA's first cut at the problem" and noting, "They do not find evidence of U.S. identification before the attack."

It is clear where the missing intercepts may have gone and where the orders came from to destroy all evidence and reports per Gotcher, Forslund and Cobbs referred to above. Helms did not buy into the mistaken identity excuse; perhaps Rostow did because he was the "political advisor" to the President. Other State Department documents in the series deal with the give and take between the U.S. government and the government of Israel to "tamp" down the harsh rhetoric resulting from the attack; in essence, diplomacy controls reality. The political side of government will dominate the military side. Judge Cristol in his book on pages 66 and 67 indicates he has a hard time reconciling Clifford's hard line against Israel in view of the fact he was a known friend of Israel.

Fig. 15, President Johnson and National Security Advisor, Walt Rostow, LBJ Library.

It is the contention of this author that the NSA tapes and transcripts discovered via the FOIA lawsuit by Judge Cristol prove beyond a doubt that the *Liberty* was constantly tracked by coastal radar. Contrary to contentions of Lunz, she was not lost track of. In addition, she was constantly surveyed from the sky by various reconnaissance aircraft; including the so-called French Noratlas Nord 2501, "flying boxcar. Specifically, as to the NSA intercepts pertaining to the two Super Frelon helicopters, 810 and 815, armed-troop laden, they

213

show the pilots being directed or "steered" toward the *Liberty* by an Israeli controller (call name: *Tribune*) who coordinated and prompted the pilots as they flew toward the "radar target". A memo from Walt Rostow to the President, dated June 10, 1967, refers to the archiving of information pertaining to the *Liberty,* including the location of files. Note footnotes 1 and 2 by going to the State Department website:[261]

258. Memorandum From the President's Special Assistant (Rostow) to President Johnson[1]

Washington, June 10, 1967, 5:05 p.m.

Mr. President:

These intercepts[2] —showing some honest ambiguity about the ship after the attack— suggest that there may have been a breakdown of communications on the Israeli side; that is, the tactical base which first received word that the ship was American may not have flashed that information to other air force and naval units.

We shall, of course, analyze this affair further.

Walt

It is clear from various documents that Walt Rostow was the prime mover in containing the fallout from the attack on the *Liberty*, without an investigation by pushing the mistaken identity and communication breakdown theories. Another document on the State Department website is a memorandum prepared by the CIA and dated June 13, 1967. This document also claims that there were no intercepts of the attack itself and pushes the mistaken ID theory:[262]

214

4. None of the communications of the attacking aircraft and torpedo boats is available, but the intercepted conversations between the helicopter pilots and the control tower at Hatzor (near Tel Aviv) leave little doubt that the Israelis failed to identify the *Liberty* as a US ship before or during the attack.

> With the outbreak of the fighting on June 5, we notified
> the American Naval Attaché in Israel that we intended to
> protect our shores from Egyptian naval attacks by
> employing a combination of naval and air units....We
> therefore asked that American ships be removed from the
> vicinity of the Israeli shore or that the Americans notify us
> of their precise location in the area near our coast. In the
> storm of battle, there was no time to check whether or not
> our request had been fulfilled
>
> Yitzhak Rabin "The Rabin Memoirs".

Chapter 8

The Mission

Why would the *Liberty's* presence in the Eastern Mediterranean pose such a threat to the Israelis that it would warrant attacking the ship? Another question would be did the issue of mission have any bearing on whether the attack was intentional or not. Mission is related to the issue of "motive". The *Liberty's* mission is one of the many perplexing mysteries surrounding the attack. I had done just enough reading to understand that the "mission" was an important part of the overall puzzle. At the end of the previous chapter, I made mention of a CIA memorandum posted on the State Department website, document No. 284, dated June 13, 1967. To understand the game playing and misdirection played by government bureaucrats one just needs to look at paragraph 9 of that memorandum.

> 9. The USS Liberty is a converted Victory
> class merchant ship utilized as a SIGINT
> collector. The unit had moved from its normal
> station off West Africa to provide additional
> SIGINT coverage of the Middle East crisis.

216

Official US statements, however, have described the Liberty as an electronics research ship which had been diverted to the crisis area to act as a radio relay station for US embassies.

The ship was not diverted to act as a radio relay station. This is an example of individuals jumping to conclusions without knowing the facts, or an example of intentional misdirection. The previously mentioned *Gerhard Report* addresses the mission issue in cryptic form.

Luckily, Jim Ennes, a survivor and author of the *Assault on the Liberty* lives in the Pacific Northwest, so I called him and arranged a meeting at his residence. He was a gracious host and we spent a couple hours together at which time he gave me three or four books to read that had sections dealing with the *Liberty*

This meeting was on March 3, 2004 a few months after reading James Bamford's book, *Body of Secrets*, and the chapter *Blood* dealing with the attack on the *Liberty*. Jim stated that the mission was simply to monitor Russian TU-95 Bear strategic bombers in the Cairo area, specifically Alexandria, to see if Egyptian or Russian pilots controlled them. Bamford, on page 208 of his book, also cites the monitoring of the TU-95s as the purpose of the mission to see if the Russians were going to be active in the war. End users of the intelligence would be the CIA, NSA, JCS and other agencies as would be appropriate, including the office of the President. Ennes admonished me to ignore anything reference Israel. At the time, I thought that strange but did not feel it was my place to challenge him. I believe he was referring to our spying on Israeli military

217

operations. It would seem to me that the end users of intelligence would want a total picture of what would be a regional war.

Now the only thing wrong with that statement was that I could find no evidence that TU-95 Bear bombers were in Egypt prior to or during the Six-Day War. There were Sukhoi-7 Soviet bombers in Egypt during the war in 1967 and the War of Attrition. In fact, Egypt had taken delivery of a package of 15 such planes from the Soviets. The Indians had used these planes during the war against Pakistan. The Sukhoi-7s were hampered by high speed landing requirements plus poor cockpit visibility that made them hard to handle.[263] Additionally, author Isabella Ginor, in her book *Foxbats over Dimona*, calls Jim on the TU-95 issue and claims they were not based on Egyptian soil. Reference is made to page 135 of her book and note 51 to Chapter 13.[264]

While the air war was essentially over on June 5th with the Egyptians losing 338 planes, mostly while sitting on the ground, 14 Soviet SU-7s and 31 Soviet TU-16 Badgers were lost, but no TU-95s. There were TU-95s Bear bombers put on alert under the command of Vasily Reshetnikov, but they were positioned at their base at Priluki, near Kiev, in the Ukraine, and able to fly five hours each way without refueling.[265] There was apparently an effort to mark these planes so they appeared to be Egyptian. Reshetnikov said his bombers were put on alert after the first Israeli strike on 5 June.[266] Further, it is reported that these bombers would be escorted by MIG-21s commanded by Yuri Nastenko. When put on alert they were told to be prepared, but were not told where they would be flying.[267] They were not positioned on Egyptian soil.[268] The piloting issue raised by Ennes could have applied to any of the Soviet planes because of the lack of qualified Egyptian pilots. It is believed that TU-95 reconnaissance planes over-flew the Sixth Fleet on reconnaissance flights as a matter of such routine that it would not require a monitoring effort by the *Liberty*.

Rashetnikov was reported by Ginor as claiming his planes were put on alert after the first Israeli strike and they "had to work Egyptian Flag", meaning disguising under who's control the planes were operating. The planes located in the Ukraine would be within striking distance of the Sinai. Author Peter Hounam reports that at the same time U.S. B-52 strategic bombers were placed on alert at Beal Air Force base in California armed with nuclear weapons.[269]

To better understand the mission dilemma, it is necessary to note that when the NSA issued SIGINT readiness alert Alfa, the intent was a general order to sweep up all possible intelligence for evaluation. It was because of the building Soviet threat that the *Liberty* was dispatched from its position off the West African coast with orders to move to Point Alfa off Gaza, El Arish, Port Said, and the Sinai giving her a better perspective of what was happening in the war. The potential for war had been heating up specifically since May 23 with certain actions taken by Nasser that raised Israeli and U.S. concerns. Simply put it would make sense that we would want to monitor the building crisis—no mystery on this point. The specific mission details are another matter.

The *Liberty*, it is claimed was capable of intercepting major Israeli communications, including Israeli Defense Forces brigade and division level communications and movement orders along with radar emissions and radio

219

transmissions from aircraft flying in the war. The *Liberty's* orders were to position her 12.5 nautical miles away from the Egyptian coast since Egypt claimed a 12-mile territorial sea limit; and she was to go no closer than 6.5 miles to the Israeli coast since she claimed a six-mile limit.[270]

Jim Ennes in his book mentions crossing with the *Valdez* en route to Point Alfa while the *Valdez* was returning home. The USNS *Private Jose F. Valdez* (T-AG-169) was named after World War II Medal of Honor recipient PFC Jose F. Valdez. The ship was also a "technical research ship" that operated during the 1960s. She was called the *Galloping Ghost of the Ivory Coast* and like the *Liberty* had been deployed to the African coast.

The *Valdez* was leaving the East Mediterranean apparently, in part, because she had mechanical operating problems. One knowledgeable person thought she had a broken screw (propeller); and Author James Bamford suggested it was because she had been on patrol so long that her bottom was encrusted slowing her speed down.[271] Regardless, before the war started she had an interesting patrol. A former crewmember who was a CT-R on board the *Valdez* described leaving Massawa, Ethiopia (Federation with Eritrea) and transiting the Suez Canal. The ship's next port was Port Said, Egypt for repairs of "some kind", noting that there was certain hostility toward Americans causing their shore leave to be limited to a 1600-hour curfew.

There were different branches of the CT (communications technician) rate or "military occupation specification": CT-R was radio, CT-L was linguist, CT-O was operations, CT-M was maintenance, CT-T was

Technical (non-Morse), CT-A was administrative. In an e-mail exchange dated 8/16/09, Alan Moore noted we all had different jobs that required top-secret clearances. He did not recall knowing a Richard Hickman, the Hebrew linguist, referred to in the previous chapter. Of course, it was over 40 years ago and he said he could not remember the names of a lot of our crew. Hickman had been on the *Valdez* but because he was a short-timer, he left the ship to report to another job at the NSA avoiding assignment to the *Liberty*.

After leaving Port Said, the *Valdez* started patrolling off the coast of Israel and Lebanon and this former crewmember recalled that they ended up in the middle of an Egyptian and Russian naval exercise. He noted that those forces made it clear their ship was not wanted in the area "...as their gun boats crossed our bow and released some kind of smoke." This was prior to the war, and then they were given orders to return to New York for shipyard repairs. He notes stopping at Barcelona, Spain and having a "Great Liberty!" and a brief stop at Rota, Spain, he says for supplies.[272]

There can be confusion as to exact dates. For example, Ennes says that the *Valdez* was tracking toward them on 4 June; however, the *Liberty* arrived in Rota on June 1 to pick up supplies and several linguists. If the ship departed Rota on June 2, it is unclear how they would have picked up data dropped off by the *Valdez*.

Bamford noted that Frank Raven, head of the G Group at the NSA was concerned about having unescorted ships in the dangerous Mediterranean. The *Valdez* was a civilian operated ship with naval technicians conducting the SIGINT operations. It was better to be open about the ship having operating problems and pulling her from the area. It took her six weeks to pass Israel, Egypt and Libya but on May 23, she was half way between Greece and Italy.[273] Raven's G Group was responsible for signals intelligence in the non-communist part of the planet.

Notwithstanding the concerns of Raven in G Group, the *Liberty* was dispatched because things were heating up between Israel and the Arabs. Consequently, the *Valdez's* stop in Rota, Spain was not only to take on fuel but to off load reams of SIGINT data for the *Liberty* and the linguists boarding at Rota.   The data contained information on who was communicating on what links, teletype, telephone, microwave according to Raven.[274] The *Valdez's* linguist included those knowledgeable in French and Portuguese. With Hickman on board, they would have had a Hebrew linguist.

The *Liberty* took on three civilian linguists and three military ones. They would become part of the NSG-855, the Naval Security Group, operating in the ship's "research department"—a misnomer also known as the "spook department". Their environment on board ship would be based on individual security clearance and need-to-know. If there was an element of "common knowledge", it was usually based upon scuttlebutt, as each had their separate job to do. SIGINT and ELINT collectors and recorders might not know what analyzers and linguists are doing, or what the P and R department was doing about putting out a product for the intelligence end-users.

What is clear, after the *Valdez* got caught in the middle of an Egyptian and Soviet naval exercise, it reinforced the U.S. intelligence communities' concern about operations of the Soviet fleet in the Mediterranean, that was considered the "Sixth Fleet's lake". In researching the *Liberty* story very little has been said about Soviet fleet operations over the years. This has been one of those mysteries bothering this author and another *Liberty* researcher and supporter. Were Soviet ships close to the *Liberty's* position once it was at Point Alfa? Ennes says very little about this in his book other than a passing mention of a Soviet ship offering to stand by the early morning of the ninth in case help was needed after the Israeli attack of June 8. As to what kind of threat the Soviets presented, we will look at that in another chapter.

Suffice to say that the Soviets had a major presence in the Mediterranean challenging the American fleet and were steadily increasing their presence all through 1967 into December when a Russian sub and an American sub, the *George Marshall,* touched—bumped together. Russian ships had been monitoring both the *Liberty* and Sixth Fleet. The *Marshall* (SSBN-654), a Polaris missile sub, was clipped by a Soviet sub in the Mediterranean Sea. The Americans knew the Soviet sub was there but could not move their massive boat away fast enough. Crewmen noted the collision was "a glancing blow" but said it still left a gash in *Marshall's* forward starboard ballast tank. [275]

One of the biggest issues having to do with the *Liberty's* mission is the question of what language specialists, linguists, were on board. The key question is whether there were Hebrew linguists along with those who knew Arabic and Russian. This is a continuing and perplexing if not confusing issue and controversy. There will be those in the know who say there was no need for Hebrew linguists because we were allies; there will be those who say there were no Hebrew linguists, and there

223

are those who say that there were only Russian and Special-Arabic linguists. Without a doubt there were Russian and Arabic linguists and possibly one who was *Special-Arabic* meaning he could understand Hebrew. There were perhaps some who had limited experience with Hebrew, in fact, Richard Hickman had mentioned one person he knew was on board but who hadn't kept up-to-date with his Hebrew. Bamford in his book noted the NSA intended to put a Hebrew linguist on board but was short of personnel. Marine Sergeant Bryce Lockwood was a Russian linguist. He claims there were five Arabic linguists and Lockwood.[276] As we will note there is some indication that Lockwood, a Marine, might have known some Hebrew.

Why would the ship be dispatched to the area if there were no Hebrew linguists? This doesn't make much sense unless there were in fact a linguist shortage, which is a definite possibility considering all SIGINT needs both in listening positions and at processing centers including those onboard air-borne collectors. Even today, our military and intelligence communities have an unfilled need for linguists because of ongoing conflicts in the Middle East. This is a critical question because it goes to the heart of the threat that was perceived by the Israelis and pertains to the motive for the attack. Bamford believes that the designation "Special Arabic" was to hide fact that we were eavesdropping on Israel.[277]

It is important to note that the *Liberty* was not the only SIGINT collector used by NSA and the defense establishment. We noted in a prior chapter the intercepts by a Navy EC-121 and flights of an Air Force C-130—as airborne collectors. Intelligence sources are not exclusive but varied, including the gathering of HUMINT or human "on-the-ground" intelligence. Was there another "collector" being used in the Mediterranean? What about "Contact X" referred to in Ennes's book—thought to be a submarine. Judge Cristol in his FOIA lawsuit cited the possible presence of the submarine USS *Amberjack*. James Bamford in his book reports that First Class Petty Officer Charles L. Rowley reported to NSA what he thought was a signal from a submarine, and then got his butt chewed out for some strange reason that remains unexplained.[278]

Ennes in his book speculated that the *Liberty* met with a submarine en route to Point Alfa. Interestingly, when Captain McGonagle requested a destroyer escort in a message sent to Vice Admiral Martin, he mentioned that the destroyer might serve as an auxiliary communicator. What was he getting at? Was the *Liberty* and Contact X supposed to be working together? Always, more questions, which seems to be the essence of the *Liberty* story—such is common when dealing with intelligence activities. A packet with sensitive instructions was supposed to have been brought aboard the ship when the linguists were picked up at Rota. We do not know what happened to that packet and whether it was even opened prior to the attack, in which case it might have been destroyed during the torpedo attack or confiscated in the cleanup of the ship.

While the *Liberty* was a full-service collector and processor, the operational plan called for the collection of signals to be transmitted to NSA for processing. Processing and reporting from onboard the ship was also part of the operation, which is the reason the satellite dish was on the *Liberty*. Whether there was a direct phone connection between the ship and the NSA is in dispute with one person who was stationed at the NSA saying he had a conversation that was direct with Captain McGonagle.[279] It would seem that messages had to be routed between points rather than going direct over long distances. Eugene Sheck was a staff officer in K-Group during June of 1967; he gave his Oral History interview on August 11, 1980, conducted by William Gerhard and others. Again, his OH was conducted with the understanding it would be kept secret. Sheck's name is spelled Scheck on the NSA website index listing those who gave oral histories. Those histories can be found on the NSA disclosure website and are in a .pdf format.[280]

Gerhard and Henry Millington, the interviewers, were in the process of writing the SIGINT history of the *Liberty* for the NSA. By the time of the Sheck interview, they had already interviewed 10 other persons. Sheck's job included the tasking of the various collector platforms such as the TRSs of which the *Liberty* was one. He notes that one reason for sending the *Liberty* was that certain signals were not being collected in the VHF/UHF range, straight radiotelephone, and VHF microwave. He noted that while there were plane collectors they had limited time on station before needing to land and refuel, whereas the *Liberty* could remain on continuous station. He noted that line-of-sight was needed; however, at this point in the interview Gerhard's question is redacted. Sheck said that the JCS/JRC controlled the placement of the ship and NSA had nothing to do with that. He further noted that HF (High Frequency) was important and gave them broad capabilities. Sheck's group was responsible for making sure that analytical element was in place, in short, data appropriate for that part of the Mediterranean. Sometime previous, the *Jamestown* had traveled through the Suez Canal and they knew the kind of communications that could be collected.

Importantly, Sheck corrected Gerhard on the point that materials from the *Valdez* and *Jamestown* were forwarded to the NSA where they were packed into a tech support packages and shipped to Rota for the *Liberty*. Sheck responded to a question as to whether his group objected to sending the *Liberty* to the area, he equivocated and noted that a General John Morrison had responsibility for sending the *Liberty*. Sheck talks about Arab-Israeli communications, and subject to a redacted question by Gerhard, Sheck says "There was [redacted] tasking." A one-word redaction could mean Israeli or Hebrew tasking—speculation.

The next question was whether NSA monitored the ship after it left Rota. Sheck said yes, via a daily SIGINT summary that included position. Farley asked if there was a direct communication link between NSA and the ship. His answer was no that they had to go through Rota or other channels. The Joint Reconnaissance Center was created in 1961, after a U-2 incident. The purpose was to track all recon efforts on a monthly basis, and this effort was monitored by key governmental leaders such as McGeorge Bundy and Henry Kissinger to make sure that the President wasn't caught off guard like occurred in the U-2 shoot-down incident under President Eisenhower involving U-2 pilot Francis Gary Powers. During the Six-Day War, the NSA representative to the JCS/JRC was John Connell. While the Director of NSA did not have a say in ship safety, it was something he could have addressed to the JCS. After the war started, Sheck called Connell to ascertain if there was consideration of moving the *Liberty*. He was advised no. He acknowledged a question from Gerhard to the effect that the Commander of the Sixth Fleet did not know what the *Liberty* was doing. NSA had technical control, but the Commander

Sixth Fleet could be asked to move the ship since she was under his operational control.

Sheck was asked how he learned that the *Liberty* was attacked. He stated just after coming to work on the morning of the eighth he was on the phone with John Connell who told him the *Liberty* had just been torpedoed. Sheck said he advised the Director of NSA, Marshall Carter, who did not know what the *Liberty* was and who got a call from the Secretary of Defense who did not know what the *Liberty* was. Everyone started to scramble to get info on the ship and the attack. McNamara: "What the hell is the USS <u>Liberty</u>?"

Sheck reported that he had word from Captain McGonagle about unmarked jets over-flying the ship that made him uncomfortable. The decision to move the ship was left with the Captain. When pressed, Sheck felt that since NSA tasked the ship it should have the right to modify the mission and he felt that in this case NSA did. When questioned about the products that the *Liberty* was accountable for, he noted, "We took off everything that was related to [redaction]." He stated that Walter Deeley was placed in charge of getting all the information on the *Liberty* for a post attack report.

One other point Sheck made before getting into damage assessment in his OH was that the *Liberty's* positioning was best for where emitters crossed on a line-of-sight basis. One would have to look at the lay of the terrain of the Sinai to properly understand this issue. To both task the *Liberty* and after the attack to justify her tasking, charts and wave propagation studies were made. Sheck said that the post attack investigators were satisfied that there was a technical reason for the ship to be where she was positioned off the coast. The atmosphere was described as one of finger pointing and trying to deflect blame for not moving the ship away from the area. That got into the missing recall message issue.

The discussion got to the question of whether to replace the *Liberty* after the attack with the USS *Belmont*, but not to position her close to the shore. They would sacrifice VHF/UHF for HF acquisitions. Sheck described how classified materials floated out of the hole in the ship's hull as it sailed toward dry-dock at Malta. Once in dock a representative from the NSA came on site and began to salvage all SIGINT materials including safes. Materials were destroyed, some being deep-sixed in weighed destruction bags; also, electronics were deep-sixed on the trip back to Norfolk. Sheck was on-sight to observe the salvage efforts to keep an eye on contractors to make sure they didn't walk off with items from the ship and to assess for General Morrison whether the ship could be salvaged and put back in the operation. The answer was, just forget it. Sheck talked with Captain McGonagle about eight days after the ship got into Malta. The Captain was still limping and had not received full treatment for the leg. He noted that the Captain was not bitter over what happened, as he did not blame the NSA. He had been antsy over the over-flights but was just interested in doing his job. He had a lot of praise for the CTs who pitched in to help with damage control.

Toward the end of his interview, Sheck remembered to bring up the issue of a submarine being associated with the *Liberty*. There are redactions at this point in the conversation, which comes after he mentions a conversation with Commander Maurice Bennett, who was the second in command of the Naval Security Group aboard the ship. The interviewers were aware of the submarine issue referring to books by Ennes and

229

Anthony Pearson. It should be of note for the reader that these individuals conducting the oral history interviews for the NSA were relying on these books about the *Liberty* for insights. This author is doing the same thing in trying to reconstruct events.

Another author, James Scott, writing about the *Liberty*, noted the following: Some of [Admiral] McCain's staff blamed his incessant politicking in part for the attack on the *Liberty*, a fact that would neither be included in the Navy's court of inquiry nor ever made public. When the conflict in the Middle East started, McCain's staff had ordered a covert submarine operating in the eastern Mediterranean to pull farther back from shore. McCain's aides requested that the admiral also move the spy ship. Unlike the submarine, which fell solely under Navy jurisdiction, the *Liberty* operated at the request of the National Security Agency, with its orders routed through the Joint Chiefs of Staff. If he moved the *Liberty*, McCain risked a clash with the Joint Chiefs or the NSA. He hesitated. "Our staff begged McCain to pull *Liberty*," recalled Rear Admiral Joseph Wylie, Jr., McCain's deputy in London. "He claimed he didn't have the authority. Enough said? He should have. And she was plugged."[281]

Sheck was asked if good intelligence was collected by the *Liberty* prior to the attack. He said not much before June 8th but good information during the morning of the eighth, this according to his conversation with Bennett. Again, we are dealing with document redactions. He indicated they had some good communications over the TRSS moon-bounce system, but for the most part, it was only available for limited use depending on the line of sight to the moon. The system was for use only by the Security Group and not general services that ran the ship.

It did have CRITICOM, critical intelligence community service, directly with NSA.

Sheck's oral history interview was over with two final comments: First, the TRS ships were expensive to operate and generated political turf related issues in terms of command control; and secondly, Gerhard acknowledged that he had access to the "Deeley Report", although it was not called that within NSA. Ennes had tried to get access to it and failed.

John Connell, the NSA representative to the JCS/JRS, gave his oral history interview on September 15, 1980. He was an exchange information officer with the DIA. There are substantial redactions in his OH. Farley, another interviewer, had a question as to whether Connell knew anything about McNamara and President Johnson calling back the planes dispatched in aid of the *Liberty*. Millington noted that there was discussion about scuttling the ship but the water was too shallow, further, General Carter and deputy director, Louis Tordella were incensed at the idea of scuttling the ship. This reference to Dr. Louis W. Tordella being upset with the scuttling idea is because it was allegedly suggested to prevent the news media from getting a looked at the damaged ship. [282]

Somewhat astoundingly, Connell, when asked said he did not know anything about the presence of a U.S. submarine. He noted that his recollection was vague after all these years. Based on Farley's questioning their focus was on the *Andrew Jackson*. Further, when questioned as to whether he had been contacted by Walter Deeley regarding the post mortem on the *Liberty*, Connell said no. Again, while Connell was vague in his recall there were an awful lot of redactions in his OH—he must have known something relevant.

231

Probably the most fruitful point to be made based on Connell's OH was the fact that NSA was either fishing to see what he knew about a submarine assignment, or NSA was not knowledgeable. Who would have been aware based upon the memorandum from the 303 Committee about a sub in UAR waters? Could it have been a CIA operation or something held closely by the JCS? Certainly, the matter of the sub remains a big mystery. One thing is clear and that is interagency communications were lacking and the "need-to-know" game was being played to the hilt—or maybe people wanted to not know and just forget. Connell had indicated when asked if he read Ennes book and he said no, he just wanted to forget—one of the benefits of retirement.

Sheck's boss, Richard Harvey was interviewed for his OH on July 16, 1980 by William Gerhard, Henry Millington and Farley. He was the Chief of K12 at NSA in charge of the Mobile Collection Division that had the tasking responsibilities for both airborne and seaborne platforms. His interview revealed an important point that arose in a question by Millington. Millington who advised they came across a report that the Israelis eventually turned over to the State Department in which they frankly admitted that their reconnaissance forces did know before the attack that this was a U.S. ship, specifically the *Liberty*. "But they, like our own command channels, the word never got down to the operating forces. As a result, the attack did occur." Of course, we have already covered the air recon and the plotting of the *Liberty*.

Interestingly, Farley asks Harvey if there was any targeting of the Israelis, and his answer was "I don't think so and I don't know why [redaction]." Farley asks why Israeli military communications were not targeted, and

232

why no Israeli linguists were on board. Harvey: "We wouldn't have had any need for it." This sort of response prompts this author to ponder the real nature of the ship's mission. Was it to serve as an auxiliary communication link to the submarine known as Contact X? Capt. McGonagle as previously noted had requested a military escort from Vice Admiral Martin that would also act as an auxiliary communication link, to what, the *Liberty* or again to Contact X. Attempting to penetrate this fog is not easy after all these years—the mission mystery deepens.

Gerhard questions Harvey on whether he was involved in setting up the processing center at Athens airport and he says yes. Gerhard then notes that a [redacted] linguist was sent there from NSA. Harvey responds yes because there was some airborne collection from "that target" [quotes are mine]. Finally, Millington asks Harvey if there were any other mobile collectors in the area and he says "None that I remember" [redaction]. He was asked would he know and he says yes because that "...was also in our shop". The assumption is the reference is to a submarine.

There were at least 10 Soviet submarines in the Mediterranean so it makes sense that the U.S. also had subs there and should have had intelligence operations at their peak effort. Again, what was the mission of Contact X if in fact there was such a thing as Ennes has reported? The United States Navy in conjunction with the CIA and NSA had a program code-named *Holystone* during the Cold War. The focus was primarily on the Soviet Union and its submarine fleet. U.S. subs involved in the program were charged with ELINT and SIGINT collection for processing at the NSA. The media divulged this highly secret program.[283] In short, it would

233

make sense to have such an operation following Soviet submarines in the Mediterranean during the lead up to Six-Day War and afterward. Contact X could have been a *Holystone* operation after having read Peter Sasgen's, *Stalking the Red Bear: The True Story of a U.S. Cold War Submarine's Covert Operations Against the Soviet Union.*

One of the most controversial things about Contact X is the reporting of a periscope around the time of the attack. The attack was allegedly filmed, and the film was transported securely to Washington D.C.[284] The fact is that the *Liberty* was attacked so early in its mission that it had little chance to carry it out, but was the perception of "a mission" a threat sufficient to warrant the Israelis to take action?

Yitzhak Rabin in his memoirs states, "With the outbreak of the fighting on June 5, we notified the American Naval Attaché in Israel that we intended to protect our shores from Egyptian naval attacks by employing a combination of naval and air units... We therefore asked that American ships be removed from the vicinity of the Israeli shore or that the Americans notify us of their precise location in the area near our coast. In the storm of battle, there was no time to check whether or not our request had been fulfilled."[285]

Information reveals that there was a codeword operation that originated at the top of our government in what was called the "303 Committee". It was composed of a representatives of the CIA, NSA and the DOD among others. Richard Helms, CIA Director, when asked about the committee said it was to approve covert operations and provide the president with a certain amount of plausible deniability.[286] National Security

Action Memorandum 303, dated June 2, 1964, addressed to the Secretary of State among others changed the name of Special Group 5412 established during the Eisenhower administration to the "303 Committee". According to the memorandum the composition, function and responsibility of the group or committee as authorized by NSC 5412/2, dated December 28, 1955 was to remain the same. The name of this group varies from time-to-time, around 1974 it was the "40 Committee" and at one time was headed by Henry Kissinger.[287]

Under the Johnson administration the 303 Committee supported paramilitary and political operations in Tibet directed against the Chinese—success was apparently minimal and the program terminated. Under President Nixon and Henry Kissinger diplomatic overtures toward China was the new policy objective. The purpose of the 303 Committee was to be a rubber stamp for well-advanced CIA plans. Whether as "Special Group 5412" or "303", a question arises to what extent CIA assassination plans against Cuba's Fidel Castro in the early '60s were discussed by the committee and thereby approved or disapproved. The history of such covert operational plans is beyond the scope of this book except to the extent that the USS *Liberty* may have been caught up in this process.

A declassified document was released through the LBJ Library dated 10 April 1967 the subject of which was the redacted minutes of the "303 Committee" meeting of April 7, 1967. Present at the meeting was Johnson's national security advisor Walt Rostow, Ambassador Kholer, Cyrus Vance and Admiral Taylor assistant director of the CIA. Two topics were discussed but only one topic was disclosed in the document. That had to do with a briefing to the committee on a sensitive DOD

235

project known as "FRONTLET 615". After discussion, the project was approved. There is a handwritten notation on the document: "Submarine within UAR waters."

What is important about this document is that it confirms a codename operation "Frontlet 615". The reference to the submarine maybe to the submarine known as Contact X referred to by Ennes in his book. There is a reference to "900 series collectors" in one of the NSA Oral Histories on the NSA website related to questions about a submarine. I am advised that "900" operations are still considered classified.[288] Whether this relates to the *Holystone* code-name is unknown by this author. The reference to "Frontlet 615" is the vaguest tip of a long hidden iceberg suspected of dealing with a cooperative plan between the CIA and Israeli Mossad that evolved into the Six-day War. The oral history statement about the 900 series collector came from Commander "Bud" C. Fossett on 15 May 1980. He served as the G Group operations or service officer at the NSA during the *Liberty* crisis. He related that an officer he dealt with at NFOIO expressed his concern about the safety of the submarine, and the person said, "You guys just keep the information flowing, we'll take care of that." My interpretation is that we are again dealing with the need-to-know constraint, otherwise butt out. Therefore, it might be assumed that NSA had nothing to do with the submarine that it was under another jurisdiction and mission. The NFOIO acronym most likely stands for Naval Field Operational Intelligence Office. While Fossett in his NSA capacity coordinated with them that does not mean information on the operation was shared. It would appear that the Navy wanted technical assistance from the NSA. The fact that the "submarine" was a naval issue is confirmed by the previous reference to Admiral McCain.

A police department is a semi-military type organization and many of the same rules apply to police operations on a need-to-know basis. The communication problems begin when others cross operations not knowing who-is-who and who is doing what. Coupled with turf issues, the organization can experience all types of problems. In police work, such events could result in "friendly fire" situations, for example during drug raids. In Fossett's interview on this point the name of the submarine *Andrew Jackson* was speculated on in the context of a code name, however, Fossett was vague on this point or could not recall.

Assuming there was in fact a submarine, how would its mission dovetail with that of the *Liberty*? Was the *Liberty* to be the communication link between the Joint Chiefs of Staff and other interested parties? Until recently, submarines had limited communication capabilities when submerged, especially if there were concern about a potential nuclear confrontation. Generally, the sub needs to be at periscope depth to communicate via satellite or otherwise. There was a long-wire system called ELF.[289]

The U.S. Navy operates two extremely low frequency radio transmitters to communicate with its deep diving submarines. The sites are at Clam Lake, Wisconsin and Republic, Michigan and are operated by the Naval Computer and Telecommunications Area Master Station—Atlantic. The Clam Lake site, located in the Chequamegon National Forest in Northern Wisconsin, is the site where testing began for ELF communications more than 30 years ago. This site has more than 28 miles

237

of over-head signal transmission lines that form a part of an "electrical" antenna to radiate the ELF signal from the two-acre transmitting facility.

Author, A Jay Cristol in a paper discusses covert intelligence resources in the Middle East. His conjecture was that a submarine of that era could operate at periscope depth to obtain VHF/UHF communications from the coastal areas of the Mediterranean. The question is what would the sub do once it collected intelligence data, how would it transmit it to say the NSA? Was the *Liberty* such a transmission link using the TRSSCOMM system? While Cristol pinpoints the USS *Amberjack* (SS-522) as the suspect sub, others speculate on other subs as being Contact X. Further, Cristol quotes a Chief Petty Officer who was onboard the *Amberjack* as saying she collected signals data but did not transmit it for fear of compromising the mission. Cristol doubts that the *Liberty* was the communication link. We do not know the working situation in part because perhaps the survivors of the attack are just not talking or they don't know because of compartmentalization of the ships SIGINT gathering function. In addition, there was a large number to personnel killed in the research section of the ship—secrets may have stayed with the deceased.

The ELF system is the only way to communicate with the submarines through deep water that is highly secure and essential in the event of a nuclear threat or war. Initial research was conducted on such a system between 1958 and 1963 and was called Project Sanquine.[290] Whether it was operational during the Six-Day War is problematic. It may not have been operational during the Cuban missile crisis. Important question: Did the Six-Day War have a nuclear component? Let the question float for a while in the reader's mind.

238

Some individuals perceived that the Israeli's, and we in the 60s, were friends and allies—in the real world that may be naiveté. Our relationship with Israel was still evolving at the time of the Six-Day War. The Israelis were and are extremely security conscious and had come to learn not to rely solely on any super-power. When it came to the bottom line, they were responsible alone for their defense and survival even though they depended on others to provide weapons and technology. Prime Minister Netanyahu meeting with President Obama has recently reaffirmed the Israeli position in a visit over the Iranian nuclear issue. Netanyahu said Israel has the right to defend itself and is "the master of its fate".[291] The Israeli position remains as it was at the time of the attack on the *Liberty*.

So once the war had begun the presence of a "spy ship" so close to their military operations could prove to be a hindrance to their war plan where time was of the essence. Notwithstanding perception and the potential of the *Liberty's* mission, the reality is that it did not get much chance to obtain worthwhile intelligence, and in fact was a failed mission, or was it? In researching the *Liberty* story, it is my impression that those who reported on it early on were mostly likely to have a "feel" for events concurrent with them happening. For example, one author who helps to shed light on the scope of the *Liberty* mission is Richard Deacon who wrote a book entitled *The Israeli Secret Service.*[292]

Richard Deacon falls into the category of early reporters on the *Liberty* attack that includes Anthony Pearson who claimed a contact with someone close to British intelligence.[293] Deacon was born in Wales and served in the Royal Navy in WWII. His duties involved fieldwork for then Deputy Director of Naval Intelligence, Ian Fleming of the *James Bond* genre of books and movies. Deacon wrote about British, Russian and Chinese secret services and was a correspondent for the British *Sunday Times*. His real name was Donald McCormick. He devotes a chapter in his book to the Six-Day War. Like many authors, he touched upon the *Liberty* as incidental to the war and the events in the Middle East.

His take on things was that on June 7 the Israelis occupied Jerusalem, the Holy City that they have coveted historically speaking. This was accomplished by "cooking" messages that caused Jordan to enter the war, wherein Israel attacked the Jordanians West of the Jordon River. However, on the night of June 7 the Mossad and Aman knew that their deception plan was exposed to the Americans. Deacon claims that the Israeli ambassador was called to the State Department and told that the Israeli attack must stop as a cease-fire was to be ordered by the UN at the request of the UAR. The Israeli ambassador tried to protest but was informed that the United States was aware that Jordan had been deceived by fake Israeli transmissions. Therefore, *Liberty* posed a threat to Israel's continuing war plan.[294] The question was how did the State Department know? Deacon points to either a satellite or a "spy ship" that could have been the source, or could it have been Contact X. This raises the question as to whether different branches of our government were operating at cross-purposes; did the State Department know what James Jesus Angleton was doing at the CIA?

Anthony Pearson reports that the *Liberty's* primary mission was to liaison with the submarine, USS *Andrew Jackson*. He notes that both ships were ordered to move

240

closer to land. Information was then passed to the NSA and Security Council at the UN.[295] Israel was in a time bind since action was pending in the UN to bring an end to hostilities before Israel could accomplish it "military goals". The insinuation here is that the war goals were not articulated by the Eshkol government, but rather by accomplishments in the field because of Israeli intelligence efforts and the IDF.

While Deacon cites June 7, the *Liberty* would have been collecting all along its route to Point Alfa. While a good reception point was off Crete, the *Liberty's* mission called for "line-of-sight" positioning off the coast. Ennes reports that Captain McGonagle and Lieutenant Dave Lewis discussed whether it would compromise the mission if the ship pulled back to a safer distance, as the Captain had reservations about being so close to a war zone. It was determined that the ship should stay on its course. Lewis wanted to work the UHF range of frequencies and needed a line of sight.[296] According to Bamford, the *Valdez* had conducted "hear ability" studies and found Crete to be a good location in which to operate.[297]

Now, the speculation begins to get into the area of motive that is reserved for the next chapter, but the mission angle is the collecting of intelligence regardless from whatever source and by whatever method.

When it comes to defining the ship's mission, even Jim Ennes is vague as I previously noted. In his book he indexes "mission" under the topic *Liberty* noting that as a "Technical Research Ship", the mission was to look into electromagnetic phenomena which was a cover story with most people including the media knowing the ship was pure and simple a "spy ship". Generally, he simply notes

241

the ship as an "intelligence" ship and on an intelligence mission. However, when it came to a question of the *Liberty's* safety in a war zone, Ennes noted that CINCUSNAVEUR warned of a need for protection, "...instructed us cryptically to use the Research Operation's Department's 'special capabilities' for early warning of possible danger, and advised that we could move to safer water if conditions became hazardous."[298]
He notes a reference to eavesdropping on "their" communications, meaning Israel and Egypt. However, when it came to the point of trying to get information on Contact X, Jim, queried his bunk mate Jim O'Connor what "X" represented, Ennes concluded he didn't have a need to know or the security clearance even though he was in charge of maintaining intelligence equipment.[299]
He reports that the press, after the attack, quoted an officer on the USS *America* as saying: "To put it bluntly, she was there to spy for us. Russia does the same thing. We moved in close to monitor the communications of both Egypt and Israel. We have to. We must be informed of what's going on in a matter of seconds."[300] Then a message came out of the Pentagon telling everyone to be quiet and go "no comment" and that it was not acceptable to answer questions about spying.

True or not, the person quoted was on target. In this modern age of nuclear weapons, the military does need to know the intelligence situation "in a matter of seconds". The need-to-know involves the complete picture not just snap shots allowing for the sensitiveness of allies. This was perhaps never truer since as we will see we came close to a nuclear confrontation more hazardous than the Cuban missile crisis of October 1962.

The *Liberty's* supposed mission does not really have to be further defined in the context of understanding the motivation for any attack. She was in fact a spy ship and she was in international waters close to two combatants, both Egypt and Israel in a rapidly developing war. Our government at the top levels, including the CIA and NSA knew something that was a closely guarded secret. That is that the State of Israel was in haste to develop nuclear weapons. The project location that our government knew about because of U-2 flights and other information was that Dimona in the Negev desert was a nuclear research and weapons development facility. Something that Israel tried to pass off as an agriculture and water desalinization facility. The only question is whether Israel had actually produced even crude devices leading into the Six-Day War. The concern would be that if for some reason the state was in danger of losing the war it would rely on a nuclear device to fend off the Egyptians and perhaps their Soviet benefactors, or at least have the "threat" of usage. It is not my intent to go into the history of Israel's nuclear program, which is marked by a policy of denial, saying that Israel would not be the first to introduce nuclear weapons in the Middle East. As we will see, three nations had nuclear capability in this war in the Mediterranean, Russia, the United States, and Israel not to mention France and Britain.

Now whether or not the White House and Defense Department considered the issue of Dimona, it certainly is something that should be expected. CIA Director Richard Helms is alleged to have stated that he knew of no nuclear capability in the Mediterranean during the Six-Day War. Talk about "misinformation". Somewhere in the intelligence community, this facility had to be monitored for a couple reasons. First, the site of the reactor was guarded by U.S. supplied Hawk missiles and French missiles. There was serious contention between President Kennedy and David Ben-Gurion over the Dimona site that was irretraceable and a serious irritation between them. The inner government of Israel was very concerned about the security of this facility as a "state jewel". In short, it would have been militarily irresponsible not to be monitoring Israel's war progression, also, in part because of discussions and cease fire pressures arising in the UN. Again, we have the seeds of a developing cover-up.

Israel may have had at least two crude nuclear weapons at the time of the Six-Day War. There was contention between Kennedy and Ben-Gurion as noted; however, it appears that President Johnson was also concerned with Israel's nuclear program. It is something that warranted monitoring regardless of any other covert operational plan existing between the CIA and Mossad directed at removing Nasser. Positioned as it was off the Sinai, was the *Liberty* and Contact X to monitor the Israeli nuclear site at Dimona? Geographically speaking the *Liberty's* position was the best for monitoring electronic signals from the Dimona site. This is a technical question considering the state of the *Liberty's* onboard electronics of the period. It is not my intent to be bogged down in technical detail, suffice to say that the nuclear issue warranted monitoring. The EC-121 and C-130 were not about to do ELINT over-flights of Dimona for fear of being shot at by guarding missile systems. U-2 flights may have been conduct but at such safe heights where photographic capabilities were possible but not ELINT.

In the aftermath of the attack the cover-up would begin to develop at NSA through the management of

Walter G. Deeley, a senior Defense Department executive of "super grade" rank who been charged with putting together a report on the attack. [301] He prompted others in the room to explain why ship was sent in harmsway. One person (Fossett) started by saying "The *Liberty* was sent into the eastern Mediterranean to provide VHF and UHF communication coverage." In fact, Fossett was involved in tasking the *Liberty's* mission. Nowhere will there be any mention of concern about Israeli's potential nuclear capability in any government inquiry about the events of June 8. The next question for the group was why it was necessary to send the ship in so close to the coast. Ennes reports that the Freedom of Information Act has failed to produce any government acknowledgement of the existence of the Deeley report.[302] As for Deeley, Cristol quotes him as saying "There would have been no reason to inform the [U.S.] embassy since she was sent to the area prior to hostilities, was a non-belligerent, and had every right to be where she was." Certainly, this begs the question in view of what happened.

Perhaps a more complex mission is suggested by Richard Deacon regarding his suggestion of a joint CIA/Mossad operational plan for the Six-Day War to get rid of Nasser. Neither side fully trusted the other, nor did the CIA want the *Liberty* to keep it abreast of every Israeli move? Deacon states: "The *Liberty's* assignment was to supply detailed intelligence on both Arab and Israeli movements on land, sea and air and signals traffic to the National Security Agency in Washington. Bamford adds that the JCS wanted to know about Soviet troops in Egypt and the deployment of Soviet missiles.[303] But the Israelis had not been informed of this."[304] This brings us back to the Israeli warning to move the ship or she would be sunk!

The ship's mission needs to be viewed in the larger context of strategic interests of the United States government and the President's National Security Council perspective and purview. Did the U.S. have the resources and ability to manage two major conflicts, the war in Vietnam and the developing Middle East crisis? President Johnson did not believe Congress would give him approval to engage the military in support of Israel.

There is an interesting and enlightening five page *Memorandum for the Record* located on the George Washington University's National Security Archive website dealing with the topic of the Israeli "bomb".[305] The source of the memo is the LBJ Library. The memo is dated May 24, 1967 just days before the outbreak of the Six-Day War. We need to look at that memo since it puts in context the issues facing the U.S. government as the Middle East crisis evolved.

Fifteen members were listed as present by name including President Johnson, Secretary of State Dean Rusk and Secretary of Defense Robert McNamara. The Director of the CIA, Richard Helms, was not listed as one of the attendees. Secretary of State, Dean Rusk, briefed the meeting noting the situation in the Middle East "as serious but not yet desperate". Reference was made to meetings of the UN Security Council and some report of flexibility on the part of Egypt that might relieve pressure arising because of the Egyptian blockade of the Straits of Tiran, with the caveat that Israel might not be interested in concessions that would head off a conflict.

It was noted that the U.S. was in touch with the USSR and "privately we find the Russians playing a generally moderate game", while publically taking a harsh line blaming both the U.S. and Israel for the Middle East

Crisis. The extent of Soviet support for Syria and Cairo was an unresolved issue. The Gulf of Aqaba was the main issue. The Johnson administration contemplated breaking the Egyptian blockade with the assistance of Britain and France but this option did not materialize. Rusk was of the impression that no government wanted war.

President Johnson noted, "I want to play every card in the UN, but I've never relied on it to save me when I'm going down for the third time." He further noted he wanted British Prime Minister Wilson and French President De Gaulle "out there with their ships all lined up too." Johnson was concerned about Congress's support for his policies in Vietnam. He parenthetically noted that key members of Congress, in particular from the Senate, did not believe that the U.S. could handle two crises. The key senators that included Fulbright thought we should get out of Vietnam in which case the choice would be support for Israel. This issue of Congressional support of a Middle East intervention on behalf of Israel would be important from Johnson's viewpoint, as we will see later.

The memo notes that Johnson told Rusk to tell Senator Mike Mansfield "this kind of music in the Senate is just want Kosygin wants to hear." Johnson wanted a military assessment from McNamara who believed the U.S. could handle both Vietnam and the Middle East crisis. Importantly, Johnson then requested a military assessment of our military posture in the Mediterranean and the current disposition of Arab and Israeli forces.

General Wheeler, Chief of the Joint Chiefs of Staff, thought it would be hard to open the Gulf of Aqaba, in part because of two Egyptian submarines operating in the

Red Sea. He noted that "we would need an ASW unit, the nearest of which is now in Singapore—two weeks away". This is a reference to an anti-submarine warfare unit. His conclusion is that Israel would use air power to open the straits and if they moved, it might not be possible to "localize a strike designed simply to open the Straits."

As a side note: Anti-submarine Warfare units could be airborne, surface ships or submarines. It is worth noting that in the memo was a reference to our large naval presence in the Mediterranean; however, no mention was made of the large number of Soviet submarines in the area, or the increasing size of the Soviet armada. The reference to an ASW unit could be to the USS *Davis*, a destroyer that was in the Med and an escort to the aircraft carrier *America*. The destroyers *Davis* and *Massey* were the first ships to arrive to provide help for the *Liberty* the next day after the attack. At any rate, the reference to an ASW unit pertained to the presence of the Egyptian submarines in the Red Sea.

A brief discussion then focused on the possible presence of "unconventional weapons" followed by what are a line and one-half redactions in the memo. It was then noted in the memo that CIA Director Helms "was quite positive in stating there were no nuclear weapons in the area." Whether Helms slipped into the meeting or was quoted is not clear. At any rate, General Wheeler noted he was less well informed "but more skeptical". The Joint Chiefs were responsible for the *Liberty's* deployment.

The above reference seems to connote several concerns: First, what does the CIA director know or not know or is hiding. Secondly, is there an "information gap" within our government at the top of the leadership? Could confusion somehow have an impact on the USS *Liberty* and its mission? It would seem that a pending confrontation of forces with nuclear capability would be a major crisis no less so than the Cuban Missile Crisis of the early '60s. A reference on the National Security Archive website notes: "Helms knew that some in his agency had suspicions about Israel's nuclear status, but he preferred not to raise these concerns at this meeting. Indeed, there are indications that around this time Israel was assembling its first two nuclear weapons."

CIA Director Helms was one of the original members of the CIA stemming from the OSS, along with James Jesus Angleton. Both had worked under "Wild" Bill Donovan the head of the OSS. Helms served most of his spy career in the covert side of the intelligence service.[306] Was he withholding information from the President and other military leaders on the issue of Israel's nuclear capability? Was a covert operation jointly involving our CIA and the Israeli Mossad in the development? Was the CIA complicit in helping Israel develop its nuclear capabilities? As to the latter question, the matter is complex and this author would refer the reader to the two books: The first book is by author Seymore Hersh and is *The Sampson Option*, and the second book is by author Avner Cohen entitled *Israel and the Bomb*.

What the President and U.S. government knew about this issue can be gleamed from a two page telegram from the State Department to Ambassador Barbour dated February 23, 1967 referring to a previous telegram from the Tel Aviv Embassy (A-478) which suggested that "Israel could be much closer to nuclear weapons capability then we had supposed." While President Kennedy was clearly at odds with Israeli Prime Minister

David Ben-Gurion over the Israeli nuclear project at Dimona, it is herein noted that President Johnson was also not keen on a nuclear-armed Israel: "The possibility of nuclear-armed Israel was not welcomed by the Johnson administration which left these reports 'pending' further assessment and verification. In this telegram, the State Department referred to these reports and asked Ambassador Barbour to press Eshkol on the matter of the next American visit to Dimona. It is evident from the cable that Israel had not responded to the American request for the visit since November 1966."[307] The Eshkol government was clearly stalling efforts by the U.S. government to visit the Dimona site.[308]

Strangely, the United States government's position regarding the Israeli nuclear project has for the most part been benign by downplaying the matter and Israel's failure to cooperate by providing information on the project. While not admitting the program, Israel's position has been it would not be the first to introduce nuclear weapons in the region.

A recent article in *Haaretz* dealing with "Former IDF chief reveals new details of Israel's nuclear program" seems to indicate the Israelis were preparing to test a possible nuclear device in the Sinai desert. Lt. General Dov Tamari was advised his mission was to "fly to a high place in the Sinai desert, unload a certain object from the helicopter, activate it and get out fast." Troops who did not know the risk were to be involved for training purposes; however, the demonstration was canceled. *Haaretz* notes few people were privy to this information, one being Israel's sixth chief of staff, Lt. General Tzvi (Chera) Tzur.[309]

The question of the Soviets motivation and intentions in the Middle East were such that it was agreed the Soviets would like and benefit from the United States being embarrassed and diverted from its efforts in Vietnam. In response to a question from the President, General Wheeler noted that a long war would hurt Israel economically. At that point, "we would have to decide whether we were going to send in forces and confront Nasser directly". Based on this quote from the memorandum, Nasser was clearly a target and if we were not in a position to send in military forces, then the obvious option left would be a CIA covert operation—my assumption. General Wheeler was not in favor of providing arms requested by the Israelis including ECM equipment.[310]

Secretary of Defense McNamara saw the situation developing somewhat differently with Israel establishing early air superiority that would deplete aircraft inventories on both sides. He felt that both the U.S. and Soviets would be requested to provide for air support. He felt that the USSR might supply Soviet-piloted aircraft. This latter point does relate to what Ennes said about trying to determine who were flying the Soviet planes supplied to the Egyptians. Therefore, this can be interpreted as being one of *Liberty's* interception objectives.

Getting back to Soviet motives, Helms had stated he felt the Soviets wanted a propaganda victory "as in the 1950's with them as peacemakers and saviors of the Arabs, while we end up fully blackballed in the Arab world as Israel's supporter".

Discussion turned to Nasser's motives, which included a propaganda victory to enhance his position in the Arab world, which prompted Assistant Secretary of State Lucius Battle to speculate that while one would expect Nasser to leave himself a way out, he hadn't done so in this case. He was either crazy or had more Soviet support behind him than "we know about".

The meeting ended with the President wondering whether he would be expected to meet Israeli Foreign Minister Abba Eban. Subsequent meetings with Eban and representatives of Israeli intelligence would raise the issue of whether or not we gave the Israelis the "green light" to attack the Arabs.

Any responsible U.S. politician and military leader would want the best intelligence on what was going on in the Israeli nuclear program considering the pending confrontation between the U.S and Soviet Union who had clearly established an active role in the Middle East as the Arabs prime backer. Anything less would be criminal malfeasance. Unfortunately, while we may assume that the USS *Liberty* and Contact-X "could" have been monitoring the Israeli missile sites and operations to make sure there was no use of nuclear weapons we are left to speculate.

Author Avner Cohen in writing about the Israeli nuclear project challenges Helms on the issue of Israel's nuclear progress. He states, "On the eve of the 1967 war, almost all the components of an Israeli nuclear weapon were in place". He further states that around 1966 the first Israeli explosive device was successfully completed, and that a French-Israeli missile designated MD-620 was in the testing stage, reportedly with some problems in the guidance system.[311] The missile was also known as the *Jericho*. Certainly, this should have been a concern of the U.S. military and political establishment and a target of an intelligence investigation. A key question is where were the missiles sited or to be located.

The Johnson administration, and in particular Rusk, in meetings with Eban in the fall of 1968 dealing with the sale of F4 Skyhawks and discussion on NPT, expressed concern that Israel was developing its nuclear program with the capability of putting nuclear warheads on the Jericho missile.[312] What was or should have been known was now put to the Israelis matter-of-factly, a confrontation they had not been use to since Kennedy objected to the Dimona project.[313] The essential point is that Israel was not cooperating with the United States in terms of providing information about the nuclear program nor its willingness to allow on sight inspections—its policy was denial and obstruction. Israel would not want the U.S. eavesdropping on communications dealing with the program, notwithstanding that in the early stages of the Dimona site development the U.S. had run U-2 over-flights.

Israel's commitment to the MD-620 project was made in 1962 and 1963 in response to the Egyptian ballistic missile program.[314] The French company Marcel Dassasult was the prime contractor, but because of a French arms embargo in 1967 the program was moved to Israel. According to Cohen, missile site development did not start until sometime after the Six-Day War. Nevertheless, it is likely that Israel took possession of a number of missiles, with the *New York Times* reporting the number at 30 missiles. Israel subsequently took over development of what would become Jericho 1 and 2 located 40 km southwest of Tel Aviv with ability to reach targets in Damascus and Cairo. Deployment of the initial

MD-620s is problematic but should have been a concern for the U.S. [315]

From the *Liberty's* designated patrol site off El Arish, could she have been in a position to monitor activities around the Dimona nuclear site? First, the *Liberty* was not suppose to be closer than 12 miles off the Gaza coast; secondly, the elevation of El Arish is approximately 121 feet (36.88) meters at the airport. The distance to Dimona rail station from El Arish is approximately 72.91 miles with the Dimona elevation being an average of 535 meters or 1800 feet. Using Google Explorer the reader can do a fly-over and note that relative flatness between El Arish and Dimona in the Negev desert, taking into account the difference in elevation. Since the *Liberty* had highly sophisticated electronic monitoring equipment, how far could she pick up signals to monitor potential missile sites and communication traffic dealing with the nuclear program? Since Commander Lewis advised Captain McGonagle that he needed a line-of-site for UHF signal reception it is noted that, the limit was line-of-sight.

Perhaps the issue is not what the ship could do, rather what the perception of her capability was in the eyes of an interested party such as Israel. Without a doubt, Israel had no more of a sensitive program than the Dimona project. [316] One author has gone so far as to state her mission was in fact to monitor those missile sites with Contact-X designated to take out the missile sites if Israel was about to launch against Cairo.

The 1981 book *Weapons* by Russell Warren Howe asserts that *Liberty* was accompanied by the Polaris armed Lafayette-class submarine USS *Andrew Jackson*, which filmed the entire episode through its periscope but was unable to provide assistance. According to Howe, "Two hundred feet below the ship, on a parallel course, was its 'shadow'—the Polaris strategic submarine *Andrew Jackson*, whose job was to take out all the Israeli long-range missile sites in the Negev if Tel Aviv decided to attack Cairo, Damascus or Baghdad. This was in order that Moscow would not have to perform this task itself and thus trigger World War Three."[317]

If the observation of Howe seems preposterous, we will later look at what the Soviets were in fact prepared to do to Tel Aviv. Did the special confidential packet dealing with secret orders that was allegedly destroyed in the attack contain information to shed light on this matter—the *Liberty's* mission—we do not know—obviously we can assume it was. When I attempted to raise the nuclear issue with *Liberty* supporters, they were not responsive. The *Liberty's* website listed Howe's book among a list of references so Howe's contentions were previously known to some *Liberty* survivors and researchers, although this author only became aware of it in May of 2010.

Considering General Wheeler's "skepticism" about Helms' contention there were no nuclear weapons in the area, the crew of the *Liberty* was surprised to receive orders from the Joint Chiefs of Staff: "Whoever heard of JCS taking direct control of a ship?...They just said that we'd get further orders at Rota."[318] Obviously, the deployment and mission was not routine! However, the ship's position assignment at Point Alfa was ideal to the mission, considering that over-flights of Israel by aircraft such as the EC-121 were out of the question. The U-2 flights previously noted began in 1958 when the first construction efforts at Dimona were beginning.[319] There

255

well may have been contention within the Johnson defense establishment, evidenced by the JCS, apparently, wanting to retaliate against Israel with a military strike on Haifa that was never carried out. Military and political elements of the government were not necessarily in harmony.

Notwithstanding lingering confusion about the *Liberty's* mission, it is more important to consider what the perception of the mission may have been in the mind of the attacking party, the Israelis, in which case we get into the matter of motive that may help us come to an understanding of whether the attack was intentional or a mistake.

The Israelis called us up one day and said, "If you don't get that ship, the Liberty, out of this place we're going to sink it in twenty-four hours."

John P. Stenbit, Department of Defense.

Chapter 9

Motive

The determination of motive is or should be an inherent component in most investigative research into human actions and decisions. It is problematic in the sense it involves the mind and the will of the actors in determining why this or that was done. It has far-reaching implications and consequences. For example, the United States dropped two atomic bombs on Japan during the war in the Pacific. Was the purpose or motive to end the war with minimal American casualties, or was it to demonstrate our superiority over the Soviets in the lead-up to the Cold War; or could it have been a combination thereof. When nations act, the ramifications are far reaching and long lasting as compared to individual actions. However, that does not necessarily hold true because the actions of individual world leaders has the propensity to drag nations along behind them such as a Hitler or Stalin—criminal dictators, or other strong and charismatic leaders. Actions coupled with motive lead to issues of right or wrong in a range of responsibility and culpability—characteristics of civilized society. In the case of the Middle East, we are still dealing with the consequences of the Six-Day War in terms of borders, land appropriation, settlement encroachments, and refugee issues.

Then there are those leaders, even in a democracy, who lie to the population and conjure up pretexts to lead a country into war. The "pretext" for action becomes intertwined with motive and becomes a manipulative tool to bring about an end result such as getting the population to support the government effort—the war. The effect can be to side step the Rule of Law, or in the case of the United States the Constitution. In most regimes, the current leader has immunity while in office unless impeached or otherwise overthrown. Motives affect behavior:[320]

> Thus, although "motive" is not an essential element of any charge, claim, or defense, evidence that a person has a particular motive can be relevant to an ultimate fact in both civil and criminal cases. The variety of circumstances in which motive might be relevant is endless, and thus any effort to catalog the possibilities would fail. The principle, however, is basic and simple: When motive is relevant, evidence tending to show its existence is usually admissible, subject to exclusion if the risk of unfair prejudice is too great.

A good place to start with the examination of motive is with Jim Ennes's book. On page 141, he refers to the following article in *Newsweek*:[321]

> SINKING OF THE LIBERTY: ACCIDENT
> OR DESIGN?
> The Israeli attack on the naval communications ship U.S.S. Liberty has left a wake of bitterness and political charges of the most serious sort. First of all, the Liberty was no ordinary vessel but an intelligence-

gathering ship on a "ferret" mission. It carried elaborate gear to locate both Israeli and Egyptian radio and radar and to monitor and tape all military messages sent from command posts to the battlefield. Although Israel's apologies were officially accepted, some high Washington officials believe the Israelis knew the Liberty's capabilities and suspect that the attack might not have been accidental. One top-level theory holds that someone in the Israeli armed forces ordered the Liberty sunk because he suspected that it had taken down messages showing that Israel started the fighting. (A Pentagon official has already tried to shoot down the Israeli claim of "pilot error.") Not everyone in Washington is buying this theory, but some top Administration officials will not be satisfied until fuller and more convincing explanations of the attack on a clearly marked ship in international waters are forthcoming.

Ennes notes that this article circulated even before the Naval Court of Inquiry went into session looking into the matter. The controversy was such that the article upset Israeli Chief of Staff Rabin and it drew an immediate reaction from the Israeli government:[322]

Such allegations are just malicious. Such stories are untrue and without any foundation whatever. It was an unfortunate and tragic accident which occurred in an area where fierce land and air fighting took place in recent days.

Undoubtedly, Rabin was personally upset as he had been under a lot of stress, in fact it was alleged that prior to the war he had a near nervous breakdown but was able to pull himself together. This information was kept from the Israeli public, and was confirmed by none other than General Ezer Weizman who had been summoned to Rabin's house where he found the Chief of Staff "silent and still" and depressed. Rabin was concerned about endangering the state by his mistakes and offered Weizman his position.[323]

While not critical to the discussion of motive, another issue is relevant. That is that the contention that the United States had been warned to keep its intelligence ships away. On the evening of June 7, the NSA learned from an intelligence report emanating from the Office of the U.S. Defense Attaché in Tel Aviv that if the *Liberty* did not change course Israel was planning to attack her.[324]

Ennes in his book reports that a CIA Naval Master Chief who had lost friends in the attack told him that the attack was no real surprise to the CIA. The man said, "Sending *Liberty* to Gaza was a calculated risk from the beginning." Further, "Israel had told us long before the war to keep our intelligence ships away from her coast. *Liberty* was sent anyway because we just did not think they were serious. We thought they might send a note of protest, or at most, harass the ship somehow. We didn't think they would really try to sink her." As will be noted shortly, author Richard Deacon raises the issue of whether the CIA was complicit in interdicting warning messages for whatever reason resulting in the failure to recall the ship. Ennes reports that there "was" a note or protest by the Israelis to move the ship, but he cannot deliver any proof and his statements fall into the realm of hearsay.[325]

An American official from the Department of Defense, John P. Stenbit, Secretary of Defense for C3I made the following statement at a seminar at Harvard University:[326]

> The Israelis called us up one day and said, "If you don't get that ship, the Liberty, out of this place we're going to sink it in twenty-four hours." We couldn't tell the ship to move when we got the data back because it was already under the water, because it took more than twenty-four hours for the data to wander in through the system and come out at the other end.

To be technically correct, while this may be called hearsay absent corroboration, nevertheless, hearsay is allowed to establish probable cause that an event did occur. In law enforcement, hearsay is allowed to obtain arrest warrants and search warrants; and is allowed in court proceedings pursuant to certain rules dealing with the exceptions to the Hearsay Rule barring such evidence. There are two underlying evidentiary issues, credibility and the propensity for prejudice. This is not an academic discussion because all Israeli reviews of the attack failed to find even a *prima facie* case for negligence. The final Israeli review was by military judge, Col. Yeshayahu Yerushalmi, who found the Israelis acted reasonably and actually put the blame on the *Liberty* for events. Yerushalmi is quoted, "I have not discovered any deviation from the standard of reasonable conduct which would justify a court martial."[327] One can refer to his written report and findings dated July 21, 1967.[328]

Just as our government moved quickly to contain and suppress information about the attack via a short and quick Naval Court of Inquiry, with no Congressional hearing on the attack itself, so did the Israeli government contain the fallout within their military establishment.

The fact is that there was a frantic effort to have the *Liberty* pulled back to 100 miles from the coast but such recall messages were not received in time, as they were misdirected. The United States Congress as previously noted investigated the communication fiasco; however, there has been no published congressional investigation into the circumstances of the attack itself—there is a distinction to make here. As Ennes points out in his book, the failure of our government to act in a timely manner to the threat would be sufficient grounds in itself to cause some to want to cover-up the embarrassment for their failure to save the ship and crew especially in the context of the plane recall.

On the subject of a warning, another ominous element further complicates the subject of the attack. Author Richard Deacon writes that the Israelis broke the *Liberty's* ciphers and that U.S. Naval Intelligence knew that; and he claims from the Israeli viewpoint the ship had to be put out of action. He further reports that the ship's crew never received the message of the Joint Chiefs of Staff authorizing a pullback. He notes that the message was sent by the CIA and was misrouted. He states another message was routed through a CIA post, sent by mistake to another CIA office in Port Lyautey in Morocco. Deacon questions: "Did the Israelis have an agent inside the CIA who was able to cause the signal to be lost? Improbable, perhaps, but it is not an impossible solution to the mystery."[329] The contention is that there were many in the military at this time that were in simpatico with the Israelis because of the treatment of Jews by Hitler prior to and during the Second World

262

War. Is this another example that the JCS and CIA were not on the same page of the game book. The JCS wanted to retaliate for the attack by bombing the port from which the torpedo boats originated; however, cooler heads prevailed and the covered-up moved forward. As Deacon noted such a response would have suited the Russians and their Arab proxies from a propaganda standpoint and sabotaged CIA-Mossad-Aman co-operation. Such a wound could have damaged our Middle East policy for years to come. In short, the Soviets would have won the "intelligence war". [330]

Deacon's question seems to implicate the CIA in a conspiracy to set the USS *Liberty* and crew up, more on this later as we are getting ahead of ourselves. The following is an excerpt from author A. Jay Cristol's book. [331]

> Without offering any source or authority for the claim, Findley asserts that CIA had learned a day before the attack that the Israelis planned to sink the ship. Captain McGonagle had heard this tale and was troubled by it. This author arranged a three-way telephone conversation between Captain McGonagle, this author, and the 1967 CIA chief of station at the U.S. Embassy at Tel Aviv. The CIA chief of station (who asks not to be identified by name) confirmed to Captain McGonagle that there was no record supporting that story and that he, who was closely involved, knew nothing about it.

Coupled with the issue of motive is the concept of "MO" or method-of-operation. In criminal law there is a concept that if the identity of a suspect is unknown, his "signature method of operation", or action, over a number of events can be used in court to establish identity and intent. The example would be a serial rapist or murderer with a pattern of unique "signature" actions. Israel has a reputation for acting brutally on the battlefield and giving no quarter nor admitting any wrong such as war crimes of which there have been many complaints over the years.[332] Refer to the harsh and deadly treatment of Indian Peace Keepers at the start of the war reported by James Bamford. The description of the needless killing of 14 Indian peacekeepers, flying the UN flag, by an Israeli tank column can be found in Bamford's book and the chapter *Blood* on page 201. He notes; one Indian officer called it deliberate, cold-blooded killing of unarmed UN soldiers. It would be a sign of things to come, referring to the Six-Day War.

Author Noam Chomsky noted for being particularly critical of both Israel and the United States when it comes to the Middle East foreign policy, describes our and Israel's subscription to the "Madman Theory":[333]

> "The fact that some elements" of the US government "may appear to be potentially 'out of control' can be beneficial to creating and reinforcing fears and doubts within the minds of an adversary's decision-makers." The report resurrects Nixon's "madman theory": our enemies should recognize that we are crazed and unpredictable, with extraordinary destructive force at our command, so they will bend to our will in fear. The concept was apparently devised in Israel in the 1950s by the governing Labor Party, whose leaders "preached in favor of acts of madness," Prime Minister Moshe Sharett records in his diary,

264

warning that "we will go crazy" ("*nishtagea*") if crossed, a "secret weapon" aimed in part against the US, not considered sufficiently reliable at the time.

Washington's support for Saddam reached such an extreme that it was even willing to overlook an Iraqi air force attack on the USS *Stark*, killing 37 crewmen, a privilege otherwise enjoyed only by Israel (in the case of the USS *Liberty*)[334]. It was Washington's decisive support for Saddam, well after the crimes that now so shock the administration and Congress that led to Iranian capitulation to "Baghdad and Washington," Dilip Hiro concludes in his history of the Iran-Iraq war. [335] The two allies had "co-ordinate[d] their military operations against Tehran." The shooting down of an Iranian civilian airliner by the guided-missile cruiser USS *Vincennes* was the culmination of Washington's "diplomatic, military, and economic campaign" in support of Saddam, he writes.[336]

The application of the *Nishtagea Theory* can be viewed in the context of our post 9/11 era. The United States, under the Bush/Cheney administration, implemented torture as a matter of its "hidden policy" in the war on terror, as well as circumventing the Geneva Convention when it was convenient—conducting renditions and the existence of "black sites" to hold detainees. Did the *Liberty* fall prey to Israel's application of the doctrine? The old saying is "all is fair in love and war"; so does that mean that civilized nations ignore the Rule of Law, the Rules of War and conventions like Geneva, as they deem appropriate? In essence, the end justifies the means. The message is, do not end up on the losing side as happened to the Germans and Japanese during the Second World War with resultant war crimes tribunals and executions. Contrast that with the many claims of war crimes against the G.W. Bush/Cheney administration that seem to be going nowhere.

In October of 2011, Amnesty International requested that Canadian authorities arrest G. W. Bush during a visit to that country.[337]

> Amnesty International today urged Canadian authorities to arrest and either prosecute or extradite former US President George W. Bush for his role in torture, ahead of his expected visit to Canada on 20 October. "Canada is required by its international obligations to arrest and prosecute former President Bush given his responsibility for crimes under international law including torture," said Susan Lee, Americas Director at Amnesty International.

We can come up with several motives for the attack in the context of the Six-Day war and we will look at each separately. Dayan will contend that the Six-Day War was won because of intelligence work, and James Bamford, the author, will note in his book *Body of Secrets* that the Israeli war plan was based on lies, in accord with the motto of the Israeli Mossad, which is *wage war by way of deception*. Was the United States ready to deal with an alliance with the State of Israel on equal terms, or was there a lack of experience in dealing in that venue, with a certain naïveté, the result being that the *Liberty* and crew were caught in the middle? Did our government, in particular the CIA through James Jesus Angleton, at the

CIA Israeli desk, defer too much to the Mossad and other Israeli intelligence agencies to direct our Middle East policy?

Author James Bamford offers one alleged motive for the attack on the *Liberty*. He reports on the slaughter of over 1000 Egyptian prisoners of war in the Sinai, because it was too difficult to take care of them. He put Ariel Sharon near this situation and says the Israeli leadership was totally indifferent, including Chief of Staff Rabin and the Minister of Defense, Moshe Dayan. The author fixes the date as June 8 in the shadow of the mosque at El Arish with the *Liberty* off shore able to pick up communications from Israeli commanders.[338] Sharon would become the Prime Minister of Israel, and one who had a reputation for alleged war crimes and complaints against him, in particular in the Lebanon occupation. He was also involved in the creation of Unit 101 authorized by General Moshe Dayan. Qibya was a major turning point as to whether the Middle East would see peace or continued hostilities. Moshe Sharett, Israeli foreign minister at the time of the Qibya massacre accused the Israeli military establishment of a cover-up.[339]

Another motive would be interference with the Israeli war plan aimed at the seizure of land. Israel lied about Egypt attacking first, Eban lied to LBJ to get US involved.[340] Land seized was the coveted old City of Jerusalem, the Golan Heights, and the Sinai, which eventually was returned to Egypt in the peace agreement between Egypt and Israel when Menachem Begin was Prime Minister. Again, the whole war effort on the part Israel was based on intelligence and deception. Any intelligence gathering effort by the U.S. directed at "the plan" would be detrimental to Israel to say the least. Was the U.S. government subject to Israeli deception? To paraphrase Charles de Gaulle of France: *Nations do not have friends, only interests.*[341]

In conjunction with the interference in the overall war plan, President Johnson had admonished the Israelis not to be the first to start the war. The big lie was that it was Egypt and Nasser that wanted to start a war with Israel.

Perhaps one of the most intriguing motives for attacking the *Liberty* was the Israeli fear that the U.S. Intelligence community and White House would learn that messages between Egypt and Jordon were "cooked" to fake messages that pulled Jordon into the war contrary to the wishes of Washington. The U.S. government favored Jordon and did not want it or Syria involved in the war effort.[342]

One of the first sources for the story about the "cooking" of communications was author Richard Deacon. He had noted that the *Liberty's* mission was to supply detailed intelligence on both the Arabs and Israel and that Israel was not told about this. However, once the war started, the Israelis broke the ciphers for both the Egyptians and Jordanians, and Israel because of the better intelligence was able to feed false information to the enemy. The author reports that in a relay station, in the Sinai, radio messages from Cairo to Amman were being blocked and "cooked" and re-routed to Amman. The gist of the plan was to give the impression that the war was going well for the Egyptians. The plan was to create confusion telling King Hussein that the Israelis were gaining ground, but that the Egyptians were counter-attacking in the Sinai and needed support from the Jordanians by an attack on Israeli positions in the Hebron area.[343] Pulling Jordon into the war was justified as a pretext, allowing Israel to attack and claim land still occupied by them today on the West Bank.

What the Israelis were risking, while their plan worked perfectly, was that the Americans would be upset with Jordon entering the war, and the possibility of the Soviets intervening on the part of Egypt or Syria. Involvement would also include the United Nations demanding a cease-fire shortening the time for Israel to obtain its objectives. Therefore, *Liberty* could have shown that the Israelis were in violation of a UN cease-fire order.[344]

Author Anthony Pearson also reports that information relayed from the *Liberty* was getting to the UN Security Council.[345] What is interesting is if one follows the various authors dealing with the topic of the *Liberty* a side mystery develops. Who printed what first and what is their underlying source? Pearson published his book in 1978, a year prior to Ennes's book. One has to use the bibliography and notes section of Deacon's book to find out when he published, most likely it was after 1977 according to a review of his endnotes. Some of these books from the '70s fail to contain footnotes, endnotes, or even a bibliography, although Deacon's book does. In Deacon's case, there is no named publisher or copyright date. He may have self-published. In addition, some of these books are out of publication and might bring a good price on the used book market. One might suspect that Pearson's book came after Deacon's or maybe it was vice-versa.

At any rate, Pearson reports that the "cooked" messages were reconstructed to show not that Egypt was getting beat, and hard pressed to give King Hussein support in the area of the West Bank. Rather, the reconstructed message was to inform Hussein that three-quarters of the Israeli Air Force had been destroyed over Cairo and that the "300-plus aircraft he was now picking up on radar approaching Jordan were Egyptian jets sent to raid targets in Israel."[346] The fact was they were Israeli aircraft returning from the destruction of the Egyptian airfields.

Pearson reports that the Israeli "cooking" plan could not fail since King Hussein had broken off relations with Syria, because of sabotage allegations against the Syrian Secret Service the week before, so Hussein had no communications with Syria. The result of all this was that the Egyptians were led to believe the Jordanians were making a successful attack in the area of Hebron; wherein, the Egyptians counter-attacked in the Sinai and got sucked into a pincher ambush set by the Israelis. Pearson then goes on to claim that Captain McGonagle believed that the alarm over serious Egyptian losses caused NSA to move both the *Liberty* and the *Andrew Jackson* as close into shore as possible.[347]

Scottish author Peter Hounam would pick-up on Pearson's reporting in his book published in 2003 entitled *Operation Cyanide*, with one difference. He cites a David McFeggan as being one of the few *Liberty* survivors who gave credence to Pearson's reporting. In my conversation with Jim Ennes I got the impression that he didn't give much credibility to Pearson's research. Originally, Pearson's reporting on the *Liberty* was for articles in *Penthouse* magazine prior to his book. There was a subsequent movie project involving an associate of Pearson dealing with the *Liberty* story that turned sour and generated hard feelings among some of the survivors. Former LVA president, Phil Tourney, alleges that some survivors were out to sabotage a movie project promoted by filmmaker Tito Howard. It seems that within the ranks of the survivors there was some concerned about being libeled with the "anti-Semite" slur.[348] Eventually, the LVA would become embroiled in a lawsuit with Howard in a California court.[349] The case was subsequently moved to the U.S. District Court Central District of California.[350]

Hounam reports the *Liberty* as monitoring the communications between Nasser and King Hussein regarding war progress. It was clear to those on the *Liberty* that Israel's success against the Egyptians was due to superior intelligence work. Hounam reports essentially word for word what Pearson relates in his book, but asks the question, can his view be seen as creditable in view of having no named sources. Hounam reports that it would be understandable to protect sources only ten years after the Six-Day War; but he says friends of Pearson claim him to be a very "diligent journalist" when he worked for the *Guardian* newspaper based in London. Some thought he had MI-6 sources similar to what he claims in his book.

Hounam notes that McFeggan was impressed with what Pearson had to report with one exception. Pearson credited Israeli intelligence for their successes in the war; however, Hounam makes an astounding statement: "In reality, it was the United States providing the expertise".[351]

Deacon claims that there was a joint CIA/Mossad plan to bring the war about; however, it appears that the State Department was still protective of Arab interests. Oil interests were, as today, of paramount concern. The State

271

Department wanted to arrange a visit of an envoy from Egypt and Jordan prior to the war. This raised concerns about the "softness" of political support in Washington for Israel, and Israel then precipitated the war. Was the CIA/Mossad plan to call for a later start to the war? The *Frontlet615* operation approved by the 303 Committee may have referred to June 15 as the start of the war. In which case did it result in the *Liberty* arriving at Point Alfa almost at the end of the war? It would appear that Israel wanted to take the initiative and started the war earlier on June 5 to give it total surprise.

Author Russell Howe reports that on June 7, Under Secretary of State Eugene Rostow called in Israeli ambassador, Avraham Harman, and warned him that Israel needed to cease its invasion of Egypt and Jordon and not to attack Syria. Harman pleaded that Israel was just "resisting aggression". Rostow "snapped back" that the U.S. knew that the Israelis had cooked communications and lured Hussein into the war. Howe reports Harman left the State Department "troubled" and reported to his government. The contention is that this prompted the attack on the *Liberty*.[352]

Another possible motive involved the pending attack on the Syrian Golan Heights. When one understands the topography of the area, it is clear that the Golan Heights is a strategic position, especially since it was used to shell Israeli farming land in the border tit-for-tat. Ennes cites an editorial in *The Shreveport Times*, dated July 18, 1967, alleging that Washington was doing more to cover-up the matter of the attack up than Israel was. It further noted that it was "shocking" that the Defense Department seemed to "absolve" Israel from any guilt. The paper noted that it appeared Israel was doing everything it could to keep the UN from learning of its plans to attack

Syria. Further, the paper noted that there was no way for the U.S. or UN Security Council to learn what Israel was doing. This was in response to Eban's June 7 telling the UN "only Israel has accepted the U.N. cease fire mandate." It fact it was massing armor and troops for the Syrian invasion. Then the paper notes on June 8 the *Liberty* is put out of commission. Ennes notes that what made the *Times* editorial different was that it wanted a better explanation from Washington and it was the only publication that speculated on the Israeli motive.[353] Vice Admiral Martin when asked about the *Liberty's* mission by the media responded: "I emphatically deny she was a spy ship."[354] McNamara then clamped a news lid on all *Liberty* stories until the official Court of Inquiry report could be published.

Perhaps the most troubling motive theory is that a "Gulf of Tonkin" type pretext was perpetrated to cause the political establishment at the White House, and in the Congress, to finally commit the U.S. to full support of Israel to buffer against a pending Soviet threat due to the Israeli invasion of Syria. In essence, the objective was to provide Israel with an "insurance policy". The claims of Hounam and Pearson including the "Gulf of Tonkin" pretext and the Syrian invasion will be looked at in the next chapter.

Suffice to say that there were several rationales for the Israeli motive to take out the *Liberty*. First, we have another articulation for the Israeli motive for the attack that actually supports the above-discussed motives. In an English version of the Russian newspaper, *Pravda* published in 9/14/2002, reference is to a prior interview with *Liberty* survivor John Hrankowski, now deceased.[355] The author noted: Mr. Hrankowski mentioned a really interesting and important fact just in passing: "American ships arrived only in 16 hours after the attack. A Soviet ship offered help to us on that night. They said that they would stay just at the horizon and, if our ship began to sink, they would help us." Hrankowski's comment led to the follow-up *Pravda* article of 9/14/2002 wherein it was reported: [356]

> This fact has drawn our special attention. Former officer of the US Navy and film producer Richard Thompson recently helped produce a film about the tragic June 8 event. Mr. Thompson recommended us to talk to Russian submariner Captain Nikolay Charkashin, who has been investigating the circumstances surrounding the Liberty tragedy during the past several years. What is more, a book by Nikolay Cherkashin, "Mysteries of Lost Warships," was recently published. This is the result of his independent investigations of Russian submarines from Empress Maria to the Kursk.

The *Prava* article included the following information: A PRAVDA.Ru journalist met with Nikolay Cherkashin, and we offer the following interview to our readers. It was rather unexpected to hear Nikolay Cherkashin say that no Russian ship was close to the USS *Liberty* that night. The following questions are posed to Cherkashin:

> **Well, let's go back to the attack on the Liberty. Could it have been a tragic accident when the US ship was mistakenly taken for an Egyptian cargo ship? Was it a deliberate attack? Provocation? What do you think about it?**

274

- Last year, a Russian translation of Joseph Daichman's "History of the Mossad" was published in Moscow. The author describes the tragedy in 1967 in detail. He admits that it was perfectly clear that the Liberty was an American ship and that the attack was committed to deprive the USA "of its eyes and ears," of the opportunity to control the situation. Daichman says the attackers had the right to act so. The Israelis feared that the Liberty would report information about the course of the war: they wanted to keep it a secret that troops had been shifted to Syria and the Egyptian border wasn't protected at all. The border was quite open for Egyptian soldiers to cross. Israel knew that American radio signals were intercepted by the Soviet Union, and the latter would certainly inform Egypt of the fact. That is why the Liberty was to be sunk to avoid leakage of important information. This is a very cynical version. I even couldn't have thought that I would ever read it.

There is also one more opinion...

- Yes, another version is that Israeli wanted to provoke the USA and involve it in a war against Arab countries. This version is still out there. Mr. Thompson supports it as well. I have known him for ten years already; by the way, it was he who told me about the Liberty tragedy. Richard Thompson is a fair and very active man, and he is persistent with his struggle for his ideas. US top officials wanted to hush up the Liberty scandal, as it was really disgusting and dirty. What is more, that was an unprecedented act, the first attack against US ships since Pearl Harbor. And the attack was committed by those whom America

275

supported so strongly. Right after the accident, the US Congress organized no investigations at all, which was mere nonsense at that time!

Interestingly, when asked by the *Pravda* interviewer, Cherkashin said after conducting his own research he could not verify any information about Ennes's claim that a Soviet ship stood by offering help on the morning of the ninth prior to any assistance from the U.S. Navy showing up. Cherkashin claims that regarding a specific ship's hull number, that: "The 626/4 destroyer wasn't at that time in the eastern part of Mediterranean. I tried to find some veterans of the Soviet Navy who had been there in the summer of 1967, but in vain. Also, nothing is also mentioned in the archives."

I had met Richard Thompson at the Liberty Veterans Association meeting in 2004 where he gave me some information on Soviet and Russian submarines including the quote from Joseph Daichman. He had been visiting Russia and researching the involvement of the Soviet fleet during the Six-Day War. I was similarly interested because of the lack of information on how the Soviet fleet figured into the war and whether research would reveal some leads on why the *Liberty* was attacked. We exchanged e-mails and Thompson mailed me his copy of the Daichman book, *Secrets of the Mossad* that was published in Russian.

The consequence of this was that I spent most of that summer scanning the book's pages and using a computer program to translate from Russian to English. The result was rudimentary, and other than verifying the quote, I did not learn much more about the *Liberty* attack. The book was a series of stories on the successes of the Israeli Mossad including a section on Isser Harel, the obtaining of a MIG from the Iraqis among other secret service stories. There was one very interesting name I found in the book and that was the name James Jesus Angleton, the CIA's chief Soviet spy hunter. We will meet him in the next chapter.

As a side note, anyone wanting to translate a foreign language to his or her language should use Google's translation service. It is much more effective than the process I used; however, scanning and use of optical conversion software may be necessary.

Richard Thompson was instrumental in the BBC production on the *Liberty* entitled *Dead in the Water*. Peter Hounam was the researcher. Unfortunately, Richard Thompson died in the motor vehicle accident on way home to Florida from attending the Liberty Veterans Association meeting in 2007.[357] Some attached to *Liberty* story wonder if his death was in fact accidental.

I made a recent attempt to use the translation service offered on Google to find information about Joseph Daichman to ascertain the basis for his information on the USS *Liberty*. I found his book on the mossad, and another book by him about Interpol (Pub. 2003) and the FBI (Pub. 2004), however, I could find no biographical information.[358] What I did find was the allegation that his literary name was a possible pseudonym of Yuri Y Ivanitchenko, with Yuri Yakoylevich CHERNER as a possible real name who wrote detective and adventures genres.[359] It is difficult to research Russian websites as they may change from time-to-time and I would take some of this information as tongue-in-cheek. Nevertheless, Daichman's statement above about the motive for the Israeli attack on the *Liberty* is consistent with the various other motives discussed.

277

In an e-mail to me dated 12/07/06, Richard Thompson stated he me Daichman in London and believed that he has since been deceased. He apparently was an Israeli Russian Jew with some involvement with the Israeli secret service, and who spent some time in Toronto, Canada.

Finally, something that has remained secret over the years that certainly must have been factored into Israel thinking and plans was the over-flight of Israel's highly secret nuclear reactor at Dimona. There were at least two reported over-flights where Israeli Hawk missiles (received from the United States) were unable to bring down the planes over-flying the site. Additionally, Israeli interceptors were unable to catch up to the over-flying planes. Who was piloting these planes would be of major interest to both the Israelis and the United States intelligence community. The Israelis were so protective of the site that they did shoot down one of their own planes that accidentally flew to close to the Dimona exclusion zone.

To illustrate Israel's sensitivity toward the Dimona nuclear facility, as noted an Israeli Mirage III type plane was shot down during the Six-Day War when it ventured too close, whether because of confusion or equipment problems.[360]

Would the fear that the *Liberty* might be eavesdropping on activities related to the Israeli nuclear program be another motive for the attack? The Israeli Air force intelligence chief was "alleged" to have threatened to attack any plane or ship encroaching Israeli territory.[361] The alleged threat was concerning a prior U.S. penetration of Israeli air space and considered "facetiously" made, according to Israeli Lt. Col. Bloch per an exchange with Commander Earnest Castle our military attaché. The personnel flying the EC-121 as previously reported took such "potential" threats seriously.

Would Israeli military shoot down an American plane? Author Russell Howe, in the prologue to his book relates an incident in 1973 Yom Kippur War where allegedly Moshe Dayan ordered 13 Jericho missiles to be armed with nuclear warheads. Dayan had received the okay from Prime Minister Golda Meir in response to the Northern Commander's inability to hold back Syrian armor. Howe relates that a Lockheed SR-71 Blackbird was conducting an over-flight when two Phantom Israeli jets took to the air in response to the encroachment. On board electronics indicated a threat when "in the clear" the Israeli controller advised the jets to "Down it". The Blackbird cleared the area and nothing happened. Howe speculates that the "in the clear" broadcast was intended to warn the Blackbird to clear the area.[362] This incident, if it happened as alleged, happened on October 12, is consistent with the Israeli military going its own route. If we discount their "go-it-alone" MO, we do so at our risk. A different interpretation of a Blackbird flight on 13 October is reported as follows, to be in aid to the Israelis.[363] The question is whether the Blackbird stories are mutually inconsistent.

> On October 13 and 15, Egyptian air defense radars detected an aircraft at an altitude of 25,000 meters (82,000 ft) and a speed of Mach 3, making it impossible to intercept either by fighter or SAM missiles. The aircraft proceeded to cross the whole of the canal zone, the naval ports of the Red Sea (Hurghada and Safaga), flew over the airbases

279

and air defenses in the Nile Delta, and finally disappeared from radar screens over the Mediterranean Sea. The speed and altitude were those of the SR-71 Blackbird, a long-range strategic-reconnaissance aircraft. According to Egyptian commanders, the intelligence provided by both reconnaissance flights helped the Israelis prepare for the Egyptian attack on October 14 and assisted it in conducting Operation Stouthearted Men.

The Israeli and CIA sensitivity about the Israeli nuclear program was highlighted in a recent news article dealing with an environmental cleanup of a nuclear waste site in Parks Township, Pennsylvania. Apparently, the U.S. Army Corps of Engineers has suspended the project due to a "severe" safety violation at the NUMEC site. NUMEC dumped radioactive and chemical waste produced at its Apollo plant in the 1960s. The dump closed in 1970.[364] Author Seymour Hersh wrote about NUMEC and the Apollo plant as being one of the sources for the Israelis obtaining of HEU (Highly Enriched Uranium) for its Dimona plant and nuclear weapons program in the '60s.[365] A recent article points the finger at the CIA as having extensive knowledge of the NUMEC operation and diversion of HEU to Israel wherein the CIA could help the Army Corp of Engineers locate dangerous waste more effectively if it wanted to.[366] The article's author, Grant Smith, notes that all FOIA requests have failed to penetrate the secrecy around Israel's illegal obtaining of HEU. He further contends that if the CIA would cough up information on the burying of nuclear waste it would be helpful to the residents of Parks Township and prevent a public health hazard that never should have existed had there been enforcement action taken in the '60s.

It seems as though the U.S. government policy is to aid and abet Israel's ambiguity about its nuclear program even to this day, notwithstanding the reality that the whole world now knows about it. The media reports Israel as having as many as 250 nuclear weapons, some on submarines. It would certainly be an Israeli motive were it concerned that the *Liberty* could have monitored communications and other signals dealing with the Dimona nuclear project. All we can do is speculate on this point. Does this portend the future as happened during the Yom Kippur War?

The short take on the motive issue is that Israeli military personnel did not want their war plans monitored. Time was of the essence. Any mix of the above motives taken separately or together could have been enough to result in the attack. Major General George J. Keegan, Jr., former Chief of Air Force Intelligence was of the belief that the Israelis were concerned that the gathered intelligence would be leaked to the Arabs, and this was the reason or motive for the attack.[367] He highly regarded the Israeli intelligence services, and yet believed the attack was intentional. Further, he had publicly stated that Israel was worth five CIAs having provided the U.S. with $50-80 billion in intelligence, research and development savings, and Soviet weapons systems captured and transferred to the U.S.[368] General Keegan is another example of United States high military brass who believed the attack was intended and not an accident. He was alleged to be an alarmist disagreeing with CIA assessments on the Soviet's nuclear position; whether they intending a "first strike" or not:[369]

Keegan was convinced that wherever the US was not on an equal footing, the imbalance gave the Soviets an advantage.

Keegan noted that an analysis of 39 large cities in the USSR had shown that each apartment building constructed since 1955 had a nuclear shelter, a network of linking tunnels, vast emergency stores of medical supplies and food, as well as alternative sources of electric power. From questioning Soviet defectors, he had learned that every large industrial plant in those cities possessed huge shelters where production could be continued in wartime. Every large town in the USSR contained linked underground central command posts. There were 75 of them. The largest, intended for the Politburo, was underneath the Kremlin compound in Moscow.

Keegan complained that even after 20 years of studying the Soviet defense infrastructure and examining photographs and documents, the CIA continued to present Congressional committees with assessments that differed from his. He believed strongly in the Soviet Union's determination to destroy the West, and he considered that everyone who helped the détente effort was strengthening the Kremlin's allies.

If Keegan was right in his assessment, then the potential for a nuclear confrontation during the Six-Day War was more than a potential "doomsday" scenario. On the other hand, Helms' public opinion that there were no nuclear weapons in the Middle East seems to put the CIA and Air Force Intelligence in different parallel worlds. Keegan's reference above to "...questioning Soviet defectors...." seems to smack of the jurisdiction of James Jesus Angleton and the Mossad under the

"Faustian bargain" we established with Israeli intelligence to interrogate émigrés coming out from behind the Iron Curtain for HUMINT.

To illustrate the scope of the danger to our national security, we only need refer to what almost happened during the Cuban missile crisis. Author Peter Janney in his new book, *Mary's Mosaic: The CIA Conspiracy to Murder John F. Kennedy, Mary Pinchot Meyer and their Vision for World Peace* notes the following commenting on the Cuban crisis:[370]

> What their intelligence had not revealed, however, was that the Russians had more than forty thousand troops in Cuba who were prepared to fight an American invasion. They were armed not only with strategic missiles (the medium- and intermediate-range ICBMs discovered by the American U-2 photography), but, completely unknown to the American military and CIA at the time, also with ninety-eight tactical, or low-yield, nuclear warheads—along with the appropriate short-range missiles and jet bombers to deliver them—which had been placed in Cuba with the specific intent of being actively used to oppose any U.S. invasion of the island.[11] Said former Defense Secretary Robert McNamara in an interview in 1998: "We didn't learn until nearly 30 years later, that the Soviets had roughly 162 nuclear warheads on this isle of Cuba, at a time when our CIA said they believed there were none. And included in the 162 were some 90 tactical warheads to be used against a US invasion force. Had we … attacked Cuba and invaded Cuba at the time, we almost surely would have been

involved in nuclear war. And when I say "we," I mean you—it would not have been the U.S. alone. It would have endangered the security of the West, without any question."[12]

In the Six-Day War, we again found ourselves on the brink of a nuclear confrontation, and our intelligence leader, Helms, is telling the President there are no nuclear weapons in the Mediterranean. Any fool knows that playing with matches around gasoline will eventually result in an accidental explosion—only here we are talking about a nuclear explosion! This is the kind of information the government does not want the population to know, and what the media fails to dig into.

I believed then, as I do today, that we held a clear title to this country. Not the right to take it away from others (there were no others), but the right and duty to fill its emptiness, restore life to its barrenness, to re-create a modern version of our ancient nation. And I felt we owed this effort not only to ourselves but to the land as well.

David Ben-Gurion's Memoirs, page 26.

Chapter 10

The Unholy Alliance

James Jesus Angleton was the CIA's top Soviet spy hunter. He and Richard Helms were holdovers from the OSS (Organization of Strategic Services) and instrumental in helping to establishing the new CIA organization formed at President Harry Truman's direction after the Second World War.[371]

Author Peter Hounam, who wrote about Angleton's involvement with the Israelis and the Six-Day War, describes him as a workaholic who also controlled the CIA's Israeli desk and who built his career exploiting contacts with the Israeli Mossad whose penetration of the Soviet Union was more successful than our own intelligence efforts.

On his death in 1986, after forced retirement from the CIA, Angleton would be commemorated by two monuments in Israel paid for by Israeli intelligence chiefs, including former, now deceased, Mossad Director, Meir Amit. One according to Hounam is opposite the walls of Jerusalem's Old City near the King David Hotel, and the other is in the Jerusalem Forest. In English and Hebrew, the inscriptions read: "James Jesus Angleton

1917-1987 In Memory of a Good Friend."[372] Just prior to the Six-Day War Hounam says Mossad Director Amit met with Angleton when he flew to Washington to assess the depth of the Johnson administration support for Israel against the Arabs.

Hounam had met with Amit twice while writing his book. The Meir Amit Intelligence and Terrorism Information Center, a NGO, can be found on the Internet.[373]

Fig. 16, Demonstrations in reaction to the Six Day War in the Middle East, outside White House, LBJ Library.

Hounam states Amit knew Angleton would open doors in Washington for him and he subsequently met with Secretary of Defense McNamara immediately prior to the start of the Six-Day War.[374] Amit's primary aim was to have the U.S. stop the Soviets from intervening on behalf of the Arabs. Because of his visit in Washington, Amit took the message from his meetings as being a green light to take whatever actions they wanted against

286

the Arabs. Amit understood that President Johnson himself had approved Israel's war plan.

OSS creator and director Wild Bill Donovan's biographer describes Angleton as follows:[375]

> Only twenty-eight years old, James Jesus Angleton already had enough quirks for a man twice his age. He chain-smoked, spoke with a slight British accent, was a chronic insomniac, quoted T. S. Eliot to relax, refused to sit beside a colleague in a restaurant booth, struck his OSS friends as overly secretive even for their profession, could be irrationally paranoid about communists, and liked to prowl Rome's streets in a black cape. After graduating with poor grades from Yale, Angleton joined the OSS and was sent to London as a counterintelligence corporal. From his first day in the London station, Angleton was a human tornado, quickly learning street skills for spy catching. Within six months he was commissioned a second lieutenant and by October 1944 he had been transferred to Rome to clean up counterintelligence operations in Italy, using the code name "Artifice."

Just how Angleton figures into the *Liberty* story is an open question. There is almost no published documentation dealing with his specific activities at the CIA Israeli Desk. In a recent George Washington University National Security Archive project release dealing with the CIA's internal history of DCI William "Bill" Colby, there are three chapters of interest posted on the George Washington NSA project website. The first is Chapter 6 dealing with Colby's termination of Angleton. Second, is Chapter 7 dealing with author

Seymour Hersh's exposure of the CIA's "family jewels" scandal, wherein Hersh told Colby he was about to expose Angleton for being associated with domestic spying. Chapter 8 deals with the issue of whether or not DCI Helms perjured himself before Congress dealing with the CIA's "Track II" covert operation to keep Chile's Salvador Allende from becoming president. Interestingly nothing in the disclosures mentions Angleton's Israeli activities.[376] Helms' credibility comes into play in the context of what he has to say or not say about the attack on the *Liberty*. As for Angleton, we were limited to what his biographer, Tom Mangold, and other authors have to say about him.[377] His erratic behavior, or MO, of withholding information from American presidents as well as other sections of the CIA, and close ties with the Israeli Mossad leaves room for much speculation.[378] Notwithstanding the continuing secrecy at the CIA, he is suspected of supporting Israel during the Six-Day War. He was not necessarily a Zionist; however, the Israelis were his key to information on the Soviets and émigrés to Israel from behind the Iron Curtain.

Mangold says, "Angleton's ties with the Israelis gave him considerable prestige within the CIA and later added significantly to his expanding counterintelligence empire."[379] Colby's predecessor, Schlesinger thought it was a "mistake to allow Angleton to continue to control his power centre so tightly" referring to his role at the Israeli account. Colby, who terminated Angleton's Israeli desk control was upset that Angleton ruled that the Tel Aviv office communicate directly through him and not with any other CIA desk including the Cairo desk.[380]

Amazingly, Angleton's biographer, Mangold, has nothing to say about Angleton's dealings with the Six-

Day War or the Israeli Mossad. However, another very recent GWU NSA release dealing with Adolf Eichmann shows that Angleton went to great lengths to ingratiate his relationship with the Israelis "To help strengthen the close ties between the CIA and Israel's intelligence agencies. The Counterintelligence Staff at the Directorate of Operations (headed by James Angleton) combed through the archives and submitted for further research other German officers' names that were mentioned in the Eichmann documents. The consequence was the discovery that some of those linked to Eichmann also had ties to the CIA and the CIA-sponsored West German intelligence service (BND)."[381] Angleton's effort to ingratiate himself with the Israelis was not without reciprocation, as we shall shortly see.

American's relationship with the state of Israel since the state's birth and recognition by the United Nations in 1948 has been problematic and mysterious. It is not this author's intention to try and summarize that history; however, a few background points need to be made to facilitate our understanding of our complex relationship with the state of Israel that is critical to understanding the USS *Liberty* saga and disaster as well as continuing conflicts in that part of the world. Israel will become our Cold War proxy in the Middle East.

Recognition of Israel by President Harry Truman was not unanimous. General George Marshall strongly opposed recognition. Stalin for the Soviet Union also recognized the Israeli state. Many Jews migrated from Eastern Europe escaping pogroms seeking a new life after the Second World War. There was a British mandate governing lands coveted by both Jews and Palestinians that would result in several wars and continuing contentions, still troublesome today with no clear solutions for the near future. For David Ben-Gurion who would become the Israeli Prime Minister, born in Plonsk, forty miles northwest of Warsaw, it was all about the Bible, the land and Hebrew.

Israel and its Arab neighbors have been in conflict for decades with the underlying concern for the Israelis being that of security, that means more land for an expanding immigrant population. The two issues go hand in hand, that of land and security; for Israelis you cannot have one without the other. David Ben-Gurion set the precedent for the Prime Minister to also serve as the Defense Minister in the early decades after the recognition of the state. To attain his goal of security he had to build up the Israeli defense forces by obtaining weapons and entering into alliances with Britain and France or any nation that would facilitate his development of a defense force for the state. France was the primary weapons supplier up to the Six-Day War until De Gaulle enforced an arms embargo on Israel; after that it would become the United States who would become Israel's main weapons supplier and benefactor and remains so to this date.

His concern for security was so occupying that he wanted under the nuclear umbrella of a super-power; he specifically wanted that coverage from the United States and not the Soviet Union. When Ben-Gurion came into power, Moshe Sharett was his foreign minister. While he wanted an alliance with the U.S., he decided no written agreement was necessary. Israel would henceforth rely on an "activist defense policy" based on deterrence with the nuclear option at its center.[382]

The following observations are from Avner Cohen in his book *Israel and the Bomb*.[383] The GWU NSA FOIA project focuses on Cohen and his book citing several

290

highlights.[384] In the period 1955-1957, a heated debate took place within the small scientific and policy community in Israel regarding the feasibility and desirability of the nuclear weapons option. When Shimon Peres put together the Dimona deal in 1957, and obtained massive French assistance, Ben-Gurion gave permission to proceed with the project. Israel was treated as a special case even by the Eisenhower administration. There was limited U.S. pressure on Israel to give up its nuclear program in favor for security guarantees. There was pressure from President Kennedy to open up the project for inspection with negligible success and obfuscation on the part of Israel.

The United States "discovered" the Dimona project in late '50s and early '60s, almost three years after it had been launched. The late discovery of Dimona is one of the colossal blunders of American intelligence. The UK confirmed to the CIA with ground photos that it was a reactor site. Israel tried to say the site was "a metallurgical research laboratory", and "an agricultural research" site. In a CIA inquiry, France denied it was helping Israel. On 12/8/60, the CIA issued a Special National Intelligence Report (SNIE) about Dimona stressing the project's repercussions. CIA director Allen W. Dulles understood that Dimona would trigger a "particularly severe" reaction from the Arabs. The *Times* magazine and London *Daily Express* reported on the Israeli reactor. Israel and France continued to stall and say the project was for peaceful purposes. Ben-Gurion's long awaited statement to the Knesset on 12/21/60 about the project said it was for research, agricultural and peaceful purposes. The subterfuge sounds familiar in the context of the present Iranian nuclear confrontation

291

involving sanctions and the threat of an Israeli military strike.

The U.S. was slow in absorbing information on the Israeli project. In early 1960, the CIA began to get information on Israeli activity but failed to pass it on—why? U-2 flights were watching a bombing range and did not fully comprehend what appeared to be a developing nuclear site. In '58, Eisenhower was briefed on the surveillance photos and said nothing. Consequently, certain individuals assumed Ike wanted Israel to have the bomb.[385] As to the above question "why", it appears that Israel had friends in high places such as James Jesus Angleton, head of the Israel desk, who failed to pass information on to other departments, and agencies including other sections of the CIA according to Cohen.

Cohen points to the *Protocol of Sèvres* as setting the groundwork for the 1956 Suez War, including a British, French and Israeli agreement to build Dimona – in which the nuclear deal was "understood". The "Deal" was for a smaller reactor. Because of the Suez conflict, the Soviets issued threats to Israel that she would be attacked with missiles; and Eisenhower intervened with a demand for a cease-fire. Israel asked what France would do in view of Soviet nuclear threat, and France could offer nothing and recommended that Israel accept the ultimatum. Shimon Peres asked the French CEA for a guarantee in exchange for withdrawal from Sinai. It was this follow-up understanding that lead to Dimona. France also was humiliated by the U.S. and Soviet threat, so there was mutuality vis-a-vis the two countries, the one re Africa and the other re the Arabs, U.S. and Soviets.

Cohen in his book reports that the Lavon Affair created political problems for Ben-Gurion, and while Kennedy pressed for visits to Dimona, Ben-Gurion kept putting the issue off. Two Americans made a May 1961 visit to Dimona and a private meeting between BG and JFK was arranged. In short, the scientists got a "snow job" as they did not challenge what they were told. The BG and JFK meeting was held at Waldorf-Astoria, wherein, BG emphasized the need for a power and desalinization plant. The road to achieving his goal was a rocky one with conflicts presented by President Eisenhower and President Kennedy who it was contended were more sympathetic to the Arab view, in part due to oil interests. Underlying these conflicts were two elements, both based on deception emblematic of a method of operation that involves ruthlessness and should clearly communicate the message that if needed Israel will stand alone to accomplish her own security.[386]

Today, this has never been clearer in the context of Iran wanting to develop nuclear weapons. Israel and Prime Minister Benjamin Netanyahu's government wants U.S. support and approval for an attack on Iran; however, they are making it clear they are prepared to go it alone.[387] This concept of seeking a "green light" and cooperation with the U.S. to accomplish their objectives, or going it alone, is at the core of the Six-Day War.

> As a digression: Ex-Mossad boss Meir Dagan says an Israeli attack on Iran would be 'stupidest thing ever'. A strike on nuclear sites would ignite regional war, he says. Told that some in Israel accused him of treason for speaking out, Dagan said, "Let them put me on trial. I'll be very happy to go on trial. It'll

be fun,"[388] Reportedly, he would prefer that the U.S. took the initiative regarding Iran. The question is whether his view is pragmatic or cynical.

The first item was Israel's willingness to act in concert with other allies while keeping the U.S. President in the dark, and the other was a desire to obtain its own nuclear deterrent capability—both linked. The first signs of a problem developed when Nasser seized the Suez Canal and shut it down to shipping in the mid-fifties. This was a concern for both Britain and France and resulted in the 1956 Suez War. Pursuant to a secret agreement known as the *Protocol of Sèvres*, Britain and France were to seize the Suez cannel and Israel was to provide a diversion by invading the Sinai—as a pretext.   President Eisenhower forced Israel to back down and return the Sinai to Egypt; in Israeli eyes, he was soft on the Arabs.   Britain and France were seeing their influence in the area on the wane.   This prompted Ben-Gurion to do an end-run around the State Department and rely on friends in the U.S. government, namely in the CIA.   Ben-Gurion knew he needed leverage and the one thing he had to trade or offer to certain nations was intelligence services dealing with what was going on in the Middle East, and Eastern Europe behind the Iron Curtain, where many of the new immigrants came from.

Ben-Gurion would try this tack with the United States government by offering to provide intelligence information on the Soviet Union. The essence of the deal was that the Mossad and other Israeli intelligence units would conduct HUMINT, human intelligence, with feet-on-the-ground in the Middle East by interviewing émigrés from Europe. In essence, the Israeli intelligence establishment would do the work of the CIA as its proxy.

294

One of the carrots dangled by the Israelis before our government was a speech by Nikita Khrushchev before the Soviet Politburo Twentieth Congress denouncing Stalin.[389] Our government had legitimate interest in the dissent building behind the Iron Curtain. This was a major event since both Europe and the Middle East were in various stages of crisis, and getting a copy of the speech was considered by Allen Dulles as a coup—it was provided by the Israelis to James Jesus Angleton.

This was an example of what would be a pattern of quid-pro-quo. This arrangement involved James Jesus Angleton as the head of the CIA's relationship with the Israeli intelligence services, primarily the Mossad and Aman. Angleton may have not been sympathetic with the concept of Zionism, but that did not matter because the relationship gave him and the U.S. a strong lever to confront the developing Soviet influence in the Middle East primarily with Egypt and Syria. The Soviet Union would become the Arabs major weapons supplier. Stemming from his wartime OSS liaison with Jewish resistance groups in London, Angleton was instrumental in arranging the working relationship with Israeli Mossad wherein the CIA would rely on the Mossad for much of its intelligence about the Arab states.[390] Angleton allegedly dealt with Ben-Gurion.[391] Angleton's tendency was to do his own thing; for example, he had to be ordered by Allen Dulles, the CIA Director, to work with Kermit Roosevelt who became the *de facto* "Mr. Middle East".

Angleton's method of operation was to keep certain information from our own government such as the timing of the Israeli invasion of Egypt during the 1956 Suez war in conjunction with Britain and France. Wilbur Crane

295

Eveland, author and former CIA operative, reports Bob Amory, the deputy director for intelligence, told him, that Angleton was in a foul mood because his Mossad contacts denied Israel was planning to invade Egypt during the 1956 Suez crisis.[392] It appears that being friends the parties were not above blindsiding each other. Angleton's main job was searching out "moles" within the U.S. intelligence establishment; however, Eveland notes it was ironical that Angleton himself was investigated as being a mole after being dismissed by William Colby when he became CIA Director.[393]

The cooperative effort between the CIA and Mossad developed under Allen Dulles and primarily focused on Soviet arms shipments to the Arabs. Ben-Gurion had refused to withdraw his forces from the Sinai and Gaza unless the United States agreed to provide Israel with the means to protect its population centers from attack by the Russian ballistic missiles that, Israeli intelligence reported, would soon be furnished to Egypt and Syria by the Soviets.[394]

Eveland was concerned that the relationship was like depending on the fox to guard the hen house. The concern was over the CIA's role in facilitating Israeli's development of "advanced weapons" that can only refer to Dimona and Israel's obtaining HEU from NUMEC and the Apollo plant in Pennsylvania—see the previous chapter. CIA Director Dulles relieved Eveland of his Middle East duties and dispatched him to Africa because of his conflict over Middle East policy.[395] Eventually Eveland would become a bitter man claiming he lost everything because of his challenging U.S. policy.

As for the Six-Day War, based on inside information, it was clear that like Britain and France in 1956, America had become a party to starting a Middle East war, and then quickly lost control of it.[396] To understand the implications of collusion on this scale, one must look at the development of the written *Protocol of Sèvres* between Britain, France and Israel in terms of the design to get rid of Nasser.[397]

Eveland concludes that Angleton was able to deal with top Israeli officials in the Ministry of Defense and the intelligence services, via his working relationship with "Eppy" Ephraim Evron, without involving Israeli Foreign Minister, Abba Eban, or the U.S. State Department and Department of Defense. Meetings in preparation of the Six-Day War included Dayan, and the efforts were to discuss the feasibility of an attack on Egypt with the objective of toppling Nasser. The Israelis were interested but unwilling to commit without further evidence that Angleton was acting with White House approval—they did not want to be stung again. This created a conundrum in terms of how far the Israelis would trust the U.S. government and vice-versa.[398] This Israeli concern was the reason for Mossad Director Amit's visit to Washington prior to the Six-Day War—to see if they had a "green light".

Eveland goes on to report that President Johnson advised Angleton to inform Evron that the U.S. would prefer Israel to lesson tensions, but wouldn't object or intervene to stop an attack on Egypt; but, the American position stipulated that there must be no military action against Jordan, Syria or Lebanon.[399] Top Pentagon officials were briefed on Angleton's discussions with Israel and became more concerned about Soviet intervention. Then the JCS sent the *Liberty* to monitor the fighting should Israel attack Egypt. Also, sent was the Polaris nuclear submarine *Andrew Jackson*. Eveland cited Anthony Pearson's reference to the sub's identity.[400] He thereby extended credibility to Pearson that Jim Ennes was not willing to do. Again, was the submarine the so-called Contact X referred to by Ennes in his book? The identity of this submarine has not been fixed since others believe it could have the USS *Amberjack*. At issue was the possibility of nuclear war developing, knowing that the CIA had helped Israel with its nuclear weapons development program at Dimona. It should be noted that if not actually aiding, it turned a blind eye. Read Seymour Hersh's, *The Sampson Option*.

While Eveland is my cited source for much of this information, he had his critics including CIA Director Helms who was not happy with Eveland's publication of information the CIA would prefer to keep undisclosed.

Again, there is evidence that the Joint Chiefs held a reservation regarding CIA and Israeli cooperation. The *Liberty* was "their" tool to monitor Middle East events. In a Memorandum for the Record, dated May 24, 1967, dealing with a National Security Council meeting to discuss the Middle East Crisis, the issue of "unconventional" weapons being introduced in the area was brought up. The President, Rusk, and McNamara were at this meeting with others. While there is a redaction at this point in the report, Richard Helms, CIA Director, "was quite positive in stating there were no nuclear weapons in the area." General Wheeler noted that he was less well informed "but more skeptical". One would think with the potential for conflict with the Soviet Union that concern about unconventional weapons would be a priority and not something summarily dismissed, especially in the context of the prior Cuban missile crisis. After all, going back to the 1956 war the main worry on the Israeli mind was the threat from the Soviets. One would think that if anyone, Helms should have been informed of the Israeli's Dimona project. Perhaps Helms delegated too much authority to Angleton—this is speculation—something that Colby was not ready to do. This ambiguity as to nuclear weapons being in the area was to carry over to a post war critique of the Six-Day War chaired by Richard Parker who would later claim he had no knowledge of Israel's nuclear program.[401]

Was the *Liberty's* mission to monitor this conspiracy and be able to make sure the White House was able to control events or limit things getting out of hand? The pattern of relationships and cooperation with Israel for the major powers was to become more than trouble-some.

A second learning lesson was missed because of the "Lavon Affair" that almost brought down the Israeli government and caused inner turmoil.

Author Richard Deacon points out in his book that because of the War of Independence in 1948 to 1949 and the Suez War in 1956 that there was never negotiated peace terms with the Arabs. The Israeli built up their technical expertise to provide a superior strength for the small nation; however, Egypt, Syria and their allies were doing the same thing via Soviet support.

During the prelude to the Six-Day War, the Israeli cabinet was equivocating on whether or not to go to war with Egypt. There was a group of seasoned military leaders, and advisors who favored war; one was Moshe Dayan who would become Minister of Defense. He had previously been the IDF Chief of Staff and later a member of the Israeli Knesset. As the stage developed for war he was out of the government, and looking for an opportunity to actively participate, even as a private or the Southern Commander. He began looking at Israel's military posture and was aware of Prime Minister Levi Eshkol's shortcomings as a war leader; Dayan had a majority of Israelis behind him. As noted above the post of Minister of Defense had been held by the Prime Minister and some including Aman, the military intelligence arm, thought this not to be a good idea. Pressure by the Mapai Party leadership brought Dayan into that position as part of a unity government; Prime Minister Eshkol did not oppose it.

Now out of office, Ben-Gurion opposed going to war for fear that it would force a confrontation with the Soviet Union. Deacon reports the intelligence establishment pushed for war less Israel lose its edge. While the denial of access to the Suez Canal was a serious blow, Nasser further added to the grounds for going to war by closing the Straits of Tiran and the Gulf of Aqaba.

Israel had learned a lesson from the 1956 Suez War that it was not enough to win a war against the Arabs, but it had to be quick and a total victory. One of the main concerns was that if the war was protracted the United Nations would press for a cease fire on terms unsatisfactory for Israel such as had been forced on them by President Eisenhower. The only way for Israel to control the situation was through a strong intelligence system that was well versed in the Arabs' military capabilities and limitations. While Israel had the best secret service system, it was not enough. It needed to get involved in diplomatic efforts and win cooperation from the western super-powers.

The Israelis did not trust the British because of their management of the Mandate and the security leaks to the Soviet Union through the spy, Kim Philby. Philby's wife was a Viennese Jewess and the Mossad was aware of Philby's communist leanings and contacts.[402] Angleton was a protégé of Philby. As noted, the Israelis had begun developing the relationship with the CIA during the Eisenhower administration. The CIA was concerned about the Eisenhower administration's appeasement toward the Arabs, perceived as disadvantageous to American military and economic interests in the view of Angleton.

The deal struck under Ben-Gurion was that Mossad would carry out our intelligence needs in the Middle East, and as to what was going on behind the Iron Curtain. Over time, this policy would prove disastrous on more than one occasion. At the center of this policy was Angleton. John Hadden, the CIA Station Chief in Tel Aviv, was Angleton's right hand man revealed by authors Peter Hounam and Isabella Ginor in their books. According to Deacon, the players in this arrangement were Isser Harel, Ephraim Evron and Angleton. I would add one other person and that was Mossad Chief, Amir Amit. Amit had succeeded Harel as the Director of Mossad.

Angleton saw our position on the 1956 Suez War as a failure of policy and decided to counteract the State Department's bias toward the Arabs by close cooperation with Israel's intelligence services. Deacon in this author's opinion has credibility because at the relative early date he wrote his book he recognized that the CIA had cooperated with Israel on the nuclear front. Evron was involved in aggressively challenging U.S. policy of

301

friendship toward Nasser that eventually led to the Lavon Affair in 1954.[403]

The Lavon Affair was an Israeli scandal involving a covert bombing campaign against American and British targets in Egypt during the summer of 1954. The false-flag operation was aimed at causing violence and instability to warrant the British to keep their forces in the Suez Canal Zone; and thwart U.S. support for Nasser and the Egyptians. Defense Minister Pinhas Lavon was forced to resign his position in the Israeli government.[404] David Ben-Gurion and Moshe Dayan were implicated in one way or another.

Ephraim Evron was Lavon's secretary who kept a low profile after the Lavon Affair, and built his worth by providing information to the CIA and to the State department of growing Soviet influence in the Middle East providing information on spies and the efforts of Russian spy ships working against Israel and the U.S. Sixth Fleet. Evron became highly regarded in Washington as the Israeli deputy ambassador. He became friends with President Johnson that included invitations to the "ranch". He was in fact the Mossad liaison in Washington.

Israel over the years developed lobbies and intelligence sources in the U.S. and invoked the support of the Jewish community in the U.S. The contention is that we did not spy on each other; however, the Jonathon Pollard incident would show otherwise. We also spied on Israel with U-2 over-flights of the developing nuclear reactor site at Dimona.[405] Nevertheless, the Israeli interest entangled the Johnson administration through two brothers Eugene Rostow at the State Department and

Walt Rostow as Johnson's national security advisor, both reputed to be supporters of Israel.

Gordon Thomas, a writer with knowledge of the world's intelligence services, is clear in stating that we are targeted by Israel's Mossad for opportunistic spying through economic, scientific and technological espionage. He cites a document written by former CIA director William Casey on March 21, 1984 to the effect that, *"A nation creates the intelligence community it needs. America relies on technical expertise because we are concerned to discover rather than secretly rule. The Israelis operate differently. Mossad, in particular, equates its actions with its nation's survival."*[406] Obviously, Casey was speaking based upon years of experience in dealing with Israeli intelligence services and whether or not it is a compliment to the Israelis is open to conjecture, as his words could also be a warning.

Deacon reports it was Walt Rostow who urged on President Johnson a view shared by both the CIA and Israel for launching a coup in Egypt to get rid of Nasser. In a memorandum to President Johnson, special advisor Walt Rostow, sums up the problem and the course he suggests:[407]

> An active attempt to stave off a Nasser takeover would amount to a sharp shift in our Middle East policy. Since 1961, we have tried to avoid splitting the area into two camps. Given all of our conflicting interests, it has seemed wiser to build a good working relationship in all capitals. Now Nasser has all but forced us to choose sides. As your message to him said, we don't want to give up entirely our effort to build some kind of

relationship with him. But the time may already have come when we must make him respect us first.

The thinking in Washington by the end of 1965 was such that pressure was on the CIA to consider a coup in Egypt to get rid of Nasser, but he was too popular and strong for that to succeed. The thinking then turned to the possibility of a war that Egypt would lose with the Egyptians getting rid of Nasser. Ahmed Shukeiry, head of the recently formed Palestine Liberation Organization was forging an alliance with Nasser with wild promises of destroying Tel Aviv.

Meetings began with CIA representatives, Evron, Amit and Brigadier-General Yariv, Director of Military Intelligence.[408] Amit had been an active member of Haganah, considered a terrorist organization during the British Mandate, and commander of the Golani Brigade in 1948, wounded in the War of Independence. He moved into the intelligence field and spent two years in the United States developing useful contacts. On his return to Israel, he was appointed head of Aman in 1961 and replaced Harel as Chief of Mossad two years later. He and Aharon Yariv, his successor at Aman worked well together. Amit and Yariv received reports from spy Elie Cohen, an Israeli hero, on what the Russians were doing in terms of SAM missile sites and Sinai fortifications and defenses.[409]

Deacon reports on listening devices planted within range of enemy camps able to pick up conversations, phones were tapped, new photoreconnaissance equipment was provided, and new techniques for jamming enemy radar were developed. Additionally, Israeli intelligence built a psychological profile of the Egyptian military personnel using computers to integrate information on potential enemies providing needed information for commanders on a speedy basis—a technology war analysis system.

During the lead up to the war, Israeli intelligence maintained contacts with the French secret service and navy. The relationship had been at its peak during the earlier Suez War, and was still in effect notwithstanding de Gaulle's pull back of French weapon support for Israel. Brigadier-General Chaim (Vivian) Herzog would become head of Aman.[410] Notwithstanding the computerization, they had a typical "information overload" problem. Herzog sought help to manage this from both France and the U.S. While the official policy under de Gaulle was neutral, Deacon reports he was still friendly toward Israel.[411]

Johnson's position was he was more sympathetic to the Israelis; he swung from Kennedy's pro-Arab policies that include a distain for the CIA going back to the Cuban missile crisis and Bay of Pigs fiasco. Rightly, both the administration and State Department were concerned with Soviet influence in the area. Johnson was prone to delegate downward, and in the area of national security, he let that rest with Walt Rostow, his national security advisor, who had agreed with the CIA regarding the Middle East concerns. Deacon makes a flat statement that the result was a secret agreement between the CIA and Israeli secret services for a limited war between Egypt and Israel that would not affect territorial lines between Jordan, Syria and Israel. The understanding was that whatever war Israel was to fight would be alone lines approved by the United States. The intent of the plan was to deter the Soviets from direct intervention. Was the code name for this plan *Operation Cyanide* as claimed by author Peter Hounam? Was the plan similar and in writing like the *Protocol of Sèvres*? Allegedly, Ben-Gurion kept a copy of that agreement to the chagrin of the British and French. At any rate an "MO" was developing. So far, there is no official confirmation of *Operation Cyanide*.

I recently came across a new book written by author Peter Janney. Janney's dad was an employee or agent of the CIA in the early '60s, named Wistar Janney. Peter Janney's book, *Mary's Mosaic*, contends that certain individuals within the CIA and military plotted to assassinate President Kennedy—not directly but through cutouts. Mary Pinchot Meyer, who had been married to CIA agent Cord Meyer, was Kennedy's favorite paramour; she was murdered a year after Kennedy was killed. Janney contends she may have had culpable information involving the CIA and James Jesus Angleton, among others that included her ex-husband Cord Meyer and Janney's dad. Angleton had been a friend of Cord Meyer and the Meyer family. Allegedly, he broke into Mary Meyer's residence to retrieve a diary after her murder. Janney is not alone in his contentions re JFK's assassination. For our purposes here, there are a couple points to be made as background.

In 1961 when John F. Kennedy became president, he inherited two explosive issues that of a totalitarian Cuba under Fidel Castro, and escalation in Southeast Asia—left over items from the Eisenhower administration. For his part, Eisenhower left office warning of the dangers to our democracy emanating from the "industrial-defense-complex"—meaning war equates to money and power. Kennedy was left to deal with these issues under the premise he would follow the advice of his national security advisors in both the CIA and military. A complicating problem was the CIA's interactions with the mafia in efforts to assassinate Castro. The result would eventually devastate this nation with the assassination of a president, to be followed by a series of high-profile murders in a relatively condensed period of our history—the sixties.

First, Kennedy upset his national security group by withholding air cover for the Bay of Pigs invasion. Individuals in the Cuban community were upset with Kennedy. Second, the national security group that involved individuals in the CIA was again upset with Kennedy for holding the CIA and military back from an invasion of Cuba during the missile crisis. Now knowing the extent of nuclear warheads in Cuba at the time, as described above, it was a good decision on Kennedy's part. Third, the CIA, took the concept of "plausible deniability" as blanket immunity with a license to kill and intervene in the internal affairs of other nations—in essence, they were out of control. Subsequently, Kennedy fired CIA director Allen Dulles, Richard Bissell, and Charles Cabell. This did not sit well with the hard-core agents who helped to establish the new CIA after the WWII. Janney reports:[412]

> ..., the president made an attempt to immediately deal with the CIA and redefine its mandate by issuing two new National Security Action Memoranda (55 and 57) on June 28, 1961, whereby he stripped the CIA of its covert military operational capacity and put it back into the hands of the Pentagon and the Joint Chiefs of Staff—at least on paper.[77] Ultimately, the memoranda may not have changed anything, other than to incur the

307

further wrath of CIA higher-ups. Kennedy then moved "quietly," according to historian Arthur Schlesinger Jr., "to cut the CIA budget in 1962 and again in 1963, aiming at a 20 percent reduction by 1966."[78]

Janney, in his book, paints Angleton in a different and new light, as the man behind the scenes pulling all the switches—the master plotter—he seemed to have his hands in everything. President Johnson becomes president and begins a more aggressive campaign in Viet Nam, then is faced with a Middle East crisis. The question is how far he put his foot directly into matters, or did Angleton, who was setting his own foreign policy, manipulate him and the administration. Johnson was the beneficiary of JFK's assassination, and peace was the victim. Some authors are putting LBJ on the edge of the plotting, if not the undercutting of Kennedy's policies. One in particular is Phillip F. Nelson in his book, *LBJ The Mastermind of the JFK Assassination.*[413] The reader can find a critique of Nelson's book and other information dealing with Kennedy's assassination on the website, *Citizens for Truth About the Kennedy Assassination.*[414]

A comment should be made here dealing with the release of government information. Certain elements in the government dig their heels in and fight legal efforts to discover information dealing with government agency conduct and policies. Information that should not be held secret in perpetuity of which the public in a democracy has the right to know. A very recent example of this is an e-mail broadcast I received because of the being on the GWU National Security Archives mail-list:

Washington, DC, May 10, 2012 -- More than year after the National Security Archive sued the CIA to declassify the full "Official History of the Bay of Pigs Operation," a U.S. District Court judge today sided with the Agency's efforts to keep the last volume of the report secret in perpetuity. In her ruling, Judge Gladys Kessler accepted the CIA's legal arguments that, because Volume V was a "draft" and never officially approved for inclusion in the Agency's official history, it was exempt from declassification under the "deliberative process privilege" despite having been written over 30 years ago.

The e-mail notice further states:

> The volume, titled "CIA's Internal Investigations of the Bay of Pigs Operations," was written by CIA historian Jack Pfeiffer in 1981. It forcefully critiqued the scathing investigative report written in the immediate aftermath of the paramilitary attack -- by the CIA's own Inspector General, Lyman Kirkpatrick -- which held CIA planners fully responsible for the worst debacle in the Agency's covert history. In court papers, CIA officials described Pfeiffer's critique as "a polemic of recriminations against CIA officers who later criticized the operation."

The GWU-NSA FOIA lawsuit did produce Volumes I, II, and IV. Volume III was released pursuant to Kennedy Assassination Records Act in 1998. These volumes are available on the NSA website.[415] This issue is very pertinent to our study of the attack on the USS *Liberty* because the National Security Agency and the CIA are still withholding information. The point is that we are still dealing with a battle to release government information that is over 50 years old. It remains to be seen if the GWU-NSA will appeal the judge's decision.

Was there a covert operation to remove Nasser, whether called *Frontlet615* or *Operation Cyanide*? Interestingly, a website has tracked our covert entanglements over the years between 1946 and 1983, beginning in 1946 in GREECE: Restore monarch after overthrow of Metaxas government—successful; 1956: EGYPT: Overthrow Nasser government—unsuccessful. An extensive number of covert operations are listed, however, there is no operation listed for dealing with Nasser in 1967. This does not mean there was not one; just that it has been buried deep in the government archives.[416]

The secret 1956 operation discussions included British, French and Israeli participants as well as Moshe Dayan, Shimon Peres and Ben-Gurion. The plan was that Israel would create a pretext for bringing in the British because of the threat posed to the canal. Patrick Dean, chairman of the British Joint Intelligence Committee signed a written summary of the understanding along with Peneau for the French and Ben-Gurion for Israel. The *Protocol of Sèvres* lacked a preamble and simply summarized the discussions and agreement of 22-24 October 1956. There were seven articles: The first said Israel would launch an attack toward the canal on the evening of October 29; next, Britain and France were to call for belligerents to stop all military action. The parties were to pull back to a particular line and Egypt alone was to allow "temporary occupation" of key possessions on the canal by Anglo-French forces to guarantee freedom of passage through the canal by vessels of all nations until a final arrangement.

The details leading up to this protocol are in the book *Suez* by Keith Kyle previously cited. My point is that the protocol begins to set up a "MO" of using a pretext to justify an end result. We do not know if there was a similar written protocol between the Johnson administration and Israel leading up to the Six-day War.

Another goal was for the U.S. to maintain good relations with Jordan and Saudi Arabia, both of whom were essentially anti-Nasser. Deacon reports that Nasser put himself on a limb by not attending a meeting of the Defense Council of the Arab League on grounds that Egypt was not ready to deal with or exchange secrets with those in the pay of the CIA and British Intelligence Services. [417]

The agreement between the CIA and Israeli Intelligence Services dominated the war situation with Israel holding the trump card and having certain reservations. There was an understanding with King Hussein that if he pursued a pro-Western approach to Arab diplomacy, in the event Egypt lost the war, there would be a U.S. guarantee that Israel would not invade them. Nevertheless, Hussein felt he needed to appear pro-Egyptian prior to the war and he signed a defense pack with Nasser on May 30, 1967. [418]

The CIA-Mossad-Aman plan envisioned a quick war starting the second week of June. This period is consistent with a document received from the LBJ Presidential Library pursuant to a disclosure request that named an operation called *Frontlet615*. Recall that this operation originated in the 303 Committee and involved a submarine in UAR waters. It is this writer's opinion that *Frontlet615* and project or operation *Cyanide* were two different matters with the former being an effort by the

311

Joint Chiefs to monitor the events of the Six-Day War and the CIA's involvement. The war did not start on 15 June but was jump-started by Israel on June 5 with surprised air-attacks on Arab air forces. The Israelis were concerned about developing talks between the U.S. State Department and an Egyptian representative.

The Israeli concern was that State Department deference to Egypt could screw the plan up thereby causing concern within the Mossad and the Israeli military establishment. A Mossad agent in Cairo reported that President Nasser was sending Zacharia Mohieddin on an exploratory mission to Washington on June 5, 1967. This event and timing was of concern to the Israelis since time was of the essence, therefore, they struck out on their own; although they had already received certain U.S. military and intelligence assistance mostly facilitated by Angleton and the CIA.

As to any scenario of plotting partners, both sides were afraid of being double-crossed by the other according to Deacon. This is where we get back into the question of the *Liberty's* mission. It is one thing to let a plan stew on the operational level while details are worked out, and another on the political level, where policy guidelines are set subject to various real world pressures and issues that can just as quickly change. Such was the situation with President Johnson who was dealing with both the war in Vietnam and his reelection effort. For the latter he need money and support from the Jewish lobby in the United States as well as for his Vietnam policies for which he was not getting Jewish support, and this frustrated him greatly.

Consequently, there was concern about the plan being leaked, so the Israelis stepped up the war to start on June

312

5, 1967. The Israeli ploy was that Nasser would preemptively strike; however, the U.S. did not buy that. The U.S. intelligence position was that Egyptian forces were in no condition to take on the Israelis. Deacon contends that as the Americans relied upon Israeli intelligence services so much that they were in the dark as to when the war would start. This was not a joint plan where the U.S. would provide ground troops as there were few in the immediate area with us bogged down in Vietnam. We had only 1400 shipboard marines in the area. More importantly, everything was carried out on the covert level, as Johnson did not believe he could get a resolution through Congress authorizing overt joint action in support of Israel. Johnson did not think he could get a *Gulf of Tonkin* type resolution (the type that escalated our involvement in Vietnam).

How smart was it to place all our eggs in one basket so-to-speak and rely on the Israelis. Reliance could be construed as the folly of the Angleton plan knowing that he tended to withhold information from the President and others in the CIA. The folly would again hit us during the bomb attack on the Marine barracks in Lebanon in 1983 killing 299 American and French service personnel, and the attack of 9/11. According to former rogue Mossad agent and author, Victor Ostrovsky, Israeli intelligence knew about the Mercedes truck rigged as a bomb used against the Marine barracks in Lebanon in which 241 marines lost their lives; but did not forward the information in a manner to forewarn of the attack. Ostrovsky notes that a "general warning" was allowed, but not a "specific warning". He reports that instructions were "No, we're not there to protect Americans. They're a big country. Send only the regular information." Ostrovsky goes so far as to attribute this order to then head of the Mossad at that time.[419] More can be found on this incident including criticism of Ostrovsky claiming he was not in-the-know, and it is reported that the Mossad director denies the allegation.[420]

As for 9/11, the 9/11 Commission report noted our lack of human intelligence in the Middle East and saw this as a serious deficiency. Undoubtedly, this was due to the Faustian bargain Angleton struck with the Israeli intelligence services wherein his superiors obviously bought into the arrangement either directly or indirectly through malfeasant management until William Colby as DCI terminated him.

The Israelis overlooked the fact that the U.S. government might want to guard against any change of plans, and the fact that the Soviets might get involved if Israel's plans spilled over to Jordan and Syria. The Joint Chiefs wanted the USS *Liberty* rushed to the war area off the coast of Gaza and the Sinai to keep an eye on Israeli war efforts. Deacon believes that CIA also wanted to monitor the situation—rightly so. Not all parts of the CIA bureaucracy were in accord since some elements still worked with the Arabs. Recall in the chapter dealing with mission that the issue of nuclear weapons was raised in a security briefing with the President. As previously discussed, the *Liberty* was to keep the NSA and JCS up to date with activity by both the Arabs and Israelis for dissemination to end users like the Sixth Fleet, DOD and CIA and the President. Israel could not afford to have the *Liberty* spying on their military because of their hidden war objective which was the seizure of land for security purposes—their hidden agenda. It has always been about land as noted by Ben-Gurion, and is even today a priority with Israeli settlement expansion in the West Bank and in

Jerusalem that is a continuing contention between the Obama administration and the Israeli government.

The final days prior to the war involved a surge of diplomacy and secret meetings in Washington. Two powers were in conflict: First, the Israeli and CIA objectives were not necessarily mutual, and Johnson's position as president was weakening over his policies in Vietnam.[421] He would face a presidential run by Robert Kennedy with Richard Nixon on the Republican side. From a landslide in 1964, he would decide to withdraw from the '68 campaign.

While planning was going on between intelligence services, the KBG was very much in the game sending out streams of reports dealing with the so-called build-up of Israeli forces on the border with Syria. Ahmed Shukeriy, the first chairman of the PLO from 1964 to 1967, began to escalate their attacks from Syria and Gaza. On May 12, a *United Press International* dispatch from Jerusalem reported a highly placed Israeli source said today that if Syria continued a campaign of sabotage in Israel it would immediately provoke military action aimed at overthrowing the Syrian regime. Author Anthony Pearson reports that this was the first suggestion that Israel might want to overthrow the Syrian government.[422]

Watching the news today, we can conclude that we are dealing with "old problems" to which there seems to be no easy solution. Syria and the Russians are still proving to be a problem with claims that a Russian company is providing Syria with a fresh supply of arms while Assad continues to kill Syrians.

Digression: Russian foreign minister, Sergey Lavrov said none of the weapons Russia currently is supplying to Syria could be used against the protesters and that the arms trade is aimed at helping Syria fend off external threats. Russia backs Assad's claim that the uprising is a foreign conspiracy and that weapons and militants have been brought into Syria from abroad.[423]

Levi Eshkol denied the border build up allegations and invite Soviet Ambassador Chuvakhin to go to the northern front and verify conditions for himself; he declined on advice of the embassy KGB head.[424] Author Anthony Pearson reports that notwithstanding the fact the British lost face in the Middle East over the Suez War, it still had strong intelligence assets through MI-6 in the Middle East, better than the CIA that relied on the Israelis. Pearson reports that MI-6 was aware of the CIA and Israeli plan for a limited conflict. Again, it appears that Deacon and Pearson are talking about the same scenario. Deacon in his book did have a bibliography and endnotes that were not include Pearson's book that had no bibliography or notes to ascertain his sources though he described them to a limited extent in his narrative. However, what both authors had in common was ties to British intelligence.

Importantly, Pearson reports that the Russians were aware of the CIA/Mossad plan based on British intelligence reports from Yemen; however, the Soviets were pushing Nasser into a war like posture by constant alarms about the Syrian border for their own reasons. The CIA knew that the Egyptian army was not in condition to fight the Israelis and the Russians did not intend to provide more than token arms to the Egyptians and advisory help if war came.[425] It appears that both the Soviets and CIA had the same goal to remove Nasser for their own separate reasons. However, Pearson believes that the Russian were going to let the Americans and Israelis to do the job of getting rid of Nasser to place a person more pliable in his place. This is not to imply that the Soviets did not have an operational plan to intervene more forcibly having placed a large armada in the Eastern Mediterranean and the placing of bombers and fighter escorts on alert.

Pearson then reports that Israel was not interested in Russian or American plans for the Middle East and just wanted land for settlements, the same issue that survives today marking differences between President Obama's administration and that of Israeli Prime Minister Netanyahu. Unresolved issues from the time of the Six-day War continue to exacerbate Middle East conflicts to current times.

On the night the *Liberty* was dispatched to Point Alfa, Abba Eban, the Israeli foreign minister, flew to Paris where he met with de Gaulle who was not about to involve France in another Suez Canal venture. France did not see the blockage of the Tiran Straits as a declaration of war and wanted to consult with the Soviets. Despite pleadings from Eban, de Gaulle felt that the world was closer to a third world war.[426] Eban flew to London to meet with Prime Minister Harold Wilson who thought issues should be handled between Britain and the United States. Wilson thought a confrontation could develop between Russia and NATO. Again, rebuffed, Eban flew to Washington to meet with President Johnson.

America had considered an effort called "Operation Regatta" to break the Tiran Straits blockade. That plan went nowhere. Johnson was in a dilemma as he and

317

advisors wanted to help Israel, but Congress would not want to see a heavy American commitment in view of Vietnam. The CIA continued with its plans with Johnson not being fully aware of the history of our relationship with Israel. According to Pearson, Eban's meeting with Johnson was arranged by Ephraim "Eppy" Evron, the Mossad liaison in Washington, and of the Lavon Affair fame, accompanied by Israeli Ambassador Avraham Harman.

Johnson was frustrated knowing the potential for war; however, he wanted to get rid of the Israeli delegation. Pearson notes that neither Johnson nor Eban had been briefed by intelligence networks about the joint war plan[427]. On May 27, Eban flew back to Tel Aviv and advised Eshkol of the disappointing results of his mission. Eshkol was facing replacement, however, a "unity government" was set up with Moshe Dayan as the Minister of Defense, again separating roles formerly held by the Prime Minister. Dayan was a hard liner with support of the generals and intelligence service leaders as well as the Israeli public.

Pearson's informant relayed information about meetings in Israel of former members of the Haganah and Palmach and Irgun, all groups that fought during the War of Independence, including Dayan, Allon, Peres, Hacohen, Weizman, Yariv and Meir Amit—the "old guard".[428] There were return visits to Washington by members of this team liaisoning via Angleton.

A key member of this team was Meir Amit who flew to Washington and met with Angleton, the Department of Defense and the CIA. The message from the Johnson administration was that Israel should not be the first to go to war if it wanted United States support. Amit wanted a

318

"green light" to proceed. He met with McNamara and was told his place was at home after Amit told McNamara that Israeli causalities would be minimal. Amit reported to the Cabinet, the consequence of which was that the war was moved up and started on June 5, with devastating air assaults wiping out the Egyptian and other Arab air forces while planes sat mostly on the ground.

Johnson had personally relayed to Evron that Congress would not support involvement without a "Gulf of Tonkin" type resolution. How did Evron interpret this comment? Did he pass this comment to Israeli intelligence personnel such as to plant a seed for a scheme of how to ensnare the U.S. into aiding the Israelis by acting as insurance against Soviet intervention?

With ambiguous signals coming from the Johnson White House, the tone should have clearly been that Israel would protect itself, while the U.S. was concerned about intervention by the Soviets—the big unknown. The *Liberty* was to provide the NSA with intercepts of both the Arab and Israelis. Once the war started, Israel had broken Egyptian and Jordanian ciphers, ergo the "cooking" of messages the essence of which was to suck Jordan into the war to allow Israeli intervention. On the night of June 7, Israel knew the U.S. had discovered their plan. The Israeli ambassador was called to the State Department and told that the Israeli attack must stop as a cease-fire was to be ordered by the UN Security Council. The ambassador was told we knew that Jordan was "tricked" into action.[429]

Was the Israeli Mossad and Aman told about the *Liberty*? The ship had been picked up by Israeli air surveillance on June 7 pursuant to an order to find "any

319

spy ship". Rabin acknowledges that the *Liberty* was eavesdropping on their commanders and plans. The pending attack on Syria was held up. The *Liberty* was attacked and Dayan then ordered the Syria attack to proceed.

Research dealing with the Israeli motive for the attack generally focuses on specific Israeli concerns; however, there could have been a simple general concern of interference with the Israeli war and diplomatic operations. Israel was concerned about leakage to the U.S. State Department and to the UN, and yet worse, the UN would pass word onto the Egyptians as it was alleged to have done in the Congo and elsewhere in Africa.

In 1980, Wilbur Eveland, a former CIA officer, published his book entitled *Ropes of Sand: America's Failure in the Middle East*, which contradicts the official position of the Central Intelligence Agency set forth in its intelligence memorandum of June 13, 1967 that the attack was a mistake reconfirmed publicly many times thereafter. As previously noted, Eveland stated that President Johnson authorized James Jesus Angleton to inform Ephraim Evron, the Israeli Deputy Chief of Mission, at the Israeli Embassy in Washington, that the United States would prefer Israeli efforts to lessen the tension, but would not intervene to stop an attack on Egypt. Eveland explains that he obtained this bit of information after he left the CIA. He states:[430]

> Under orders from the Joint Chiefs of Staff, the USS Liberty was rushed to the waters off Israel's shore to permit this sophisticated communications-monitoring vessel to follow the fighting should the Israelis attack Egypt. The Liberty wasn't sent alone, for an even

more important reason. Stationed below her was the Polaris nuclear submarine Andrew Jackson, for the Pentagon knew that the CIA had aided Israel in acquiring a nuclear capability. Moreover, the U.S. had provided the Israelis with missiles, to which atomic warheads could be attached. Thus, in case a bogged-down Israeli army decided to use ballistic missiles to win a war against the Soviet-equipped Egyptian army, the U.S. was in a position to warn both Israel and Russia that the introduction of nuclear warfare would produce instantaneous retaliation. . . . Message intercepts by the Liberty made it clear that Israel had never intended to limit its attack to Egypt....To destroy this incriminating evidence, Moshe Dayan ordered his jets and torpedo boats to destroy the Liberty immediately. . . .

Then the U.S. Government shrouded the entire Liberty matter in secrecy under a cloak of national security considerations. Why? Defense Minister Dayan had stated his government's position bluntly: unless the United States wished the Russians and Arabs to learn of joint CIA-Mossad covert operations in the Middle East and of Angleton's discussions before the 1967 fighting started, the questions of the lost American ship and how the war originated should be dropped. That ended the U.S. protestations.

Professional reviews of the Eveland book are critical and doubt that he had plausible access to information to back up his "revelations." CIA Director Richard Helms, referring to the Eveland book at a conference organized by Ambassador Richard B. Parker and held on the twenty-fifth anniversary of the 1967 war at the Center for the Study of Foreign Affairs of the Department of State's Foreign Service Institute in Rosslyn, Virginia, said: "Let me put to rest one or two things. First, books like Miles Copeland *The Game of Nations* [London: Weidenfeld and Nicolson, 1969], Eveland *Ropes of Sand*, and others: The Central Intelligence Agency has had the misfortune to have had certain former employees who have written mischievous books, not necessarily based on fact, a lot of it just plain fiction." [431]

One would assume that the director of a clandestine organization would want internal affairs and covert operations kept from the public eye, even to the point of withholding the truth from Congress. [432]   As an example of the "game", Miles Copeland in his book *Without Cloak or Dagger,* in his index hides the identity of Angleton by referring to "Mother", his code-name. [433]   Whereas, Eveland clearly identifies Angleton in his book *Ropes of Sand,* of course Eveland had a contentious relationship with Angleton that eventually sent his career into decline over U.S. Middle East foreign policy.

At the heart of this contention is a comment made by Tahsin Basheer at Parker's conference on the Six-Day War, a comment Helms took exception with. Basheer referred to a quote from Eveland's book, alluding to conspiracies as he quotes Eveland: "Angleton concluded that General Abdul Nasser was responsible for the West's only problem in the area. If Nasser could be eliminated, the Egyptian Army defeated without overt major power assistance, the Arabs would be left with no alternative to making peace with Israel." [434] Basheer was a member of Egypt's UN delegation in 1967.

At the Parker conference, Helms denied there was a U.S. Israeli plot in 1967. He dismissed as nonsense the idea, mentioned in the Andrew and Leslie Cockburn book *Dangerous Liaison* that the CIA's James Angleton would have colluded on his own with the Israelis to bring down Nasser. The authors claim, "The 1967 war was launched with American permission to 'break Nasser in pieces'."[435] He also commented that there was no substance to the accusation contained in Stephen Green's book *Taking Sides*, that a U.S. reconnaissance squadron had flown missions for Israel during the war. Neither Helms, nor Robert McNamara, had ever heard of such missions, which would have been impossible without the knowledge of either of the two.[436] The covert activity of the reconnaissance mission was not only mentioned by author Green, but also by Peter Hounam in his book. Mossad Director, Meir Amit's, take on the conspiracy was that "...the main thrust of Israeli-U.S. intelligence liaison had been exchanges about the Soviets. He apparently felt that his earlier comments in panel 3 of the conference had answered the conspiracy allegations."[437] Therefore, both Helms and Amit, directors of their respective intelligence agencies, continue to adhere to the cornerstone of spying—deniability.

The issue of whether President Johnson gave a "green light" to Amit, when he visited Washington just prior to the war, Amit stated: "My goal in this meeting is to give an answer to the simple question whether I, Meir Amit, got a green, yellow, or any other light from the American authorities to wage a war, especially from my friend Dick Helms. I want to say now, before I start, the answer is no. Not a green, not a yellow or any other light. To convince you, I have the original report that I wrote on June 4,

1967. This is copy number two out of eight. This is written here and whoever reads Hebrew can read it."[438]

As a side note: Eveland ended up bringing a lawsuit against the Director of the CIA. He represented himself *pro-se*. His original complaint name William J. Casey and others including Richard Helms and James Jesus Angleton. Eveland based jurisdiction on the Racketeer Influenced and Corrupt Organizations Act (RICO), 18 U.S.C. Sec. 1961 et seq. Allegations fell into two categories: First, Eveland goes on to allege generally that Kissinger has assumed the powers of the President and has enabled the government of Israel to dominate the conduct of United States foreign policy. The second category involves allegations that government officials engaged in tortuous conduct against Eveland. Such activity includes libel, slander, character assassination, the publication of false charges, and attempted murder and other life-threatening actions. Specifically, Eveland alleges that Kissinger acted to discredit Eveland as a national security risk, did away with Eveland's "business interests and professional position", caused Eveland to live below the poverty level and engaged in measures to eliminate Eveland.

The Court held: "In summary, we find that Eveland's suit is barred by the political question doctrine in so far as it concerns foreign policy in the Middle East. His claims for money damages are barred by principles of sovereign immunity and the lack of personal jurisdiction over the individual defendants. The requests for specific relief also are barred by sovereign immunity. The judgment of the district court is therefore Affirmed."[439] Obviously, there is a price to pay for challenging those in power—tragic.

324

Eveland's effort to base jurisdiction on the RICO statute is interesting as the court notes:

> Eveland's RICO claims also were properly dismissed under the political question doctrine. The only intelligible mention of RICO in the complaint is a statement that "Henry Kissinger, and those who have worked with him, and still are, have sold America to a RICO-controlled organization: the present government of Israel." It is clear that such an allegation concerns foreign policy and again reflects Eveland's attempt to air his differences with the government's conduct of Middle Eastern foreign policy. Eveland cannot use RICO to seek judicial redress for such a political question.

An interesting obituary dealing with Eveland's death on January 2, 1990 can be found on the Internet, *In Memoriam A Respectful Dissenter*: *CIA's Wilbur Crane Eveland*.[440] There are a couple of interesting items learned from the obituary and his lawsuit. First, he alleges that James Jesus Angleton, per Eveland's lawsuit complaint, conspired with the Israeli Mossad to falsify documents indicating Eveland passed classified information to British double agent, Kim Philby. The second item is in the obituary and referenced in the Court of Appeals decision in footnote No. 1 that his wife was murdered. He added this charge to his complaint on his appeal; and his obituary states: "Eveland subsequently charged that her respirator was turned off by a member of the intelligence community, who coolly admitted the murder to Eveland."[441]

No further information is provided, but his dissent from our Middle Eastern foreign policy going back over the years is certainly evident by his actions and statements. My final comment on this matter is that Eveland represented himself pro-se in a complex litigation that went against him for the most part on substantive procedural grounds.

In the denial game, where there is smoke there most likely is fire. While Helms' comment was a dig at Eveland, it should be remembered that he denied that there were nuclear weapons in the Middle East region when asked by the President; and Parker, a researcher and authority on the Six-day War later admitted he had no knowledge that nuclear weapons were an issue in that war. Notwithstanding the foregoing, Helms was unequivocal about the attack on the *Liberty*: "I had no role in the board of inquiry that followed, or the board's finding that there could be no doubt that the Israeli's knew exactly what they were doing in attacking the Liberty. I have yet to understand why it was felt necessary to attack this ship or who ordered the attack."[442] He refers to a "board of inquiry" that made a finding that the Israelis knew what they were doing. It is unclear as to who conducted this board of inquiry. Strangely, this comment about the "board of inquiry" does not jive with the CIA Memorandum of 6/13/1967 referred to above with differing conclusions.

Notwithstanding the Helms' position, the June 1967 war had an important nuclear dimension. New and little-known Israeli and American sources suggest that Israel had improvised two nuclear devices and placed them under alert. Author Avner Cohen suggests that some time prior to the Six-Day War Israel had achieved a rudimentary nuclear weapons capability, and during the tense days of the crisis in late May, it placed that capability under "operational alert." By the eve of the war, Israel had two deliverable explosive devices.

A new set of American-Israeli understandings on the nuclear issue came into being in 1970 through meetings between President Richard Nixon and Prime Minister Golda Meir. The United States no longer pressed Israel to sign the NPT; it also ended the visits to Dimona. In return, Israel is committed to maintaining a low profile nuclear posture, no testing, no declaration, and no acknowledgment. With these, "Don't-Ask Don't-Tell", understandings nuclear opacity was born. Those understandings persist today.[443]

Therefore, in this context of the U.S. relationship with Israel how would Angleton have had any impact on what happened to the USS *Liberty*, a question we posed earlier. He could have been involved in the planning process with Israeli intelligence. He could have coordinated and facilitated U.S. units providing intelligence, photo recon, and equipment such as communication equipment to aid Israeli intelligence.[444] Author Hounam believes that any resources needed from the U.S. would have been authorized by the 303 Committee.

Could he have tipped off the Israelis of the ship's assignment to Point Alfa? Could he have somehow facilitated setting the *Liberty* up as a "Gulf of Tonkin" type pretext? President Johnson had advised "Eppy" Evron that Congress would not authorize a U.S. intervention on behalf of Israel without a "Gulf of Tonkin" type resolution.[445] Did this plant a seed?

A search of the Internet via Google shows a couple of items. A *Spotlight* report of Nov. 21, 1977 implicated the

327

CIA's counterintelligence chief, James J. Angleton, in having conspired with Israel in orchestrating the attack on the *Liberty*. "An Israeli loyalist who headed the CIA's liaison with Israel's intelligence agency, the Mossad, and who also played a key role in helping Israel develop its nuclear arsenal (in defiance of President John F. Kennedy), Angleton believed the destruction of the *Liberty* could be used as a 'Pearl Harbor' or 'Remember the Maine' type incident to inflame American passions against the Arabs."[446] This author makes no comment on this information in terms of credibility.

Misinformation and deception has always been a Mossad trademark. The most prominent victim was the U.S., thanks to an agreement negotiated by CIA Assistant Director James Jesus Angleton that Israel and America would not spy on each other. The Mossad always ignored the pact in America, but until Admiral Stansfield Turner nullified the agreement a generation later, when he was Jimmy Carter's CIA director, the CIA apparently relied on Mossad data. After Angleton died, a memorial was erected to him in Jerusalem, as previously noted.

Under the circumstances and because of enduring secrecy it would be understandable for some of the *Liberty* survivors to believe they were setup. This is something that as of this date cannot be proven even though our government has a MO of utilizing the "pretext" to embark on a military venture.[447]

It is contended that Angleton helped to protect Israel's nuclear secrets.[448] As for Angleton there is no evidence he was involved in the *Liberty* attack, and anything to the contrary is mere speculation. Author Seymour Hersh who implicated him in illegal CIA domestic spying writes that he handled his Israeli desk account properly.

328

However, Hersh reports that some of Angleton's files found wrapped with black tape indicated a suspicion of American Jews in the government that amounted to a matrix of position and "Jewishness" of senior officials in the CIA and elsewhere who had access to classified information of use to Israel. Those that rated high were classified for scrutiny. Hersh reports the matter was not investigated further on Angleton's retirement. Perhaps, notwithstanding his quirks it shows his primary interest was ferreting out possible moles in the CIA.[449] There are plenty of reasons for the government not to make disclosures that could cause embarrassment.

John Ranelagh, author of *The Agency*, makes an interesting observation re the attack on the USS *Liberty*: "Friendship between metropolitan centers of power did not necessarily mean friendship at the edges… Friendship between America and Israel did not prevent the Israeli Air Force from attacking the USS *Liberty*...." He contends the attack was intended to keep the intelligence the *Liberty* collected from forcing Israel into an unsatisfactory peace.[450]

(CENSORED) commented on the sinking (sic) of the US communication ship, Liberty. They said that Dayan personally ordered the attack on the ship and that one of his generals adamantly opposed the action and said, "This is pure murder." One of the admirals who was present also disapproved the action, and it was he who ordered it stopped and not Dayan. (CENSORED) believed that the attack against the US vessel is also detrimental to any political ambition Dayan may have.

CIA Report of unevaluated
information, October 1967.

Chapter 11

The Order: "Sink It!"

Both authors, Jim Ennes and Peter Hounam, give a codename to the joint CIA/Mossad war plan—*Operation Cyanide.* In a 2002 supplement to his book, author Jim Ennes, reports that all efforts to learn about "Contact X", the mystery submarine tracking below the *Liberty*, have turned up little public information. Ennes claims he received information from a former submarine crewmember confirmed by other confidential sources. *Liberty* survivor, Charles Rowley, also confirmed the story of a submarine according to Hounam.[451] The submarine in question was the *Amberjack*; however, Ennes says the sub's commander denies it. "The submarine, he says, was on an especially sensitive mission called "Project Cyanide".[452] Ennes verifies the release from the Johnson library of a document dealing with another codename, *Frontlet615*, as previously mentioned authorizing a submarine in UAR waters. Some speculation is that the submarine was actually the Polaris sub *Andrew Jackson*, and that it was the sub authorized to conduct a top-secret mission in Egyptian territorial waters. Such is the world of government covert operations—strictly a need to know, and to the extent possible the public has no need to know what the government is doing in all too many cases.

Hounam cites that Charles Rowley, in the spook spaces, relayed an encrypted signal from a mysterious submarine that led to rousting President Johnson in the middle of the night; the content of the message is unknown. This being the case, it would tend to confirm that Contact X used the *Liberty* as a communication relay link, which makes sense due to a submarine's limited communication capabilities when submerged.

Project Cyanide is discussed in a BBC production called *Dead in the Water,* about the *Liberty,* and in a new book by prize-winning investigative reporter, Peter Hounam, called *Operation Cyanide.*[453] A word of caution for the reader: The use of two codenames can be confusing as to their context since we are to speculate about a covert operation. We know that *Frontlet615* pertained to a sub in UAR waters because we have a partially declassified memorandum to that effect released by the LBJ Library. Does *Project Cyanide* also pertain to it or to a larger joint CIA/Mossad plan, or could it be the other way around? There may be no easy answer absent government disclosures.

Peter Hounam is a hero to *Liberty* survivors for his diligent efforts to penetrate the "big lie". He was Chief Investigative Reporter at *The Sunday Times* in London. He was involved in the TV documentary production *Dead in the Water* (2002) as the main researcher, and is the author of five books including *The Woman from Mossad.* This book told the story of Mordechai Vanunu the Israeli whistleblower who was the first person who

331

publicly exposed Israel's nuclear bomb program at the Dimona reactor site in the Negev desert where he worked, with photographs to back up his claims. Hounam at the newspaper was involved in the Vanunu story; and in his book about Vanunu, he detailed an Israeli Mossad "honey-pot" operation where a female operative lured Vanunu out of Britain to Rome where he was kidnapped, returned to Israel for trial and imprisonment as a traitor.

On February 2, 2004, the Israeli government was set to release the former technician jailed for 18 years, mostly in solitary confinement, after he exposed the country's covert nuclear weapons program. The Israeli paper, *Yediot Ahronot,* reported Vanunu was to be freed in April, and placed under tight surveillance. Israel's security forces would bar Vanunu from giving press interviews, publishing or travelling overseas. Additionally, Vanunu would be required to check in with the police on a regular basis. After his kidnapping, Vanunu was subjected to a secret trial and jailed in 1986 for treason. He had revealed previously secret details about Israel's covert nuclear weapons program and the role of its Dimona atomic reactor to London's *Sunday Times*.

Vanunu testified in a lawsuit against *Yediot Ahronot* after it allegedly reported he provided information to Hamas on how to make explosives.[454] Hounam, assigned by the *Sunday Times*, would visit Israel upon Vanunu's release after eighteen years of imprisonment (11 years in solitary confinement), to meet with him for an interview. In a dramatic twist, Hounam found himself under arrest and accused of nuclear espionage, undoubtedly, for his role in exposing the program via the newspaper he worked at. After participating in an interview conducted by an Israeli journalist, while driving through the outskirts of Tel Aviv, he was pulled over and arrested. While one copy of the interview tape was confiscated, another copy got through to London via a courier.

About his arrest, Hounam said he broke free and ran into the hotel restaurant and warned a person he knew of his pending arrest. He had a hood placed over his head and was dragged from one "windowless dungeon" room to another, being shackled, he was interrogated. His situation became international news, and with interest from Israeli media and diplomatic efforts, he was freed after 24 hours.

After his experience, Hounam could only imagine what kind of treatment Vanunu received from the Mossad in 1986. He relates the paper's initial contact with Vanunu as follows:[455]

> I had met him in Sydney, Australia, recorded in detail everything he knew, and taken him to London to be cross-questioned by experts. As a potential Mossad target, he accepted tight security precautions, but he later grew impatient. Strolling alone around Leicester Square in London, he met an attractive blonde American tourist called Cindy. They had a coffee, and arranged to go to the cinema. Vanunu had stupidly walked into a classic Mossad honeytrap.
> He said nothing to me of his dangerous liaison until it was too late. After hearing about his meetings with Cindy, I warned him she might be an Israeli agent but he dismissed the notion. I suggested meeting them for dinner that evening but he cancelled. Then he disappeared. It was several weeks before

Israel announced it was holding him on treason and spying charges.

The *Sunday Times* printed the Dimona nuclear story even though their star witness went missing. Hounam stated that he has been living a quieter life since his Israeli arrest incident, but obviously, from his story in the *Telegraph* he was not intimidated. Former Mossad agent turned author, Victor Ostrovsky, reports in his book *The Other Side of Deception*, that Israeli Prime Minister Shimon Peres knew there was no way to put the Vanunu story back in the *genie bottle* and wanted to take advantage of the situation by letting the Arab world know that Israel had the ability to annihilate them. Peres wanted it both ways, with the world fearing Israel and yet Israel having the ability to keep denying the nuclear weapons program. Hounam thought that Peres wanted the story suppressed. Ostrovsky reports a rift between then Foreign Minister, Shamir, and Peres, with the former wanting Vanunu killed and the story suppressed. Shamir wanted Israeli sayanim, Robert Maxwell, to run a story in his paper, the *Daily Mirror*, discrediting Vanunu. Ostrovsky confirms an Israeli *kidon* team was dispatched to London to lure Vanunu to Italy to be kidnapped and returned to Israel to stand trial.[456]

As for his part, publisher Robert Maxwell, at the age of 68, was presumed to have fallen overboard from his luxury yacht, the *Lay Ghislaine*, while cruising off the Canary Islands on November 5, 1991. He was buried on Mount of Olives in Jerusalem.[457] While the official cause of death was accidental drowning, some thought he was murdered, possible by Israeli agents as a pushback. Some thought him to have been an Israeli agent.[458] The alleged motive for his death was that he had financial troubles and was putting the squeeze on the Mossad to help him out for all his prior efforts on behalf of Israel.

Vanunu's and Hounam's story is relevant to our look into the attack on the USS *Liberty* because of the sub-title of Hounam's book, *Operation Cyanide,* and thesis that the bombing of the USS *Liberty* nearly caused World War III.

It was and is Israel's official government policy to refuse "unrestricted" inspections of Dimona, even to representatives of the U.S. government, and it has refused to acknowledge its nuclear weapons program to this day or to participate in the Nuclear Non-proliferation Treaty (NPT). Israel's policy is one of nuclear "opacity" saying it would not be the first to introduce nuclear weapons into the Middle East. Israel has never officially acknowledged its nuclear program; however, Israel is alleged to have had one or two crude weapons at the time of the Six-Day War as discussed in the prior chapter.

In recent times there have been more media stories dealing with Israel's nuclear arsenal. While Israel is not a participant in the NPT; nevertheless, in the context of the present controversy dealing with Iran's nuclear program there has been additional statements that Israel should come clean and sign off on the treaty. Israel's position is that "opacity" suites its strategic position. It is reported Israel now has some 200 nuclear weapons with air, land, and sea delivery systems including Dolphin class submarines purchased from Germany[459].

We have previously discussed disclosures by authors Deacon and Pearson regarding the issue of "cooked" messages as a deception method applied to communications between Nasser and Hussein of Jordan.

335

Hounam relates the story of a communications expert who had free-lanced for both the U.S. and British governments. This individual's experience goes back to the late 1960s. Hounam reports that this person's involvement in the Six-Day War got him a prominent scar across his belly, and his 1966 deployment by the United States to help Israel helps to explain much about the secrecy behind the *Liberty* affair. Hounam reports the individual confirmed to him that this was a joint plan by elements of military intelligence in Israel and the United States to engineer a war with Egypt and depose its leader Gamal Abdul Nasser who, the U.S. believed, was a dangerous puppet of Moscow" and espousing Arab nationalism.[460]

Hounam reports in August of 1966, the individual was secretly sent as an advisor to the Israeli Army. He found the agitation between Israel and its Arab neighbors as no greater than usual, but when he arrived in Tel Aviv he found a "a total commitment to a state of readiness" among the military. He discovered he was part of a multi-national force of so-called advisers. Some described as Brits and Aussies who were intelligence and communication specialist.

Hounam reports the person said senior officers were from the United States and were in charge of a covert operation. The person did not release names because some were still working at the time Hounam interviewed him. Further, it was claimed that some of the Brits might have been from MI-6, which would tend to substantiate the flow of information that Deacon and Pearson picked up on, and noted in their books a decade or so after events of the Six-Day War.

336

The person related to Hounam, "I tutored young Israeli officers in a number of situations and venues." As related, they were provided with state-of-the-art communications equipment from the U.S., which, he divulged, was specially designed to distort or "cook" signals. One of the team was fluent in Egyptian who could imitate voices—for example, those coming from the Egyptian high command.[461] The person further advised that he had met with Meir Amit, head of Mossad in 1966, in the preparation for the conflict with Cairo.

Hounam reports the person's impression was the United States was pushing to eradicate Nasser, and that Israel was not the prime mover. It was his impression that more assistance would be provided, as the U.S. got more involved.

Hounam: "Would that *Liberty* attack have prompted that assistance?" The interviewee responded: "There's just so much speculation on that", he said, "You'd be amazed at some of things that were discussed-who perhaps promulgated it [the war]; who masterminded it; who supported it; who logistically assisted... Well, it would have taken a hell of a lot [of resources] for somebody to press a direct confrontation."[462]

The individual described as "horse shit" the commonly held notion that Israel fought this war on its own: "Anybody working around intelligence knows it isn't true." Hounam goes on to state: "He repeated that Operation Cyanide was a secret plan to start a war against Egypt, I asked if he had heard there might be an attack on a United States ship as a pretext for bringing the U.S. into the war?" The response was "Not until later on." He goes on to tell Hounam that Israel's only goal was to "grab territory", and it was elements in the U.S. who were pushing them to invade Egypt.[463] This is amazing, as we will later see when another author alleges, with new information, that the KGB and Soviet Union was pushing Israel into attacking Egypt. A consensus of several authors concludes that both the U.S. and Soviets wanted to get rid of Nasser for their own reasons.

In response to questions from Hounam, he said that the United States did not want Israel to attack Jordan or Syria. Hounam: "Was King Hussein pushed into the arms of Nasser by provocation?" The reply: "Absolutely". Hounam: "Was the Israeli cross-border raid on the Jordanian village of Samu an example?" Reply: "From time to time they would execute things like that, he added, as a provocation". Hounam: "Cyanide was the main name?" Reply: "Sure".[464]

The individual related that Meir Amit was involved with different objectives and that the Israeli Prime Minister Levi Eshkol and other government leaders were not consulted, at least in the early stages. At some point, this person was wounded in a field operation that limited his further involvement in the Six-Day War.[465]

Hounam would report that additional U.S. assistance to Operation Cyanide would include photoreconnaissance assistance in the form of assigning the 17th Tactical Reconnaissance Unit to Israel. This was also reported by author Stephen Green. This photo recon effort was essential to help Israel in its success in destroying the Egyptian air force on the ground.[466] Helms and McNamara would deny this—as expected—called "plausible denial".

On May 30, Mossad Chief Meir Amit was dispatched to Washington at the suggestion of Aman boss Yariv because there was confusion in Tel Aviv about the United States attitude toward the Israeli standoff with Egypt. The first person he met with was James Jesus Angleton a "trusted brother" according to Amit in his conversation with Hounam.[467] Angleton took Amit to Richard Helms the CIA director and into a meeting with 30 or 40 people where Amit recalled they were in essential agreement. After the meeting, he met with Secretary of Defense McNamara. Amit told Hounam, "I told McNamara, look we don't want even one soldier of you. All we want from you is to stop the Russians coming into the arena, and...to help us after the war." McNamara asked how many casualties would Israel suffer and Amit said "Less than the War of Independence". Amit says he asked, "Mr. Secretary, what do you advise me?" McNamara: "No, you go home; your place is there now." Amit told Hounam, "I drew the conclusion that it was a green light."[468] The gist of the meeting with McNamara is memorialized in the following document on the State Department, Office of the Historian website:[469]

124. Memorandum for the Record
Washington, June 1, 1967.
SUBJECT
Conversation between Major General Meir Amit and Secretary McNamara—late afternoon, 1 June 19672
Amit said that he met with McNamara for 40 minutes and told him three things: first, a short description of the military situation, second, the impact of the Israeli mobilization on Israel's economy and the fact that it could not be sustained for a long period, and third, "I told him that I'm personally going to recommend that we take action, because there's no way out, and please don't react. He

told me it was all right, the president knows that you are here and I have a direct line to the president." He said McNamara asked only two questions: how long a war would last, to which Amit replied, "Seven days," and how many casualties Israel would sustain. Amit said, "Here I became a diplomat. I said less than in 1948, when we had 6,000."

Deputy Director of the CIA, Vice Admiral Rufus Taylor, was the author of the above memorandum. There are nine itemized points underlying the understandings emanating from this meeting. Paragraph No. 9 notes, Amit raised the issue of meeting with the President, but was advised by Admiral Taylor that was not possible. "He expressed satisfaction with the entire interview and wondered aloud if he shouldn't have tried to see the President also. I told him such a move would be entirely out of the question, totally inappropriate, and that the President was quite well aware of Amit's visit and would receive from the Secretary all of the information Amit had conveyed." It sounds like Taylor was attempting to preserve President Johnson's "deniability" status; however, this memo put Johnson clearly "in-the-know".

Amit said that during the meeting McNamara consulted with Johnson several times so there is no doubt that Johnson was on top of the situation and giving his version of a "green light". At the same time, Rusk as Secretary of State was trying to avoid war by seeking contact with a representative of Nasser. Amit denied that Angleton was responsible for providing covert assistance but reports that Angleton visited after the war and was taken on a sightseeing trip. Recall the previous mention of two memorials in Israel dedicated to "their friend".

Author Russell Warren Howe writes that Angleton, the head of CIA covert activities, was the fulcrum of communications on the American side. He further reports, "Angleton was sentimentally sure that he could believe in the promises of Jerusalem"; however, the NSA wanted the *Liberty* moved into the area as a check "on Israeli good faith" and for general intelligence purposes to cover both Arab and Israeli communications traffic.[470]

One of the persons accompanying Amit was Ephraim Evron, the Mossad liaison in Washington.[471] As previously mentioned one of Johnson's concerns was political—getting him reelected in the context of the turmoil over Viet Nam. Evron met with the White House staff to arrange the visit of Abba Eban immediately prior to the war. Evron, on this May 26 visit was surprised that the President wanted to see him. Evron, the Deputy Chief of Mission at the Israeli embassy under Ambassador Avraham Harman, related that Johnson talked "in Texan terms" and he used "diplomatic terms". Johnson related, "I, Lyndon Johnson, have to get congressional approval if I want to act as President of the United States. Otherwise, I'm just a six-foot-four Texan friend of Israel." Evron noted that this description stuck with him. Johnson went on: "But you and I, the two most powerful people in Washington, are not going to get the Congress to pass another Tonkin resolution." Evron related, that knowing little about the Tonkin resolution and how Johnson got the resolution and the mood in the country, he thought, "He's telling me that Congress is never going to give him permission to use military force."[472]

Johnson had gone to Canada to meet with Canadian Premier Lester Pearson who had played a role in ending the Suez crisis in 1957 to obtain support for launching a new war against Egypt. In not getting that support, Hounam suggests that Johnson's next step was to seek a pretext for winning Congressional support. He suggests that the sinking of a U.S. surveillance ship and the death of 294 Americans would undoubtedly be a suitable *casus belli*.[473] So here, we are confronted with an American motive for the attack on the *Liberty*, not an Israeli motive! This, frankly, is the feeling of a number of *Liberty* survivors—that they were setup by their own government—a very *Machiavellian* approach by government. This "floating" allegation along with the failure of Congress to investigate the attack is an unhealed open wound for *Liberty* survivors and family members and supporters. It is certainly the basis for the government not wanting to open the *Liberty* Pandora Box.

The reference to a the Gulf of Tonkin resolution occurred to escalate U.S. involvement in Vietnam when in August 1964, two U.S. destroyers, the *Maddox* and *Turner Joy*, in the Gulf of Tonkin believed they were under attack by North Vietnamese motor torpedo boats. Governmental use of "the pretext" to justify action is not unusual; rather it is typical of a *modus operandi*. Hounam may stretch matters a little when he equates the U.S. attack on a Russian ship, the *Turkistan*, makes it more plausible for a Soviet attack on the *Liberty*.[474] Speculation runs rampant throughout this saga. The U.S. Air Force attack on the *Turkistan* occurred on June 2, 1967 while the ship was in Cam Pha, North Vietnam; probably too short a time to link it with the attack on the *Liberty*, from a suggestive standpoint.[475]

To summarize, the contention is that the U.S. administration wanted Nasser removed from office and was willing to support a covert operation to accomplish that objective. Israel had its own objectives, which involved gaining land for settlement expansion and border security as well as possessing Old Jerusalem. As President Johnson had noted Congress would not support military action in support of Israel to head off the potential for Soviet intervention. Was a pretext plan implemented to insure U.S. intervention to run interference for Israel? There are two sides of this coin if plausible, that the U.S. plan was to create a pretext, or on the Israel side to implement the pretext in order to carry out the implication of Johnson's comment to Evron about needing a Gulf of Tonkin type resolution.

Under this theory, the plan would be to have the *Liberty* attacked and the blame put on either the Egyptians or Soviets freeing Johnson's hands to do whatever he wanted including dropping an atomic bomb on Cairo. Hounam claims that "this" plan went array when the Israeli operation failed and the ship did not sink.[476] This is an astounding allegation that has resulted in little to no scrutiny by the media over the years.

Johnson's discussion with Evron about Congress not supporting intervention on behalf of Israel was not the only such furtive conversation with Evron. Author Seymour Hersh reports in his book that during a 1968 meeting with Israeli Prime Minister Eshkol at this Texas ranch, Johnson discussed with Evron, who was at the meeting, Israel's desire to get U.S. F-4 jets. Johnson reportedly told "Effy" that Israel was going to get the F-4s but Johnson wanted something from Israel first. Johnson wanted access to Dimona. Within weeks of the Eshkol summit, the CIA presented the President with an estimate that for the first time Israel had four nuclear warheads. Johnson told Helms to bury the report and Helms obeyed the order.[477]   Such was the nature of our relationship, that Israel had no better friend that President Johnson.

We have previously written that author Richard Deacon claims the order to attack the *Liberty* was all done orally with no written record.   Obviously, that would make sense since a major government MO is to make sure that "deniability" was available at hand, as a governing term.   CIA Director Richard Helms has said that the "303 Committee" was created just for this purpose—to afford the President deniability.

A comment is in order. Hounam's description of the message "cooking" follows the earlier contentions of Deacon and Pearson. Hounam does cite Pearson in his book. On the matter of which submarine linked up with the *Liberty*, Hounam notes that Pearson believed it to be the USS *Andrew Jackson*.   He notes that Ennes was aware of this contention by Pearson, but Ennes did not put much stock in what Pearson had to say because of his "doubtful provenance of his research".   During my research, I found a tendency by Ennes to downplay anything having to do with Pearson.   A person named Tito Howard who put together a video dealing with the *Liberty* story knew him.   There were some conflicts between Howard and the LVA dealing with the rights to that video. Pearson's book came out just prior to Ennes's book. Jim Ennes had invested at least 10 years of effort in his book and was concerned with credibility— provenance.

My feeling is that what Pearson reports should not be discounted out-of-hand. Of interest to me was the fact

344

that in checking Hounam's endnotes I found that author Anthony Pearson died in the early 1980s after complaining to a friend that he had been poisoned by a cup of coffee. The friend took him to the hospital and Pearson died a couple days later. Hounam reports that Tito Howard heard Pearson died because of two strokes in 1984; however, Howard believes the death story was fiction and that Pearson continued to live in his native Kenya.[478] Hounam reports that Pearson died while doing another investigation that was critical of Israel. Further, Hounam notes that while Pearson may have made some careless errors and may have been discounted by others, he notes "One of the mysteries of the *Liberty* affair is therefore whether Pearson had an 'inside track'."[479] That inside track for him and Deacon was most likely British intelligence contacts.

The Anthony Pearson and Tito Howard connection is convoluted when one digs a little deeper. Hounam reports that the friend who took Pearson to the hospital was a person named Nicholas Davies, who at one time was the foreign editor for the London *Daily Mirror*.[480] Authors, Ari Ben-Menashe, Seymore Hersh and Gordon Thomas in the pages of their books, link Davies to the Mossad—actively recruited or as a potential recruit. Allegedly, he, Davies, was linked to arms trafficking. In addition, the *Daily Mirror* would eventually be purchased by Robert Maxwell who Gordon Thomas dedicated a book to dealing with his role as a benefactor of Israel and a spy for Israeli intelligence. Thomas relates the story that Maxwell when going broke attempted to put "the arm" on the Mossad for financial help and was killed while on his yacht by Israelis.

345

Author Seymour Hersh fingers Nicholas Davies as the one who compromised Vanunu to the Israelis.[481] Because Hounam worked in the London newspaper world, he would probably know these people.

Ben-Menashe who was an Israeli spy, in his book *Profits of War*, links an Anthony Pearson to Davies. Ben-Menashe claims Davies was recruited by the Mossad in the 1970s and that "The connection had come through a former British Special Airborne Service (SAS) officer, Anthony Pearson…"[482] The connection of these names is interesting and Ben-Menashe may be referring to some other Pearson.

Nevertheless, "our" Anthony Pearson got around and had contacts. Similarity of names and confusion is not unusual. In attempting to locate Davies, I ran into the fact that distinction should be made between Nick Davies an investigative reporter and Nicholas Davies of the *Daily Mirror*. Nick Davies is still an active journalist. Therefore, the Pearson reference may well be two different people. Certainly, the date and manner of his death is wrought with confusion.

It would appear that Anthony Pearson just vanished off the face of the earth with no record easily searched. Thanks to Google's search engine, entry of the term "writer Anthony Pearson Nairobi Kenya" did turn up a link to him including a reference to him working for the *Guardian*. Two URL links are referenced via a forum on fishing noting he wrote several books on fishing in the late '60s and early '70s. The discussion indicated that he had a serious following of fishing advocates interested in learning more about his books and what happened to him. Two comments standout: First, he took literary license with the facts, and second that he died of a brain tumor in a London hospital in the '90s. Forum participants sought to get more information from someone claiming to know of him. There is a discussion reference to one of his books dealing with fishing off the Kenyan coast. The discussion thread provided no further information and dated in the period from 2008. There is a posted cover-photo of one book entitled *Successful Shore Fishing* by Anthony Pearson with a cover photo apparently of the author. This photo is compatible with the photo of Pearson on the back of his dust-jack of his book dealing with the *Liberty*. According to one forum poster, dated, 3/23/2008, notes [A copy of "Successful Shore Fishing" by Anthony Pearson 1967, 1 Ed. currently is on Fleabay for £7.49. Whilst having a quick Google I also found another title by him, *Davy Jones' Locker*.[483]] We are talking about the same Pearson in the context of the *Liberty* story and fishing.

If as noted above that Tito Howard was correct in his claim that the earlier death of Pearson was a fiction, then, it is possible that there is some validity to the forum discussion referred to above that he died possibly around 1990. Peter Hounam in his book noted that Pearson wrote a fishing column for the *Guardian* after he joined it in 1963.[484]

The interest in Pearson is that both my and Hounam's feeling is that "he got it right" in his book *Conspiracy of Silence: The Attack on the U.S.S. Liberty*. He copyrighted his book in 1978 a year before Ennes published his book. Quartet Books Limited, a member of the Namara Group of London, first published the book. He dedicated the book to his mother and father. The author's note says Pearson became a journalist "accidentally" in Nairobi, Kenya when he was sixteen.

He trained as a reporter for the *East African Standard*, became a staff reporter for the *Guardian*, a special foreign correspondent for the *Manchester Evening News* and a freelance war correspondent contributing to British, American and European newspapers and magazines. He did two articles on the *Liberty* for *Penthouse* magazine. He covered the Middle East consistently since the Six-Day War and covered the October 1973 war. He notes that "Over the past ten years he has become a specialist in terrorism and guerilla warfare, having had practical experience when covering what he calls 'street fire fight war'. He says, 'I am now more soldier than journalist'." At the time, he wrote the book he was thirty-seven years old and an inveterate wanderer. "I live where I happen to drop that night." His home is Nairobi, Kenya.

Pearson and Nicholas Davies both worked on the *Guardian*. Another author, Russell Warren Howe in his book *Weapons* reports on Anthony Pearson's version of events including the submarine USS *Andrew Jackson*. He cites the action of the Joint Chiefs of Staff as authorizing a strike against the MTB base at Haifa by two wings of A-4 Skyhawks from U.S. carriers. He further notes the Skyhawks would have to cross over Egypt to reach the spot—with permission obtained from the White House through Moscow.[485] As is known, these air launches were recalled by McNamara "and" Johnson. Why the planes would have to fly over Egypt from where the Sixth Fleet was position off Crete is an open question. In addition, whether these flights ordered by the JCS were the same carrier flights launched in aid of the *Liberty* is unclear. It is possible that reference is to the same context.

Howe pulls no punches and reports that the compensation paid to survivors and families was actually

348

paid by the U.S. government, perhaps from funds intended for Israel. Howe: "Washington let the matter drop. Had Israel been called to account, it could have riposted—as the Johnson White House knew—by revealing U.S. connivance with Israel in various plots to overthrow Nasser." The U.S. desire to over-throw Nasser seems to be a consistent theme.

Again, Howe reports that the story of the attack on the *Liberty* was first "unearthed" in the British press. For his book, Pearson interviewed one of three Mirage pilots, a Baltimore-born American who had immigrated to Israel in 1966. Pearson learned that one of the other pilots was a U.S. Vietnam veteran. Of interest is the fact that Pearson recounts that during his investigation, his private office in London was burglarized, and some of his *Liberty* files taken.

Howe contends that the London *Sunday Times* believes that the murder, in Cairo, in December 1977, of its chief foreign correspondent, David Holden, may have been a Mossad job, with Holden mistaken for Pearson.[486] Unfortunately, tracing Pearson's history is difficult. Pearson did not come out with his book on the attack until 1978; however, his *Penthouse* stories came out in 1976. His choice of the *Penthouse* venue was because it was one of the few publishers that would carry his story. More on the circumstances of his eventual death would be good to know because of his early writing about the USS *Liberty*.

I was able to find a book review by Ennes, dated 1995, of *The Secret War Against the Jews* by John Loftus and Mark Aarons, St. Martin's Press, 1994. Jim makes a few unflattering comments about Pearson claiming him to be paranoid and fearing the Mossad was after him.[487] The

349

apparent animus between Ennes and Pearson is interesting. Interesting in the sense that Russell Howe published his book in 1980, making the link between David Holden, Anthony Pearson and the Mossad. Maybe Pearson had reason to be paranoid of the Mossad.

Howe does not tell us the reasons Holden could have been mistaken for Pearson. Holden was a distinguished correspondent for the *Sunday Times*, the paper that Peter Hounam worked at. Holden's body was found on a Cairo street in December 1977 nine hours after his arrival to report on Israeli-Egyptian peace negotiations. He was shot in the back. Sir Harold Evans, editor at the time, speculated there was no reason for the killing. However, the speculation included the fact that it was believed "an intelligence agency" had infiltrated the London office of the *Sunday Times* to spy on the investigation of Holden's murder. Evans feared a staff member was feeding material to a foreign spymaster—a sting was set up wherein documents stopped vanishing—leading to the speculation that British agents were involved.

His abduction and murder appeared well planned and involved several stolen cars. It was no secret when Holden would arrive in Cairo as his itinerary and other documents turned up missing—it appeared that there might be a spy on the *Times* staff. Scotland Yard's C-10 unit was called in. After a period of surveillance, no suspect turned up who could have been stealing documents. Evans consequently began to suspect MI-6 had played some role in the abduction of Holden.

After the passage of years and no solution, Evans began to suspect that the CIA was involved because it and the FBI blocked efforts to see American intelligence files on Holden under the U.S. Freedom of Information

Act. Eventually, Evans was to conclude that Holden died not for journalism but for some secret cause, he may have betrayed. The murder is still unsolved.

It stands to reason that because of Britain's and European history that spying is more than a part of everyday life, more so, perhaps than in the U.S. The article on Holden in the *TIMESONLINE* (9/6/2009) gives no clue as to how the murder of Holden and a possible threat on Pearson's life are linked. [488]

One mystery related to Pearson's life and actions has to do with the claim of being broke, the reason for doing the *Penthouse* articles, and his apparent "high living" at five-star hotels and the expensive flat he rented in Cheyne Place, London. Hounam notes that he never seemed to make enough to support his lifestyle. Could this be a tip off that he led a double life? Colleagues contacted by Hounam were not aware he was interested in the *Liberty* story.

While Pearson's *Penthouse* articles were published in May and June of 1976, they did not refer to any submarine in conjunction with the *Liberty*. The submarine story did not come out until his book published in 1978. According to Hounam, Pearson's source appeared to be a MI-6 officer named McKenna; and McKenna's source was a "Mr. Clarkson", who in 1967, had been working under the cover of the British Council in Tel Aviv.

Hounam attributes the story from Clarkson as being third-hand, but one element was the USS *Andrew Jackson* that had apparently filmed the attack on the *Liberty* but was under orders not to break silence unless a "Red Alert". The *Andrew Jackson* was alleged to have left Rota at the same time as the *Liberty* to liaison with her. Hounam reports that Pearson contended that on June 12 an officer from the sub was flown to Washington with a canister of film that included the attack.

Hounam acknowledges that while Pearson had been in contact with Ennes in 1978, he was right in doubting him since McKenna and other Pearson informants were dead or not identified. While readers and researchers fall on either side of Pearson's credibility, Ennes doubts him because his research put the *Andrew Jackson* in the Atlantic. What troubles me is Ennes contention that since he was the "intelligence officer" on the *Liberty* and would "be-in-the-know", he, in his book contended he did not have clearance to know about Contact X. Hounam in his book on page 127 talks about people who saw the film, and found a crewmember who said that the *Andrew Jackson* did sail out of Rota and spent time in the Mediterranean in April, May and June of 1967.

Hounam speculates that the mission of the sub was to counter the Soviets and possibly Israel, alleged to have had at least two nuclear bombs. The ship's mission was to provide a counter-weight to a dooms-day scenario.

Hounam then cites Wilbur Eveland, the former CIA agent, as being convinced that the above scenario was plausible. Remember, because of Helms' and Angleton's policy of relying on Israeli intelligence for it sources of information, parts of the U.S. government, in particular the Pentagon was left in the blind. The Pentagon knew that the CIA had aided Israel in acquiring a nuclear capability or at least helped to hush it up. Additionally, Hounam points out that the U.S. had also provided missiles to which a nuclear warhead could attach; then

Israel had its own MD-620s based upon French technology.

The concern was that if things bogged down for Israel it might tend to rely on its missiles to win the war against the Soviet equipped Egyptians. There is a contention that Shimon Peres had suggested that Israel detonate a nuclear weapon as a demonstration prior to the Six-Day War. Dayan rejected the suggestion that Peres cannot talk about, in part for fear of Soviet reprisal.[489]

A Polaris submarine secretly in a war zone was no small matter. It provided the U.S. with substantial negotiating power. The sub could not betray its presence via radio contacts, however, considering communication considerations it could relay via the *Liberty*.

On June 8, the day of the attack, we know that Chief of Staff Rabin was in the command post at the Kirya, and Minister of Defense Moshe Dayan was at Taiman field in the Negev desert. Taiman field is near Beer Sheba and is now known as Sde Teyman a privately operated field. We know Dayan was there because the Israeli transcripts tell us he was there.

At 1000 on June 8, Sinai time, Rabin orders a halt to the Syrian advance by the Northern Commander who is not happy with that order because of built up momentum.[490] According to Captain McGonagle two jets circle the *Liberty* at high altitude. At 1100, Lunz removes the *Liberty* from the plot table at Naval HQ. At 1100, the 744-bomb squadron at Beale Air Force base in California is put on alert per author Peter Hounam.[491] At 1120, Division 914 motor torpedo boats are placed on alert. At 1124, the Israeli Southern Command notifies that El Arish is bombarded from the sea. At 1127, the IDF HQ

353

in Tel Aviv gets the report from the Southern Command of the bombardment.[492]

At 1130, the *Liberty* is at Point Bravo on a course of 283 decrees and hears explosions off El Arish. The attack on the *Liberty* begins at 1358 Sinai time. The *Liberty* is subjected to approximately an hour and one-half attack by aircraft and motor torpedo boats of the Israeli armed forces. The ship's communication system is knocked out. A radio link is jury-rigged and a call goes to the Sixth Fleet.[493] The Sixth Fleet launches attack aircraft two different times to be recalled, allegedly by Secretary of Defense McNamara on orders from President Johnson. At 0400 6/9/67, Dayan reconsiders and orders the attack on Syria.[494] He will become the prime suspect for ordering the attack on the *Liberty*.[495]

Hounam poses the question as to why Israel ceased attacking the ship allowing it to limp away; noting that the feeling of the crew was that the word of the attack got out to the Sixth Fleet that began to launch planes to come to the ship's rescue, and that Israel noticed the call for help. The Sixth Fleet was sending aircraft authorized to use deadly force against anyone attacking the ship—this would have brought about a direct confrontation between the two countries involved in the *Operation Cyanide* conspiracy.

Hounam speculates that Rabin and Dayan did not know the planes had been ordered recalled by Secretary of Defense McNamara. Hounam speculates further that there was a direct link between the Pentagon and the Israelis and they would have known the planes were recalled in which case they could have proceeded, except for the fact the attack was now known by the Johnson administration.

Another theory is that Admiral Shlomo Erell aborted the attack as noted in the raw intelligence report received by the CIA noted at the top of this chapter. He had his son on one of the torpedo boats. Erell had left HQ and gone to the harbor and when he returns it is believed he ordered a halt to the attack, perhaps a sort of "minnie-mutiny" that rippled through out the military command structure.

Hounam notes that while helicopters with armed troops headed toward the *Liberty,* the MTBs continued the attack and the cease-fire order was not strictly a naval decision. He goes on to speculate that Rabin and Dayan had no idea that the U.S. was prepared to drop nuclear weapons on Cairo and feared that Israel would be the next target if the Soviets decided to retaliate against Tel Aviv or Dimona.[496] This author finds the contention that the U.S. considered dropping a nuclear weapon on the outskirts of Cairo as problematic and speculative.

Hounam reports that a CT named David McFeggan suggested that it was someone else in our government who ordered Israel to cease the attack, and that came from the State Department allegedly not knowing about *Operation Cyanide.* Was that person Dean Rusk who was furious with Israel over the attack? Hounam suggests it could be Cyrus Vance who would resign within hours. On the other hand, could it be McNamara who later left the administration over disagreements about the Six-Day War. McNamara when asked about the *Liberty* always claimed he had no memory of it.[497]

Hounam posits that Johnson was upset his covert policy was upset, that Israel had to grovel and apologize, and that planes were recalled from Cairo—if that in fact was the scenario. A cover-up was demanded, with the U.S. left in a position of being blackmailed by the Israelis if they pushed too hard over the *Liberty* affair. As it was, the State Department had to put pressure on Israel to obtain reparations for the dead, wounded and damage to the ship.

What was the motive for the order to attack the ship? Was it prevent the United States from learning that Israel was attacking Jordan and going to attack Syria in contravention of an agreement with the United States. Was it to hide Israel's effort to obtain covenanted territory; or was it a version of the Gulf of Tonkin Resolution posited by Hounam with a version A and B? The A version would be that the U.S. wanted a pretext to get into the war; and the B version would be that through Israeli intelligence channels the Israelis decided to follow the Evron report that Johnson needed an excuse to go to Congress for approval to fully aid the Israelis thereby boxing the U.S. in.

With 34 dead and 175 wounded the ships limps to port for repair after aid arrived by ships of the Sixth Fleet.

Another set of factors to consider is the Israeli concern that developed in the middle of May 1967. Nasser became more concerned with Israel's nuclear program. He wanted to develop his own nuclear capability by getting a reactor from the Soviets. They did not agree to this and offered simply to put Egypt under the Soviet's nuclear guarantee, much like Ben-Gurion wanted of the United States.

356

Concern developed, that Egypt might give thought to bombing Dimona. The claim has come out that on May 17 and May 23 there were over-flights of Dimona where the Israelis could not shoot down the intruder. This set off alarms high in the Israeli government and started the clock running separate from any joint CIA/Mossad plans.

The other part of this scenario was that the *Liberty* and Contact X were jointly tasked to keep an eye on Israel's actions in the context of the Dimona factor. Tasking the ship to the Egyptian waters raises the question for what reason? There is a line of sight from the ships position across the Negev desert to where the reactor was located and guarded by U.S. provided Hawk missiles. Considering Israel's security policy to ultimately rely on her own abilities and not to rely on any superpower, would she if threatened by destruction resort to use of her crude nuclear weapons? Did Shimon Perez, as previously noted, suggest a nuclear demonstration to head off the confrontation? In the 1973 Yom Kippur War, Dayan is reported to have ordered nuclear warheads be placed on 13 Jericho missiles.

This contention or theory has been pooh-poohed, however, former CIA agent Eveland thinks otherwise. Richard Parker, a researcher into the Six-Day War did not consider what role the nuclear factor might have played; and further, CIA Director Helms denied any knowledge of Israeli's nuclear capability. While ambiguity controlled, could the United States simply ignore the issue and have any credibility in view of a potential nuclear confrontation between three nuclear powers? It is suggested that Avner Cohen's book *Israel and the Bomb* be consulted.

All elements in the Israeli command structure were concerned about the Soviets and wanted the U.S. to counter that threat. The Israeli motivating factors were present, while difficult in view of the continuing cover-up; one can pick their own motive for Israeli actions. The order being verbal fit nicely into the shelling of El Arish and Israel's engagement rules regarding fast moving ships. It makes no sense to say a "lower level" commander may have ordered the attack without authorization. The lower level commander would most likely be unable to divert Israeli air and naval forces without clearing it with the "Supreme Command". The prevailing opinion on who ordered it falls on Dayan, however, Rabin was in control in the "Pit" and involved in the operation. Yet, he would be the one who set up the Colonel Ram Ron internal review with a total conflict of interest on his part. Credibility is totally lacking. While Dayan was a strong leader and not reluctant to read-out subordinates, his subordinates did not always follow his orders. He does not refer in his memoirs to the *Liberty*. Again, speculation runs rampant; however, the reality is in the words:

Israeli Transcripts:

1400 Sinai time:

MENACHEM: Shmulik [a diminutive for Shmuel, Kislev's first name], she's burning. [Menachem is obviously excited.] The minute *Kursa* is finished, we're sending in *Royal*.

KISLEV: Right. Sink her.

MENACHEM: Sink her. Okay.

"President [Lyndon] Johnson is not going to war or embarrass an American ally over a few sailors."

Chapter 12

The Cover-Up

The Six-Day War was for all practical purposes over on the 10th of June, 1967 with a cease fire agreement that essentially left Arab/Israeli borders where they are today with the exception of the Sinai that was returned to Egypt. The cover-up started immediately even before the Naval Court of Inquiry had a chance to convene. It was quickly agreed that the attack was a "tragic mistake". As can be seen in the below State Department telegram, Israeli ambassador Harmon noted that Israel would investigate the attack, however, he wanted any discussion to "follow line that this was a tragic mistake". Under Secretary of State Eugene Rostow, brother of Walt Rostow, agreed the incident was a "tragic mistake", however, he acknowledged the attack was "mysterious". [498] While some top U.S. officials did not buy into the mistaken ID claim, and while they concluded it may have been ordered by some low level commander, there was in fact no U.S. investigation.

The Naval Court of Inquiry convened by the U.S. Naval Commander-in-chief, Europe, in London at the hour of 2314, June 10, 1967. The claim will be that President Johnson ordered the matter covered up. The JAG Chief Counsel to the Court, Captain Ward Boston, made this claim in an unprecedented written declaration.

Court personnel were ordered not to contact any Israeli about the attack. The record shows the Government of the United States has taken a more aggressive course of action to cover-up than have the Israelis who put blame on the U.S. for having the ship in the area. Raising this issue is not to in anyway mitigate the responsibility of the Israelis.

257. Telegram from the Department of State to the Embassy in Israel

Washington, June 11, 1967, 4:24 p.m.

210199. Memcon between Amb Harman and Under Secretary Rostow, June 10.

1. Under Secretary [Eugene] Rostow presented Amb Harman text of USG note concerning *Liberty* incident (sent septel). Before reading note Harman noted GOI was appointing committee of inquiry to investigate incident.

2. Harman said he would refrain from commenting on note but expressed hope that any publication of it would follow line that this was a tragic mistake for which GOI accepted full responsibility. Rostow agreed incident tragic mistake but added that circumstances surrounding it very mysterious. Word used in our note was "incomprehensible" and we hope board of inquiry would take appropriate action against responsible parties when investigation concluded.

3. Rostow said USG presenting this case to GOI in same manner in which it would present similar case to any other government.

4. Harman noted three things: GOI did not know location of ship, location was scene of active hostility, and GOI had promptly apologized for this tragic episode.

> 5. In closing Harman again reiterated GOI desire to handle incident as tragic mistake for which GOI accepted full responsibility.
> Rusk

The Mirage and Mystère Israeli jets had devastated the *Liberty's* complex antenna system in the first minutes of the air attack, and knocked out all communications making it all but impossible to get a call for help to the Sixth Fleet. When Captain McGonagle had requested a destroyer escort, Admiral Martin previously assured the *Liberty* that he would have planes over her within minutes if the ship were to come under attack. Ennes reports that the radio room crew had to piece together a working communication transmitter and an antenna that had to be long-wired; but as radiomen James Halman and Joseph Ward tried to establish voice contact with the Sixth Fleet, they found the frequencies blocked by a buzz-saw-like sound; apparently, the Israelis were jamming the frequencies.[499]

According to Chief Smith the *Liberty* started calling for help at 1158Z or 1358 Sinai time, continuing for more than two hours, remaining silent only when the ship was temporarily without electrical power. The *Liberty* radioman transmitted *"Flash, flash, flash. I pass in the blind. We are under attack by aircraft and high-speed surface craft..."* This message was repeated over-and-over. Ward came on the air again at 1405Z (1605 Sinai time), this time adding, *"Torpedo hit starboard side."*[500] Smith testified before the Court of Inquiry that went he went outside the radio room he saw the flag flying and he also testified that he thought they were being jammed.[501]

The carrier USS *Saratoga* operating with Vice Admiral Martin's Sixth Feet forces near Crete responded saying: *"Rockstar,* this *Schematic,* say again. You are garbled." "Authenticate *Whiskey Sierra,"* demanded the operator on the *Saratoga.* "Authentication is *Oscar Quebec,"* Halman responded. *Saratoga* then rogered *Rockstar* at 1209Z (1409 Sinai time). Ennes reports that *Saratoga* relayed *Liberty's* call for help to Admiral McCain in London, and "only" for information to Rear Admiral Geis, who commanded the Sixth Fleet carrier force, and Vice Admiral Martin on the cruiser *Little Rock.* To maintain the context and perspective there is agreement that the attack began around 1358 local time.

Liberty continued to call for help and the *Saratoga* advised that she was relaying the message and asked *Liberty* to authenticate again. Ennes reports the operator frustrated and angry held the radio button down and called, *"Listen to the goddamned rockets, you son of a bitch!"* *"Roger, Rockstar, we'll accept that,"* the reply came according to Ennes.[502]

The Israelis certainly knew the ship had called for assistance and efforts were stepped up to sink her. According to the Israeli transcripts, there was an hour and nineteen minute break in the air controller tapes between 1605 and 1724, most likely a critical conference was taking place in the Israeli command structure trying to figure how they would deal with the situation. The ship was not sinking—the evidence kept floating. Ennes notes that the Sixth Fleet says, *"Sending aircraft to cover you"* at 1305Z (1505 Sinai time).[503] Planes will be launched twice to come to *Liberty's* aid only to be recalled in an extraordinary way by Secretary of Defense McNamara.

Author and publisher Alexander Cockburn in an article on McNamara's death reported that he was the one who orchestrated the cover-up of the *Liberty:*[504]

362

Just before this '67 war the Israelis were ready to attack and knew they were going to win but couldn't get a clear go-ahead from the Johnson Administration. As the BBC documentary The 50 Years War narrates, Meir Amit, head of Israel's Mossad, flew to Washington. The crucial OK came from McNamara, thus launching Israel's long-planned, aggressive war on Egypt, Jordan and Syria, which led to present disasters. It was McNamara, after Israel's deliberate attack on the US ship Liberty during that war (with thirty-four US sailors dead and 174 wounded), who supervised the cover-up.

McNamara had been interviewed a number of times and was asked about the *Liberty*. He steadfastly maintained he knew nothing about the *Liberty* events of June 8.

Word would finally get to President Johnson and the White House Situation Room that the *Liberty* had been attack and speculation would be that it was the Egyptians or Soviets. The first sign of a problem developed after Johnson was advised of the attack. The following is attributed to the President's Foreign Intelligence Advisory Board: "…also granted that Israeli forces had reason to think that the *Liberty* was an Egyptian supply ship."[505] "They assumed that the Israelis saw their attack on the *Liberty* as an act of self-defense. Fearful that the American ship was monitoring and transmitting information about Israeli military preparations against Syria, the Israelis felt compelled to silence the *Liberty*: If its intelligence inadvertently fell into the hands of the Arabs, they could use it to inflict significant casualties on Israeli forces, and U.S. government forewarnings of Israeli military plans might make it more difficult for Tel

Aviv to secure its war aims."[506] Clark Clifford was chairman of this board in which case it would seem that author Dallek's attribution mitigating the Israeli attack is out of sync with what the individuals believed. Much of what was done by the board is still classified. However, in a memorandum from President Johnson, dated May 1, 1968, on the board's leadership being transferred from Clark Clifford to General Maxwell D. Taylor, he noted:[507]

> Pursuant to my appointment of General Maxwell D. Taylor to serve as Chairman of the President's Foreign Intelligence Advisory Board, as successor to Secretary *Clark M. Clifford*, I wish to emphasize the importance which I attach to the foreign intelligence function in government and to the mission of the Board. In this period of rapid political and economic change, the operation of government is more dependent than ever before on reliable, timely intelligence leading to a wise evaluation of the world situation. Under the coordination and guidance of the Director of Central Intelligence, all members of the U.S. foreign intelligence community contribute to this essential service.

Confusion would reign over the number of casualties. Egypt's air force had been devastated on the first day of the war and the Soviets did not have a carrier or planes in the area that could have attacked the ship. Many Soviet planes had been caught on the runways of the Egyptian air force bases and were destroyed.

Israel would acknowledge that it was responsible for the attack. At 1614, Sinai time a flash precedence message was received from the American embassy in

Israel reporting that GOI apologized for attacking an unidentified "maybe Navy" ship.[508] President Johnson received this message just prior to a meeting of his Situation Room personnel. The cover-up would immediately begin.

Lloyd Painter was saddened that the skipper was not among those who were candid about the attack. "I witnessed a cover-up take place of the highest magnitude, I witnessed someone receiving the highest medal of the land, someone being promoted, someone given his choice of duty in the Navy for his silence...the Captain never stepped forward until the end of his life, and I only think what could have been if he'd stepped forward in 1967."[509] Painter upon leaving the Navy would join the Secret Service. I had exchanged e-mails with him and was aware of his strong feelings about a cover-up.

In the murky waters of the intelligence world, author Peter Hounam posits another nugget: He reports that a U.S. intelligent agent who studied the attack on the *Liberty* said that the Captain knew more than he admitted. He said McGonagle was briefed to expect a superficial strafing attack on the *Liberty*, which would be a pretext for attacking Egypt—however; he did not expect the onslaught that occurred. "...he knew he had been sent to the Eastern Mediterranean as part of a deception plan."[510] If true, this is a devastating claim that implicates the Captain and our government in a conspiracy that would set the crew up to be murdered and maimed. Hounam attributes the information on the Captain to an unnamed U.S. intelligence agent.[511] While such claims would cry out for an investigation, it also reveals an ugliness that no one wants to open up, especially after all this time.

The use of the "pretext" by the government to justify a course of action is not new or unusual. For example, there is documentation of such a practice during the Cuban missile crisis of the early Sixties pursuant to a plan called *Operation Northwood,* a plan to justify an invasion of Cuba during that crisis in 1962.[512]

> These proposals - part of a secret anti-Castro program known as Operation Mongoose - included staging the assassinations of Cubans living in the United States, developing a fake "Communist Cuban terror campaign in the Miami area, in other Florida cities and even in Washington," including "sink[ing] a boatload of Cuban refugees (real or simulated)," faking a Cuban airforce attack on a civilian jetliner, and concocting a "Remember the Maine" incident by blowing up a U.S. ship in Cuban waters and then blaming the incident on Cuban sabotage. Bamford himself writes that Operation Northwoods "may be the most corrupt plan ever created by the U.S. government."

The pretext footprint and MO was associated with the Vietnam War and the Gulf of Tonkin incident, and the weapons of mass destruction (WMD) claim in preparation for the Iraq war. It is the administration of President Johnson where the "pretext was honed". This coupled with the claims of Phillip Nelson in his book; *LBJ The Mastermind of the JFK Assassination* strikes at the character of Johnson and marks his Machiavellian tendencies—not a flattering portrayal.

According to Hounam's source, the war was not meant to begin on June 5 when the *Liberty* was still far from Point Alfa, but rather on the 15th. This is consistent with the *Frontlet615* document out of the 303 Committee, as the name indicates, as referred to previously. This person claimed that the U.S. was supposed to be engaged from day one with amphibious Marines to conduct an invasion in support of Israel. The source said *Frontlet615* was a secret political agreement approved by the 303 Committee by which the U.S. and Israel agreed to destroy Nasser.[513] Hounam claims that while the former was the political name, *Operation Cyanide* was the military operational codename. We discussed all this in the previous chapter. One problem with this is that per the memorandum dealing with the record of the National Security Council meeting of May 24th, 1967, General Wheeler noted while we had a "powerful naval force in the Mediterranean; that our land forces are few, limited to about 1400 marines now ashore at Naples..."

Hounam further states that the source claimed that Israel acted prematurely because she feared Nasser would sue for peace and disrupt the plan; recall that Secretary of State Dean Rusk sought an opening and invited a representative of Egypt to Washington. This did not please the Israeli military establishment and may have caused the attack date to be moved up; nor did it please President Johnson. McGeorge Bundy, special national security advisor to the President noted in his oral history interview:[514]

> The President was driven up the wall in a lower-key sense of importance by a State Department announcement that we were neutral in thought and deed and word, which was not what his friends in New York wanted to hear. So he heard about that from the Arthur Krims and the Abe Feinbergs of the world.

Obviously, the reference was to Johnson's Jewish friends and supporters. As noted in the President's Daily Diary on June 8, 1967, at 1141 p.m., a telephone call was logged from Mrs. Arthur Krim. The President then retired at 1150 p.m. Among the President's advisors, there was an "appearance concern" as noted by Bundy in his OH interview:[515]

> Well, there were complications about who was talking to who down there. It was mildly embarrassing that three of the people most closely involved with the problem were Jewish. That would have been dandy if the President had been adopting an anti-Israeli policy, but he wasn't. He needed someone with a different apparent image, and I did do the job anyway. You can come back to it if you want to.

McGeorge Bundy is referring to the fact that per his oral history interview he was asked to come back to government service to assist with managing the crisis in the Middle East. He states that it was McNamara who asked him to consider coming back and taking over. Bundy says that Walt Rostow was handling the Vietnam War and has his hands full, and therefore he took over the handling of the Middle East crisis. As to the sensitivity issue, it has been noted that the Egyptians had accused the United States of supporting the Israeli side.

However, Hounam asks the question of why attack the *Liberty* if Israel had already won the war. He claims that the answer in part came from John Hadden, the CIA Station Chief in Tel Aviv. After requiring that Hounam turn off the tape recorder, he went on to say that, Dayan refused to cross the Suez Canal and push the offensive all the way; and the White House was furious with Dayan who was not prepared to continue to Cairo and unseat Nasser "as had been agreed". Hadden noted that Israel was more interested in grabbing land. This would be the Golan Heights and portions of Jordan including Old Jerusalem.[516]

Again, McGeorge Bundy's oral history interview put this view into context by noting a reference to the President, and to Bundy's viewpoint:[517]

> He has told people that he thinks this was the most serious diplomatic crisis of his time in the White House. I honestly don't share that view. I think it was--the Russians used some fairly brisk language down toward the end of the week, but they knew and we knew that the game was just about played out, and certainly the Israelis did. I am not one of those who thinks that there would have been global war over the Middle Eastern crisis if it had gone on another day or two, but it wasn't certainly worth having it go on. And we gradually increased the pressure on the Israelis to stop. They gradually acquired most of what they wanted. The Soviets were discomfited but by no means driven to the wall on the question, and the ceasefire came. But it was coolly handled by the President. It was a very intense week, but not a dangerous week in the sense that the Cuban time was dangerous.

Hounam reports the United States was not dragged into this war, but was in fact the prime mover and the attack on the *Liberty* was to give the U.S. an excuse to finish a job it started in 1966. This concept of *Frontlet615* smacks like the agreement between the

French, British and Israelis for their involvement in the 1956 Suez War and the *Protocol of Severes*. Our CIA had been involved in plans to remove Nasser ever since the failure of the Suez War collusion and fiasco entered into between Britain, France and Israel. One can say that the Six-Day War was a replay of the Suez War, but with a different lead actor—namely the U.S.

Again, Hounam raises the question of whether the President would sanction the use of nuclear weapons in such circumstances; however, he points out if the plan was to attack the ship and cause casualties, then circumstances had to be cataclysmic. Hounam was told the target was West Cairo and a large military base where Russians were stationed that was outside city boundaries and away from major population centers. Under the right circumstance and spin, would the U.S. population end up supporting the President? Hounam seems to ponder this position and asks whether it was credible than an American President would use nuclear weapons under this scenario. He notes his informant understood it was a plan of last resort.[518]

Recall the U.S. objective was to get rid of Nasser. Whether any of this is accurate to any extent, the readers will have to make up their own mind. There most likely was a series of scenarios and options as in most covert plans. The result was that there was an international clamor to end hostilities, Nasser had agreed to a cease-fire, Dayan halted his troops at the Suez Canal and moved forces to the border with Syria. The U.S. did not have sufficient forces to move over land to accomplish the overthrow of Nasser although a carrier task force was in the Atlantic heading to beef up the Sixth Fleet as observed from the *Valdez*.[519]

Hounam reports that John McNaughton, General Counsel in the Department of Defense, who was considered a civilian war planner, was one of Johnson's "ideas men". Actually, he was an assistant secretary of defense, who according to State Department documents was involved in assessing failures in Vietnam. According to Hounam, in 1965, he began looking at ways to extract the U.S. from Vietnam, realizing victory was unlikely. In a memo to McGeorge Bundy, Walt Rostow's predecessor as National Security Advisor, he suggested that to recover its standing and divert attention while it retreated, America might launch "diversionary offenses" elsewhere in world. Hounam gives him the benefit of the doubt by saying maybe he meant "diplomatic offenses"; then surmised it made no sense in the context of the rest of the memo.[520]

Hounam questions how far Johnson was willing to go by putting a squadron of B52s on alert at Beale Air Force base in California loaded with H-bombs targeted against the Soviet Union. Would it be a surprise to know that the Soviet Union had put its strategic bombers on alert also in the Ukraine and had nuclear submarines prepared to nuke Tel Aviv? Johnson was a beaten man who would not run for reelection and did not understand why he, such a friend of Israel, could not get the Jewish support for "his" war in Vietnam.

There was a lull in the air controller communications as previously pointed out in Chapter 5 from 1605 to 1724, one hour and nineteen minutes; after which time it has been reported that Commander E. E. Castle, the U.S. Naval Attaché in Tel Aviv, was flown by an Israeli helicopter to the ship to ascertain if there were casualties. Captain McGonagle waived off the helicopter. 1549 Sinai time, 0949 Washington time, National Security

371

Advisor Walt Rostow advises President Johnson of the attack on the *Liberty*.[521] Some timeline context is in order:

- Admiral Martin recalls all planes for no further launch at 1559.
- At 1615, the State Department advised the Soviets of the attack and planes flying toward her aid.[522]
- At 1614, there is a flash message from American embassy that Israel apologizes.[523]
- At 1616, the JCS authorizes the use of force.[524]
- At 1645, *Liberty* advised assistance on the way.[525]
- At 1700, the 744th bomb squadron is taken off alert status. LBJ arrives at the situation room at 1706.[526]
- At 1710, Ambassador Barbour cables a suggestion to keep the attack quiet.

The *Liberty* is escorted to a port at Malta where bodies will be removed from the research area where the torpedo had hit, and the recovery and destruction of cryptographic information and equipment will continue. The ship will have received over 800 cannon and rocket hits. The torpedo hole will be plated over and the other holes patched. The ship will be sent to Norfolk for eventual scrapping. Sensitive equipment will be deep-sixed and other material burned by the truckload in an incarcerator once in Norfolk. Crewmembers will be sent to hospitals and later dispersed to other assignments.

In 1967, there was no Internet and easily used e-mail for the crew to keep in touch and join as a group. The government did not want them collaborating with each other. *Liberty* survivor, Phillip Tourney, three-time president of the LVA will claim that he was sent on several days of liberty to get him out of sight from interviewers looking into the attack.[527]

There will be a contention that they were advised not to discuss the attack and in particular not to talk to the media. A Naval Court of Inquiry will be established under Admiral Kidd to look, not into who attacked the ship, but rather incidental issues of how the crew saved the ship and communication problems. Some survivors will state that they were not threatened or intimidated, however, in one case the person was allegedly sent to a hospital in Germany under an assumed name. Tourney is specific in terms of the intimidation provided by Admiral Kidd, in the "interest of national security" as he is alleged to have said to the survivors he was talking to about the attack.

There would be no criminal investigation conducted by the FBI or other appropriate authorities as took place with the attack on the USS *Cole*.[528] The NCOI will call only 21 witnesses and present 49 exhibits.

The traditional Naval Court of Inquiry would be quickly convened and just as quickly adjourned having made its cursory findings and conclusions. Years later in 2003 the Chief JAG advisor to the court would issue an affidavit and declaration saying that it was a sham and a cover-up was ordered by sitting President Lyndon Johnson—very strong words.

Once Israel had extended its apology for the attack, Chief of Staff Rabin would order an inquiry. Yet, as was previously noted he was in charge in the "Pit", a clear conflict of interest on his part because he was in the chain-of-command. Rabin on another occasion, in an unrelated matter, had been admonished by the civilian court in Israel. We will concern ourselves with two of the inquiry reports, one by Colonel Ram Ron and one by military judge, Yeshayahu Yerushalmi. Both of these inquiries would be under the military system in Israel. The Israeli civilian court system had nothing to do with the attack.

Normally, in a situation like the attack on the *Liberty*, Congress would get into the act and begin a series of hearings. However, in an unprecedented manner Congress would not investigate the circumstances surrounding the attack and would limit inquiries into matters such as problems with military communications system. The survivors of the attack would for years attempt to pressure Congress to conduct an investigation, all to no avail alleging that Congress was corrupted by the Jewish and Israeli lobby in this country. That there is a cover-up cannot be doubted, however, the reasons are open to question and review. Others, such as author A. Jay Cristol, would claim there were numerous Congressional hearings into the attack. This is simply a smokescreen and not true. No Congressional hearing was conducted to look into the Israeli actions or the actions of our government dealing directly with the attack; nor were any witnesses from the crew ever called before Congress. Can it be a surprise that Congress would not open an investigation dealing with the *Liberty*, when it has failed to re-open an investigation into the assassination of President Kennedy based upon new information?

With the contention that the U.S. government and Israel were in collusion to remove Nasser it is obvious that secrets were to be kept, especially with the involvement of intelligence agencies who operate in a murky, sub-rosa environment.

The person making the threat has his fingerprints all over the command and control processes surrounding the attack. Now the same person participates in the internal review process, in essence the "code of silence" governs. The U.S. for its reasons goes along with it. The President does not want to embarrass an ally, because of mistakes or because of need to hide covert participation in the war and attack. In fact, those high in the administration consider sinking the ship before it reaches Norfolk so the media cannot get a chance to examine it and shock the American public with their findings—this did not happen.

Certainly, there were ample grounds for an investigation and in reality, the facts beg for such an investigation. Over the years, subsequent presidents will claim that there is no new information or reason to re-open the case of the attack on the USS *Liberty*. It is simply an effort to stall and continue the cover-up.

Additionally, there were and are a number of government career personnel in high places at the time who believed that the attack was intentional. Some of them, such as Clark Clifford, the chairman of the President's Foreign Intelligence Advisory Board, have expressed themselves; but none have made getting to the bottom of issue and the truth a project that they themselves wanted to pursue.

Those who believed there was compelling evidence that the Israeli attack was a deliberate attempt to destroy an American ship and kill her entire crew includes: Secretary of State Dean Rusk; Undersecretary of State

375

George Ball; former Director of the CIA, Richard Helms; former NSA Directors, Lt. General William Odam, USA (Ret.); Admiral Bobby Ray Inman, USN (Ret.); Marshal Carter; former NSA deputy directors Oliver Kirby and Major General John Morrison, USAF (Ret.); and, former Ambassador Dwight Porter, U.S. Ambassador to Lebanon in 1967.[529] If such a distinguished group of governmental leaders believed the attack was intentional, why did the cover-up succeed?

Generally, the cover-up of the attack on the *Liberty* would occur as most cover-up do, by obscuring, misdirection if not outright lying, by gathering and sequestering all available information and evidence, and by conducting a phony court of inquiry, while calling for investigative reports by those who can be trusted to "not dig too deeply". Johnson ordered all information pertaining to the attack sequestered.[530]

Of course, the Navy would need to conduct an official "court of inquiry" to find the underlying cause of matters. We will look at that first. Essentially, a military court of inquiry is a fact-finding body convened to investigate an incident involving substantial loss of life or major property damage, and one that could involve serious international and legal consequences. It is a purely administrative body and not judicial in nature such as a court martial would be. The court's report is advisory for subsequent decisions and actions as may be warranted, such as a court martial or other governmental response. In the case of the USS *Liberty*, the process started with a Court of Inquiry convened at the direction of Vice Admiral McCain at his London headquarters. It started with a June 10th, 1967 letter to Admiral Kidd from Admiral McCain charging Kidd to "inquire into all the

376

pertinent facts and circumstances leading to and connected with the armed attack; damage resulting; and deaths of and injuries to Naval personnel." This would appear to be an all-encompassing charge; however, it would be much less. The court would consist of Kidd as the president, Captains Bernard J. Lauff and Bert M. Atkinson as members. Captain Ward M. Boston, Jr., would be the senior JAG adviser along with assistant counsel, Lieutenant Commander Allen Feingersch. Chief Petty Officer Joeray Spencer was the assigned as recorder.

The process was prefaced by Admiral Kidd meeting with groups of crewmembers aboard ship, taking his stars off his collar and prompting crewmembers to "just tell it like it was". On finishing, he would put his rank insignia back on the collar and then admonish the crewmembers not to speak to anyone about the matter for fear of them being court-martialed or otherwise being subject to "action", leaving the latter thought to ruminate in their minds. After all, the crew was active duty military personnel subservient to the military code of justice and interested in successfully getting a service pension at the end of their career—they took their oath to the country seriously.

In a hasty manner, the complete inquiry process would be over June 18 with Admiral McCain's approval. A top-secret 707 page transcript would be developed followed by a 28 page unclassified version. For the most part, we now have access to the full transcript.

More importantly, we have the affidavit and declaration of Captain Ward Boston claiming that the Court of Inquiry was a sham and a cover-up ordered by President Johnson and Secretary of Defense McNamara.

Author James Bamford who sat on the State Department panel in January 2004 dealing with the Six-Day War and the attack on the *Liberty* read Boston's declaration into the session record.

Captain Boston makes the most serious charges against the President of the United States, as Commander-in-Chief, and against Secretary of Defense McNamara. Specifically, he alleges the following:

> Notwithstanding the seriousness of the attack, he and Admiral Kidd were given only one week to gather evidence knowing that it would require at least six months doing the job properly.
> Both he and Kidd discussed the case at length in the evenings and believed that the attack was intentional. He recalled Kidd repeatedly referring to the attacking Israelis as "murderous bastards".
> While he and Kidd believed it necessary to travel to Israel to do a proper investigation, they were denied permission by Admiral McCain. Not only were they not to travel to Israel, they were admonished not to contact the Israelis about it.
> Boston states that he personally knows from conversations with Admiral Kidd that both President Johnson and Secretary McNamara ordered them to find that the attack was a case of "mistaken identity". Further, Kidd told him that he was forced to sit down with two civilians from the White House and Defense Department and told to re-write portions of the report.
> Boston states that Kidd told him he had been ordered to "put the lid" on everything having to do with the attack on the USS *Liberty* and

they were never to speak of it and were to caution everyone involved to never speak of it again.

Boston further states that the transcript released to the public is not the same one he certified and sent off to Washington.

There can hardly be a more serious blight on the record of the United States Navy and the personnel involved to have an official court of inquiry called a sham. The questions regarding the conduct of the Commander-in-Chief and Secretary of Defense are the most serious. McNamara simply puts off all questions as to the *Liberty* and says he cannot recall; McNamara is now deceased. Of course, Lyndon Johnson is long deceased and cannot respond to these allegations, so we are left to look at his record to the extent that it is exposed regarding the matter.

While the Naval Court of Inquiry issued 52 findings, most dealt with communication issues, and not the attack and who perpetrated it.

Perhaps the most telling and devastating indictment of the U.S. handing of the *Liberty* affair comes from former, and now deceased, Admiral Thomas H. Moorer who put together an *ad hoc* independent commission to look into the matter. In a June 8, 1997 memorandum on the attack, he stated he never believed the attack was a case of mistaken identity. "That is ridiculous....The *Liberty* was the ugliest, strangest looking ship in the U.S. Navy. As a communications intelligence ship, it was sprouting every kind of antenna. It looked like a lobster with all those projections moving every which way."

He said Israel knew perfectly well that the ship was American considering the many over-flights and that

Israel knew the ship could intercept messages from all parties and potential parties to the war. Further, Admiral Moorer refers to the pending Golan Heights attack that Israel knew President Johnson did not want to happen. Admiral Moore writes, "And I believe Moshe Dayan concluded that he could prevent Washington from becoming aware of what Israel was up to by destroying the primary source of acquiring that information the USS *Liberty*."

Admiral Moore stated, "What is so chilling and cold-blooded, of course, is that they could kill as many Americans as they did in confidence that Washington would cooperate in quelling any public outcry." This statement puts the Johnson administration in the middle of a conspiracy to obstruct justice.

Was Admiral Moorer qualified to make his comment and observations? Note the following quote from his memorandum:

> As we know now, if the rescue aircraft from U.S. carriers had not been recalled, they would have arrived at the *Liberty* before the torpedo attack, reducing the death toll by 25. The torpedo boat commanders could not be certain that Sixth Fleet aircraft were not on the way and this might have led to their breaking off the attack after 40 minutes rather than remaining to send the *Liberty* and its crew of 294 to the bottom. Congress to this day has failed to hold formal hearings for the record on the *Liberty* affair. This is unprecedented and a national disgrace. I spent hours on the Hill giving testimony after the USS *Pueblo*, a sister ship to the *Liberty*, was seized by North Korea. I was asked every imaginable question,

including why a carrier in the area failed to dispatch aircraft to aid the *Pueblo*. In the *Liberty* case, fighters were put in the air not once, but twice. They were ordered to stand down by Secretary of Defense McNamara and President Johnson for reasons the American public deserves to know.

The treatment of the crew by their government was appalling. Admiral Moorer noted that the Naval Academy failed to record the name of Lt. Stephen Toth in the Memorial Hall because he had not been killed in battle. Admiral Moorer noted, "I intervened and was able to reverse the apparent idea that dying in a cowardly, one-sided attack by a supposed ally is somehow not the same as being killed by an avowed enemy." He further notes that six of dead from the *Liberty* lay under a tombstone at Arlington Cemetery describing only that "died in the eastern Mediterranean". Of course, Captain McGongale was also slighted when President Johnson did not present his Medal of Honor at the White House. The Captain's medal was awarded in obscurity at the Washington Naval Yard.

Admiral Moorer, a former Chief of the Joint Chiefs of Staff, in addition to the above memorandum went further with an independent commission making findings dealing with the attack, recall of a military rescue support aircraft, and the subsequent cover-up by the United States Government. The findings were published on Capitol Hill October 22, 2003.[531] The participants were Admiral Moorer, US Navy Retired and former Chairman of the Joint Chiefs of Staff; General Raymond G. Davis, United States Marine Corps, former Assistant Commandant of the Marine Corps; Rear Admiral Merlin Staring, US Navy Retired, former Judge Advocate General of the

Navy; Ambassador James Akins, former US ambassador to Saudi Arabia; certainly, a very distinguished panel. After reviewing records, documents and statements of Americans and Israelis, the commission makes the following findings (summarized here):

1. After eight hours of aerial surveillance Israeli launched a two hour attack killing 34 and wounding 172 of a crew of 294;

2. The air attack lasted approximately 25 minutes during which unmarked Israeli aircraft dropped napalm, fired 30mm cannons and rockets causing 821 holes, more that 100 of which were rocket size. Survivors estimate 30 or more sorties were flown by a minimum of 12 attacking planes which were jamming all five American radio channels;

3. The torpedo attack involved not only firing torpedoes but the machine-gunning of *Liberty's* firefighters and stretcher-bearers and life rafts that had been lowered in the water;

4. There is compelling evidence that Israel's attack was a deliberate attempt to destroy the ship and kill her entire crew;

5. "That in attacking USS *Liberty*, Israel committed acts of murder against American servicemen and an act of war against the United States";

6. Fearing conflict with Israel, the White House deliberately prevented the U.S. Navy from coming to the defense of USS *Liberty* by recalling Sixth Fleet military rescue support while the ship was under attack;

7. The ship was saved from almost certain destruction by the heroic efforts of the Captain and crew. That surviving crewmembers were

threatened with court-martial, imprisonment or worse if they exposed the truth, and were abandoned by their own government;

8. That due to the influence of Israel's powerful supporters in the United States, the White House deliberately cover-up the details of the attack;

9. The *Liberty* has been the only serious naval incident not investigated by Congress because of continuing pressure by the pro-Israel lobby in the United States;

10. The cover-up has been without precedent in American naval history and is now supported by statements of Admiral Merlin Staring and Captain Ward Boston the Chief counsel to the Naval Court of inquiry;

11. The cover-up continues to this date;

12. That a danger to our national security exists whenever our elected officials are willing to subordinate the American interests to those of any foreign nation, and specifically are unwilling to challenge Israel's interests when they conflict with American interests as evidenced by failure to defend the USS *Liberty*.

13. The commission calls upon the Department of Navy, the Congress and the American people to take the following actions: That a navy count of inquiry operating under Congressional over-sight take public testimony from surviving crewmembers and to thoroughly investigate the attack with full cooperation of the NSA, CIA and military intelligence services and to determine Israel's motive in launching the attack.

14. Further, that "every appropriate" committee of Congress investigate the actions of the White House and Defense Department that prevented the

rescue of the USS *Liberty*, thereafter threatened her surviving officers and men if they told the truth.

At the time of the announcement, it was in memoriam for General of the Marine Corps Raymond G. Davis, one of America's most decorated military heroes and Medal of Honor recipient, who passed away on September 3, 2003.

The commission acknowledged Captain Ward Boston who had come forward with his declaration dated 1/8/2004 claiming the attack was intentional and not a case of mistaken identity. Boston claimed that the evidence so pointed. Boston stated, "Admiral Kidd and I believed with certainty that this attack, which killed 34 American sailors and injured 172 others, was a deliberate effort to sink an American ship and murder its entire crew".

"I am certain that the Israeli pilots that undertook the attack, as well as their superiors who had ordered the attack, were aware that the ship was American." Captain Boston stated that he has personal knowledge that Admiral Kidd found the attack to be "a case of mistaken identity" in 1967 only because he was under direct orders to do so by Defense Secretary McNamara and President Johnson.

Lieutenant Commander David E. Lewis, USS *Liberty's* chief intelligence officer (severely wounded in the attack) has reported a conversation with Admiral Lawrence R. Geis, the Sixth Fleet carrier division commander, who visited Lewis after he had been medically evacuated by helicopter to the aircraft carrier USS *America*. According to Lewis, "He (Admiral Geis)

384

said that he wanted somebody to know that we weren't forgotten...attempts HAD been made to come to our assistance. He said that he had launched a flight of aircraft to come to our assistance, and he had then called Washington. Secretary McNamara came on the line and ordered the recall of the aircraft, which he did. Concurrently he said that since he suspected that they were afraid that there might have been nuclear weapons on board, he reconfigured another flight of aircraft - strictly conventional weaponry - and re-launched it.

After the second launch, he again called Washington to let them know what was going on. Again, Secretary McNamara ordered the aircraft recalled. Not understanding why, he requested confirmation of the order; and the next higher in command came on to confirm that... President Johnson...with the instructions that the aircraft were to be returned, that he would not have his allies embarrassed, he didn't care who was killed or what was done to the ship...words to that effect. With that, Admiral Geis swore me to secrecy for his lifetime. I had been silent up until I found out from Admiral Moorer that Admiral Geis had passed away."[532]

This statement by Commander Lewis has recently been corroborated by Tony Hart, a Navy communications technician, stationed at the U.S. Navy Base in Morocco in June 1967. Mr. Hart connected the telephone conversation between Secretary McNamara and Admiral Geis and stayed on the line to keep them connected. Hart has been recorded as saying that he overheard Admiral Geis refusing McNamara's order to recall the Sixth Fleet rescue aircraft while the ship was under attack. Mr. Hart reported that McNamara responded, "We are not going to war over a bunch of dead sailors."[533]

Does the above reference to planes armed with nuclear weapons give credence to Hounam's theory that we were close to a nuclear confrontation with the Soviets? Secretary of Defense McNamara as stated said he does not remember anything about the *Liberty*. McNamara died July 6, 2009 at age 93; noted for criticism for his management of the Vietnam War causing the deaths of millions of Vietnamese. McNamara's words have survived his death to enlighten us. Less than enthusiastically, he sat for a couple of oral history interviews, one in 1975 conducted by Walt Rostow, and one in 1993 by Robert Dallek. Based on these interviews, there are two points to be made, first reference our policy toward Israel and second dealing with the attack on the USS *Liberty*.

First, McNamara was not keen on going to war on behalf of Israel, nor was Congress. It was his belief that both the Israelis and Soviets were unclear as to our intentions in support of Israel. "But our own record indicates that our own people were unclear as to whether we would or should respond to support Israel with military force. The Israelis were unclear as to our intentions and probably the Russians as well. I believe this is an extremely dangerous situation for all parties: Israel, the U.S., and the Soviets. It existed then and, in my opinion, it exists today."[534] McNamara thought, as did Senator Fulbright, that it was better to have a defense treaty with Israel.

As for the attack on the *Liberty*, let McNamara's words speak for him. This was a special interview conducted by President Johnson's biographer, Robert Dallek (D is Dallek and M is McNamara):[535]

1. D: The *Liberty*, you have--

M: I've heard so much about the *Liberty* my mind is clouded on it. I have no independent--

D: Richard Helms talked to me about that.

M: Helms would know far more than I. I don't mean I didn't know at the time, but I have heard such absurd stories about the *Liberty* that--I was told a few months ago that we knew that the Israeli planes were going to attack the *Liberty*, and the American planes were going to take off a carrier to prevent the Israeli planes from attacking, and Johnson called them back. I believe that is baloney. But I mention it only in the sense that I am so confused as to what actually happened I don't want to even pretend to have [inaudible] source of information.

D: I think that was part of one of those journalistic exposés on television about it.

M: That's exactly what it was. Today I'm so confused that I don't have an independent view as to what happened.

D: There is a very substantial record in the Johnson Library about that and I'll be reviewing it. I just thought of it because Helms told me something about that which I found interesting. What he asserted to me was that the Israelis knew perfectly well what they were doing, and they attacked the *Liberty* because they felt that it was an electronic spy ship that was passing information back to Washington; that they were afraid the Egyptians and Syrians were going to pick it up, and the Israelis were about to attack the Golan Heights.

M: I have no knowledge one way or the other, but I find that pretty hard to believe, and I am no admirer or supporter of the account[?]. But

387

I just find it such poor judgment, if that was the case.

D: I'm glad to have your perspective on that.

M: I underline what I said before: My mind is so confused by all these damn stories I've heard, I cannot tell you what my knowledge was at the time.

D: That's the danger of doing these oral history interviews; that one just takes it as gospel that--

M: This is one reason why I almost always refuse to participate in oral history now, because most of it is so--what I call unscholarly.

D: You have to be very careful. Believe me, [on] anything we talk about, my first priority is to look at the document. I can barely remember what happened to me two weeks ago, let alone you to go back twenty-five or thirty years and put this all together.

McGeorge Bundy, with his hands on the controls, had this to say in an 11/10/1993 interview conducted by Robert Dallek asking about the attack on the *Liberty*. Note that Dallek again refers to CIA Director Helms:

What about the *Liberty*?

B: Very tough, and very mysterious, and Johnson was very careful about that. He wanted not to jump to conclusions.

D: As to why the Israelis--?

B: As to how it happened and what the cause was.

D: Richard Helms has told me that in his estimate this was purposely done by the Israelis; this is his conclusion. He was very eager to talk about this when I saw him. I asked him why he thought this was the case,

388

and he emphasized that the Israelis were about to move against Syria when this occurred, and he felt they were very concerned that the *Liberty*, monitoring Israeli military moves and intelligence, might spill the beans in some inadvertent way, so that the Syrians would know the Israelis were coming and that, according to Helms, the assumption was that they had to put this ship out of commission in order to protect their forces from possible danger--

B: I don't even remember hearing that theory. I may have heard it from somebody, but I don't have any recollection of having heard it, and I certainly haven't had it live in my own mind in the last ten or fifteen years. I read that same story, either in the papers or somewhere.

D: Johnson you don't think necessarily came to that conclusion, or--?

B: I certainly have no affirmative evidence that he did, in my own head.

D: So he was cautious, as to--

B: I didn't say that, because I--I think he was cautious, but I just don't have any recollection of his being exposed to that theory and what his reaction was.

D: Do you know if he ever came to any--at the time--conclusion as to--did he take the Israeli explanation--?

B: I really don't know what he thought about it. I think the written record shows what he did about it, and I can't go behind that.

D: So you really didn't speak to him about it.

B: I can't say that; I don't remember speaking to him.

D: You don't remember, then, I see. So you may have had conversations--

B: I could easily have; I don't remember them.

D: Obviously I have to consult that documentary record and see what's there, as to what—but I was struck by--

B: There's nothing here; that's all I'm saying.

D: I wanted to ask that, because Helms was so emphatic.

B: It very often happens that the guy who's close to a particular piece of information will have a very clear recollection of what he thought about it and what he said about it, and how much his saying so had an influence on events. I don't have any such recollection.

It is amazing that smart men like Bundy and McNamara can exhibit such loss of memory when they are so good on other details. It is almost as if they are afraid of touching the "third-rail" so to speak, or lacked courage. Prior to public service, McNamara was one of the "Whiz kids" who helped rebuild Ford Motor Company after World War II, and served as Ford's President before becoming Secretary of Defense.[536]

What does CIA Director Helms have to say in his book? He states that "The day after the attack, President Johnson, bristling with irritation, said to me, 'The New York Times put that attack on the Liberty on an inside page. It should have been on the front page!'" He further states, "I have yet to understand why it was felt necessary to attack this ship or who ordered the attack."[537] Helms had been more forthright with Dallek than he was in his book. Helms has said that he didn't want to be involved in litigation over the matter.

There can be many reasons for staging a cover-up, especially in the world of politics, which is rampant with the many such scandals. The first sign of a cover-up is when one runs head on into the "wall of secrecy" or the

390

so-called "conspiracy of silence". This is exactly the situation we have with the attack on the USS *Liberty*.

There is one countervailing factor that needs to be put into perspective and that has to do with national security. The cloak of "national security" can cover many sins, whether it is justified or not, it is a reality. The claim of the Moorer Commission is that our national security has been put in jeopardy by the actions of the Johnson administration. Further, the claim is one of a political nature; however, one can see why the Johnson administration would not want anyone looking in on *Operation Cyanide* if our government was complicit in the Six-Day War.

Congress passed the Freedom of Information Act under the premise that in a free society the citizens have a right to know what their government is doing. Exemptions were created in the law for allowing the country to protect itself by allowing the government to implement defense and security policies—most of the public accepts that as a fact.

However, when the guise of national security is used to cover political sins and other sinister acts is when democracy and freedom are put at risk—it evolves around the plea of "trust me" or trust your government to know what is best. There is reason to believe that the CIA is the worst violator of the Rule of Law. The Senator Frank Church Congressional investigation into the CIA was a major event, and today we have the contention that the CIA systematically provides no information or disinformation to Congress.

A major part of the *Liberty* story is the attempt to penetrate that wall of secrecy, yet on the other hand, some of the *Liberty* crew have in fact acted to perpetuate that wall, for whatever their reasons. Jim Ennes in an e-mail to this author acknowledged the fear or threat for violating the secrecy obligation they had as service personnel. He responded to my inquiry as to whether or not the crew might still be under threat of sanctions for revealing information at this late stage. "Yes. We are sworn to lifetime secrecy under penalty of $10,000 fine and ten years in prison."[538]

To understanding the cover-up is to understand that the *Liberty's* mission is strictly one component of a much larger scenario—that of our foreign policy objectives. Was Johnson's foreign policy and security advisor, Walt Rostow, his wall of deniability? I would suggest that is a fair question to ask.

The attack on the *Liberty* has to be contrasted with other cases of attack on our intelligence apparatus, for example, the capture of the USS *Pueblo* by an adversary, North Korea, a nation that also shot down and killed the entire crew of the EC-121. Was Israel really our ally, or simply a manipulator of our politicians?[539]

I do not know how there could be a stronger indictment of a Commander-in-Chief and President and his administration. Did any of this have to do with Johnson deciding not to run for president again? We don't know because there are still documents in his library from the Six-Day War period that have not be cleared for disclosure, a process that might take years, if disclosure ever happens. One can assume that to open the *Liberty* matter would eventually result in opening the record of our covert cooperation with the Israelis. I do not believe that will happen anytime soon.

Both versions don't contradict each other. Both objects could be pursued at once, and two birds could be killed with one stone. Israel wanted to stop leakage of information and, at the same time, established a precedent for US troops to fight against Arabs. If the Americans landed, the Soviet troops would also have done the same, and a great stir would have started then.

Captain Nikolay Cherkashin, Russian
Submariner.

Chapter 13

Desant: Soviet Landing

Over the years as the *Liberty* story has evolved, little has been said about one major element, and that has to do with what the Soviet fleet was doing in the Western and Eastern Mediterranean and Red Sea. The Soviets had some 70 ships and at least 10 nuclear and diesel submarines present in the area as a "combined Eskadra". The first significant appearance of Soviet sea power in the Mediterranean came in 1967 during the Arab-Israeli conflict. During the Six-Day War, the Soviets increased their force in a show of support for the Arab states. The Soviets were to demonstrate their willingness to influence major events in the area by projecting their use of military power. During that crisis, the Soviet Mediterranean Squadron numbered up to some 70 units, some of which were in Port Said and Alexandria, to prevent Israeli attacks against those ports.[540]

Did the Soviets, electronically, or otherwise witness the attack on the *Liberty*, or did the Soviets have some role to play in the attack? Were they intercepting *Liberty's* transmissions and reporting to the Arabs? The

393

claim is that after the attack one Soviet destroyer stood by her, offering help, until the early morning hours of June 9. U.S. carrier planes were dispatched twice to be recalled with no U.S. military help quickly coming to the *Liberty's* aid.

The role and objective of the Soviet leadership in the Middle East was to create a "situation in which the U.S. would become seriously involved, economically, politically, and militarily, in which case the U.S. would suffer serious political reverses as a result of siding against the Arabs." The Soviets thought Nasser "must go"; and that his own disillusioned people would "most probably" assassinate him in the near future. However, the Soviets had made certain miscalculations of the Arabs ability to unite in their own self-interest.[541] The veil of secrecy perpetuated by the Soviets, the U.S. and Israel has obscured the full scope of Soviet involvement in the Six-Day War.

Dr. Isabella Ginor and her partner Gideon Remez, have spent the last few years studying the role of the Soviet Union in perpetrating the Six-Day War, including the involvement of the Soviet fleet and aircraft. Isabella Ginor is a research fellow at the Harry Truman Research Institute at the Hebrew University of Jerusalem. She was born in the Ukraine and immigrated to Israel in 1967. She has specialized in Soviet affairs and she appeared at the State Department January 2004 conference on the Six-Day War and the attack on the USS *Liberty*. Gideon Remez was a radio journalist for 36 years with Israel's premier national radio network. He was a paratrooper during the Six-Day War. The authors live in Jerusalem. Throughout this chapter when I am referring to the authors in the plural, I am referring to Ginor and Remez. They have done much to lift the cloud of secrecy by

394

painstakingly piecing information together bit-by-bit. They are not alone in deserving credit for lifting the fog over events in the Middle East war.

Another researcher, and *Liberty* supporter, Richard Thompson, until his death in 2007 because of an auto accident, returning home from a LVA reunion, had made several trips to Russian to interview Soviet military veterans as to their knowledge of events in June of 1967. He also deserves much credit for exposing the Soviet role, especially the naval role in that war, in particular dealing with the Soviet submarine activity.

On May 17, a fast moving jet, at high altitude, over-flew Israel's national secret, the nuclear reactor and weapons facility at Dimona in the Negev desert. Neither Israeli jets nor U.S. supplied Hawk missiles could shoot the high-flying-fast-moving plane down. The same thing occurred again on May 26. Incidentally, when an Israeli plane accidentally flew into the prohibited zone around Dimona, Israeli missiles shot it down. Was Nasser planning a preemptive strike on the Israeli nuclear facility; and what about a plane that the best U.S. missile system could not shoot down? How did these events factor into Israeli plans and did it portend ominous concerns on the part of the Israelis about Egyptian and Soviet intentions. All along, the Israelis said all they wanted from the U.S. was to counteract the Soviets.

The story of the *Liberty's* saga would be incomplete without understanding the role of the Soviet Union in the Six-Day War. In the various books, dealing with the attack there is incidental mention of the Soviet Union's involvement with Egypt and Syria other than as a weapons supplier, sponsor—and agitator. In the prior 1956, Suez War, the Soviets threatened intervention and

395

strangely allied with the Eisenhower administration in bringing that war to halt eventually returning the Sinai to Egypt, assuring unfettered access to the Suez Canal. One thing is clear, and that was there was continuity between the Suez War and Six-Day War in terms of what the intelligence services of the U.S., Israel and the Soviets were doing behind the scenes. Within the CIA, elements, in particular under the leadership of James Angleton wanted to see Nasser out of power to blunt Soviet influence in the area. It appears the Soviets became increasingly disenchanted with their Egyptian proxy.

Dr. Ginor and her partner uncovered the provocative role that the Soviets played in bringing about a nuclear confrontation. From our standpoint, all of this is background to the *Liberty* affair—the attack on the ship did not occur in a vacuum. One question stands out having to do with the Israeli concern about the Soviet threat: How could Israel keep track of a large threatening Soviet armada, and yet lose track and misidentify a single clearly marked United States ship such as the *Liberty*— defies logic.

Another obvious question for anyone researching the attack on the *Liberty* is whether there were other ships close to her, and whether there was Russian intercepts of the communications emanating from Israeli controllers, the planes and motor torpedo boats attacking the ship that would help illuminate matters. I had previously referred to a *Liberty* supporter and researcher named Richard Thompson, who was instrumental in producing the BBC documentary production of *Dead in the Water,* with author Peter Hounam as the researcher. Thompson was intent on discovering information on the Soviet involvement, especially as to her submarines that were in the Mediterranean during the war. He had made several

396

trips to Russian and met with retired Russian naval personnel including the granting of an interview on his efforts to the Russian newspaper, *Pravda*.[542]

This article was a follow-up to another *Pravda* article of an interview with *Liberty* survivor John Hrankowski who stated a Soviet ship had offered help when no American help arrived for close to 16 hours after the deadly attack. There is a question as to that ship's identity. Was it a Soviet missile destroyer 626/4, or an oil tanker, the *Nikolaj Podvojskij*? The NSA reports that the only Soviet ship near the *Liberty* was the tanker *Nikolaj Podvojskij*.[543] The *Podvojskij* would not be mistaken for a destroyer; it had been built in 1966 by a Yugoslav shipyard—could it have also been a Soviet spy ship—a trawler?

The authors report the following in an online abstract article dealing with their research referring to documents released by the NSA:[544]

> The released documents do name at least one more Soviet ship that was "in the area of the USS Liberty immediately after the attack," besides the two for which we already had evidence. This third ship, Nikolai Podvoysky, is identified by shipyard records as a tanker -- whose presence in the area could only be to refuel warships. The document in question is one of several where the context indicates that the deleted passages pertain to the Soviet angle of the Liberty's mission or of the circumstances around the attack. Unless the Nikolai Podvoysky was mistakenly identified as a trawler, which in turn was assumed to be an intelligence-gathering ship--both of which are also mentioned as approaching or

397

following the Liberty--one or two more Soviet ships were also present.

The *Pravda* reporter was aware of the BBC production on the *Liberty* and he stated that Mr. Thompson recommended they talk to a Russian submariner, Captain Nikolay Cherkashin who was himself investigating circumstances surrounding the *Liberty* tragedy. The article noted that Cherkashin had recently published a book entitled *Mysteries of Lost Warships* resulting from his independent investigation of Russian submarines from *Empress Maria* to the *Kursk*. A *Pravda* reporter interviewed Cherkashin who unexpectedly said there was no Russian ship close to the *Liberty* that night. He reportedly said, "What happened to the *Liberty* is an astonishing and unique fact, but Soviet sailors had no connection with it." However, according to Thompson's version, two Soviet ships were allegedly in the area and offered help but the Americans refused. Cherkashin to *Pravda*: "In my mind, this information isn't true. No Soviet ships were in close vicinity during the attack. Moreover, the very fact of the attack against the USS *Liberty* was practically unknown to the Soviet people. Probably, only the Soviet defense minister, Chairman of the Soviet government Kosygin, and several top officials in the government knew about it, that's all."

We know that Kosygin was aware of the *Liberty* attack on June 8 because of communications between President Johnson and Kosygin using the *Molink*, which stands for Moscow Link, or the Hot Line. The following summarizes use of the Hot Line: [545]

Here's how it works. On those rare occasions when an official Soviet Government message

398

is received, MOLINK (short for Moscow-link) immediately translates it into English and sends both the Russian and English text by an untappable fax line to the Situation Room in the White House basement, which is staffed around the clock by military personnel. If the message were to suggest an imminent disaster, such as an accidental nuclear strike, the MOLINK team would call the Situation Room duty officer and "gist" the main elements to him for prompt relaying to the President; this is quickly followed up by a meticulously translated message. When away from the White House, the President can be quickly "patched" into MOLINK through special equipment that accompanies him at all times.

The exact number of times the hot line has been used is secret because only the President is authorized to declassify such information. But some instances can be culled from Presidential memoirs. Perhaps the most intense period of use came during the Arab-Israeli Six-Day War in 1967. The very first official message ever transmitted was received in Washington on June 5. Just before 8 A.M., President Johnson recalled in his memoirs, "The Vantage Point," Defense Secretary Robert McNamara called him in his White House bedroom and announced: "Mr. President, the hot line is up." After an Israeli pre-emptive strike against Arab countries, the Soviet leader Alexei Kosygin sent a message saying that his country's forces would stay out of the pending conflict if the United States agreed to do likewise. The President readily agreed.

A few days later, after a United States communications ship was accidentally torpedoed off the Sinai Peninsula, an American carrier task force moved into the area to rescue survivors. Worried that the Soviet Union might misinterpret the Sixth Fleet's maneuvers as intervention, President Johnson sent a message explaining the action. And when it appeared that Israeli troops might advance on Damascus, Johnson assured Kosygin he was pressing the Israelis for a cease-fire, and the Israelis did stop short of the Syrian capital. Secretary McNamara later said that the hot line had proved "very useful" in preventing what could have become a direct American-Soviet confrontation.

The above reference to U.S. and Soviet engagement, along with the reference to the *Liberty* might indicate that the potential for a Soviet involvement was tepid to the say the least. This would seem to reinforce some thoughts and observations reported earlier herein where McGeorge Bundy had noted President Johnson's "cool" handling of the crisis.

Thompson provided me with a copy of a Molink communication in Russian dated June 8, 1967 transmitted by Soviet Molink – 12:20 PM, received by US Molink – 12:23 PM addressed to White House President L. B. Johnson. The provided translation said, "Dear Mr. President. Your telegram concerning the incident of the American ship "Liberty" which was torpedoed near Port Said was received and transmitted immediately to President Nasser for his knowledge. With respect, A. Kosygin 8 June 1967."

This is a good place to examine in depth the role the Molink, or Hot Line, played in the Six-Day War and the *Liberty* matter. A declassified White House

Memorandum dated November 4, 1968, obtained from the LBJ Library pertains to "SUBJECT: The Hot Line Exchanges". The memorandum is an effort by Mr. Nathaniel Davis to contact Ambassador Llewellyn E. Thompson who was in Bethesda Naval Hospital to obtain the ambassador's "recollections" of the Hot Line exchanges between President Johnson and Premier Kosygin. First, Kosygin expected Johnson to be physically present at the receiving end. Johnson asked how to address Kosygin and he was advised as "Comrade"—a protocol mistake that was overlooked. Five exchanges are summarized as follows:[546]

1. June 5, 8:47 a.m.: The topic was cease-fire or cease-fire <u>and</u> withdrawal. At June 6, 10:02 a.m., the President suggested to the Soviets a resolution UN Ambassador Goldberg gave to Federenko wherein Federenko agreed to a simple cease-fire in New York. The question is whether Federenko was authorized to do so and would he get in trouble. The Situation Room was elated.

2. June 6, 7:45 p.m., Johnson reinforced the resolution to Kosygin and suggested they support the Security Council's efforts toward peace and to nail down a cease-fire.

3. June 8, 9:48 a.m., Kosygin called for withdrawal. In his reply on June 8, 11:00 a.m. President Johnson informed Kosygin of the torpedoing of the *Liberty* and the dispatch of aircraft to the area. Ambassador Thompson commented that he felt this was a successful use of the Hot Line to avoid danger of war arising out of a misunderstanding. Thompson said this made a "big impression" with the Russians.

4. June 10, 8:48 a.m. This message was from Kosygin saying the Russians were ready to act independently if Israeli didn't stop actions against Syria in the "next few hours". Thompson point out that the threat "including military" actions would be taken. He noted how the Soviets were more sensitive to the plight of the Syrians than of Egypt's situation. Speculation in the Situation Room was that Russians might think the U.S. wanted to knock off the Syrian government. Thompson noted that Helms was brought in to provide insight into how much progress the Israelis were making.

5. June 10, 9:30 a.m. Thompson noted how calm and reasoned the President was. Televised proceedings at the Security Council reflected that Israel advised General Bull that Israel would accept any recommended cease-fire. Tension in the Situation Room soon eased. Discussion was whether it would be better for the Israelis to continue to move on Damascus, and this was not pursued.

Note item No. 3 above deals with advising Kosygin of the attack on the *Liberty* and the dispatch of planes. President Johnson advised Kosygin at 1100 that planes were dispatched to the aid of the *Liberty*; that would be 1700 Sinai time. My timeline shows that Admiral Martin issued a "recall" and no more launches of VQ-2 flights from Athens until further advised at 1559 Sinai time and 9:59 DC time. This refers to the EC-121 and C-130 flights. At 1015, the NSA director advises McNamara of the attack. At 1016 Washington time, the JCS authorizes the use of force. At 1040 Washington time, all carrier planes have been recalled. A flash message from U.S. embassy in Israel advised the Israelis apologized for the attack at 1041. What is going on here as the *Liberty* was still at risk? The planes going to the aid of the *Liberty* were recalled before President Johnson advises Kosygin planes are going to the aid of the ship. Walt Rostow advised the President at 0949 of the attack on the *Liberty*. It is alleged that both McNamara and Johnson participated in the order to recall the carrier planes. During this critical period, Walt Rostow, McNamara, and McGeorge Bundy were in contact with the President. The President then meets staff in the Situation Room at 1106 local time.

The President and the politicians in Washington D.C. have now *de facto* abandoned the USS *Liberty*. All military efforts to go to the aid of ship and crew have been over ruled by these very politicians, why? The finger points to a very small circle of advisors.[547] U.S. Sixth Fleet ships would not arrive until the next day. We do not know if any additional deaths occurred during the wait for the arrival of Sixth Fleet ships.

Clearly, the use of the Hot Line played a major role in events where a nuclear crisis was narrowly averted. The critical point of confrontation with the Soviets was after Israel attacked Syria and on June 10. Was the *Liberty* sacrificed, as a "damaged pawn", on the Middle East chessboard? The point of collision with the Soviets was on the 10th when McNamara turned around the Sixth Fleet to the east. President Johnson met with advisors in the Situation Room from 0857 to 1155. Those present were Under Secretary Katzenback, SecDef McNamara, Clark Clifford, McGeorge Bundy, Walt Rostow, Ambassador Thompson and CIA Director Helms. In a Memorandum for the Record, Helms notes the following:[548]

403

While the President was out, Secretary McNamara asked whether we should turn the Sixth Fleet around to sail toward the eastern Mediterranean. Thompson and Helms agreed. Helms pointed out that Soviet submarines monitoring the Fleet's operations would report immediately to Moscow, that the task force had stopped circling and had begun heading eastward.

The President returned and McNamara mentioned this possibility. The President said, "Yes, go ahead and do it." McNamara picked up a secure telephone and gave the order.

[*3 lines of source text not declassified*]

Recalling the atmosphere of the meeting, Mr. Helms said that conversation during the first couple of hours was in the lowest voices he had ever heard in a meeting of that kind. The atmosphere was tense. As the morning wore on, everyone relaxed a bit as it became clear that the fighting was petering out.

In difference to the U.S. leaders, it may be that the *Liberty* was inadvertently caught-up in this confrontation between the U.S. and Soviets, no small matter—in essence, she was sacrificed. With the potential for a nuclear confrontation, everything is up for play. On the proverbial chessboard, the "King" is under siege. With the Sixth Fleet maneuver, the Soviets were checkmated—or so it seemed. This was one of Israel's objectives for the U.S—to buffer the Soviets.

Getting back to the *Pravda* article, the reporter wanted to find evidence among Russian sailors, but it was in vain. The article notes: "Headquarters Commander of the 5th operative squadron Admiral Platonov was the first to lead his squadron to the site on June 26; however, nothing is mentioned in his memoirs about Soviet sailors offering help to the *Liberty*. If that really happened, I think he would have mentioned it for sure." It is this author's belief that the *Pravda* article translation (the translation results in rough grammar) should be substantially summarized below because it has not been widely disseminated in the United States and its content is explosive:[549]

The *Pravda* reporter poses the following questions to Cherkashin:

[Pravda] Who do you think spread that version?

I myself would also like to know the answer to that question. Fleet Admiral Ivan Kapitanets, for example, mentions nothing at all about the June 8 events in his memoirs. In his book *"War At Sea"*, he wrote that he led Soviet ships to the western part of the Mediterranean Sea on June 1. "On June 4, we were ordered to put the ship in the state of a complete war alert within 12 hours. Probably, Moscow knew something just 24 hours before the tragic event. This time was required to check the ammunition. The Arab-Israeli 7-day war started on June 5. I received an order to travel to the Antikitir Strait, receive landing forces, and be ready to land them in the port of Ataki for the sake of protect Soviet people there. On June 7, we arrived to the Antikitir Strait." And not a single word is said about the events on

June 8, 1967. When I asked him about the USS *Liberty* and a Soviet ship, he said he had known nothing about the event; it was a revelation for him.

[Pravda] Who was the first to spread information about a Soviet ship that offered help to the USS *Liberty*?

I think it was former *Liberty* officer Lieutenant James Ennes (Nikolay Cherkashin showed a translation of the book *"Assault on the Liberty"* by James H. (Ennes). He describes in detail what happened with the crew during the Israeli attack, and he describes the event from different angles.

James Ennes:

"For one day and night when the ship was slowly moving northward, no other ships or planes could be seen. At midnight, the *Liberty* came across the 626/4 a Soviet missile destroyer that signaled in English. The following information was exchanged by both ships:

626/4: Do you need help?

Liberty: No, thanks.

626/4: I will stay at the horizon and be ready to help if you need it.

The Soviet ship followed a parallel course at a distance of several miles for the next six hours. At dawn, the *Liberty* radar station discovered the American destroyers *Massey* and *Davis*. The Soviet destroyer turned eastward and joined the ships of the 6th fleet. Aircraft carriers were not far behind the destroyers, and wounded sailors from the *Liberty* were delivered by helicopters to the aircraft carrier, to its hospital. The *Liberty* continued its course to Malta, where, as the crew was told, the assault would be investigated by a Navy court."

[Pravda] But the hull number was even mentioned!

(Cherkashin) Yes, we know the number. The matter of the fact is it is still a secret to whom it belonged. The 626/4 destroyer wasn't at that time in the eastern part of Mediterranean. I tried to find some veterans of the Soviet Navy who had been there in the summer of 1967, but in vain. Also, nothing is also mentioned in the archives.

[Pravda] Well, let's go back to the attack on the *Liberty*. Could it have been a tragic accident when the US ship was mistakenly taken for an Egyptian cargo ship? Was it a deliberate attack? Provocation? What do you think about it?

(Cherkashin) Last year, a Russian translation of Joseph Daichman's *"History of the Mossad"* was published in Moscow. The author describes the tragedy in 1967 in detail. He admits that it was perfectly clear that the *Liberty* was an American ship and that the attack was committed to deprive the USA "of its eyes and ears," of the opportunity to control the situation. Daichman says the attackers had the right to act so. The Israelis feared that the *Liberty* would report information about the course of the war: they wanted to keep it a secret that troops had been shifted to Syria and the Egyptian border wasn't protected at all. The border was quite open for Egyptian soldiers to cross. Israel knew that American radio signals were intercepted by the Soviet Union, and the latter would certainly inform Egypt of the fact. That is why the *Liberty* was to be sunk to avoid leakage of important information. This is a very cynical version. I even couldn't have thought that I would ever read it.

[Pravda] There is also one more opinion...

Yes, another version is that Israel wanted to provoke the USA and involve it in a war against Arab countries. This version is still out there. Mr. Thompson supports it as well. I have known him for ten years already; by the way, it was he who told me about the *Liberty* tragedy. Richard

Thompson is a fair and very active man, and he is persistent with his struggle for his ideas. US top officials wanted to hush up the *Liberty* scandal, as it was really disgusting and dirty. What is more, that was an unprecedented act, the first attack against US ships since Pearl Harbor. And the attack was committed by those whom America supported so strongly. Right after the accident, the US Congress organized no investigations at all, which was mere nonsense at that time!

[Pravda] Do you think it is possible now to start a new investigation of the tragedy but on a higher level?

If someone in the government is concerned, an investigation can be initiated. But currently the USA has no time for it; it is preoccupied with the war against terrorism. However, we can call the *Liberty* tragedy an act of terrorism as well. By the way, it seems to me that the 9/11 attacks at the WTC and Pentagon are very much like the tragedy with the USS *Liberty*. This also seems to have been a well weighted provocation. The USS *Liberty* was a very old ship that operated since WWII. Probably, that is why it was the *Liberty* that was sacrificed.

[Pravda] Do you mean that America was ready for that kind of attack?

409

I think America knew. Even sailors anticipated the tragedy and felt depressed. When the ship stopped in Spain, a famous prophetess told the *Liberty* sailors that the ship wouldn't return home. Richard Thompson has been investigating the *Liberty* tragedy for several years. As a result, he has arrived at the conclusion that the attack had been a well-planned action of the Israeli and American special services. The USA was up to its neck in a bloody war in Vietnam and wouldn't get involved into a lingering Mideast conflict. That is why it rejected direct military support to Israel. However, there were quite enough hawks in America of that period who wanted to turn a regional war into a large-scale battle. Especially at the cost of an old ship built in 1945.

[Pravda] Which version do you prefer?

(Cherkashin) Both versions don't contradict each other. Both objects could be pursued at once, and two birds could be killed with one stone. Israel wanted to stop leakage of information and, at the same time, established a precedent for US troops to fight against Arabs. If the Americans landed, the Soviet troops would also have done the same, and a great stir would have started then.

The Soviet submarine K-172 under the command of Nikolay Shashkov armed with missiles and nuclear warheads was at the very same moment in the Bay of Sidre. The submarine received instructions to surface and deliver a blow against the Israeli coast if the Americans landed troops on Syrian shores. The submarine had eight nuclear missiles on board. However, as we know the Israeli coast means the whole state of Israel stretched along the sea. Israel would have been completely destroyed if such blows were delivered by the Soviet submarine. I wrote about Nikolay Shashkov; the publication was called *"The Man Who Was to Destroy Israel"*. The publication produced a strong response from society. I received inquiries from the Israeli Embassy, and many journalists wanted just to see the man who was to liquidate the Israeli state. The K-172 crew had to operate under emergency conditions; the submariners nearly died of high concentration of mercury vapor in its compartments. Several people were poisoned with the vapor, suffered from hallucinations and giddiness, and no explanation could be found to it. Can you imagine what submariners suffering from hallucinations could have done with nuclear warheads? They were to have been immediately sent to hospitals. However, as the situation in the region was still tense, the Soviet Navy commander-in-chief asked the submariners if they would be able to stay in the area for several more weeks, and the submariners agreed. Even when doctors were sent to the submarine, they failed to find the cause of hallucinations and giddiness. Nobody even guessed that was mercury, and people spent two months in the compartments poisoned with mercury vapors.

Submariners from the Soviet B-31 submarine had to face an even harder situation. When the war began, the submarine was transferred from the Atlantic Ocean to the eastern part of Mediterranean Sea. A disastrous fire broke out somewhere in the Tunisian Strait; it took over 24 hours to extinguish the fire. Five master sergeants and sailors perished because of the fire. And, for the first time since WWII, perished sailors were buried at sea. Large-scale repairs were started on the submarine, and, after that, the submarine set off for the Bay of Sidre. Therefore, Soviet submariners experienced very difficult situations, and many of them fell indirect victims to that Mideast war. However, none of these submariners also heard about the *Liberty*. To tell the truth, it wasn't a matter of their concern.

[Pravda] The USS *Liberty* is a bloody secret of the Cold War. Was there any Soviet destroyer at all, or it was just a myth? Captain Nikolay Cherkashin thinks that it is impossible to find a 100% answer to the question, as too much time has passed since the tragedy.

412

Author's Note: The Antikitir Strait is Antikythera or Anticythera, a Greek island lying on the edge of the Aegean Sea between Crete and Peloponnese.[550] The U.S. Sixth Fleet had been circling in the area of Crete prior to being redirected by Secretary of Defense McNamara to confront the Soviets.

At the time Thompson was doing his research, Dr. Isabella Ginor was researching and writing about the Soviet Union's involvement in the Six-Day War. She published in the *Middle East Review of International Affairs* two articles of particular interest, with the first being entitled: *THE RUSSIANS WERE COMING: THE SOVIET MILITARY THREAT IN THE 1967 SIX-DAY WAR.*[551] The second article was *THE COLD WAR'S LONGEST COVER-UP: HOW AND WHY THE USSR INSTIGATED THE 1967 WAR.*[552]

Ginor is a noted media and academic analyst of Soviet and post-Soviet affairs. She collaborated with her partner, Gideon Remez in a break through book on the Soviet involvement entitled *Foxbats over Dimona: The Soviets' Nuclear Gamble in the Six-day War.*[553] In short, their theme is that the Soviets instigated the Six-Day War by pushing Israel into it. If that is the case, then we have two super-powers both plotting in the Middle East, not reactively, but proactively.

The authors first got interested in their Soviet research when they happened on some information about a former Soviet naval officer who was to lead a "desant" [Russian: Десант for landing], or landing party of volunteers onboard a frigate in the Mediterranean during the Six-Day War, landing on the coast of Israel specifically off Haifa. The essence of Ginor's and her partner's effort

413

was going to be a revisionist version of history. Because of her birth in the Ukraine, she was uniquely qualified for this research. Captain Yuri Khripunkov was the Soviet source for this theory in an article in a Ukrainian paper, and the authors needed to overcome their own skepticism before plunging into their research.

I would note that while she had the unique advantage of familiarity with the geography and language, one can now research topics in Russian and other languages on the World Wide Web and have Google automatically translate the page into English—a very valuable research tool.

According to accepted wisdom, while the Soviets through the KGB did foment rumors of a large build up of Israeli troops on the Syrian border, Moscow acted to prevent war, or according to the CIA was blustering and would not actively engage in hostilities. When hostilities did break out Moscow cooperated with the U.S. to end them, primarily using the Hot Line or *Molink* as previously described. The prevailing Washington view was that Moscow was moving toward détente and although it was still competing with Washington for worldwide influence, the risk of a head on clash between nuclear super-powers was out of the question.[554]

On first blush, it would seem that Moscow had been stung in the Cuban missile crisis, or so it seemed, until Kennedy removed certain missiles from Turkey and promised not to invade Cuba. However, was another super-power confrontation, this time in the Mediterranean possible? The authors found that checking Russian archives that were supposed to be open after the demise of the Soviet Union was not easy. They found that the Soviet political establishment did not like to put things in writing, or did it ambiguously in a self-protecting fashion—known as CYA. In the Soviet Union, the rule was propaganda and disinformation in order to survive.

Upon publishing their book *Foxbats*, the authors ran into skepticism; however, they noted one military historian supported their efforts and was of the belief that the onus had shifted to those you who challenge their thesis and research. Some of their documentation was not found in Moscow but in other Warsaw Pack member's archives such as Poland and East Germany. One particular document was General Secretary Leonid Brezhnev's speech to a closed session of the CPSU Central Committee on June 20, 1967. It disclosed Moscow's May 1967 warning about Israel's offensive intentions, which was designed to get Egypt and Syria to begin to take appropriate countermeasures. The authors note this would signify that the warning did not originate with low-level officials.[555] Their research is still confounded by continuing secrecy by all governments involved in the crisis including that of the United States

In a Russian article published May 21, 2007 written by Viktor Baranets entitled *Forty Years Ago, the USSR Wanted to Bomb Israel*, Michael Oren is quoted as challenging the findings of the authors [Russian to English translation]:[556]

Facts and hypotheses - not the same thing
Michael Oren, an Israeli historian and author of "Six Days of War: June 1967 and the formation of the modern Middle East":
For many years I thoroughly engaged in this problem, but do not have any documentary evidence to support the hypothesis Remez and Ginor about the aggressive plans of the USSR.

415

Although I worked in the Soviet archives, but few documents were declassified. I believe that there were several reasons why the Soviets sought to war, but this was not among them ...

The authors concluded that the Israeli preemption was not expansionist, but rather the result of provocation by Soviet-Arab efforts. One is not required to accept all the authors' contentions, as it is possible the parties had their own self-interest motives.

They do determine that Israeli's nuclear posture before 1967 was a factor in Soviet planning. The nuclear factor was real, however, the authors seem to be unaware or ignore the joint US/Israeli intelligence plan for the war referred to as *Operation Cyanide* or *Frontlet615* in the prior chapter. On the other hand, the reality of history and actions evident by the media record, is that Israel has benefited from land gains made during that war, evidenced by the recent contentious exchange between President Obama and the Israeli Prime Minister (May of 2011), wherein the President referred to a return to 1967 borders "with swaps". The Israeli PM responded that those borders were "in defensible". All parties to the conflict had their motivation and perspective.

While there had been Hot Line exchanges with Kosygin and Johnson, there were "threats" that the Soviets would get involved, especially after the invasion of Syria. At 8:48 AM, June 10, the White House over Hot Line, the *Molink*, received a warning from Soviet Premier, Alexei Kosygin demanding an immediate halt to Israel's invasion of Syria threatening action that might lead to nuclear confrontation. According to the U.S. ambassador to the USSR, Llewellyn Thompson, the scene was one of "great concern and utmost gravity" at the White House situation room. Notwithstanding rational concern, the threat was perceived as bluster at this stage of the war.[557]

The authors cite a CIA document excerpt acknowledging Soviet intentions to involve itself in the crisis by landing sailors and paratroopers in Syria to halt the Israeli advance. The document "tongue-in-cheek" acknowledges some pressure may have been brought to bear by the Soviet threat, however, it notes the Israelis had already agreed to a cease-fire.[558]

Authors Ginor and Remez, will challenge Western historiography that has been rooted in three assumptions over the years. First, the Soviet warning to Egypt in mid-May 1967 that Israel was massing troop on the Syrian border that triggered the war was a miscalculation; second, that the USSR did not want full-scale hostilities; and third, Moscow had not done any planning directed toward intervention.

The authors challenge those assumptions as misplaced. They report that the Soviets had readied strategic bombers and nuclear-armed naval forces that backed up the threat, and assigned secret aircraft to conduct reconnaissance over the Dimona nuclear weapons factory and reactor. Recall the contention of author Peter Hounam that B52s were put on alert at Beale Air Force base in California during the Middle East crisis on June 8.[559]

The sudden Israeli destruction of Arab air forces caught the Soviets off balance. Victory was not possible for Egypt, and was it worth confronting United States? Therefore, "it", the plan was implemented in minor part

417

as a deterrent on June 10 with regard to the Israeli attack on Syria. The dismal failure of the Soviet plan resulted in their covering up their intended intervention. The fact is that all three participants were involved in an elaborate mutually beneficial cover-up that included facts surrounding the attack on the USS *Liberty*. The cover-up of the attack on the *Liberty* is essential to maintain the larger cover-up of U.S. and Israeli cooperation during the lead up to the war. To isolate the *Liberty* out of the context of the U.S. and Soviet confrontation is I believe a mistake.

The authors remind us that the Soviets long had an interest in the Middle East, the Mediterranean and the Palestinian issue. Jews had suffered pogroms in Russia since at least 1880. In 1947, the Soviets under Stalin did a "tactical shift" and supported the establishment of a Jewish state. The goal was to strengthen the USSR and subvert British influence during the waning period of the British Empire. Stalin felt he could make Israel a subordinate satellite and Cold War naval base and port.[560]

After the UN General Assembly approved the partition plan on November 29, 1947, the U.S. withdrew support and enacted an arms embargo. The Soviets via Czechoslovakian arms suppliers aided the Jewish underground. Israel declared independence on May 14, 1948 after the War of Independence. Stalin recognized the state *de jure* while the U.S. recognized it *de facto*. Israel turned over Russian church property to the Russian church thereby creating an intelligence apparatus reaching into Eastern Europe that survives to this day.[561] The "intelligence product" was what Ben-Gurion enticed the U.S. CIA with in trade for mutual assistance during the James Jesus Angleton era wherein Angleton headed up the Israeli desk at the CIA, working with the Mossad and Aman.

Ben-Gurion steered the country away from Soviet socialistic influence in favor of the West. As was previously noted, Ben-Gurion wanted Israel under the U.S. nuclear umbrella. Of interest is the fact that in a run-up to a meeting between Egyptian President Hosni Mubarak and President Obama, Egypt made it clear in 2009 that Egypt rejected a U.S. offer to guarantee defense of the region against atomic weapons as part of a comprehensive Middle East peace plan. A nuclear umbrella is usually used for the security alliances of the United States with non-nuclear states such as Japan, South Korea, much of Europe, Turkey, Canada, and Australia, originating during the Cold War with the then Soviet Union. For some countries, it was an alternative to acquiring their own nuclear weapons. In doing so, Mubarak reaffirmed Egypt's pledge underlying the country's commitment since 1974 for the establishment of a "nuclear-free Middle East."[562]

The nuclear issue has become more complex over the years with Iraq and Iran's efforts to develop nuclear power and weapons—a competitive heritage from Israel's Dimona project begun in the 1950s; something that former CIA Director Allen Dulles feared would happen.

With Ben-Gurion's policy of moving away from the Soviets, as both Prime Minister and Defense Minister, he initially had to look for support from Western Europe, including nuclear reactor assistance from France. The Soviets stepped up their courtship of the Arabs, most of whom were anti-Western and with socialistic tendencies according to the authors Ginor and Remez. Both sides were taking steps to arm themselves.

For the United States, the lack of our aid to Nasser over the building of the Aswan dam and other items turned Egypt toward Russia complicating our Middle East foreign policy. In 1955, Nasser had concluded arms deals with the Soviets even before he formally took power. An arms race was setting up in the Middle East. Nasser nationalized the Suez Canal on July 26, 1956 wherein, Britain, France and Israel launched a campaign against Egypt—the Suez War.[563] Russian advisers were in Egypt and were to abstain from direct involvement.[564] Nevertheless, the authors claim Russian pilots flew against the Israelis and the British. The Soviet's main tactic was bluster and bullying in the manner of Nikita Khrushchev.

Ginor and Remez equate the 1967 war as akin to the Cuban '62 missile crisis as evidenced by the use of the Hot Line, the *Molink*, resulting from that earlier crisis. The Soviet objective in 1967 was to limit Israeli borders to those of 1947, after having attained more territory in the '48 war than intended by the partition act. Another Soviet objective was to destroy the Israeli nuclear facility at Dimona, the consequence of which resulted in Soviet over-flights without the Israelis being able to shoot down the recon planes. Israeli apprehensions were peaked with concern that Egypt would attack Dimona and the fear of direct Soviet intervention. Moshe Dayan was particularly concerned about the Soviet intervention problem. The Israelis wanted the U.S. to counter the Soviets.

The Israeli nuclear program, started without formal government approval, would be a source of contention within the inner circles of power. It not this author's objective to historically correct or enlighten on that issue. Suffice the concern was real and Avner Cohen in his book on Israel's nuclear project is of the opinion that they had two crude nuclear weapons going into the Six-Day War.[565] Michael Oren notes concern about Dimona and Labor Minister Yigal Allon's concern that Nasser might attack the site the moment America challenged Nasser's blockade of the Straits of Tiran.[566] This was not the first time that the nuclear threat entered the Middle East. The authors, Ginor and Remez claim there was a Soviet nuclear threat made to deter France, Britain and Israel during the 1956 Suez War; so there would have been an historical context and precedent for concern over the nuclear issue. Additionally, the Soviets had reason to be concerned about missiles and nuclear weapons in proximity to its borders.[567]

While the contention appeared to be that Egypt alone was concerned about Dimona and the Israeli research reactor at Nahal Sorek, Ginor and Remez report that the USSR did abet Egypt's nuclear motive for the war. They contend Russia's nuclear threat deterred France, Britain and Israel during the Suez crisis more than Western pressure, and that the Russian ultimatum was hushed up in Western literature. Such bluster worked and prompted Khrushchev to try the ploy in Cuba in 1962. The suggestion by the authors is that this prompted Israel to seek its own nuclear deterrent as France had done.[568] It is clear that governments tend to follow a set pattern of conduct, in essence an MO or method of operation—one those methods is nuclear blackmail.

An issue developed over whether Isser Harel, the former Mossad Director and intelligence advisor to the Prime Minister, had been involved in tipping off the

421

Soviets about the Israeli secret nuclear effort. Shimon Perez was a prime sponsor and protector of the Dimona project. Were the Harel releases to deter the Russians by giving them a warning of Israel's nuclear ability without "advertizing" the bomb?[569] The authors deal with the Harel nuclear issue in more detail in their abstract published after their book dated 10/28/2008.[570]

In response to Nasser's request for nuclear weapons, Andrei Grechko, the Soviet Defense Minister, during a visit to Egypt pledged "the use of Soviet nuclear forces to safeguard Egypt should Israel develop an atom bomb". The guarantee came from a meeting in May 1966 in a visit to Egypt by Soviet Premier, Alexei Kosygin. While neither Kosygin nor Grechko could make such a promise without the approval of Politburo, operationally the plan was implemented by moving the Soviet fleet into the Mediterranean, and later into the Red Sea.[571] Traditionally, super-powers project their potential power and foreign policy using naval forces. The authors report that as the crisis developed, on May 24, 1967, CIA Director Richard Helms was quite positive in stating there were no nuclear weapons in the area, something I have restated several times.[572]

The authors Ginor and Remez, in their research, sought to establish the following points among others:

1. The war resulted from the Soviet-Arab effort to provoke Israel into a preemptive strike;
2. The Soviet motive was to destroy Israel's nuclear weapons development before it became operational;
3. The Soviet effort was accelerated by ambiguous messages from Israel about its intent to develop such weapons;

4. Soviet nuclear weapons were readied for use against Israel in case it already possessed and tried to use such devices;
5. The Soviets prepared for a marine landing (desant) with air support on Israel's shores;
6. The Soviets used their most advanced aircraft to do recon flights over Dimona;
7. The Soviet plan was to be unleashed once Israel was branded the aggressor after her preemptive attack, with the Soviets tipping the balance in favor of an Arab counterattack.

In view of the evidence that has been developed and reported over the years, the issue of nuclear weapons were certainly on the table as to all three countries, notwithstanding efforts to play it down, **in fact the potential for nuclear confrontation is exactly what has been covered-up**. One can expect that Helms knew more that he was willing to admit. On the other hand, the authors quote Richard B. Parker, one of the authoritative researchers on the Six-Day War as saying in 1994 that none of his Egyptian sources ever mentioned the nuclear issue, so consequently; he never entertained the idea that nuclear weapons played a role in starting the conflict.[573] The American policy was "see-nothing-say-nothing-do-nothing", thereby facilitating Israeli's "opacity" policy on her nuclear development objectives. There are reports that the CIA and our government facilitated Israeli's nuclear program.[574]

The authors' report that a *New York Times* article noted that the Israelis wanted to obtain French missiles with a 500 mile range capable of reaching Egyptian targets, and could reach the southern Soviet Union. It would seem to make sense that the U.S. government would be monitoring Israel's missile capability as part of the *Liberty's* mission based upon JCS objectives to monitor events in the war theater. General Wheeler doubted Helms' assessment that nuclear weapons were not present in the area.

On 2/23/66, the Baath party took control of Syria by a coup; wherein General Hafez al-Assad became defense minister, with soviet influence reported to have been involved. In part, the 1967 crisis was tied to this since the Soviets did not want any threat to that government.[575] Ginor and Remez report that Russian propaganda pushed the issue of Israeli troop concentration on Syrian border beginning in May of 1966.

The first measure taken to implement the new Soviet policy in Middle East was placing Soviet naval ships in Mediterranean; some had been there since two years prior, grouped under command of "semi-independent" formation. Only after the war would it become the "Fifth Eskadra". Prior to the war, it was simply the "combined Eskadra", with ships from Northern and Baltic fleets as well as Black Sea Fleet. This followed in July 1966, by formation of the first "brigade" (the 197th) amphibious landing ships with the Black Sea Fleet, and the formation of the first naval infantry battalions.[576]

The Soviet navy would provide the nuclear "umbrella" for Egypt.[577] The underlying Soviet objective and motive was to establish bases in the Mediterranean. Consequently, Moscow turned to the Arabs exploiting Egypt's aversion to European imperialism and America's support for Israel. Economic difficulties in the early 1960s and the devastation caused by the Six-Day War pushed Nasser closer to the Soviets.[578]

There is a contention that removal of the UNEF from Sinai and closure of Tiran Straits was "inspired" by the Soviet military. This was called the "Grechko-Amer" plan shaped between 22 and 25 November 1966. November 4, 1966 Egypt and Syria signed a defense pack calling for thousands of Soviet advisers. Israel captured plans calling for an offensive operation. The plan called for Arab initiation of action.[579]

The Soviet General Staff on 12/22/66 issued a directive followed up on 1/26/67 that was to unite the Black Sea Fleet's submarines divided into four detachments, into the "14th division", based in three Crimean ports under a single commanding officer directly subordinate to the fleet commander. The purpose was to counter the Sixth Fleet in Mediterranean. In April Brezhnev demanded the Sixth Fleet's removal from the Mediterranean.[580]

The authors claim that as Soviet advisors arrived in Syria the U.S. was not up to speed in knowing what was going on. In the meantime, Palestinian intrusions continued and there was a major dogfight between Syrian and Israeli planes with a number of Syrian planes shot down within sight of Damascus on 4/7/67.

Further, the authors contend that Israel tested a nuclear device in February of 1967. The CIA reportedly was aware in February 1967 that Israel could have bomb components in 6 to 8 weeks. The Soviets were aware in the spring of '67 they were working on a "deliverable" weapon. Nasser in a February 5, 1967 comment to the *London Observer* said, "If the Israelis proceed with the production of an atomic bomb, the final solution would be preventive war and eliminate the danger."[581] So again, for Helms to say in a national Security Council

425

meeting dealing with the crisis in the Middle East on May 24 1967, with the President, that there was no nuclear issue is astounding.

Soviet Fleet commander, Admiral Gorshkov was in Kosygin's delegation the year before when the Soviet "nuclear umbrella" was promised to the Arabs, and now it was being implemented. The aim was to strike a blow at the U.S. via Israel at the expense of Nasser.[582] The "combined Eskrada" as of June 1 was put at 30 surface ships excluding auxiliaries and 10 submarines, all at battle readiness, and more to follow if crisis worsened. The count would later be at 70 with Rabin himself noting there were 70 Soviet ships in the area.

A legitimate question is posed as to the condition the Soviet fleet noting the submarine problems reported in the *Pravda* article. There were ammunition and gunnery problems with Soviet Fleet commander, Admiral Gorshkov's ship, the cruiser *Slava*. A person named Alexander Rozin has developed extensive information on the Soviet ships in the Mediterranean including U.S. ships.[583] The information is in Russian but can be translated by using Google's translation function. His personal quest deals with the Soviet navy during the Cold War, especially dealing with Soviet submarines—this appears to be his hobby.

The deputy commander of the Black Sea Fleet, Vice Admiral Viktor Sysoyev hoisted his pennant on the *Slava*, taking command of the reinforced but still unnamed Mediterranean flotilla.[584] Ginor and Remez write in their book that there was a transfer at sea of ammunition for *Slava's* 155mm guns, and that these may have been nuclear shells. The crew and a group of cadets did the transfer at sea in the area of Crete at enormous effort. Eventually, the cadets transferred to smaller ships to serve as a possible landing force.[585]

Fig. 17, Soviet Cruiser *Slava* (Glory – Molotov)

Source: http://en.wikipedia.org/wiki/Soviet_cruiser_Molotov.

Certainly, the Sixth Fleet commanders were concerned with interference and harassment by Soviet ships; note Admiral Martin's concern about his ability being limited.[586] Ennes in his book refers to being followed or sighting Soviet ships as the *Liberty* made way toward her target area.

Subs and ships going through from the Black Sea had to comport to the Montreux Convention, one sub at a time on surface. The Montreux Convention was a 1936 agreement that gives Turkey control over the Bosporus Straits and the Dardanelles and regulates military activity in the region. The convention is still in effect today with certain amendments; it guarantees the free passage of civilian vessels in peacetime. The convention has been a source of contention for years especially for the Soviets who needed access to the Mediterranean.[587] The Black Sea fleet did not have nuclear subs; those came from the Northern Fleet via Gibraltar with K-52 passing under a

427

passenger liner. Allegedly, no logbooks were kept. Diesel sub B-105, also, S-38, and S-100 arrived in the Mediterranean in June.

Nuclear sub K-172 was dispatched from the Northern Fleet Arctic base to the Mediterranean under Commander Nikolai Shashkov. He noted being ordered to "be ready to fire nuclear missiles at Israeli shore", by Fleet commander Gorshkov, if Americans and Israel landed on Syrian coast. Shashkov arrived in Med on March 30; his missiles had limited range of 600km.[588] Sub K-131 was sent from Barents Sea at end of April. Diesel subs B-31 and B-74 were also sent to Mediterranean. Soviet ships and subs were also in Red Sea. These kinds of major naval movements would have required Politburo approval according to the authors. The authors quote Shashkov: "...in a critical situation, the Soviet Union would support them by any means, including nuclear. [They] also guessed from where the strike on Israel would come— from the sea."[589]

Yuri Khripunkov's ship, SKR-6 was a brand new Petya II class antisubmarine frigate along with her sister ship; SKR-13 were sent to Med and told to stay there.

Captain Ivan Kapitanets who retired as Admiral of the Fleet in 1967 was skipper of *Nastoychivy*, a Kotlin class destroyer converted to launch anti-aircraft missiles. In the afternoon of June 10, a Soviet class Kotlin destroyer, Number 514 (I question whether this hull number is correct), ceases tracking the aircraft carrier *Saratoga*.[590] Another Kotlin class destroyer interdicted the carrier *America* and her escorts and had to be warned off by Admiral Martin advising the Soviet commander that he risked a collision—he backed off.

Khripunkov knew there was a BDK large landing ship with tanks and a battalion of infantry. See comments of Professor Aleksandr Kislov, a member of Russian Academy of Science.[591] Additional landing craft and regular marines were onboard, stationed at anchored at Port Said. Monitoring these units could have been part of the *Liberty* mission—logically it would make sense to do so. How far was Port Said from El Arish? It would have been within *Liberty's* intercept range. The *Liberty* mission included monitoring Soviet activities in the area.

The Russian fleet lacked direct air support thus Sixth Fleet was tactically the stronger of the two navies. The *Moskva* had yet to enter service as the first Russian carrier; the *Moskva* was a helicopter carrier commission in 1967. However, there is evidence land based aircraft were being readied. Aleksandr Vybornov is said to have commanded a possible Soviet Air Force deployment to support Arab forces in Middle East. In April, Egypt got 15 Sukhoi-7 attack aircraft but did not have time to master them[592]. Were these the planes that the *Liberty* was to monitor rather than TU-95 Bears per Ennes? Alternatively, was it the TU-16 heavy bomber, which was somewhat smaller that the TU-95s but faster. Interestingly, 31 TU-16 Badger bombers are listed as being destroyed in the early Israeli attack, but no TU-95s were listed.[593]

According to the authors, General Vasily Reshetnikov commented on the targeting of Dimona by Soviet strategic bombers. He knew nothing of Dimona as a nuclear center, but knew of it via the working maps as a "battlefield object" on Israeli territory, and that special mention was brought to his attention it was guarded by Hawk missiles. They go on to stated the General said

429

there were 30 planes armed with "fougaz" (napalm bombs); and were positioned in the northern Caucasus describing the actual base at Mozdok—still a Russian air base. Importantly, the authors note a correction as to the type of plane they were talking about. In their abstract, they say it is the shorter range but faster TU-16s and not TU-95s as they originally reported in their book. Deployment of General Reshetnikov's planes began during the week of June 3rd and 4th prior to the Israeli preemptive air attack. The authors seem to clear up the confusion by reporting in their abstract published after their book that the Egyptian Air Force also had the TU-16s, which according to the authors "made camouflaging of the Reshetnikov planes plausible." Since 90% of the Egyptian Air Force had been destroyed, the planned reinforcement of the air force was not implemented.[594]

Fig. 18, Tupolev TU-16

Source: http://www.botinok.co.il/node/31548. (Ru)

The Russians claim that Israeli battalions on Syrian border triggered Nasser to move troops toward Sinai. This Soviet passed message via several channels was intended to trigger an Egyptian response. Refer to the speech by Brezhnev to Central Committee on June 20, 1967. Based on Stasi and Polish transcripts later found, the Soviet aim was "to create situation where U.S. would become involved economically, politically and militarily".[595] It seems the essence of the disinformation was a signal to Egypt and Syria to do certain things.

The authors report Brezhnev, after the initiative foundered, did not specify what was expected of Egypt and Syria following its messages reference troops gathering on Syrian border. However, Egypt took three actions: 1) 5/14/67 moved troops into Sinai; 2) on 16th asked UNEF to leave; 3) on 22nd closed Straits of Tiran. The question is did the Soviets approve of these actions. The authors report they acquiesced in two and three, and probably did as to No. 1 to insulate against an Israeli attack on Syria.

A watershed event occurred on 5/17/67, when the Israeli cabinet was informed of two unprecedented photoreconnaissance over-flights of Dimona. The authors note that the first published account of this event was made by Michael Brecher in 1980 based on a comment made by military intelligence chief Aharon Yariv.[596] This was the first direct Soviet military intervention under General Vybornov's mission. Israeli apprehension increased and they called up reserves at a level that could not be sustained over extended period for economic reasons.

There was such concern that Arabs would be emboldened in reliance on Soviet help; and consequently Ambassador Eban handed Ambassador Barbour a letter for LBJ seeking U.S. assurance of a commitment to Israel, and advising the Soviets of U.S. support. The authors report the Israeli's fear of a bombing raid on the reactor and that they could not tell the Americans who were unlikely to take a firmer stand if the main threat was against a target of which they were tepid or ambivalent. Consequently, the U.S. was probably not aware of the threat to Dimona or chose to ignore it. Yarvi: Egypt was not concerned for the Syrians, but rather the Israeli nuclear program, and for first time, there was a "connection with it to the Soviet initiative."[597]

Of particular interest is that the authors note Meir Amit, Mossad Director, tried to convince the CIA's John Hadden that Soviets had a grand design. Amit considered this a confrontation between the U.S. and the Soviets. Hadden said if you attack, the U.S. would land forces on Egypt's side in order to defend it. Later Hadden denied saying this, and he blamed it on the note taker, future Mossad leader, Ephraim Halevy.[598] Note how this fit in with Hounam's contention re Angleton and *Operation Cyanide*. Hadden's whole attitude and response here and with Hounam seemed strange. Angleton was supposed to be his boss; yet, there were parts of the CIA still working the Arab side of things. A concerned was that the CIA was playing both sides and could have leaked information to the Arabs.

Is this ambiguity a lingering problem from tactical and strategic perspective for the Mossad on up the Israeli military ladder wherein there is a perceived need for "insurance" to offset the Soviet threat over Syria? It would seem that a major problem with intelligence operations is the perceived or real ambiguities, which often lead to blowback as has been rampant in our Middle East foreign policy over the years.

The contention is that Egyptians practiced bombing Dimona and Soviets knew about it. The Israelis obtained maps with Dimona and Nahal Sorek marked as targets, with missile sites.[599] Dimona was the first Israeli site protected by Hawks obtained from U.S. in 1965. Israel kept the over-flights "top secret". The Israeli, French made Mirage IIIC was comparable to the MIG-21 in the range of 50000 to 60000 feet at mach 1.7 to 2. As to the May 17 flight, Israel did not notify the U.S., but later U.S. Ambassador Barbour cabled that Israelis were "frightened by four MIG over flights" and, that they could not intercept them, but there is no evidence that he told U.S. the flights were over Dimona. While some MIG-21s flew diversion, probably with Egyptian pilots, on both May 17 and 26, one plane was not seen nor kept up with—what was it?

The authors claim it was possibility a MIG-25, an experimental aircraft. The *"Foxbat"*, the NATO designation, had a ceiling of 75000 at mach three, and was based in Yemen thus avoiding damage on first day of the war. Hawk missiles were fired but could not hit the plane.[600] However, the Hawk battery commander said no Hawks fired except at one of their own Ouragan fighters after the war started.[601] One of the plane's missions could have been to provoke a missile firing to test its parameters. We had previously referred to a Mirage III being shot down over Dimona, or was it a Mirage Ouragan, we do not know.

JCS Chairman General Wheeler was aware of two over-flights. The authors speculate that the sudden appearance of a heretofore-unknown Soviet plane might have been of such concern to the JCS that it helps to explain why the *Liberty* was hastily dispatched to the Mediterranean. It is their opinion that this would definitely put Soviet activity as a top mission priority.

433

[handwritten at top: Egyptian manned TU-95 TU-16 overflights of SARATOGA June '67]

The authors question Ennes's version of the mission, which is at least five TU-95s were based in Egypt and flown by Arab pilots. The U.S. believed that they were actually under Soviet control. As was noted, the authors contended no TU-95 Bears were in Egypt and none were on the list of destroyed planes.[602] In my visit with Ennes he advised me it was the mission to track who was operating the TU-95s. Perhaps clearing up the confusion the planes might have been TU-16s. One could assume the *Liberty's* mission to be more encompassing.

In their chapter 14, page 138 entitled "Posed for Desant", the authors refer to Israeli efforts to bring the "main project" on line into operational readiness. They cite Cohen's contention of the possible completion of two weapons. Were they to be used to counter gas use? It is thought Israel "put nuclear weapons on alert" during Six-Day War, and the CIA was not aware of this; although the authors cite Cohen to say the U.S. was aware of this—an ambiguity.[603] The authors further pursue the understanding of Soviet submariners as to what their orders were in the event of either the U.S. landing troops in Syria, or the Israelis use of nuclear weapons on Egypt or Syria. Those orders were to "obliterate" it—Israel.[604]

The Soviet fleet was put on "battle alert" on June 1 with 40 ships plus 10 subs in the Med. Turkey was notified on May 31st that 10 more ships would arrive via the Bosporus and Dardanelles from the Black Sea including a Kildin-class destroyer designated 626. The authors claim this was closest ship to *Liberty* off El Arish.[605] They claim four destroyers were involved in the transient. This seems to refute what Nikolai Cherkashin said earlier in this chapter. The ships included the Soviet's own intelligence gathering ships.

434

Using Google's translation function on Alexander Rozin's web page, it would appear that he is in agreement that Soviet destroyer 626 was in the Mediterranean and dogging the carrier *America*. Again, we run into uncertainty and ambiguities, which may be difficult to resolve due to translation problems.

After extensive Internet surfing, I will nominate my opinion as to the identity of the Soviet missile destroyer known as 626. My "guess" is it was the *Prozorlivyy*. It is a Kildin (NATO designation) class destroyer constructed at Nikolaev Shipyard, Project 56M, commissioned 12/30/58 and decommissioned 6/24/91. It had a crew of 300. Poject56M was for four ships. In 1966, her hull number was 626 and she was part of the Baltic Fleet. Her hull number changed again sometime in 1967 to 525. After checking a large number of pictures, I found only one example of the Soviet Navy using a number over number (000/0), it was not 626/4.

A picture is as follows showing a hull number of 351, which she had in 1982 according to documentation. Soviets ships periodically changed their hull numbers.[606] "A word on hull numbers: it does not appear that the Russian Navy uses consistent hull numbers. The numbers change as the vessel moves under the operational control of another fleet, or something similar, which is why those numbers do not appear in many of the standard references. For the really major capital ships (such as the "Admiral Kuznetsov") which generally stay attached to the same fleet, perhaps the hull numbers will be more consistent."[607] Whether this is, the ship that stood by the *Liberty* the morning of June 9 is still an open question. I can find no recorded history of the ship in the

Mediterranean in 1967; that does not mean she was not there.

Fig. 19, Kildin Class Soviet Destroyer *Prozorlivyy*

Source:
http://commons.wikimedia.org/wiki/File:Prozorlivyy1982.jpg

Capt. Ivan Kapitanets of Northern fleet on the destroyer *Nastoychivy* was given orders with 12 hours to come to full battle alert and join the "combined fleet" to defend Soviet citizens. Soviet Arabic interpreters moved from Cairo to Alexandria to be put on ships. One person mentioned a "desant force", a landing force, to land off Haifa.

The discussion of landing plans, whether true or not and whether realistic or not was to include volunteers from the "combined fleet" without training and proper equipment in essence a suicide mission. However, there was also a BDK (landing ship) with tanks and infantry.

After the June 5 attack, the plan was dropped because Israeli air strikes were too effective.

On June 10, the USSR broke relations with Israel to be represented by Finland. It appears that this move was preplanned for the Bloc. The Hot Line was used on the Russian end and coordinated with the Politburo that came to believe it would accomplish little to continue the plan and risk a clash with U.S. Israel had to act fast because the deterrent value of the Sixth Fleet was deteriorating because of presence of the Soviet fleet.

The Sixth fleet had pulled back after Arab complaints that the U.S. and British planes were helping the Israelis. Johnson was concerned about the Soviet press contending that the U.S. was helping the Israelis. Johnson on Hot Line: "You know where our carriers are." The Americans pulled back to no closer than 100 miles, and more. Soviet Vice Admiral, Viktor Sysoyev was asked to verify if U.S. planes were involved and responding to Moscow, he advised "no". This posed a predicament for Soviets.

The Arabs were upset that held back from initial attack and now with no Soviet assistance did not want to confront Sixth Fleet and the potential for a nuclear confrontation. The problem for the Soviets was Egypt and Amer were ready to give up during 2nd day of war. The action moved to UN where Russia wanted Israel to pull back and implement a condemnation of Israel. There was a conflict in Politburo on what to do. The MIGs and bombers from USSR were kept on alert but never ordered out.[608] The SU-7s may have seen some action but avoided being shot down on bombing run over tanks at a refueling depot.

Soviet ships were 50 to 100 miles from Israeli coast. An Israeli General Yoel Ben-Porat said his unit tracked radio messages from three Soviet ships in Eastern Med, but was unable to crack their code. Sub K-52 on 5-6 June was off Tel Aviv as was K-131. Capt. Gennadiy Zakharov (later admiral), said they were to hit Israel's oil facilities.[609]

Admiral Shlomo Erell had referred to an attack on either Russian or American sub on June 8, with a resulting oil slick. It was not believed to be Egyptian.[610] The authors see this sub incident on June 8 as a distraction for Admiral Erell since he now had to deal with *Liberty* issue.

The Authors contend, "Continuing debate over Israel's motive in attacking *Liberty* tended to obscure the Soviet context throughout this affair." They acknowledged Israel attacked the ship but put Soviet fingerprints on matter, and while mentioned in isolation they have not been linked together until now, but clues may open new inquiry into background of Israeli attack.[611]

The authors note that the "Soviet" aspect had been omitted from most *Liberty* references as I have contented and as Richard Thompson continued to pursue in his own rite. However, the Soviets started to know about *Liberty* when she passed through the Straits of Gibraltar on June 2 as the crew noted certain Soviet ships were in their proximity. Those were intelligence-gathering ships. The *Liberty* was concerned that her transmissions could be picked up as the Soviets had at least a week to determine its signal frequencies.

Note the comments of Rocky Sturman as to how hard it would be for the Israelis to pick up five of *Liberty's*

438

frequencies in order to jam them, not from planes but from shore. On the other hand, the frequencies could have been picked up by Soviets. According to the authors, if the *Liberty* was monitored it could have been done by the *Proletarsk*. [612]

Rabin was concerned about a landing in El Arish area in context of the claimed bombardment. Israeli surveillance competency needs to be questioned on this point. Rabin thought they had attacked a Russian ship. Did the Soviets set the *Liberty* up? Was the ship they thought they saw, Kapitanet's *Nastoychivy*? The authors per Kapitanets put his ship off Tel Aviv, 50 miles north of the *Liberty*, with a landing force of cadets and not off Syrian port of Latakia.[613] There appears to be a contention between Kapitanets and Cherkashin as to *Nastoychivy's* location and the role she may have played in the *Liberty* affair. Was the *Nastoychivy* destroyer 626/4 that offered help to the *Liberty*—ambiguity prevails? A picture of the *Nastoychivy* can be found on Wikipedia showing her hull number was 610.[614] My research indicates that the *Nastoychivy* never used hull number 626.

On June 10, all Soviet naval forces were directed to the Syrian coast; however, the Soviet Fleet would have little effect. The Soviets offered to break relations with Israel to satisfy hawks, Andropov and Grechko. Gromyko was concerned about a confrontation with U.S. It was communicated to Israel and the U.S. that the Soviets would use force if Israel did not cease its attack on Syria. There was Kosygin's "threat" to Johnson. Anatoly Dobrynin, the Soviet Ambassador to the U.S. disclaimed a threat was intended.[615]

If the Soviets intervened on behalf of Syria, it would threaten the very existence of Israel. McNamara said he did not have specific intelligence on Soviet intentions; however, the U.S. interpreted matters as evidencing the Soviets considered Syria more critical than Egypt.

A critical and secret dispatch was received from Ambassador Barbour that noted limited Israeli penetration intent. Helms could not offer any intelligence, but the tension was noted, while down played by others. Dayan placed limits on the Syrian intrusion because of the Soviet threat.[616]

In the White House situation room there was uncertainty as to whether it was an Egyptian or Soviet attack on the *Liberty*; that immediate emergency was alleviated with a sigh of relief when it was learned that it was the Israelis who attacked the ship. Attention focused back on the Soviets to back up Syria unless Israel stopped its advance into Syrian territory. The U.S. pressured Israelis to accept a cease-fire when Undersecretary of State Nicholas Katzenback was dispatched from the situation room to call in the Israeli ambassador. When informed of the seriousness of the Soviet threat Israel relented after achieving limited objectives on the Golan Heights.[617]

Secretary of Defense McNamara ordered the Sixth Fleet to turn around and head toward Israel in the event of Soviet intervention—the collision point! McNamara: "if want war will get war". Soviet subs would have noted the change in the fleet's direction and were in a position to confirm to Moscow the existing U.S. threat in defense of Israel in the event the Soviets aided a Syrian attack on Israel.

Khripunkov's frigate was ordered to abandon its landing mission to evacuate Soviet personnel from Damascus, to later return. Use of the Hot Line allowed cooler heads to prevail and a direct U.S. Soviet nuclear confrontation was alleviated. In 1991, one of last acts of USSR before she ceased to exist was to recognize Israel.

What is clear is that the authors, notwithstanding all their research, did not factor in any concept such as *Operation Cyanide* in the Six-Day War; to the effect that the United States wanted Nasser replaced and was attempting to undercut Soviet influence in the Middle East—the Angleton "foreign policy" ploy. Israel was concerned, but knew it could handle Egypt and Syria absent Soviet intervention; and Soviets wanted Nasser out for a more pliable leader as a puppet and wanted to destroy the Israeli nuclear program and extend its influence into the Middle East. The USS *Liberty* and crew survived a deadly attack, yet the authors, Ginor and Remez, in their research and publications seem to accept that the Israeli attack was a case of mistaken identity. They need to take a more comprehensive approach to their continuing look into the events of the Six-Day War and the attack on the *Liberty*. For example, they fail to include any reference to James Jesus Angleton and the role he may have played in the Six-Day War sitting at the Israeli Desk at the CIA. They seem uniquely qualified to penetrate the multi-government cover-up because they have shown dedication and personal persistence in their endeavor.

The question remains whether or not Captain Nikolay Cherkashin was correct in his assessment that both theories were correct: Israel did not want the ship eavesdropping, and wanted a pretext to assure that the U.S. would counteract the Soviets over their Syrian invasion and the Soviet's demand to desist. Was the *Liberty* set up?

Sayanim derives from the Hebrew word *lesayeah*, meaning "to help." The reference is to Jewish helpers who do things for the Mossad and Israel.

Victor Ostrovsky, *The Other Side of Deception*, page 27.

Chapter 14

SAYANIM

Victor Ostrovsky, a self-proclaimed former Israeli Mossad rogue agent, provoked controversy within the Israeli intelligence establishment, by writing two, "tell-all", books about the Mossad. In his book, *The Other Side of Deception*, he described the concept of *sayanim*. In a footnote, he says it derives from the Hebrew word *lesayeah*, meaning, "to help". They are not paid, so it can never be said they are doing what they are doing for money.[618] Further, they are not to know the whole operational picture when asked to assist or provide resources.[619]

He described the concept using the Jonathan Pollard spy case as the example; Pollard is an American Jew who was working in U.S. naval intelligence. The FBI captured him in 1986 after he was denied asylum in the Israeli embassy in Washington. Ostrovsky describes a "Mr. X", not necessarily one person, who would instruct Pollard as to what to bring out as hard intelligence copy. He notes a *sayan* is to serve not ask questions. The concept of *sayanim* transcends borders and the clock, meaning they are available "on call". A suggestion for the reader is to use Google to keyword search *sayanim*. One

443

such site is *VT, Veterans Today*, with an article entitled, *Sayanim: Israeli Operatives in U.S.*[620]

According to former CIA Director, George Tenet, Pollard had become a bargaining chip in the Middle East "peace process". To Tenet's surprise, Israeli Prime Minister Bibi Netanyahu had brought up the Pollard issue in a meeting with former President Clinton. He noted that if Pollard were released, he, Tenet, "…would be effectively through as CIA director." In short, his credibility within the CIA would be worthless. To the Israelis Pollard having spied for them on "his" country was a soldier not to be left on the battlefield. Pollard is still serving time in a federal prison.[621] Such is the audacity of Israeli leaders in putting U.S. leaders in a compromised position making a joke out of our acting as impartial "peace brokers" in the Middle East peace process. It is a myth that we do not spy on each other, notwithstanding platitudes to the contrary.

There has been a recent allegation that Israeli Mossad agents used false CIA identification to pose as American spies to recruit members of the terrorist organization Jundallah to fight their covert war against Iran in a "false flag" operation.[622] Of course, an Israeli representative denied it per a *Haaretz.com* article dated January 15, 2012.[623]

Ostrovsky is very frank when it comes to talking about the ability to mobilize the Jewish community to come to the aid of Israeli state. He describes "the community" as being divided into a three-stage action team. To illustrate his point he refers to an effort by King Hussein of Jordon to obtain a two-billion-dollar arms purchase package from America. He states, "We had guaranteed the prime

444

minister that this would not happen." He then explains that the "action team" would consist of individual *sayanim*; then the large pro-Israeli lobby would support whatever direction the Mossad pointed. Finally, B'nai Brith would solicit support from non-Jews and tarnish as anti-Semitic whoever couldn't be swayed to the Israeli cause.[624] The key question is to what extent this action team was mobilized to refute the contention the attack on the *Liberty* was blatant and intentional. The lack of a Congressional investigation into the attack would tend to speak for itself.

If author Peter Hounam can be considered a "friend" of the *Liberty* survivors and supporters, then A. Jay Cristol is considered by the survivors to be a propagandist for Israel. Who is A. Jay Cristol, and what was his task in what I call the *Liberty* "information wars"? These information wars would take place not only in the print media, but also on the Internet via websites and discussion forums, radio waves, and in a series of movie documentaries made for TV. Certain individuals in support of the *Liberty* survivors had hoped to bring the *Liberty* story to the movie theater—so far, that has not developed. The information wars are not just one sided.

Cristol is the author of the book *The Liberty Incident: the 1967 Israeli Attack on the U.S. Navy Spy Ship* published in 2002.[625] *Liberty* survivors and supporters take strong exception to the thesis of his book that the attack was a case of mistaken identity and an accident in the *fog of war*.

Cristol includes the name of Admiral Isaac C. Kidd, Jr., head of the Naval Court of Inquiry, in the memorial to his book along with Vice Admiral Donald D. Engen, as

445

"Giants in the history of the United States Navy". It is alleged that Admiral Kidd is the person who followed orders to facilitate the cover-up even though he may have personally thought the attack was intentional. While Cristol's purpose seems to be solicitous to provide credibility to his book; former JAG legal advisor to the Naval Court of Inquiry, Captain Ward Boston, in his declaration claims that Admiral Kidd spoke to him referring to Judge Cristol as a possible Israeli agent and didn't regard him with much esteem.

A. Jay Cristol served as a federal bankruptcy judge for the Southern District of Florida, a federal employee; he also claims to be a naval aviator and former member of the Navy's Judge Advocate General Corps. He retired as a captain in the U.S. Navy Reserve. While Judge Cristol is controversial, there is antipathy between the two camps; the focus here will be on the issues. A context is appropriate.

In the Preface to his book, Cristol described how one of his professors while attending courses in international studies, Dr. Haim Shaked, solicited him to write his book.[626] Dr. Shaked suggested that with Cristol's background as a naval aviator, U.S. Navy lawyer, and lecturer in the law of naval warfare, civil lawyer, and federal bankruptcy judge that he was well qualified to research and write on the *Liberty* affair. Cristol said he was at first reluctant because of the passage of time and whether anyone would be interested in the subject.

Finally, Cristol agreed and was warmly received in Israel as he name-drops and notes:

I began with a trip to Israel through my friends in the Israel Navy, many doors were

446

opened to me, and I was able to sail on an Israel Navy antiterrorist Dabour patrol boat to the scene of the *Liberty* incident near El Arish. I was also able to meet Meir Shamgar, the president of the Supreme Court of Israel, the equivalent of the U.S. Chief Justice, who had served as Military Advocate General of the IDF during the 1967 war. President Shamgar introduced me to Ambassador Ephraim Evron, who provided information that enabled me to locate the 1967 CIA chief of station at Tel Aviv. The CIA chief introduced me to Captain Ernest Castle, the 1967 U.S. naval attaché in Tel Aviv. Captain Castle, then teaching at the University of South Carolina, suggested that my research project had already gone far beyond the parameters of a master's degree and proposed that it be converted to a Ph.D. program, which I completed successfully in 1997."[627]

Author Peter Hounam commented in his book, *Operation Cyanide*, contemplating his writing project: "Richard Block, an Air Force Captain, had kept his experiences of 8 June 1967 to himself until provoked by a book, written by Miami Judge, Jay Cristol, which claimed that the attack was provably an accident. Block confronted Cristol at a book-signing in Coral Gables, Florida, in July 2002 and accused him of ignoring evidence that showed Israel acted intentionally."[628] This comment sets up the estrangement between camps, or rather, contrary views of the evidence in the context of the information wars. Review of the evidence minus the obvious bias, difficult as it may be, would be an appropriate objective for all interested in the *Liberty* story—unfortunately, we are not yet at that point.

447

Hounam noted that in approaching Israeli authorities, he was rebuffed and somewhat frustrated over the fact that the Israel had been differential to Thames TV that produced a documentary on the *Liberty* in early 1980s entitled *Attack on the Liberty*; and that Cristol had been feted by Israelis as he worked on his thesis.[629] Clearly, he felt that the Israelis were embarking on a public relations ploy.

The fact that Israel through its agencies would solicit a public relations venue or an opportunity for misinformation or disinformation would not be unusual in view of the Mossad's motto of *by way of deception thou shall do war*.[630]

By way of contrast, another author had been solicited by Israeli intelligence, the Mossad, to write a book. Gordon Thomas the author of *Gideon's Spies: the Secret History of the Mossad* acknowledged in his section *Notes on Sources* that he was solicited by Zvi Spielmann, who assured him he would have a complete free hand in writing about the Mossad and Israeli intelligence services. Thomas noted his grant of access to the Israeli intelligence establishment.[631] Thomas well known for writing about intelligence matters would not tackle the project without having a free hand. In a communication, I asked why he did not write about the USS *Liberty*; his response was that he would not unless he could establish beyond 50% what actually happened.

One can surmise that the Mossad's motive in part was in response to one of two books published by self-designated "rogue agent" Victory Ostrovsky in 1990 and 1994 that upset the Mossad and the Israeli intelligence hierarchy. Israel tried to prevent in a Canadian court his publishing of one of his books.[632] Since publishing his books, Ostrovsky has kept a low profile by conducting an art gallery and publishing business in Scottsdale, Arizona. When I visited him at his art gallery and asked about the attack on the *Liberty*, he merely said that the people he knew would not intentionally engage in such an attack.

In the case of Cristol being tasked, the Israeli defense hierarchy was upset with the publication of Jim Ennes's book *Assault on the Liberty*, and obviously felt that their side of the story had to be told.[633]

While there has been criticism of Cristol, he and whoever assisted him, have done a lot of research—a time consuming project—a devotion of years out of one's life. Nevertheless, it may be that what he has found actually helps to establish that which he tries to disprove or down play—that is my opinion. A typical comment from a *Liberty* survivor might be, "...Not that Cristol BS!" Cristol is the preverbal advocate; after all, he was trained as an attorney and served as a judge—that is why he was solicited for his book project. In his book, he tried to methodically deal with all efforts to prove the attack was intentional rather than a "friendly fire" incident—in essence acting as a defense attorney.

For an illustrative critique of Cristol and his book by *Liberty* supporters, check the following internet website: http://www.usslibertyinquiry.com/commentary/cristol/critiquecristol.html.

Perhaps the best service that Israel and Cristol could have performed is to have published the so-called transcripts between air controllers and attacking aircraft and motor torpedo boats in Appendix 2 of his book. We

449

addressed those in chapters 5 and 6. To put the transcripts into context, *Liberty* survivor Joe Meadors, vice president of the LVA at the time, wrote a letter to Israeli historian, Dr. Ahron Bregman dated January 30, 2003, who was residing in London. Meador's inquiry had to do with the credibility of Cristol's portrayal of the transcripts between Israeli air controllers and pilots and torpedo boat operators. A copy of Dr. Bregman's reply letter can be found on the Internet at: http://www.ussliberty.org/bregman.pdf.

In Dr. Bregman' response letter dated February 5, 2003, he stated that the difference between his and Cristol's interpretations of voice communication was one of "tone". Bregman stated, "Yes, the tone seems to be one issue on which we disagree, but then tone is very important for in these tapes the tone sometimes makes the music". He goes on to say: "It is sufficient to listen to the tone of Robert (here I am using the names used by Cristol in his book) at 1353 where he says: 'What do you say?' to realize that, in fact, he refers to the previous suggestion of L.K. that it might well be that the ship is American."

Bregman says that when it suits Cristol, he uses "tone" when at 1412 Cristol reports that Kislev says, "Leave her", and Cristol adds in brackets "There is a dramatic change in the tone of Kislev's voice." Bregman concludes that tone (or voice inflection) is important in analyzing the tapes. As I re-read this letter from Dr. Bregman, sometime struck me as being important, and that was Cristol's use of the name "Robert", in the sense that maybe that is not how the tapes went. Normally, in police work we call someone by a call sign that might be a designator or number, such as "District 1" or "Motor 9" or simply 185—not a personal name. This is important because only a select few have been granted access to the "raw" Israeli transcript tapes, one of the persons being Dr. Bregman. Is Dr. Bregman inferring that the actual tapes use different call signs? It would be unusual to use actual names as I have noted. Dispatchers do not use their own names when calling a working or field unit. Cristol claims the transcripts are accurate, but that cannot be verified unless the Israelis were to release them to the broader public or independent commission for review. To my knowledge, no *Liberty* survivor has heard these transcripts, although they could read them in the appendix to Cristol's book.

Bregman in his letter goes on to say: "But it seems that Cristol and me differ on substance as well. You see Cristol is not a plumber, or a mechanic but rather a judge – a Federal Judge – and as such his is the world of words and he fully understands – I am pretty sure – the meaning of words and the need to be accurate when using them. But when it comes to the audiotapes it seems as if Cristol no longer understands the importance of words and in his text there are omissions and the text itself is sometimes heavily edited." The examples used by Dr. Bregman in his response to Joe Meadors are as follows:

Cristol's version:
13:54
L. K.: What is that? Americans?
SHIMON: What Americans?
KISLEV: Robert, what did you say?
[No one answers.]
Bregman's version:
13:53
L. K.: What is it? American?
Shimon: How do you mean, American?

451

Kislev: Robert, what do you say? [namely, what's your opinion and clearly a reference to the query just raised regarding the ship's identity – AB]
Robert: I didn't say [the tone: I don't want to know – AB]

Bregman:
"Why did Cristol edit the text by saying that "no one answers" where in fact Robert does answer by saying "I didn't say" in a tone which suggests "I don't want to know" or "no comment"? Dr. Bregman provides another example:

Cristol's version:
14:13
MENACHEM: Kislev, what country? [Menachem has become concerned.]
KISLEV: Possibly American.

Bregman's version:
14:14
Menachem: Kislev, what state?
Kislev: Probably American
Menachem: What?
Kislev: Probably American.

Bregman:
"Why did Cristol shorten this passage?? In order that the word "American" will not ring in our ears for too long? True, this latter passage is far from being a "Smoking gun", but why to edit such a critical moment in the event??

Bregman:
"If Judge Cristol was chosen to be the messenger whose task it is to put an end to a terribly painful debate then – in my opinion – the opposite was achieved."

452

The letter to Meadors was signed "Best Wishes, Yours, Dr. A. Bregman". Dr. Bregman is the author of *A History of Israel* and speaks Hebrew. As an historian of note, his work has to be up to a high standard to be accepted in the world.

As noted by Dr. Bregman, if Cristol "is the messenger", the opposite was achieved—as messenger for the Israeli military establishment. As an attorney, he does a good job of highlighting the key issues and then misdirecting the reader just as a defense attorney would do to the jury in a court of law. Contrary to Cristol's claim that the transcripts were accurate, Bregman by his above examples shows Cristol did some selective editing.

His defense against the accusations of the USS *Liberty* survivors, family members and supporters, is to present the State of Israel and its defense forces in a more favorable light in the eyes of the American public. It is further intended as a lobbying effort to cut off any debate, communication, and consideration of a need for a Congressional or other investigation into actions of the Israeli government dealing with the attack and cover-up. It should be mentioned here that any reference to the Israeli government in the context of the USS *Liberty* should be to the military establishment. The conduct of the Six-Day War was left by the politicians to the military with Moshe Dayan eventually becoming the Minister of Defense, a position often held by the Israeli Prime Minister.

In Chapter 8 of his book, *Survivors' Perceptions*, Cristol, again, as defense attorney, points out that the crew are a fine group of men who risked their lives in the service of their country. However, he acknowledges their bitterness and various grievances as a "result of their

453

traumatic, tragic experience....It is probably worse when they are the victims of friendly fire." Pointing out their suffering from post-traumatic stress syndrome, "The severe trauma experienced and the lingering after-effects are, undoubtedly, deserving of sympathy but do not enhance the ability of the victims to impartially analyze the incident."

While acknowledging their suffering he seeks to undermine their credibility in the most subtle of ways. Many of the survivors wanted to testify before the Naval Court of Inquiry as to events of June 8 and were not allowed to do so. One survivor, Phillip F. Tourney, in his book claims while he wanted to testify about events of the attack, however, he was sent on leave to Naples and Rome, and was not interrogated after a group meeting with Admiral Kidd who headed up the Naval Court of Inquiry. Having arrived back at the ship after his Italian visit he learned, to his dismay, that the "investigation" had already taken place. He surmised that "they" did not want his presence to testify to the Israeli strafing of the life rafts, an action that could constitute the basis for an alleged war crime.[634]

While eyewitness identification and testimony can be problematic, it does not preclude the witnesses' ability to testify subject to being impeached, having their creditability undermined. Cristol goes on to use the "triple hearsay" rule of evidence to undermine the credibility of Jim Ennes who was wound in the attack and points out his "harsh line against Israel". He refers to an Ennes footnote wherein Ennes writes that Senator William Fulbright told one of the *Liberty* survivors, a Lieutenant Maurice Bennett, "The President knew the attack was deliberate and ordered it covered up for

454

political reasons."[635] According to Cristol, the triple hearsay was reporting that Bennett-said-Fulbright-said-Johnson-said. William Fulbright, deceased, had chaired the Senate Foreign Relations Committee; and Cristol does not miss a beat as he reports that Fulbright and Johnson's relationship had "cooled" because Johnson did not appoint the senator as Secretary of State.

What Cristol is attempting with via his book is to impose an evidentiary standard appropriate for an actual criminal trial, not for the investigative stage. Fortunately, the "investigative" standard is not set that high. Cristol goes to great lengths to post on his website correspondence noting that several presidents contend there is no new evidence to warrant opening the matter of the attack on the *Liberty*.[636] Quite to the contrary, there has been plenty of new evidence slowly emerging over the years, especially in view of the fact that there had never been a forensic investigation of the attack. Admiral Kidd and his investigative team were not allowed to go to Israel to interview those involved in the attack; further, there is new evidence that the tapes of the actual attack were destroyed or lost; and that the identity of at least two of the Israeli pilots, including General Specter, has emerged in recent years.

It is problematic to have two separate and sovereign jurisdictions involved in such a matter, normally it would warrant some cooperation at the high governmental levels; however, when it comes to a cover-up the sky is the limit in terms of CYA.

Subject to the various exceptions, hearsay testimony is not allowed to prove the truth of the matter at issue in a court of law because of lack of credibility or introduction of prejudice. However, hearsay, even triple hearsay, is

455

allowed for the purpose of establishing probable cause for obtaining arrest or search warrants as part of the investigative process, or bringing about an indictment by a grand jury. Cristol invokes the Hearsay Rule several times in his book in efforts to refute Ennes who was wounded early in the attack, as well as the witness of others. In an administrative hearing or preliminary hearing to determine whether there are grounds to proceed further, the rule is not applicable and Cristol's use in his reporting is self-serving. However, he further contests statements of *Liberty* survivors by citing for example his interview with Lt. Bennett quoting him as saying he was never in the presence of Fulbright. Since we are playing a game of legalities, only a deposition would serve to clarify the ambiguity on the issue of reliability of one's memory of past events.

Cristol is entitled to write about his version of events, but the reader needs to be on guard for the sophistication of a writer defending a fixed position, that of "accidental attack"; note Dr. Bregman's comments above. Cristol will go as far as posting on his website copies of the medical records of the crew to show the extent and nature of their injuries.[637] A question exists as to how he obtained what should have been confidential medical records. Interestingly, he caveats his access to these records by noting: "The Court of Inquiry lists 171 injured personnel but redacts the names of the individuals. The names were disclosed prior to the enactment of the Privacy Act." This document is an un-redacted list of the 171 injured. One can conclude that his purpose is to support his argument that the crew suffered psychological trauma and are therefore lacking in credibility as witnesses—a typical defense attorney tactic. For current information on the public's access to military medical records, one should check the National Archives website.[638]

In his book, Cristol, in Chapter 8 entitled *Survivors' Perceptions,* is careful to praise the *Liberty* crew, while at the same time undermining their credibility as witnesses to the attack. He saves his harshest criticism for Ennes for whom he claims has taken "an irrationally harsh line against Israel."[639] He falls short of directly alleging anti-Semitism against Ennes or the crew; however, he does that later beginning to rely on the anti-Semitism argument in some of his speeches. For example, in an article in the *Jerusalem Post,* Cristol is quoted as saying "But I was soon shown how active the conspiracy theorists and hate mongers were about keeping the story alive." Anyone who does not agree with this position is lumped in those two categories. He is further quoted in the article:[640]

> The victims of the tragedy are typical of victims of friendly fire. They find it difficult to believe that they were wounded or their buddies were killed by mistake. In this case the victims have been imposed upon, used and abused by groups with their own agendas. First, are those who are on the Arab side of the Arab/Israeli conflict and who try to use the tragedy to drive a wedge into the otherwise excellent relationship between the United States and Israel. Next are those persons who are anti-Semitic or anti-Israel. And finally there are the conspiracy buffs. For the reasons indicated these three groups have continued to probe the wounds of the victims for their own purposes and are not concerned with healing or closure.

457

Cristol takes on Captain Ward Boston who was the Chief JAG, military legal advisor, to the Naval Court of Inquiry looking into the attack on the *Liberty*. Boston had executed a declaration stating that the Court of Inquiry was tainted. His declaration is dated January 8, 2004, at Coronado, California. The document was read into the record of a January 2004 State Department Conference on the Six-Day War and the attack on the *Liberty* by author James Bamford.[641]

Boston states his belief is that the attack was intentional. He states that both he and Admiral Kidd, the presiding officer of the court of inquiry, needed to travel to Israel to interview those involved in the attack. "Admiral Kidd later told me that Admiral McCain was adamant that we were not to travel to Israel or contact the Israelis concerning the matter." He further stated, "In particular, the recent publication of Jay Cristol's book, *The Liberty Incident*, twists the facts and misrepresents the views of those of us who investigated the attack." Boston's declaration is online and available to the public.[642]

Cristol certainly had the right to defend his book. Judge Cristol serving as a "defense attorney" for the Israeli version of the attack attacks Captain Boston publicly to "impeach" him for his declaration referred to above, with his own commenting document posted on his, Cristol's website, wherein he labels Boston a liar and accuses him of perjury by implication.[643] Matters have sure gotten nasty.

The *Liberty* affair has simmered and then boiled at different times over the years; it boiled to the surface again during the 2004 State Department Conference referred to above. Judge Cristol was a panelist; however,

458

Jim Ennes did not attend the session although other *Liberty* survivors did including Phillip Tourney who served several terms as LVA president. The State Department made a substantial number of records available on its website.[644] A representative of the NSA announced that there were no additional documents to be release on the *Liberty* matter; however, that did not hold as another batch was posted on the NSA website in 2007. The 2003 release dealt with the transcripts of Israeli helicopter flying toward the wounded *Liberty* that had been released pursuant to Cristol's FOIA lawsuit. The CIA released several documents in 2006.

Before leaving the topic of Judge Cristol, one more chapter in his book is of importance, and that is Chapter 11, entitled, *Did Dayan Order It*. Again, in true defense attorney style he raises the issue and proceeds to misdirect.

He starts out with the statement that some conspiracy theorists claim that the Minister of Defense, Moshe Dayan, ordered the attack. Refer back to the Chapter 11, herein, dealing with the "order". Cristol focuses on one person making the claim who was the national chairman of the American Palestine Committee. Cristol writes that in September 1977, Norman F. Dacey paid for an ad in the *New York Times* when Dayan was schedule to visit the United States; the ad saying, "Are We Welcoming the Murderer of Our Sons?" The ad claimed that the committee had obtained three "unevaluated" intelligence documents from the CIA under the FOIA. As a side note, Dacey was famous for his campaign to get people to avoid probate by executing "living trusts."

Cristol reports: "The release of these documents was highly unusual. He had never been able to obtain the release of a CIA unevaluated intelligence document nor any further information on the facts and circumstances surrounding this particular release for the *New York Times* ad."[645] As is often usual with the release of government documents, these documents had certain portions blocked out or redacted so that not all the information in the original document is readable. Any governmental release is supposed to comply with the Freedom of Information Act and various exemptions there under. The first document referred to the opinion of the Turkish General Staff (TGS) and stated in part:

> 2. The TGS is convinced that the attack on the U.S.S. Liberty on June 8, 1967 was deliberate. It was done because the Liberty's CCNMO actively was having the effect of jamming Israeli Military communications.

A copy of the actual document is included here as an example. The reader can go to the CIA FOIA website and browse the various documents that have been released. The CIA web site is http://www.foia.cia.gov/search.asp. Rather than paste the various documents into this book, I will merely paraphrase them to the extent appropriate, or create a hyperlink to the CIA document. Here is the link to this CIA Intelligence Information Cable of June 23, 1967.

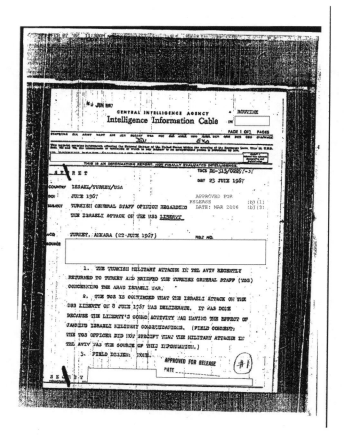

Neither the name of the informant nor the exact place from which the information was obtained is readable. The second unevaluated intelligence document stated, "Israeli forces did not make mistakes." Cristol notes that like the first document, both the name of the informant and the source of the information were redacted. It was dated July 27, 1967.

Cristol does not cite the second document noting the date of information was early June 1967, so I will summarize it here:

461

SOURCE (Censored)
1. (Censored)
2. (Censored) attack on the USS Liberty by Israeli airplanes and torpedo boats. He said that "you.ve got to remember that in this compaign, there is neither time nor room for mistakes," which was intended as an obtuse reference that Israel's forces knew what flag the LIBERTY was flying and exactly what the vessel was doing off the coast. (Censored) implied that the ship's identity was known at least six hours before the attack but that Israeli headquarters was not sure as to how many people might have access to the information that LIBERTY was intercepting. He also implied that there was no certainty of control as to where the intercepted information was going and again reiterated that Israeli forces did not make mistakes in their compaign. He was emphatic in starting to me that they knew what kind of ship the USS LIBERTY was and what it was doing offshore.
3. (Censored) [my comment: deals with burning oil fields]
—end-

This particular document dated 6/27/67 would seem to have more credibility attached to it because item No. 3 deals with the informant making an inquiry as to when two oil fields in the Gulf of Suez would be reopened for production. These fields had been set on fire by the Arabs with the Israelis putting the fires out. The effort was to get them back into production.

This appears to be a detailed and extensive statement from an informant, which should form the basis for a more detailed investigation. Absent the release of more information from the CIA, it can be stated that there

462

appears to have been no further investigation, except that according to former CIA director Richard Helms, there is one CIA report that has not been released as of current times. There is some confusion as to what document that might be by date.

From a purely investigative perspective, these "information reports" would be similar to any police department's miscellaneous information or intelligence reports. They stand alone to be eventually linked up with an "incident report", past, present, or future for follow-up. Cristol's claim that subsequent presidents claim that there is no new evidence to warrant reopening the *Liberty* attack is folly on his part. The conclusion of the Naval Court of Inquiry was already cast in stone with such information never being presented to the Court or any other investigative body. In the '60s, the FBI under Hoover and the CIA did not cooperate because of jurisdictional issues. Under the Johnson administration, it would have been "politically" charged for anyone to initiate a further investigation.

Helms is one of the government officials who held the belief that the attack was intentional; however, he could not understand why they attacked the ship. He refers to a board of inquiry that he had no involvement in.[646] He implies the "board' findings showed the attack was intentional and that Israeli forces knew what they were doing. It is unclear if he is referring to the Naval Court of Inquiry or to some "in house" board. To quote him is necessary: "I had no role in the board of inquiry that followed, or the board's finding that there could be no doubt that the Israelis knew exactly what they were doing in attacking the *Liberty*. I have yet to understand why it was felt necessary to attack this ship or who ordered the attack." Helms referred to an interim intelligence memorandum that concluded that the attack was a mistake and "not made in malice against the U.S." He further notes that when more evidence was available, more doubt was raised. His deputy, Admiral Rufus Taylor, wrote to Helms, "To me, the picture thus far presents the distinct possibility that the Israelis knew that the *Liberty* might be their target and attacked anyway, either through confusion in Command and Control or through deliberate disregard of instructions on the part of subordinates."[647]

Cristol mentions Helms in one context in his book and does not mention Helms' conclusion as noted above.

The third document referred to by Cristol in his Chapter 11 is dated November 9, 1967, with the date of information being Oct. 67. The Subject says: (Censored) /Attack on USS Liberty Ordered by Dayan. This is noted as unevaluated information. Cristol says the newspaper advertisement included paragraph 2 of the redacted document.

> [Deleted] commented on the sinking [sic] of the U.S. communications ship Liberty. They said that Dayan personally ordered the attack on the ship and that one of his generals adamantly opposed the action and said: "This is pure murder!" One of the admirals who was present also disapproved the action and it was he who ordered it stopped. [Deletion] believe that the attack against the US. Vessel is [deletion] detrimental to any political ambitions Dayan may have.

In this particular CIA Information Report, paragraph 2 references one of the Israeli generals claiming that "This is pure murder", and that the admiral also present agreed, and it was he, not Dayan who ordered the attack to cease.

The advertisement ends with the statement "It is time for the U.S. Government to end its silence on the *Liberty* tragedy. It is time the American people were given the truth!" A separate news article in the same issue of the *New York Times*, on page 7, described the American Palestine Committee as "a nationwide committee of Americans trying to help the Palestinians to get back into their homeland." The Associated Press and United Press International picked up the story of this ad, and articles about it appeared in the *Washington Post* and other Washington, D.C., newspapers.

Cristol reports that on the day the advertisement appeared in the *New York Times*, the director of the Central Intelligence Agency, Admiral Stansfield Turner, appeared on the ABC television program *Good Morning America*, hosted by Steve Bell. Cristol notes it is rather sad that it was only on January 28, 1985, that the CIA approved for release a transcript of that portion of the *Good Morning America* show, more than seven years after it had been heard and seen by tens of millions of TV viewers! The transcript is enlightening:

> Transcript—Good Morning America
> September 19, 1977
> **Steve Bell:** There is a particular incident that has just come into the papers this morning; namely, that a group of Palestinian supporters in the U.S. has taken out an advertisement in The New York Times which uses raw CIA data gained from the Freedom of Information Act. The accusation is made that Moshe Dayan specifically ordered the attack on the

465

USS *Liberty* in the 1967 Middle East War. Can you give us any enlightenment on that? **Admiral Turner:** I certainly can and I am glad Steve that you emphasized the word raw intelligence data. We are required under the Freedom of Information Act to produce to those who ask for it intelligence documents which can be unclassified. In those which we released there were several which indicated a possibility that the Israeli government knew about the USS *Liberty* before the attack. Also, we released an evaluated over-all document which said very clearly that it was our considered opinion that the Israeli government had *no such knowledge* at that time. Approved For Release Date 28 Jan 1985 (Emphasis added)

This reference and appearance of CIA Director Turner caused some controversy with a member of Congress, Senator James Abourezk, of South Dakota, per correspondence exchanged between him and the director. The gist is whether the CIA was trying to withhold information requested by the committee pursuant to the FOIA. Abourezk was chairman of the committee charged with dealing with enforcement of the FOIA. There appears to be a document dated 6/21/67 that had not been released by the CIA that deals with the *Liberty*. Cristol refers to a document dated 6/23/67 that has not been released, it may be the same one dated 6/21/67. Turner claims that there were a number of documents dealing with the *Liberty* dated prior to 6/21/67, but none changes the CIA position that the attack was a mistake—in his minds-eye. The question is whether he was "stiff-arming" the Senator. To access these documents the reader can go to the CIA FOIA website and keyword search USS LIBERTY. You will get a large list of

466

documents. In the second of two search boxes, use the Keyword ABOUREZK. You will turn up seven documents.

Again, the question is whether there was any follow-up investigation to these "leads". Information only remains "unevaluated" until evaluated pursuant to an investigation. Turner in the Abourezk correspondence offers a rationalization as to why the unevaluated "information reports" were not followed up. Essential Turner claims that they were hearsay and that the information did not change the determination that the attack was a mistake.

Obviously, the *Liberty* did not sink as referred to in the memo, which has no bearing on the issue of the informant's information, as he may not have known about the outcome. Further, the reference to a general and admiral, while speculative, might refer to General Hod, head of the air force, and Admiral Erell, both of whom followed orders. While Dayan has been labeled a suspect, his career was certainly not affected, as pointed out by Cristol in his book.

In CIA Director, Stansfield Turner's letter to Senator Abourezk, dated February 27, 1978, he describes a CIA records system that is less than responsive to FOIA requests. It appears that at the time of attack on the *Liberty*, and probably for years after the CIA had a decentralized record keeping system. Turner admits that there was no "master index" for the filing system and that each employee would have to be requested to search his or her particular case files. This problem may well have related to findings of the 9/11 Commission and the inability to share intelligence with other agencies.

Further, Turner defers to the judgment of experienced CIA analysts in determining whether information is relevant. He claims they determine the three information reports contained hearsay. Any competent law enforcement investigator knows that many cases are built on hearsay supporting probable cause; hearsay needs to be corroborated with other information.

It appears that the missing 6/21/67 memorandum may be included in documents released by the CIA in 2006. This document is entitled Directorate of Intelligence Memorandum that is four pages long and seems to be the work of an analyst dealing the Israeli Col. Ram Ron Report of 6/16/1967. In the General Comments section (10, 11, and 12), the following observations are noted:

1. The Israelis admitted there jets were ordered to attack an unidentified vessel.

2. This was not a case of over jealous pilots acting on their own. The CIA did not know if the pilots were advised of the *Liberty's* presence in the area.

3. It is questionable military policy to attack a unidentified ship solely based on a radar track of its speed, and an erroneous report of positions being shelled.

4. It was self-serving to claim the ship could not be identified because of smoke when the attack was what caused the smoke.

5. The claim that the ship was not identified until 44 minutes after the attack is an error.

6. The attack was not made in malice and was a mistake, but was gross-negligence.

468

No wonder the memorandum of 6/21/67 was withheld until 2006. It would have complicated the "political agreement" between the GOI and the Johnson administration to call it a case of mistaken identity thereby burying the issue.

It is important to recognize that these various documents were created in very short period after the attack and in proximity to the close of the Naval Court of Inquiry. Two points are important: First, immediately after the attack it was agreed at the highest levels of government that the attack was a mistake, and second, evidence was not followed up on. One additional CIA document is to be referenced, and that is the Intelligence Memorandum of 6/13/1967 previously referred to. This memorandum says the *Liberty's* mission was to act as a relay for U.S. embassies. The document notes the convening of the Naval Court of Inquiry, and "alludes" to the possibility of mistaken identity. Again, an example of reaching for an early conclusion to the "political problem".

What we know, in preparation for war, is that as Defense Minister, Dayan, following a Cabinet meeting, returned to Tel Aviv and met with the Chief of Staff, Rabin, to review the projected action in the south. He then flew north for a meeting with "Dado", Major General David Elazar of the Northern Command to hear his proposals. Dayan made it clear, contrary to Elazar's wishes, to not activate the Syrian front. Rather he was to take a "defensive" posture.[648]

Further, we do know that Rabin ordered a halt to the Israeli attack on Syria on the morning of June 8 at around 10:00 AM.[649] Rabin was in the "pit" at the Kyria during the attack on the *Liberty* and wanted to know what was being done reference the report of the coast being shelled from the sea. Subsequently, the next day Dayan ordered the attack on Syria resumed. According to his own words, "due to changed circumstances" with the conduct of the war being so favorable, he ordered forces to go into action against Syria. This was not withstanding the fact that Nasser and Syria had announced they would accept a cease-fire.[650] His objective was to protect those Israeli settlements that had been subject to harassment from the Syrian side of the border.

What is worth noting is Dayan's personal method-of-operation, especially regarding the Six-Day War, was to meet with his commander "to personally convey instructions". In his book on his life, he makes little mention of activities on June 8. He does not refer to the USS *Liberty*, and he tends to describe his actions in broad general tones without a lot of detail. Rabin was under Dayan, the Minister of Defense, and would have to follow his orders and directions regardless how they might have been communicated. Rabin was the overall operational commander as chief of staff.

The Israel Navy had only one admiral, Shlomo Erell. Erell was in Haifa on June 8, 1967, and Dayan was en route to Hebron. There was no admiral present with Dayan at the Kirya in Tel Aviv.

Per the CIA Document, "It was he [the admiral] who ordered it [the attack] stopped and not Dayan." Cristol comments that what is known about Dayan's temper and style of command, it is most difficult to imagine a subordinate countermanding his order in his presence.

Cristol's conclusion: The unidentified informant was wrong, or inaccurate, about every other assertion made. It

470

suggests that the assertion that Dayan personally ordered the attack suffers from lack of credibility. It appears that the unidentified informant was uninformed or spread misinformation about every single detail in the document, and his evaluation of Dayan's political future was far off the mark. How much weight, should be attached to the source's reported comment that "Dayan personally ordered the attack on the ship?" None.[651]

Cristol cites Dayan's autobiography, *Story of My Life*, published in 1976, as saying that on June 8, he learned that Hebron had been captured, and he promptly set off for Hebron. Hebron is located in the southern West Bank.

Shortly before noon on Thursday, Central Command reported to General Headquarters that its Jerusalem Brigade had linked up with Southern Command, having advanced south from Jerusalem and seized Bethlehem, Hebron, and Dahariah. He promptly set off for Hebron, meeting Uzi Narkiss [The general in charge of the Central Command] in Jerusalem and driving South with him.

Cristol notes that the Israeli Defense Forces History Department reports that on the morning of June 8, 1967, Dayan went to Jerusalem, where he had Major General Uzi Narkiss transport him to Hebron. It is about a fifteen-minute drive from the Kirya to Sde Dov Airport, located on the north side of Tel Aviv, on the coast. It is a little over thirty miles from Sde Dov to Jerusalem as the crow, or helicopter, flies. A Super Frelon helicopter cruises at between 138 and 155 miles per hour; thus Dayan's flight time to Jerusalem was about twelve to fifteen minutes. His route then went south less than three miles from Jerusalem to Bethlehem, then another five miles to the

471

Gush Etzion site, or EtzionBloc, where he and his entourage stopped for lunch, and finally on to Hebron, about ten more miles.

Cristol details Dayan itinerary for June 8 and asks the question: Is there any evidence that supports Dayan's alleged evil deed? He elaborates about a photograph of Dayan in *Life* magazine published as a special edition about the 1967 war that included a picture of Dayan having lunch that day on the road to Hebron. Cristol with good sleuthing finds the photographer and interviews others as to Dayan's whereabouts. He notes, thus, there are corroborating witnesses to Dayan's location and inability to give an order to attack the *Liberty* on June 8, 1967, between 1300 and 1400.

He further notes, Dayan first heard of the *Liberty* incident when he reached Beer Sheba in late afternoon. From there they flew by helicopter back to Tel Aviv. Upon arriving, they went to the Kirya. Shortly thereafter, Dayan left headquarters at the Kirya to spend the night with his girlfriend in Tel Aviv. Cristol does not tell us how Dayan learned about the attack on the *Liberty*. Certainly, it would seem he would learn about it one way or another. He could have heard about it orally the same as an order to attack the ship could have been orally made at any point in time.

Cristol notes his research indicates Dayan's total lack of involvement in the *Liberty* incident seems to be clear enough based on the evidence discussed above. He concludes that Dayan and his party were without the ability to communicate with the rest of the world from midmorning until they arrived in Beer Sheba. How naïve does Cristol think his readers are? Imagine the Israeli Minister of Defense is without communications during a

472

major war, one where Israel is alleged to have two nuclear devices, and is worried about Soviet intervention. Cristol then relies on the "watch" ruse dealing with enlarged pictures. He claims a close examination of the picture shows at least three people wearing wristwatches. He asked Rubinger, the photographer, if the photo could be enlarged to show the time on the watches when Dayan was eating lunch. In the *Life,* magazine picture Dayan's watch was at an angle and could not be effectively enlarged, but Rubinger advised that he had taken multiple shots of that same scene, all within a minute or two. Those pictures could be enlarged along with the pictures of the other watches. The time on the watches, including Dayan's own watch, was 1325, about seventeen minutes before the first order was given sending Mirage IIICJ aircraft in search of a warship off El Arish.

Using the "watch ruse", Cristol says Dayan was eating lunch at 1325, seventeen minutes before the first order was given sending planes to attack the ship. However, per the Col. Ram Ron Report, at 1205, Captain Rahav orders the MTBs to head toward El Arish to check on the shelling report and at 1341, the MTBs spot "the target" via radar at a distance of 20 miles. According to the IDF History Report, at 1317, the MTBs are told of the shelling and to listen to channels 86 and 186 for planes that would be dispatched after target was spotted. The IDF History Report states the planes were dispatched at 1348. However, evidence is that the planes and MTBs were picked up by *Liberty's* radar together at 1353. *Liberty's* fate was set. Cristol's ruse with the watches means nothing in terms of how the "order" was implemented. The "order to attack" the *Liberty* and the "order to dispatch" planes and MTBs to implement the attack are two distinct and separate acts based on command and control positions.

On page 209 of Cristol's book dealing with the Israeli transcripts in Appendix 2, he refers air controller's telephone conversations (commencing at 1342 Sinai time) and pilots' transmissions on the attack channel frequency at (commencing at 1329 Sinai time). The transcripts start at 1343. While keeping track of all these time references can be difficult for the reader, just watch out for the slight-of-hand misdirection.

So, the question remains, did Dayan do it? While we cannot say with certainty that he ordered the attack, nevertheless, Appendix 2 of Cristol's book dealing with the transcripts may shed some light on this matter of where the Minister of Defense was and whether he could have been advised or himself been monitoring events, note the following excerpt from the Israeli transcripts:

1419

KISLEV: Robert, do you have contact with O*fot* 1 and 2?

ROBERT: Okay, Im trying. None yet.

SHIMON: Kislev, I have O*fot* 2 in Taiman Field. [Taiman is an air base in the south near Beer Sheba.]

ROBERT: Okay, I'm trying. None yet.

SHIMON: Kislev, I have *[Ofot]* 2 in Taiman Field.

KISLEV: Not him.

1425

KISLEV: Robert, Two *[Ofot,* a Super Frelon 807] is in Taiman Field?

SHIMON: Yes, with the Minister of Defense.

SHIMON: Frelon from Air Force Base 8 [Tel Nof, located south of Tel Aviv] is ready to leave for the ship. Shall I send him out? Operations notified Base [censored].

KISLEV: Okay.

1429

KISLEV: Robert, is there any contact with the Super Frelons?

SHIMON: Yes.

Cristol says Dayan was on the road to Hebron and eating lunch at 1325. While the attack on the *Liberty* started at 1358, it certainly took some preparation and directional positioning. Per the Israeli transcripts, Dayan is placed at Taiman air base near Beer Sheba at or around 1419. The distance between Hebron and Taiman is approximately 25 miles. The attack is in progress with the torpedoing occurring minutes later.

Per the transcript excerpt, the Minister of Defense, Dayan, has been pegged as being mentioned in the transcript dialogue, whether incidental or not. In this time span, we have another reference to something being censored, why? This is not a smoking gun; however, just prior to the mentioned of the Minister of Defense, we are advised that there are no NSA intercepts of the attack—strange. Those recordings would have shown that attacking forces had known the *Liberty's* identity.

Cristol notes that there are corroborating witnesses to Dayan's location and inability to give an order to attack the *Liberty* on June 8, 1967, between 1300 and 1400. Again, he is the misdirection expert.

When all is said and done, what is Cristol's point? If Dayan, as the leading suspect is at point "X", wherever that is, why couldn't he as Minister of Defense simply pick up a phone, or verbally give the order to attack a ship off the coast of El Arish because it is allegedly shelling the shore. His Chief of Staff Rabin was in Pit at the Kirya as Michael Oren tells us, apparently coordinating the attack with the air controllers.[652]

> In the Pit, meanwhile, news of the purported shelling [of El Arish] unsettled Rabin, who had been warned of a possible Egyptian amphibious landing near Gaza. He reiterated the standing order to sink any unidentified ships in the war area, but also advised caution: Soviet vessels were reportedly operating nearby.

Dayan and Rabin had communicated earlier around midnight of the June 7 to early into the morning of the 8th dealing with the Syrian issue among other matters. The two did not agree as to how Syria should be handled.[653] Around 1000 the morning of the eighth, Rabin ordered a halt to the Syrian operation.[654] The surveillance of the *Liberty* had already begun as the ship was over-flown at 5:15 AM local time by the flying boxcar type plane, the Nord Noratlas 2501, as part of the early morning costal surveillance patrol. One might suggest her fate was sealed in that midnight exchange. Both men, Israeli heroes, have long since departed, and the record for history is murky at best. A recent *Jerusalem Post* report

476

came out critical of how the IDF history departments work at cross-purposes failing to fully establish a record of past events so the military can effectively learn from those events.[655]

As author, Richard Deacon has suggested, everything is oral, no written orders: "If it's a warship, sink it". The defense had better rest its case before it reveals too much. Notably, Cristol in the preparatory comments to his transcripts notes radio traffic as early as 1329 but does not include this in his Appendix 2 to his book. The transcripts start at 1343. This editing-out plus use of the term UNKNOWN in the transcripts raises issues of credibility—his defense of Dayan proves nothing. However, the unevaluated CIA report is just that—unevaluated.

Another book was written heralding the accomplishments of the Mossad. That book, *History of the Mossad*, was authored by a Joseph Daichman. He was referred to in the prior chapter dealing with the *Pravda* article about the USS *Liberty*. This author is unable to find any information on this author and the name is believed to be a pseudonym. The topics the author includes in the books are major Mossad accomplishments written about by Gordon Thomas and Ostrovsky such as the coup in obtaining a MIG-21 by defection of an Iraqi pilot. An e-mail check with Yossi Melman, an Israeli journalist dealing with intelligence matters and co-author of the book *Every Spy a Prince* along with Dan Raviv, has no knowledge of Daichman and his book. A search of Russian websites locates one indicating that Daichman was accused of plagiarizing from Melman's work.

When talking about "friends" of Israel, as I pointed out the *Liberty* survivors also have their friends. Richard Thompson using the letterhead *USS Liberty Friends* sent me information dealing with his research into Russian sources that he used in the BBC production on the *Liberty*. To illustrate the "friends" of Israel concept, he enclosed a copy of an e-mail he received. The subject was USS *Liberty* CIA documents labeled "Operation Cyanide". The context of the communication was prior discussions Thompson had with a certain person who wrote, "Yes, people are getting closer to the truth. Let me mention two major pertinent points...I've discussed with you before in one form or another." I am paraphrasing the following:

Point 1 deals with his request to open an OSI "Zero File" during the Six-Day War reference an USAF Lt. Colonel whose Israeli code-name was "Deleted". The author could not recall his real name and only dealt with code names. The author contends that the issue dealt with a security leak to the Israelis pinpointing "each and every gap in Egyptian radar, which was used by Israel to "sluice-in" their pre-emptive first strikes at the blinding crack of dawn on June the 6th—2-3 days after the Egyptians had ordered their Sharm-Al-Sheik garrison (in "soft-code broadcast") to stand-down, obviously intended for interception by USS Liberty, Israel and other intelligence monitors and as a signal to defuse the crisis." The author says he personally received this information at the time via NSA and assumed the crisis was over.

In the e-mail, the author says the Pentagon SSO officer he referred the investigation request to, came back to him and said, "There will be no case opened". The author says he and the SSO officer were "communicating by our gazes and gestures—that the dual loyalty had reared up its ugly face once more and we'd better shut up. The author revealed the name of the USAF SSO officer, a Colonel.

For Point 2, this person contends that to his knowledge there "was no A-bomb-laden aircraft coursing towards Cairo." [My comment: This is in the context of the thesis of Peter Hounam's book *Operation Cyanide*]. This person reports he would know this directly or indirectly, more likely directly because of his access to the USAF Command Post during the Six-Day War. He further contends that the USS Liberty attack did not seem to involve any U.S. government connivance. "Now that the public is getting close to the truth, let's not soften the final incriminatory results by saying it was a US-Israel scam. If there was any scam, it was exclusively Israeli and done behind the backs of the USAF Command Post, which is tantamount to doing it behind the back of the President and many Cabinet officials." The author continues: "...the USS Liberty was thoroughly destroyed by the Israelis on purpose to eliminate incriminating evidence. Evidence that pointed at their starting a war after the other side had stood down as requested by the global community. All the collateral signs indicate that the attack may also have been designed, in the heat of battle, as blatant signal of defiance, and Russian-style admonition, aimed at loyal American officers who did not follow certain political (sectarian?) inclinations."

This person goes on: In those days, my contention was that "Deleted" could have knowingly yet "in conscience" revealed, albeit without USAF knowledge and authorization, top-secret (and above) SIGINT and other ELINT findings to Israel regarding the "gaps" in the Egyptian radar network....which allowed them to minutely time penetration of those narrow "sluices" and knock out the Egyptian Air Force in a matter of hours.

In the above text, the reference to June 6 should be June 5 the first day of the war. The person writing the e-mail notes he never expressed his notions of a possible connection between the *Liberty* sinking and the attempt to protect the source of U.S. information Israel obtained dealing with the radar-gap. This "Deleted" is alleged to have been a USAF Lt. Col in Aerial Surveillance "or something like that". "The Person" at the time of the e-mail claims he is 65 and that "Deleted" must be 75 and the SSO officer is 80. I need to note that while this e-mail has been copied onto the USS Liberty Friends letterhead, there is no date and no sender's name. It is conceivable that the e-mail is dated around 2000 or 2002.

In my opinion, the point of referencing this e-mail is to associate it with the theme of Peter Hounam's book. It should be noted that to this author's knowledge, except for the contentions of author Peter Hounam in his book referring to the U.S. providing aerial photography assistance during the war, and the work of his informant, that this is the third example of help being provided to the Israelis from within the U.S. military circles—there were probably more.

I did not have the opportunity to discuss this e-mail with Thompson, and frankly was not able or ready to put it into a context or verify its provenance. The implication is that a *sayanim* was at work within the U.S. military; or, on the other hand, it could have been a sanctioned covert activity as part of Operation Cyanide, or both.[656] The truth can be elusive.

Wallace evaded capture for years, until finally in 1305 he was betrayed and captured as he slept by a well in Robroyston, near Glasgow. He was tried for treason and brutally executed on the 24th August 1305. After the trial, he was taken to Smithfield, and subsequently hung, drawn and quartered, then beheaded. As a warning to all others, the ruthless King Edward I sent the body parts of William Wallace to Berwick, Stirling, Perth and Newcastle to be put on display. His head was impaled on a spike on London Bridge.[657]

Chapter 15

War Crimes: The Advocate

The trial and sentencing of William Wallace, symbolic of the power of the absolute sovereign monarch, is a good illustration why our ancestors founded this country with a written constitution intending to limit the power of government. The President of the United States, as Commander-in-Chief is not a sovereign in the same sense as King Edward. Our system is founded on the principle of checks-and-balances with the citizen retaining certain inalienable rights as well as protections under the Bill of Rights. One branch of government is supposed to be a check on the other, for example, by congressional investigations of the executive branch of government, or judicial review. When the system fails, it results in a breach of the Rule of Law and injustices sprout up— anathema to democracy.

The survivors of the attack on the USS *Liberty* believe that their government failed them by not holding the government of Israel accountable for the murder of 34 crewmembers and the wounding of 175 others, not to mention the traumatic effect on families and survivors

482

years after the event. Suspicion exists that the monetary payments received from the Government of Israel, were actually provided by the U.S. government, administered through the State Department, as part of our aid package to the Government of Israel. Regardless, financial reparations do not resolve the question of whether or not there was the commission of murder, war crimes and obstruction of justice. The *Liberty* survivors continue to call for a Congressional investigation of the matter.

What was the responsibility of our Command-in-Chief and President, Lyndon Baines Johnson? What was the over-sight responsibility of the Congress and following Congresses, that have failed to investigate the events of June 8 1967? To this day many survivors, their family members and other Americans still cling to some hope that justice will be done in their lifetime. The Liberty Veterans Association (LVA) promotes the idea that Congress should finally hold a hearing on the attack. The LVA's statement of purpose is: "...obtaining a Congressional investigation into the attack, and...*TO BRING THE TRUE STORY OF THE ATTACK ON THE U.S.S. LIBERTY AND HER HEROIC CREW TO THE AWARENESS OF THE AMERICAN PEOPLE.*"[658] It is long past the time that both the governments of the United States and Israel open up the records and cease this on-going cover-up. Even author Michael Oren the current Israeli ambassador to the U.S. says it is time to end this matter.[659]

Obviously, looking into the circumstances of the attack on the *Liberty* would risk opening the broader picture of what our actions were during the Six-Day War in support of Israel. The generally accepted theory is that we supported Israel as opposed to the position that we

483

were promoting our own agenda to get rid of Nasser, albeit as a covert effort.

The full story of the events surrounding that war remain untold, however, the consequences of that war continue to govern events in the Middle East to this day with no foreseeable resolution. Can the United States be an effective "peace broker" as long as our government promotes a foreign policy of duplicity? The 2011 "Arab Spring" highlights the complexity of our foreign policy dilemma as our government supports the removal of certain dictators and yet remains ambiguous in our support of others, such as our policy toward Egypt and Libya, and our ambivalence toward suppressive regimes in Bahrain and Syria. It is one thing to promote a foreign policy with public statements and yet another when it comes to behind-the-scenes action—a cynical yet pragmatic approach to foreign policy.

Recently, President Obama called for a Middle East peace process reverting to the 1967 borders with "swaps". The Israeli Prime Minister claims this approach is "indefensible" during a recent visit to the U.S. where he publically chastised the President in front of the news media. The result has been no progress with the Palestinians going to the UN with a request for statehood, almost assuredly resulting in a U.S. veto, or a perpetual state of bureaucratic limbo for the petition. As of early 2012, the peace process appears all but dead. Ultimately, the U.S. could threaten to withdraw funding from the UN if it recognizes a Palestinian state.

It is clear that the United States had its goals for the events of June 1967, as did the State of Israel and the Soviet Union. We had two nuclear super-powers and one small nation want-to-be nuclear power with possibly two crude devices at the point of confrontation that could have been catastrophic for humankind. One mistake, one miscommunication, can ignite the process. The *Liberty* and crew were caught in the middle, where it was initially thought either the Egyptians or Soviets were responsible for the attack. It can be argued that the *Liberty* was "politically" sacrificed as an incidental footnote to the war.

A report alleging war crimes was filed with the Secretary of the Army and the Department of Defense pursuant to the appropriate procedure and protocol, dated June 8, 2005—thirty-eight years after the attack, by the Liberty Veterans Association as petitioner. Nothing has been heard from the Department of Defense reference that filing. Former LVA President Gary Brummett advised the following status report as of April 9, 2012: "The Bush WH advised case closed no further action will be taken (comment deleted)."

An unrelated letter from the Department of Navy addressed to The Honorable Rob Simmons, House of Representatives, and dated March 16, 2005, states the official Navy position. This letter responds to an inquiry from Mr. Simmons based on the Admiral Moorer's Independent Commission findings of a cover-up. Interestingly, the response confirms that the only investigation was into the communication failures and the heroic efforts of the crew to save the ship. **"The Court of Inquiry was the only United States Government investigation into the attack. The Navy plans no further investigation into the incident**."[660] [Author's Emphasis]. This statement seems to go contra to the claim of Israeli advocate, A. Jay Cristol, of multiple investigations.[661]

485

The United State's position on war crimes has been effectively modified in two ways: First, during the G.W. Bush administration, when it drafted amendments to a war crimes law that would eliminate the risk of prosecution for political appointees, CIA officers and former military personnel, according to U.S. officials and a copy of the amendments. Officials say the amendments would alter a U.S. law passed in the mid-1990s that criminalized violations of the Geneva Conventions, a set of international treaties governing military conduct in wartime.[662] The conventions generally bar the cruel, humiliating and degrading treatment of wartime prisoners without spelling out what all those terms mean.

Secondly, by the United States use of the veto in the United Nations and World Court by protecting Israel from war crimes allegations and jurisdiction.[663]

It is not the intent of this author to address an in-depth study of the elements of a war crime; however, a topical outline follows:[664]

1. Willfulness, or mens rea, denoting a criminal intent.

2. Willful killing.

3. Violation of the Law of War or International Humanitarian Law.

4. There must be proportionality.

5. Legitimate military targets.

6. Military necessity.

7. No indiscriminate attack.

486

8. Specific individual illegal or prohibited acts.

9. Sick and wounded should not be subject to attack.

10. There must be a legitimate military objective.

11. No wanton destruction.

12. No extra-judicial executions.

Each element or subject area can include a great deal of jurisprudence; just looking at the list flags several items that could apply in the *Liberty* attack. A suggested source for more information is the American Society of International Law.[665] Regarding the attack on the *Liberty*, and the filing of the war crimes complaint, what was and is the responsibility of the U.S. Government as the injured party? The murdered and maimed victims were employees of the United States government.

Rhetorically, it was the duty of the Commander-in-Chief to make sure that aid got to the ship, and to enforce certain laws dealing with the murder of U.S. service personnel. Did President Johnson through his administration perpetuate a cover-up for personal political reasons and gain? Did he or his immediate advisors, directly or indirectly participate in the cover-up of war crimes? Did the failure to provide air cover directly result in more deaths and casualties. Yet, worse, was the *Liberty* and crew used as a pretext to get the U.S. into the war in direct support of Israel, a conspiracy whereby American service members were murdered and maimed physically and psychologically. So many questions and yet after all this time so few answers—the stalling continues.

What are the limits on government power, specifically as to the President, in catastrophic situations such as a nuclear confrontation or contagion? It is clear that the Six-Day War did have a nuclear threat component. Nevertheless, presidents do not have absolute immunity for their actions or omissions:[666]

> Under the circumstances of this case, we cannot agree that petitioner's interlocutory appeal failed to raise a "serious and unsettled" question. Although the Court of Appeals had ruled in Halperin v. Kissinger that the President was not entitled to absolute immunity, this Court never had so held. And a petition for certiorari in Halperin was pending in this Court at the time petitioner's appeal was dismissed. In light of the special solicitude due to claims alleging a threatened breach of essential Presidential prerogatives under the separation of powers, see United States v. Nixon, 418 U.S., 691-692 (1974), we conclude that petitioner did present a "serious and unsettled," and therefore appealable, question to the Court of Appeals. It follows that the case was "in" the Court of Appeals under § 1254 and properly within our certiorari jurisdiction. [n23]

The constitutional battle over the presidential powers has generally focused on the issue of war powers:

> "The Framers of the Constitution vested in Congress the sole and exclusive authority to initiate military hostilities, including full-blown, total war, as well as lesser acts of armed force, on behalf of the American people. The constitutional grant to Congress

of the war power, which Justice William Paterson described in *United States* v. *Smith* (1806) as "the exclusive province of Congress to change a state of peace into a state of war," constituted a sharp break from the British model. The Framers were determined to deny to the president what Blackstone had assigned to the English King—"the sole prerogative of making war and peace." The president, in his role as commander in chief, was granted only the authority to repel invasions of the United States. But what the Framers sought to deny to the president has become a commonplace. Indeed, executive usurpation of the war power in the period since World War II has become a dominant characteristic of American foreign relations as presidents have routinely committed acts of war without congressional authorization."[667]

"On behalf of the American people" is the controlling phrase—the government acts on behalf of the people. The historical resistance to giving one man the unilateral authority to wage war is waning in our country for various reasons, notwithstanding the fact that our Constitution is a "limiting document".

There is no evidence that anyone supposed that his office as Commander in Chief endowed the President with an independent source of authority. . . . The President had no more authority than the first general of the army or the first admiral of the navy would have as professional military men. The President's power as Commander in Chief, in short, was simply the power to issue orders to

489

the armed forces within a framework established by Congress.[668]

The current controversy before the President and Congress surrounds the War Powers Resolution (1973), and what defines hostilities that would invoke the act. Take the recent Libyan situation as the example where President Obama committed U.S. military assets pursuant to a UN resolution without approval of Congress.[669]

Contrary to what President George W. Bush said and thought, the President is not the sole "decider". Government and its agencies tend to push the limits of the law, and this is true in other countries including Israel. The Six-Day War almost resulted in a military coup against Prime Minister Eshkol.[670] U.S. officials expected the Israelis to investigate and punish those responsible for the attack. The *Liberty* attack was handled totally within the Israeli military establishment when Chief of Staff Rabin assigned Colonel Ram Ron to conduct a preliminary investigation. He concluded, "I have no doubt that the *Liberty* did try to conceal her identity and presence in the area both before she was spotted by the Torpedo boats and even after she was attacked by the Air Force and the Naval Force and thus greatly and decisively contributed to her identification as an enemy ship and determined her own fate."[671]

Colonel Ram Ron was appointed to this task by Rabin on 6/12/67, and submitted his report within 8 days of the attack. His investigation was as cursory as the U.S. Naval Court of Inquiry. His report stated he interviewed 12 individuals, none of whom included pilots or General Hod commander of the IAF, nor Rabin.

490

The Israeli military prosecutor filed formal charges recommending court martial proceedings against a number of Israeli military personnel. Among those charged included the Acting Chief of Naval Operations who failed to notify the head of the naval department that the *Liberty* was observed in the early morning hours.[672] The list of charges is as follows:[673]

1. **Charge:** The first charge related to the failure of the Acting Chief of Naval Operations to report to the Head of the Naval Department that the American ship, *Liberty*, was seen in the morning hours of the day of the incident sailing in the vicinity of the Israeli coast.

2. **Charge:** That the Acting Chief of Naval Operations failed to report to the Head of the Naval Department that the hull markings on the ship observed by one of the attacking aircraft were similar to those on the *Liberty*.

3. **Charge:** That the Naval Liaison Officer at the Air Force Headquarters was negligent by not reporting to the Air Force the information about the presence of the *Liberty* in the area.

4. **Charge:** That the Naval Department's order not to attack the ship (the *Liberty*), "for fear of error and out of uncertainty with regard to the true identity of the ship," was not delivered to the torpedo boat division.

5. **Charge:** That it was negligence to give the order to attack a warship without previously establishing, beyond doubt, its national identity and without taking into account the presence of the American Ship, Liberty, in the vicinity of the coast of Israel.

6. **Charge:** That it was negligent to order the torpedo boat to attack the ship upon an unfounded presumption that it was an Egyptian warship and

this as a consequence of not taking reasonable steps to make proper identification.

The gravamen of the Israeli charges is "negligence", which falls far short of alleging war crimes. Subsequently, there was the Judge Yersushalmi inquiry and report that concluded that there was no *prima facie* evidence of wrongdoing to commit anyone to trail, and that IDF had acted in a reasonable manner—putting off the blame on the U.S. He concluded, considering the alleged shelling of coast, that the *Liberty* was there to remove Egyptian soldiers from the shore and she "lagged" behind the other vessels involved. His report was dated July 21, 1967.

One can view his decision as "the system protecting itself". Would the result have been different if culpability of Israeli military personnel had been brought before the civilian justice system in Israel?

The fallout from the *Liberty* attack was similarly contained within the U.S. military system. As previously reported, the Naval Court of Inquiry investigative personnel were not allowed to go to Israel in interrogate those involved. Notwithstanding the claim of many Congressional investigations, there was no "forensic' investigation". The unrequited claim is that the attack resulted in allegations of murder and assault, and that covering up such claims would constitute an obstruction of justice at a minimum. The Congress as a matter of checks-and-balances had a duty to hold hearings on the conduct of the Executive Branch in covering the matter up. It seems that when it comes to the State of Israel there is a double standard and our constitutional checks-and-balances fail along with the Rule of Law. This is the first time Congress failed to hold hearings into an attack on an American ship.

It took 38 years for the survivors to seek redress by filing a war crimes report with the U.S. government that has a legal duty to investigate.

The text of the war crimes report can be found at http://ussliberty.org/report/report.htm. The report was filed on behalf of the USS Liberty Veterans Association, Inc., a California non-profit corporation, as petitioner. Formally, this is a report and not a complaint, as one would find in a court of law; however, it does require attention and action. It was addressed to the U.S. Department of Defense and the Office of the Secretary of the Army pursuant to DOD Directives Numbers 5100.77 and 5810.01B (29 March 2004) that deals with the reporting of war crimes complaints against U.S. military personnel. The directive reads: *(3) All reportable incidents committed by or against members of (or persons serving with or accompanying) the US Armed Forces are promptly reported, thoroughly investigated and, where appropriate, remedied by corrective action.*

It is clear from these directives that the United States Military is to follow the DOD Laws of War Program, and any breeches are to be reported. One confusing matter involving casualties has been cleared up by this report, and that is that 175 personnel were wounded in the attack, and not 171 as commonly reported.[674] I recently checked with Dave Lewis (4/5/12) via e-mail to see if he could help explain the change in the number wounded. He said, "The reason for the change Bob is new people coming forward to get Purple Hearts. I believe the number of wounded is now 174."

Jurisdiction for following up the report with legal action can be found in the Federal Criminal Code, at 18 United States Code, Sec. 2441:

18 United States Code, Sec. 2441. - War crimes
(a) Offense. -
Whoever, whether inside or outside the United States, commits a war crime, in any of the circumstances described in subsection (b), shall be fined under this title or imprisoned for life or any term of years, or both, and if death results to the victim, shall also be subject to the penalty of death.
(b) Circumstances. -
The circumstances referred to in subsection (a) are that the person committing such war crime or the victim of such war crime is a member of the Armed Forces of the United States or a national of the United States (as defined in section 101 of the Immigration and Nationality Act).
(c) Definition. -
As used in this section the term "war crime" means any conduct -
(1) defined as a grave breach in any of the international conventions signed at Geneva 12 August 1949, or any protocol to such convention to which the United States is a party;
(2) prohibited by Article 23, 25, 27, or 28 of the Annex to the Hague Convention IV, Respecting the Laws and Customs of War on Land, signed 18 October 1907;
(3) which constitutes a violation of common Article 3 of the international conventions signed at Geneva, 12 August 1949, or any protocol to such convention to which the

494

United States is a party and which deals with non-international armed conflict; or

(4) of a person who, in relation to an armed conflict and contrary to the provisions of the Protocol on Prohibitions or Restrictions on the Use of Mines, Booby-Traps and Other Devices as amended at Geneva on 3 May 1996 (Protocol II as amended on 3 May 1996), when the United States is a party to such Protocol, willfully kills or causes serious injury to civilians.

The contention is that pursuant to U.S. law, government officials had a duty, not the discretion, to take action on the report. The passage of time would not be an issue since there is no statute of limitations for murder. A report or complaint is just that, it is not adjudication. It requires follow-up and an investigation by the Executive branch. The prior Naval Court of Inquiry did not investigate the issue of war crimes as has been acknowledged.

Irrespective of International Law issues, 18 U.S.C. Sec. 1114 deals with the protection of officers and employees of the United States, and whoever kills or attempts to kill such officer or employee while engaged in the performance of their duties shall be punished in the case of murder, manslaughter or attempted murder and manslaughter. The word "shall" is used, so again, enforcement of the law is mandatory. According to 18 U.S.C. 1111 in the case of murder, it shall be punishable by death; therefore, as a capital crime there is no statute of limitations per 18 U.S.C. 3281. As to lesser crimes such as manslaughter, negligent homicide, and assault, there would be a statute of limitations issue. In the case of the USS *Liberty*, to the extent there is a basis to charge murder of the crew there is a lingering cloud from a legal

495

standpoint. This discussion is problematic since one has to find a U.S. Attorney willing to seek an indictment. Therefore, we are faced with the same conundrum faced by those who wanted to indict G. W. Bush and others in his administration for war crimes and crimes against humanity for pursuing an unjust war. The reality is that the government invokes the law when it suits the government.

The essential allegations contained in the report filed with the Secretary of the Army by the LVA in its representative capacity are: 1) The USS *Liberty* was a neutral ship in international waters and an attack on her was *prima facie* a war crime; 2) The Israeli MTB crews shot at rescuers and firefighters on the deck of the ship; 3) The MTB crews fired on the ship's life rafts.

We have noted what the GOI did regarding a review of the Israeli Defense Forces' actions in attacking the *Liberty* in the chapter on the cover-up. Obviously, in the context of following up the war, the GOI, meaning the military establishment was not about to hang its own out to dry in the public forum. That is not to say that the civilian side of the Israeli government was reluctant to hold commanders responsible. The case of a Colonel Meir was handled by the Civilian court in Israel after some pressure and criticism had been brought to bear.

For an illustrative case, see the article on *Command Responsibility*, by Nomi Bar-Yaacov, citing the Israeli handling of the Col. Yehuda Meir case.[675] This case is of particular importance in the context of the USS *Liberty* matter, and is distinguished because the *Liberty* attack was handled solely within the "military system", whereas public pressure pushed the Meir case into the Israeli civilian court system, which then ordered a proper consideration of the case.

In January 1988, barely one month into the *Intifada* uprising against Israeli occupation of the West Bank and Gaza Strip, Col. Yehuda Meir ordered troops under his command to round up twenty Palestinian men from Hawara and Beita, two Arab villages in the West Bank, bind them in handcuffs and blindfolds, and break their bones. The unit commander reporting to Meir passed on the order to his troops, but told them he did not require them to comply. Some soldiers refrained from doing so, but others carried out the order with such zeal that they broke their truncheons. The defense minister at the time, Yitzhak Rabin, publicly spoke of the need to "break the bones of Intifada rioters." Although Meir was not present during the incident, he was the superior commanding officer in the area.

It took some months before military police, following a request by the International Committee of the Red Cross (CRC), launched an investigation. The army chief of staff summoned Meir and offered him the choice to appear before a disciplinary military court for a severe reprimand and discharge from the army, or to face a court martial. Meir accepted the first option, under which he was to go to work for the State security service until he could begin retirement on his colonel's pension.

When word of the behind-the-scenes deal became public, the Association for Civil Rights in Israel petitioned the Israeli High Court of Justice, demanding that Meir be court-martialed.

The High Court ruled unanimously that Meir should be tried in a special military tribunal for torture, intentionally causing bodily harm, grievous assault—all, incidentally, grave breaches of the Geneva Conventions—and unbecoming conduct.

"These actions outrage every civilized person, and no lack of clarity can cover it up" Justice Moshe Bejski said. "Certainly, if the order is given by a senior officer, that officer must be aware that the morality of the Israeli Defense Forces forbids such behavior."

Following the High Court's decision, Meir went on trial before a special military tribunal in Tel Aviv in April 1991. He was found guilty, demoted to private's rank, and deprived of his colonel's pension. The facts indicate that Minister of Defense, Rabin, while setting the policy that lead to Meir's orders, did not suffer any adverse action.

Meir's case points to two critical issues of international humanitarian law (IHL). Can obedience to superior orders be a defense against allegations of war crimes? In addition, how far up the chain of command does "command responsibility" reach?

The answer to the first question is that a claim of superior orders cannot serve as a defense against an allegation of grave breaches or other serious violations of IHL. It should be noted, however, that the illegality of the orders was blatant and undeniable in Meir's case. In other cases, the illegality may not be so apparent, and a war crimes prosecution may fail if the subordinate is not shown to have acted "willfully" in the sense of knowing or having reason to know that the order was illegal. In addition, although a claim of superior orders cannot serve as an affirmative defense, it may be part of a claim of duress—such as a threat to execute the subordinate for

498

failure to carry out orders—that may be offered in mitigation.

The second issue is how far up the chain of command responsibility may extend for ordering a war crime. Article 86 of Additional Protocol I to the 1949 Geneva Conventions states: "the fact that a breach of the Conventions or of this Protocol was committed by a subordinate does not absolve his superiors from penal disciplinary responsibility as the case may be if they knew, or had information which would have enabled them to conclude in the circumstances at the time that he was committing or was going to commit such a breach and if they did not take all feasible measures within their power to prevent or repress the breach."

This rule applies to officers. Therefore, command responsibility extends as high as any officer in the chain of command who knows or has reason to know that his subordinates are committing war crimes and failed to act to stop them. Although Israel has not ratified Additional Protocol I, it is clear from the Israeli High Court decision that its domestic law embraces these internationally recognized standards for superior orders and command responsibility.

Under the 1998 statute of the new International Criminal Court, a military commander is liable for crimes that he "knew or should have known" about under circumstances at the time, and only for those crimes committed by forces under his "effective command and control." He is liable if he "failed to take all necessary and reasonable measures" to prevent and repress such crimes that subordinates "were committing or about to commit" or for failing to report such crimes to proper authorities.

Various cases have raised difficult questions, starting with the famous Yamashita case heard by the International Military Tribunal in Tokyo following World War II. That tribunal held a senior enemy commander to what many critics, including a dissenting U.S. Supreme Court opinion, thought to be an extraordinarily high standard of responsibility for actions of subordinates, even under circumstances where Admiral Yamashita had lost almost all command, control, and communications over his subordinates. In practical terms, command responsibility is not taken to extend as far up the chain of command as might logically be implied, that is, to commanders in chief, and is generally confined to officers in some meaningful supervisory capacity.

Meir argued in his own defense that he was acting in accord with his understanding of orders given by his superiors. The tribunal rejected his argument. The judges concluded that political and high-ranking military officials had not given orders to break bones. Consequently, the State prosecutor's office decided not to pursue charges against Ehud Barak, the chief of staff at the time, Rabin, the minister of defense, or Maj. Gen. Yitzhak Mordechai, the commanding officer of the central zone.

Officers and soldiers who carried out Meir's orders in the Hawara and Beita affair were tried in special military courts. Their arguments that they were merely "obeying orders" were rejected and they served time in prison.

While the Meir case is an example of how the civilian side of the Israeli judicial system dealt with the breaking of bones, a more egregious act involving the attack on the *Liberty* was the torpedo boats strafing the deck of the ship while crew were rescuing the injured and fighting deck fires was well as strafing deployed life rafts.[676]

A key provision of the Law of War prohibits attacks on neutral ships in international waters. Without getting technical, a brief discussion of the Law of War is useful to help frame the issues. Some of this information was taken from the *Liberty Court of Inquiry* website forum and is presented as a quid-pro-quo exchange between an advocate and skeptic. The information provided is critical to the understanding of the war crimes complaint filed by the LVA. The perspective is primarily that of the advocate. The exchange was on a public forum where input was solicited from the public. The dialogue has been reformatted from the original website forum; the gist of the argument has not been altered. It is believed that the source forum is no longer active nor available on the Internet.[677]

*** Start of Forum Discussion ***

The Advocate: International law does not provide for a "good faith mistake" defense when a party refuses to comply with international legal requirements. The attackers are required to ascertain the nationality of the target before attacking. By their own admission, the Israelis did not do that. By failing to ascertain the nationality of the ship they attacked in international waters, they assumed responsibility for what followed.
I do not use terms like war crime lightly. This was a war crime. It was not an error. It was not a mistake. It most definitely was not friendly fire. It was a war crime.
Let us take this one-step at a time. No one disputes that USS *Liberty* was in international

501

waters. The Israeli forces pursued a ship, known to be in international waters, with the intent of attacking it. The Israelis admit that they made no effort to ascertain the nationality of the ship in international waters. They were under a legal obligation to do so before attacking.

The ship was moving at a speed of approximately five knots. Those incompetent naval personnel made a 600% error (twice) in calculating the ship's speed is of no consequence. When the aircraft arrived, they could see that the ship was moving slowly and that there was no need for haste. Without knowing the nationality of the ship, and without waiting a few minutes for the torpedo boats to arrive and positively ID the ship, the aircraft attacked. They had no legal right to do this and there was no rational basis for attacking at that time. That was their prerogative, but by attacking without knowing the nationality of the ship, they assumed all liability for what happened next. The characterization of the Israeli actions as a war crime is wholly consistent with decisions made previously in trials of war criminals. For example, see: http://www.usslibertyinquiry.com/law/rae der.html in the case of German Admiral Raeder, a war crimes charge was sustained where similar facts were present. Quoting from the Court's decision:

"Raeder is charged with war crimes on the high seas. The *Athenia*, an unarmed British passenger liner, was sunk on 3 September 1939, while outward bound to America. The Germans 2 months later charged that Mr.

Churchill deliberately sank the *Athenia* to encourage American hostility to Germany. In fact, the German U-boat U-30 sank it. Raeder claims that an inexperienced U-Boat commander sank it in mistake for an armed merchant cruiser, that this was not known until the U-30 returned several weeks after the German denial and that Hitler then directed the Navy and Foreign Office to continue denying it. Raeder denied knowledge of the propaganda campaign attacking Mr. Churchill. The most serious charge against Raeder is that he carried out unrestricted submarine warfare, including sinking of unarmed merchant ships, of neutrals, non-rescue and machine-gunning of survivors, contrary to the London Protocol of 1936. The Tribunal makes the same finding [guilty] on Raeder on this charge as it did as to Doenitz, which has already been announced, up until 30 January 1943 when Raeder retired."

The Skeptic (a forum participant): I would not dispute that the attack on USS *Liberty* involved negligence on the part of certain Israeli personnel, perhaps to a criminal extent. For one thing, the pilots were given authorization to attack "IF it is a warship". Apparently, their verification of this fact went only so far as to ascertain that it was not an Israeli vessel. In an apparent effort to beat the Navy to the punch (get on the scoreboard, if you will), the gung-ho Air Force pilots rolled on the ship. The whole thing snowballed from there.

I'm not a lawyer, and I'm not up on international law, so while you may be technically correct in your characterization

503

(once again, I don't know), I'm not as comfortable in throwing the term around in any event. For one thing, the phrases "war crime" and "war criminals" have an historic and well-documented connotation with war-time atrocities (e.g., systematic mass-murder of civilians, torture/summary execution of POW's, etc.). While the attack on the *Liberty* may have involved a military "crime" which occurred during a "war", I would submit that such does not significantly distinguish the incident from that which occurs in all wars.

My guess is that many "friendly fire" incidents, when disassembled down to their nuts-and-bolts, reveal a breakage of command and control somewhere in the mechanism. In other words, someone (or some persons) were not doing what they were supposed to be doing, and people died as a result. We've seen this sort of thing time and time again - both within our own armed forces and in those of other countries. While military personnel who are found guilty of negligence (or what-have-you) in such cases may indeed be guilty of crimes committed during a war, they are not commonly referred to as "war criminals".

So, in a sense, I think it DOES matter whether one believes that it was a "tragic accident" or a planned attack.

The Advocate: Something that often gets lost in the discussion of the Israeli attack on USS *Liberty* is that it was a war crime. It doesn't matter whether you believe that it was a "tragic accident" or a planned attack, the fact remains that the uncontroverted facts establish conclusively that the attack constituted a war crime.

504

Israel admits that its forces deliberately attacked a ship of unknown nationality in international waters. They committed a war crime. It doesn't matter how they got there or what they thought. They committed a war crime. They knew the ship was in international waters. They failed to make a positive identification of the ship's nationality. They deliberately attacked the ship. They committed a war crime.

Does anyone dispute the characterization of Israeli Air Force pilots and Israeli Navy crews as war criminals? [The question is thrown out to the forum].

[**Author's note:** To put the discussion into a real world context, note the following: A relevant and material point is based upon statements of a participant in the attack—The commander of motor torpedo boat Division 914, Moshe Oren: I just finished reviewing the documentary video *Attack on the Liberty*, a 1987 Thames Television production for the Discovery Channel. This is a particularly important documentary because it records statements of key players, both on the U.S. and the Israeli side. For example, Moshe Oren, the MTB Division 914 commander, was interviewed on the Thames video. He was the commander of the motor torpedo boat division that fired torpedoes at the USS *Liberty*.

As to the issue raised in this thread, he stated that the "actual order was to find and destroy it"; "It" being the *Liberty*. Further, he states on the video (and production script) they were not told of the ship's ID, but that it was possibly an enemy ship. He gave the command to fire torpedoes.

In the video, the context for the narrator's question to Oren, years after the attack, is that he is interviewed on board what appears to be a motor torpedo boat at sea (he is in civilian clothes). The narrator's question relates to the claim that El Arish was being shelled by "it", the "target"--the target being the USS *Liberty*. Of course the *Liberty* had no guns capable of "shelling the shore".
The Issue and Question: 1) Are "his statements" made against his "penal interest", and, 2) would they be considered incriminating and admissible under the "Rules of Evidence" in the context of the advocate's quoted statement above and in the prior postings? Of course, the assumption being that the Rule of Law still governs in both countries.]

The Advocate to the Skeptic: If you amend that to "an attack upon any neutral vessel on the high seas or in international airspace without first having positively ascertained the nationality of that vessel is, in fact, a "war crime" (and not to be referred to as a "tragic error" or "friendly fire"), then I agree 100%. More importantly, so does the entire body of international law.

The Skeptic: And is it your contention that an attack upon any vessel (sea, land or air) without first having positively ascertained the nationality of that vessel is, in fact, a "war crime" (and not to be referred to as a "tragic error" or "friendly fire")?

The Advocate: In the interest of intellectual honestly, let's call this attack what it was: a

506

war crime. This is not a hyper technical interpretation of that term, but rather one that is well within the universally accepted definition. It is important that we use proper terms if we want to understand things.

People who defend the Israeli actions use terms like "innocent mistake," "tragic error," and "friendly fire." The attack was none of those. It was a war crime. Once everyone understands that we can proceed with an analysis of what happened and what should be done about it.

For this reason, I want to ask everyone again, is there anyone who disagrees with the characterization of the Israeli attack on USS *Liberty* as a war crime? If so, please step up and explain why this is not so. If not, then we can take this as agreed upon and proceed to other aspects of the case.

The Skeptic: Where are you going with this?

The Advocate: I don't wish to be insulting, but I have to believe that you are desperately trying to shift the focus because you are unable to reply on the merits of the argument. No one could be as obtuse as you would appear to be from your replies.

This is now at least the third time that you have suggested that a posting said something other than what was written. You suggested that [name deleted] had accused the Captain of committing perjury. He made no such accusation. You suggested that I was holding Israel to a different standard than other countries. I have not done so and I do not do so. Now, you want to characterize my earlier

507

remarks concerning the definition of a war crime into something I never articulated.

For purposes of the Laws of War, there are three distinct areas where combat could potentially take place:

Within the jurisdictions (including territorial seas and airspace) of the combatants – commonly known as a war zone;

In international waters or airspace;

Within the sovereign territory (including territorial seas and airspace) of other countries.

Combat within the sovereign territory of other nations is explicitly prohibited by international law. If the country where the combat takes place does not actively work to prevent it, that country could lose its neutral status.

Combat within a war zone, if conducted in accord with the Laws of War is legal as between the combatants. While neutrals must accept a higher risk of getting caught in the fighting if they voluntarily enter the sovereign territories of the combatants, it is still a violation of the Laws of War for a combatant to attack a neutral.

Finally, international law protects neutrals that remain in international waters or airspace. Combatants are explicitly prohibited from attacking them. International waters and international airspace are defined terms and their definitions have never been subject to challenge.

Let me run through this one more time. Combatants are absolutely prohibited from attacking neutrals, particularly in international territory. If you are a combatant in international waters or airspace and you observe a ship, how can you tell if it is

508

neutral? The answer is simple: you look. If the presumed neutral ship fires on the aircraft or ships making such an inspection, then that ship forfeits its neutral status. Otherwise, it remains neutral until proven otherwise.

In the case of the attack on USS *Liberty*, the ship was unarguably in international waters. The ship did not fire on the aircraft before or after they began their attack. The ship was moving slowly and was nowhere near an enemy port. The oncoming Israeli gunboats could (and in fact did) intercept USS *Liberty* within minutes of the start of the attack.

The Israeli commanders made the decision to forego confirmation that the ship was hostile. They cannot now hide behind their refusal to perform their legal obligation as a defense to the war crime of attacking a neutral ship in international waters.

You seem to have trouble understanding this concept, so let's try it again. A combatant may not attack a neutral in international waters. Are we clear on this or do you dispute it?

If we agree, then we proceed to the next step: how does a combatant know that it is not attacking a neutral ship in international waters? The most reasonable answer is that they take a moment to observe the ship. Does it display the flag of a hostile nation? Has it fired upon the ships or aircraft making the inspection?

If the combatant elects to forego making a positive identification of the nationality of the ship, then it assumes all liability for what happens subsequently if it attacks. If the ship, in fact, turns out to be hostile, no problem. If it turns out to be a neutral, however, we call that attack a war crime.

509

Are you not capable of understanding that the Laws of War were designed to limit combat to the belligerent parties only? That is why there is an absolute (no exception) prohibition on attacking neutral shipping.

Let me ask you a very simple question. Do you personally believe that the attack on USS *Liberty* was justified or proper? If you do, are you not appalled that the people responsible for more than 200 American casualties not only avoided punishment, but were wholly exonerated by the Israeli government? Are you not disgusted that the United States government has failed to live up to its legal obligations and seek the punishment of the people responsible for the attack?

As a lawyer, I deal with statutory law and precedent decisions. There is a precedent in a case involving the mistaken sinking of a neutral ship on the high seas. A German U-Boat commander sank a merchant ship after mistaking it for an armed cruiser. His superior officer was found guilty of committing a war crime.

*** End of Forum discussion ***

Therefore, the discussion, as is typical of many forums on the Internet, can be free flowing, controversial and contentious. While the discussion is thrown out to the public, the forum format may or may not generate contra-arguments.

After the attack, the State Department took over the responsibility of negotiating with the government of Israel for reparations for the families of those killed and for the wounded as well for the damage to the ship. That was also a contentious process. Some family members wanted to sue the GOI, however, most settled by accepting a check from the State Department. The problem is that the State Department was an interested and conflicted party, involved in the cover-up notwithstanding that Secretary of State Dean Rusk believed that the attack was intentional. Actually, the State Department was in the best position to leverage pressure on Israel to tender settlement funds, notwithstanding Israel's resistance.

Unfortunately, it would be difficult if not impossible to bring a lawsuit against a foreign nation, subject to very narrow exceptions such as being listed as a sponsor of state terrorism. There is such a thing as the Foreign Sovereign Immunities Act (FSIA) that would be used by the State Department and Department of Justice to block any such suit on grounds of national sovereign immunity and lack of personal jurisdiction. In a surprising manner, dealing with the fallout of 9/11, a lawsuit alleging certain Saudi Arabian defendants, including the Kingdom of Saudi Arabia, of involvement in the events of 9/11, has been block by the U.S. Government. The case is *In Re Terrorist Attacks on September 11, 2001*, 538 F.3rd 71 (2nd Cir. 2008). The lawsuit has been backed up with factual affidavits of two former U.S. Senate members, leaving 9/11 families and survivors to wonder what is going on with our government.[678] I suspect the result would have been the same for *Liberty* survivor claimants even though FSIA had not been enacted until 1976.[679]

While discussion has focused on Israel, the real issue here is the responsibility of our government. If President Johnson did not want to embarrass and ally and if members of his advisory inner circle gave serious consideration to having the *Liberty* scuttled before

511

returning to her homeport in the United States, then, to the extent the President participated he was involved in an obstruction of justice. Were it not for a compromised Congress, it would and should have been grounds for an investigation and possible basis for impeachment. Certainly, the circumstances involving the attack on the *Liberty* was more egregious than messing around with a female intern.

The cover-up has been perpetuated through other presidents and congresses, with some saying there has been no new evidence, thus keeping the lid on something that must remain hidden. Author Peter Hounam: "It is surely time America, Israel and anyone else involved in Operation Cyanide told the truth-the-whole-truth about this fiasco. If not, can we ever be sure that the nuclear button is in safe hands? And will we ever unravel the real causes of the Middle East Crisis?"[680]

Like Peter Hounam on the last page of his book, I would like to reiterate, that it is now time for our governmental leaders to muster political courage and let light shine in on this tragic saga. Let the surviving crew members, families and friends, and above all the American public know the truth of the events of June 8, 1967 where 34 American sailors were murdered with 175 fellow crew members being wounded, having their lives disrupted, losing confidence in the government they so ably served—they were true "Cold-War Heroes".

What would the Johnson administration motive be for covering up details of the assault on the *Liberty*? The primary motive for the administration's actions was not to embarrass an ally, and he did not want to embarrass himself and his administration. Johnson needed Jewish support for both the Vietnam War and his reelection bid.

He did not have their support for the Vietnam War. A "political" rational does not relieve the President from following the law as previously stated above re the killing or harm to American officers and employees of the government.

A particular insight into Johnson's thinking comes from the Oral History of his aid, Harry McPhearson who acted as a conduit and go-between with the Jewish community.[681] He notes how Israeli minister and Mossad liaison, Ephraim "Eppy" Evron, and Johnson became unusually close friends. McPhearson arrived in Tel Aviv at three o'clock in the morning of June 5, 1967 and found all to be quiet—prior to the start of the Six-Day War. He would awake to the sound of air raid sirens at eight in the morning. McPhearson stayed for most of the war and notes the Arab's belief that we had something to do with the start of the war; he says he was not the person who brought the "go" signal to the Israelis. Importantly, McPhearson claims credit for getting the word to President Johnson that it was the Israelis who preempted the war.

McPhearson described himself as the administration's "semi-Semite" liaison with the Jewish community. McPhearson famously quotes: "...that some place in Lyndon Johnson's blood there are a great many Jewish corpuscles. I think he is part Jewish, seriously, not merely because of his affection for a great many Jews, but because of the way he behaves." McPhearson goes on: "We couldn't say anything about the fact that the Sixth Fleet had been turned East, aimed at the Russian fleet, to head off the Russian fleet before it got to Alexandria. We couldn't say what we had said on the Hot Line about the necessity for Russia to keep its mitts off the Middle East, because of our relations with the

513

Russians and because we were trying to settle the Middle Eastern situation."

McPhearson wanted to get the story out to the Jewish community how Johnson had saved Israel and he pleaded with the President to authorize Evron to "spill the beans". Evron carried the message: "I can't tell you anything about the facts, but let me tell you, I'm the Minister of Israel. I have the strongest interest in the United States helping Israel and I can tell you that Lyndon Johnson saved Israel." McPhearson quotes Evron: "And Eshkol did say it. And Lyndon Johnson's popularity rating in Israel, as the Jews would say, 'Oi vey, if he could be transferred here.' The most popular man in Israel on the popularity polls is Lyndon Johnson. Second is Eshkol. Third is [Moshe] Dayan and it goes on down the line like that. But Johnson is first. Quite a change from that period, that early period, around the six-day war when they really didn't know."

Whether there was a national security element to the cover-up is an open question and one for which more information is needed. National security is a big rug under which to bury the activities of politicians to keep them from embarrassment. If the system of checks-and-balances had been working and a proper Congressional investigation had been conducted, we would not be looking at this matter. The problem is that once *Pandora's Box* is opened, it cannot be closed.

A key question is, did Israel have any legal argument for its actions? One argument has been suggested:[682]

> What Israel was claiming by implication was an exclusion zone on the high seas directed toward intelligence-gathering vessels, thus

giving her the right to force them to leave by threats or to destroy them if they did not. Restated, the Israelis' implied claim was that the United States had no right to conduct electronic intelligence gathering from a maritime exclusion zone of undefined character or limits in the southeastern Mediterranean.

The author of the article breaks this issue into two parts:[683] First, the lawfulness of the intelligence gathering functions of the *Liberty*, and second, the location in which she operated.

As to the activity,

> Absent hostilities, intelligence gathering on the high seas is lawful; it becomes illegal only when it interferes with the activity of another lawful user of the high seas or when it infringes upon protected features of the public order in the coastal state, thereby upsetting the balance of interests. Since intelligence gathering from the high seas is normally conducted in an unobtrusive and non-interfering manner, there is generally no support for the proposition that electronic intelligence collection from the high seas is of a nature that would justify an attack or interference, particularly when the states are at peace with each other, and when there is no trend to the contrary.

As to location,

> Since the *Liberty* was not in territorial waters nor in a contiguous zone, as defined by the Territorial Seas Convention, the only basis for

515

the Israeli hostile action against a nonbelligerent warship must be found in a claim of self-defense applied to the high seas. Applying the criteria for a maritime exclusion zone to the implied exclusion zone that the Government of Israel sought to assert against the *Liberty* reveals that this zone did not meet the basic requirements.

What about the issue of "anticipatory self-defense"?

The attack on the **USS**. *Liberty* was not a justifiable act of anticipatory self-defense. The *Liberty* committed no aggression against Israel. The Israeli attack was not preceded by justifiable peaceful procedures. The attack was unnecessary because it was based only on a speculative threat and conducted after Israel's legitimate war aims had been achieved. Any coercion against the ship would have been unjustified. Since there was no justification for the attack as an act of self-defense under article 51 of the U. N. Charter, and since the attack was not committed as part of a decision of the U.N. Security Council, it was an unlawful use of force by a member of the United Nations.[684]

· The attack on the *Liberty* and the cover-up is the result of a complete breakdown in the Rule of Law. Just as King Edward's execution of William Wallace in 1305, the arbitrariness and abuse of power is just as prevalent in today's world.

516

The Flying Dutchman, according to folklore, is a ghost ship that can never go home, doomed to sail the oceans forever. The Flying Dutchman is usually spotted from far away, sometimes glowing with ghostly light. It is said that if hailed by another ship, its crew will try to send messages to land or to people long dead. In ocean lore, the sight of this phantom ship is a portent of doom.

http://en.wikipedia.org/wiki/Flying_Dutchman.

Chapter 16

Cold War Heroes

Should the USS *Liberty* be analogized to the *Flying Dutchman* and the "portent of doom" claim? With a sense of hyperbole the question can be asked in the context of whether a free society can continue to be free if justice is denied, the Rule of Law is undercut and the "big lie" prevails.

In the post 9/11 world review of intelligence operations, it is clear that the United States intelligence agencies were caught flat-footed resulting in major structural changes being recommended by The 9/11 Commission Report.[685] The National Security Agency admittedly was not prepared to deal with the terrorist threat posed by elements from the Middle East in terms of its signals intercept mission. There was a lack of trained linguists for countries like Iraq, Afghanistan, and Yemen, the focal point of various terror related activities; conversely, the CIA was deficient in terms of HUMINT, human intelligence, not having effective human agents and assets on the ground in those same Middle East countries. The hope is that problems are being rectified.[686]

Another problem regarding America's Middle East intelligence gathering is that during the height of the Cold War we opted to let Israel handle "our" intelligence gathering needs. This policy may have been convenient at one time but leads to a false sense of security where we may be getting a filtered product. Did this relationship and vulnerability have any effect on what happened to the USS *Liberty* in June of 1967 during the Six-Day War?

If we were to recall a "B" movie from say the 1940s we might conjure up an image of the "spy" as sinister individual, lurking around the corner under a street lamp with the hat brim pulled down over the eye and the collar up on the trench coat. On the other hand, we might think in terms of "Ultra" the [687]codename for the "Enigma" product, the high-level cipher machine of Nazi Germany, and the breaking of Japanese codes by tedious hand methods. Forget all that, those images are in the past.

Today's "spies" and spying is much more sophisticated involving high technology and multiple methods of obtaining information for computer processing and delivery to governmental consumers who make foreign policy and national security decisions. Nevertheless, technology does not replace feet-on-the-ground needed to gather human intelligence for corroboration of collected information.

Technology in use today and under continuing refinement could regulate our lives to an "Orwellian hell" if unchecked. The question is whether our Constitutional protections under the Bill of Rights can keep up with technological advances that may compromise them.

518

Recently, the government has proposed storing data on American systems gathered from multiple sources, even though no terrorism is involved. They would be allowed to keep information on you and me for seven years to be "data mined" via software algorithms—for what purpose?[688]

Just imagine drones controlled by local governmental authorities over-flying your back yard. Everything we do or say can be monitored in one fashion or another not only by government but also by private entities as evidenced by the recent Rupert Murdock News Corporation hacking scandal. We have quickly moved from the "analog" world to the world of computer bits and bytes, meaning that data can be stored to be quickly retrieved using filters against matching keywords or "trigger" word criteria. The question is, who would want to abuse the process, and whether the "information grab" would be so overwhelming as to make it useless—unless specifically targeted—a data glut problem! The public has little or no awareness of the fact that "everything communicated" can be vacuumed up by one technology method or another for storage and processing. We have now learned that millions of cell phones have embedded software to track our location, key strokes, text messages, etc. We are surrendering our freedoms for technical convenience, comfort and a false sense of security. Nevertheless, one needs to be "connected" in a global world we are now living in—a trade off—is it worth the downside?

In a recent *Wall Street Journal* article, it was reported that the NSA and other intelligence officials are petitioning President Obama to play a bigger role in protecting computer networks in the U.S, an expansion of NSA powers into the domestic forum. What are the checks-and-balances for the protection of civil liberties? Apparently, the Department of Homeland Security will get the primary role for handling cyber security, with the NSA providing intelligence and technical assistance—the government gets bigger and bigger.[689] All of this may be well meaning, however, the problem begins when mindless bureaucrats get their hands on the controls with no supervision. Is a National Security Court the answer or would it simply become a "star chamber"?[690]

The fact is that government wants and has the computing power to manage most of the data glut. The process just became more interesting in the post 9/11 environment when President George W. Bush announced on February 17, 2005, his choice of John Negroponte to be the new intelligence czar in charge of 15 different government intelligence agencies. Perhaps more interesting was the fact that Bush nominated Lt. General Michael Hayden, former head of the National Security Agency, to be Negroponte's deputy, subsequently to becoming director of the CIA in 2006, now retired. Hayden was the longest serving director of the secretive code-breaking agency, the NSA. His presence may have been intended to assure others who may be concerned with both the idea of an "intelligence czar", and the person nominated to be the first occupant of that position[691]. James Bamford has credited Hayden with running a more open public relations orientated operation in part because of the need for public support of his huge budget—secret as it is.

The 1960s was the height of the "Cold War". There were numerous intelligence gathering events and covert operations, known, partially known or still unknown occurring in that context. There was the Bay-of-Pigs

520

fiasco involving the aborted CIA program to invade Cuba in 1961, followed by the 1962 Cuban missile crisis, the assassination of President Kennedy with allegations of CIA involvement; and of course, continuing Vietnam escalation with carpet-bombing as the method of operation, riots in American cities, and conflict in the Middle East. One might say an interesting time that continues to this day, but with more complications, and perhaps fewer chances for lasting peace—the world becomes more dangerous, not less so.

It was a time of deadly nuclear brinksmanship and the doctrine of "mutually assured destruction" know by the acronym MAD, in short, nuclear intimidation and blackmail. We tend to think in terms of the known in the current context, with limited awareness of a near nuclear confrontation with the Soviet Union during the Cuban nuclear missile confrontation between President Kennedy and Khrushchev. We have been looking at another nuclear confrontation that was every bit as dangerous, but which is little known by the general public—that was during the Six-Day War—the potential for confrontation had been downplayed.

Cold War competitiveness was in full swing, with us bogged down in Vietnam, and the Soviets wanted to get us further bogged down in the Middle East. A CIA memo report addressed to the White House Situation Room, and dated June 1967, from a Soviet informant, stated, "The Soviet replied affirmatively, stating that the USSR had wanted to create another trouble spot for the United States in addition to that already existing in Vietnam. The Soviet aim was to create a situation in which the U.S. would become seriously involved, economically, politically, and possibly even militarily and in which the U.S. would suffer serious political reverses as a result of its siding against the Arabs."[692]

The memo further stated that the "Soviet" thought that Nasser "must go" and that his own disillusioned people would most likely assassinate him in the near future. He further stated that the Arabs are incapable of unity even when their vital interests are at stake.

This memo would appear to be an example of CIA HUMINT. It contains the name "Rostow assumed to be Walter Rostow, President Johnson's chief advisor and special assistant. Soviet activities in the Middle East were becoming a major concern leading up to the Six-Day War.

Still reeling from Sputnik, and the U-2 shoot down of Francis Gary Powers, national security groups were making plans to re-group. The Russian space coup with Sputnik I tended to open the Congressional purse strings.[693] The result was a major effort to improve U.S. intelligence gathering capabilities. The result was many events with untold stories, many heroes, and unfortunately, resulting in many dead American service personnel. One can visit the Cold War Museum website to read about the missing-in-action or MIAs, by name and by incident.[694]

In my visit to the 37th Liberty Veterans Association reunion, I was able to pick up a Cold War Memorial Calendar—2004 Edition, and noted some of the comments on it, one of which is as follows:[695]

"We have a patrol tomorrow that takes us across the Bering Strait (sic) and around the Russian coast as far as we can go. I certainly

522

don't look forward to them 'cause flying conditions' here are absolutely terrible."

Navy Lt. Jesse Beasley wrote this to his wife in a 1953 letter, he and his crew were subsequently lost on a mission over the Yellow Sea January 4, 1954. The calendar further contains the following comment on the backside:

The Cold War – It wasn't just "ideological struggle"

It wasn't just "peaceful competition"

It wasn't just "Olympic Boycotts"

It was serious, deadly, and global. It last over 45 years

The North Koreans attacked and captured the USS *Pueblo* AGER-2 in January 23, 1968 with the lost of Seaman Duane Hodges and the crew of 82 held captives for 11 months. The *Pueblo* incident fully exposed our SIGINT seagoing platform programs and actually resulted in the end of that platform program. This was less than a year after the attack on the *Liberty*. The same tendencies to retaliate by the JCS were there but again held in check. Other incidents can be cited remembering these were casualties, not of an ally, but cold war adversaries:

January 4, 1954: Navy PV2-5 aircraft lost off Korea, 10 killed in action.

January 10, 1965: U-2C shot down over China, 1 killed in action.

April 15, 1969: US Navy EC-121 shot down over Sea of Japan, 31 killed.

523

Each is a story in itself. One day I picked up our Sunday newspaper to read a local article about another Cold War incident. The article dealt with an Air Force crewmember, Clifford H. Mast, having been shot down during the Korean War on July 4, 1952.[696] He was shot down and believed captured with information of what happened to him suppressed by the Air Force, according to the article. Recently the federal Defense Prisoner of War/Missing Personnel Office enlisted the help of Russian archivists in researching the cases of 10 missing U.S. Servicemen including Mast.[697]

Mast, born April 25, 1927, originally enlisted in the navy, but later joined the Air Force and was serving on a RB-29 Super-fortress reconnaissance plane on a mission when shot down.[698] "So Tired" was the plane's name. He had joined the military at Fairchild AFB, Spokane, Washington October 8, 1951 and eventually joined the 91st Strategic Reconnaissance Squadron, the "Demon Chasers". On that fateful day, he flew out of Yokota Air Base Japan in the nose gunner position. He had volunteered for the flight, as it was not his regular assignment. A MiG-15 shot down the plane. The RB-29 was no match for the MiG-15, subsequently; jet-powered aircraft eventually replaced the prop-driven plane. Of the 13-man crew, two are listed as MIA with no body returned-BNR. Eleven were repatriated at the end of the war, but the status of Mast and a Sergeant Albright remains a mystery. Did Mast manage to bail out? According to the DPMO there are 7500 unaccounted for veterans of the Korean War.

A deciphered telegram turned over to the U.S. after the fall of the Soviet Union says the crew admitted to dropping spies onto the territories of China, Tibet and the

Soviet Union. It further mentions the use of radiological, bacteriological and chemical warfare allegations, which the U.S. has repeatedly denied. Information indicates he may have survived the shoot-down. The gist is that it is the U.S. government, for whatever reason, that is the obstructionist in the search for information on the Clifford Mast mystery—this according to the newspaper article—after all these years.

With the continued passage of time the focus is on the tragic family matter of trying to learn what happened to a relative—the sense of longing and lack of resolution. Cousin Amy of Spokane, Washington says "Everyone must have a purpose in life, and Clifford is mine...I will keep pursuing it until he comes home or his death is rectified."[699] Notwithstanding the passage of years, Amy's quest is to bring certainty and resolution to her relative's story. A fate faced by many loved ones and families of the Cold War Heroes!

The unresolved issue is whether Mast stayed with the plane and died in the crash, or whether he was able to parachute and land alive to be captured. The story of Mast, and "So Tired", RB-29 #44-61727, can be found on the rb-29.net website.

The unit was called upon to conducted psychological leaflet drops with its assigned RB-29 aircraft. Not only did the 91st drop Korean "Psyops" leaflets throughout the Korean peninsula and into Manchuria and China; Russian language leaflets were dropped as it was suspected that advisers from the Soviet Union were assisting the Chinese and North Korean communist forces. In addition to bomb damage assessments, targeting and aerial photography for the Bomber Command and FEAF, the 91st conducted Electronic Intelligence (ELINT) and

525

"ferret" missions in theater mapping RADAR emissions of air defense sites.[700]

A mission description is as follows:[701]

> Our job was to take aerial photos of the suspect airfield and not be caught. There were MiG fighter aircraft at the base, which worried us somewhat. The course we were to fly was designed to imitate a Northwest Airlines flight en-route to Alaska, a flight that might have drifted off course. Hopefully, we would appear to be committing a harmless violation of their coastal waters.
> Just opposite Sakhalin, still beyond the 12-mile statutory limit usually respected by international law, we applied more power, increasing our airspeed and turned toward our target. We began a wide sweeping turn, hoping it would show on the Russian radar that we were turning back on course. At the same time, our turn permitted our K-18 and K-20 wide-angle cameras plenty of opportunity to take photos of the suspect airfield below. [702]
>
> Six months later, our intelligence people advised me that nothing unusual had been discovered by the photos we took that day. All the film was destroyed and not a word was mentioned of our flight, except perhaps in this writing.

The information on the rb-29 website is a collection of comments by various contributors trying to piece together an historical context and consequently, the stories may be fragmented.

Soviet transcripts of the event follows: "...elements of the 351st lAP encountered a USAF B-29 while on a combat sortie. At 2246 hours, Major Anatoly Karelin (Russian Ace) observed one B-29 in the searchlight beams near Khakusen at an altitude of 7200 meters and attacked it. Orienting on the flaming aircraft, the pilot conducted three more attacks and shot down the B-29. The bomber started to break up midair and fell two kilometers west of Khakusen. Four engines and the burnt fuselage were found at the crash site. Eight crewmembers of the B-29 were taken prisoner by our Chinese comrades."[703]

Fig. 20, RB-29 from Wikipedia, the free encyclopedia.

Boeing RB-29 (s/n 44-61727) from the 91st Strategic Reconnaissance Squadron over Korea.

Every month of the calendar previously referred to reflects multiple similar incidents occurring over the Cold War years. Probably the most published event in this category was the shoot-down over Sverdlovsk, USSR on May 1, 1960 of U-2 pilot Francis Gary Powers.

At the time there was the fear of the so-called "missile gap"; consequently, new technologies that allowed better

527

surveillance and early warning were budgeted for.[704] The U-2 program was one of them. It was also a time of high paranoia.

The U-2 spy plane was a super-secret program of sending a high-flying pilot controlled imaging platform over the Soviet Union taking pictures of strategic targets. It was developed by Lockheed Aircraft Company in Burbank, California and would be able to fly and glide for almost eleven hours.[705] It could cover more than five thousand miles at heights greater than 65,000 feet. President Eisenhower, the World War II Supreme Commander in Europe, knew the value of overhead reconnaissance from bombing runs over Germany. With the lack of aerial intelligence of the Soviet Union, he ordered the CIA to do something about it. The U-2 project followed.[706]

Richard M. Bissell, the economist and innovator of the U-2 program wanted a reconnaissance platform that did not have to skirt borders but could over-fly the target country, hopefully out of missile range. Powers' flight was the twenty-fourth such mission over the USSR since the program was started four years prior.[707]

Powers was one of the most experienced U-2 pilots with close to 600 hours at the controls. His shoot-down would have major impact on the Cold War and our intelligence gathering programs. There had been a "thawing" in relations between the Eisenhower administration and that of Nikita S. Khrushchev in the late 1950s. Khrushchev visited the United States in September of 1959. He invited Eisenhower, his children and grandchildren to visit the Soviet Union.[708]

528

The shoot down resulted in an end to the thawing and resumption of tensions with Khrushchev going to the United Nations to denounce the over-flights. Eisenhower's administration had been caught in a boldface lie claiming an American cover-story of the plane being on weather reconnaissance and straying off course—a classic case of "blow-back".[709]

Eisenhower took personal "political" responsibility with the brunt of the fault falling on the shoulders of the CIA. The over-flights were temporarily halted at a critical time, but previous flights proved highly valuable in obtaining information on the Soviet manned bomber and intercontinental ballistic missile programs along with other much valuable information.

The U.S. government had to admit that a worldwide network run by the CIA was able to penetrate the Soviet Union, as Eisenhower put it; it was a "vital but distasteful necessity in order to avert another Pearl Harbor."[710]

Gary Powers survived to be put on trial, subsequently to be released in a prisoner trade.[711] The episode was extremely embarrassing for the Eisenhower administration, and resulted in major changes to our intelligence gathering programs. The move would be toward space with the eventual launch of so-called sophisticated spy satellites such as *Gambit* and *Corona*.

As a side note of the interplay between technology and human intelligence, it was contended that the Soviets might have learned about Powers' U-2 over-flights from one of two employees in contact with Soviet agents, who had requested and received information on the U-2 flights. They were NSA employees who apparently failed to return from vacation and defected to the Soviet Union.[712]

This mystery pertaining to the Power's shoot-down is further compounded by the contention of author Phillip Nelson that Lee Harvey Oswald and James Jesus Angleton are referenced as both connected to this incident.[713] It is suggested that the reader Google the combined names of Francis Gary Powers and Lee Harvey Oswald for further controversial information.

> It was likely that the shoot-down of the U-2 incident caused Angleton to facilitate Oswald's quick reentry into the United States in 1962 for the express purpose of using him as a "patsy" for the original plan to simulate an assassination of Kennedy as a pretext for an invasion of Cuba.

The U-2 as an imagery intelligence-gathering vehicle would prove to be important in other photoreconnaissance events. One we know about from history as being the Cuban nuclear missile crisis with the Soviet Union, and the other would be the lesser-known matter of the first observations and information having to do with Israel's nuclear bomb development program in the Negev desert near Beer Sheba at Dimona. Seymour Hersh in his book, *The Samson Option,* reports in detail how the U-2 was used to discover and watch the "deep dig" and pouring of lots of concrete in the middle of the desert.[714] The Dimona story will become a big factor in trying to understanding the events that led to the attack on the USS *Liberty*. We have already addressed that in part.

Photo interpretation of the Israeli complex development was sensitive because any photo interpretation no matter how sophisticated needed to be coordinated with HUMINT—human intelligence. The sensitivity was due to the special relationship and coordination between the CIA and Israeli Mossad, the latter handling the interrogations of immigrants from behind the Iron Curtain migrating into Israel, for the CIA. This is a reference to the early comment about the U.S. relying on Israeli Cold War intelligence. It appears that we provided money and equipment as part of the quid-pro-quo. This human intelligence was needed to properly interpret what was being seen in the U-2 imagery as Soviet nuclear facilities were carefully camouflaged. An Israeli refugee's random comment often resulted in a major discovery.[715]

As a hint of the "sticky-wicket" involving anything about Israel, Hersh reports that Arthur C. Lundahl, the CIA photographic expert was never asked to do a follow up on his Israeli intelligence findings regarding the Israeli Dimona nuclear project—there was "no additional requirement. No request for details." In fact, added Lundahl, over the next years, "nobody came back to me, *ever*, on Israel. I was never asked to do a follow-up on any of the Israeli briefings."[716] Of course, briefings were for Eisenhower, Allen Dulles, the CIA Director and John Foster Dulles, the Secretary of State. This is amazing when one thinks about, but it is only the tip of the iceberg to come. Reasons for this attitude on the part of high-level government officials can be speculated to include genuine sympathy for the Jewish Holocaust survivors, and our Cold War intelligence needs.

Finally, at a point in construction of Dimona, while imagery told interpreters there were two sites under construction, the second being the chemical re-processing facility to make bombs, the intelligence gathering process was incomplete. Our getting physical access to the site was more than problematic. Since, even to this day, Israel denies having WMDs, there would be ramifications for the USS *Liberty* as we have already seen.

Programs following in the path of the U-2 included the SR-71 Blackbird, noted for its sooty, heat-resistant titanium skin, which glows cherry-red when it flashes across the sky at Mach 3.32. As successor to the vulnerable U-2, it can photograph 100,000 square miles of the earth's surface in less than an hour from the height of more than 85,000 feet. In addition to imagery, with its SIGINT sensors, the plane can chart electronic battlefields and peer over a border with side-looking radar.[717]

While the U-2 was primarily an imagery program, subsequent programs like the SR-71 included the development of low orbit satellites of a group called "Key Hole" whose mission was to take photos of ground-based targets with astounding resolution. They also would later include a SIGNIT function as needed. Two such programs were the Corona and Gambit program as noted. While the Corona program has been declassified, the Gambit missions are still for the most part classified.

This technology developed in the 1960s allowed for missions days or weeks long. Film packets would be dropped from the satellite and "hook" by a plane or picked up from the sea for delivery and processing.

However, the real workhorses were the "SIGINT/ELINT" EC-47s, fat EC-130s, and the hunchback EC-121s. These planes were limited by the fact that they required full crews of communication technicians and had limited time "on station". Further, they were vulnerable to harassing flights of adversaries and susceptible to being shot down as noted above in the reference to the Cold War Museum events.

The main point to remember is that now our intelligence-gathering machine knows few limits and is multi-faceted. At any given point in time resource might be "layered" with low flying planes, SR-71s at higher altitudes and satellites above them. This gigantic vacuum cleaner would be supplemented with sea going ships and submarines as well as shore based listening stations and of course HUMINT. As a side note, the U-2 saw additional service in Iraq in recent years helping UN inspectors look for that countries' hidden WMD program.

Foreign policy is driven by the value of intelligence gathered via this multitude of methods. Poor intelligence meant and does mean poor governmental decisions having to do with areas of national security. Without getting into the political manipulation of intelligence, this was made extremely clear in the context of 9/11 and the rush to go to war in Iraq.[718]

Photo imagery by itself has limits and this is where the other techniques become complementary with one corroborating the other. Notwithstanding how good the systems are, there are risks: First, that we are smart enough to be able to read the intelligence, and second, that directed covert activities do not run amuck and result in the inevitable "blow-back" when things go wrong. A key issue involving repeated events is the inter-agency sharing of information; failures can be catastrophic.

For the layperson, a brief definitional description of SIGINT is in order. Signals intelligence comprises areas of communication intelligence (COMINT), electronics intelligence (ELINT), foreign instrumentation signals intelligence, and information derived from the collection and processing of non-imagery infrared and coherent light signals.[719] In short, it means to eavesdrop on every form of information transmitted in the electrical environment from telephone calls, to television to radiation of atomic explosions to communications over various frequencies involving any activity related to national security.[720]

In the world of intelligence there is a constant struggle and need to find a balance as to what is acceptable in a free society when there is a need for secrecy, where there are "hidden or dark budgets", monies off the books so to speak that are hard to account for. Lacking Congressional oversight things can turn to the dark side—the checks-and-balances issue.

The fact is that our freedoms as we know and expect them are in a delicate balance with the government's attitude being "trust us". Vigilance of government is really the key word, and nothing should be taken for granted because the abuses will eventually become known. When Congress passes a bill like the Patriot Act without fully reading or understand it, then we are in trouble as a nation. Presidents tend to want complete power to deal with threats falling on their shoulders. G. W. Bush's attitude was that he was the "great decider", a dangerous frame of mind for one as powerful as the President.

One non-governmental organization delving into secret government files is the National Security Archive Project at George Washington University. A look at their

534

website will reveal many previously secret documents and programs.

The most recent disclosure by the GWU-NSAP, dated April 3, 2012, has to do with a previously secret memo drafted by Philip D. Zelikow, counselor to then-Secretary of State Condoleezza Rice. His memo had to do with his challenging the Department of Justice's approval of CIA "enhanced interrogation methods. The G.W. Bush administration wanted all copies of the Zelikow memo destroyed, however, pursuant to an FOIA request to the State Department, a copy was found and published by GWU-NSAP on its website.[721]

Notwithstanding the risks, political and otherwise, the need for accurate and up to date intelligence is a critical commodity for any commander-in-chief. Multiple sources are the optimum for corroboration purposes. The story of the USS *Liberty* makes the point and also illustrates how control over the intelligence gathering process can be used to suppress the truth from getting into the public forum—clearly an abuse.

It was into such a world that the USS *Liberty AGTR-5* came into existences as a SIGINT floating platform.

For years, the Soviets had been shadowing our fleets with their own fleets of antenna-laden trawlers, or moving into coastal water areas close to military installations to pick up coveted and revealing electronic signals. In April of 1960 the *Vega*, a six-hundred-ton Soviet trawler with eleven antennas protruding cruised down the East Coast to within an intercept range of the naval base at Norfolk, Virginia.[722]

535

Author James Bamford proceeds to tell how Frank Raven in charge of G Group at the NSA succeeded to a new responsibility for monitoring 100s of nations rather than monitoring only one. While the Soviet Union had been ringed with listening stations there were many gaps as to other countries. For example, the NSA had only two listening posts in all of Africa—near Asmara on the Eritrean plateau in Ethiopia and Sidi Yahia in the Moroccan desert.[723] To overcome this lack, the NSA decided to copy the Russians and build its own fleet of eavesdropping ships. *Liberty's* initial assignment was to the African coast.

Once approval for the plan was obtain, Raven and others began looking into "slow moving tubs" that could spend a lot of time at sea. These ships could fill the void left by planes with short "on station" time that had to be scheduled with appropriate relief planes. Several ships were commissioned including the *Private Jose F. Valdez* (T-AG 169), *Sergeant Joseph E. Muller* (T-AG 171), and the *Lieutenant James E. Robinson* (T-AG 170). A second generation of ships would be developed that included the U.S.S. *Oxford* (AGTR-1), U.S.S. *Georgetown* (AGTR 2), and the U.S.S. *Jamestown* (AGTR 3). The final two ships to round out the fleet were the U.S.S. *Belmont* (AGTR 4) and the U.S.S. *Liberty* (AGTR 5). Our focus here has been on the USS *Liberty* (AGTR-5).

Throughout the '60s into the present day, the intelligence needs are the same, but the technologies have evolved with greater sophistication. The digital world has allowed for the creation of tools for remote monitoring and control that are truly the fulfillment of earlier space-age dreams. However, the reliance on electronic methods to the exclusion or undercutting of human intelligence carries as a heavy burden as noted in

536

the U-2 case involving Gary Powers. Some government agency or individual will always be involved in traditional counter-spying capers like the Jonathan Powers case.

The *Liberty* story is worthy of any spy scandal ever known, with evolving claims of murder and war crimes, cover-up, blackmail and certainly the hint of treason.

The June 8th 1967 attack on the *USS Liberty* by Israeli aircraft and motor torpedo boats is complicated by allegations against the crew of being less than creditable witnesses because of their trauma, and anti-Semitic for their charges and recriminations against the State of Israel.

Israel acknowledged the attack when caught red-handed but plead error and a case of mistaken identity. President Lyndon Baines Johnson stating, "He would not embarrass an ally", quickly shoved the matter under the rug from a "political standpoint". Did he really make that statement or is it mythology? What followed was a "sanitizing" of all existing records of the attack in the context of our covert involvement, leaving open the question of an Israeli motive, and the reasons and motives for the cover-up by the United States government.

Pursuant to a State Department "managed" settlement, the families of dead crew members did receive compensation as did the crewmembers who were wounded. It would not be until many years later under the Carter administration that damages were paid for the ship's loss.

The damage to the USS *Liberty* was so extensive that the ship was decommission, scrapped, while crewmembers went about their damaged lives, and moved on under the intimidation of the Navy with a threat of repercussions if the matter was openly discussed. The ship's commanding officer would be awarded the Congressional Medal of Honor in a backhanded fashion—not in a traditional White House ceremony with presentation by the President himself.

It is very ironic that President Johnson would so slight the Captain and his crew over how the Medal of Honor ceremony was held, considering it is alleged that Johnson, while a member of Congress, received a Silver Star fraudulently. The medal was awarded when Johnson took an airplane ride during the Second World War while on a fact-finding tour in the Pacific, claiming he came under fire for a few minutes that did not happen—a reported lie like so much of his life.[724] It is interesting that the article dealing with Johnson is on the historical website of B-26 Marauder.

Congress would for the first time "refuse" to investigate circumstances surrounding the attack, looking into only certain matters dealing with communication failures. The claim would be that continuing Congresses were "bought off" by the Israeli government and Jewish lobby in this country.

Not everyone remained silent. In 1979, survivor Jim Ennes would publish his book *Attack on the Liberty*, and a campaign would begin with the formation of the Liberty Veterans Association in 1982 for the purpose of getting the *Liberty's* story told and petitioning Congress and the President for an investigation of the attack—all to naught.

In 2004, the 37th reunion of the LVA (Liberty Veterans Association) surviving crewmembers and

538

families was held in Nebraska City, Nebraska at the end of May. Again, the traditional ceremony of calling out the names of the dead would proceed with survivor Glenn Oliphant calling the names as he stood in a dark suit at the podium. Seated at a front table would be survivor Lloyd Painter tolling the ship's bell. Survivors, friends and supporters, and family members would come to front of the room and place flags represent the 34 dead crewmembers on to a pegboard:

William Allenbaugh

Philip Armstrong

Gary Blanchard

Allen Blue

. . . .

For a complete list of the USS *Liberty* dead crewmembers, go to the following website: http://www.ussliberty.org/casualty.htm.

The Liberty Veterans Association, LVA, had been formed in 1982, fifteen years after the assault, at their meeting in Washington D.C. Their goal was and is to obtain a Congressional investigation into the attack and to bring the true story of the USS *Liberty* and heroic crew to the attention of the American people where the media has failed them.

It was obvious that the years have taken their toll in terms of frustration, anger, fatigue and resignation among some; still others wanted to carry on a fight for the ever-elusive justice.

Obviously, notwithstanding the cover-up and certainly because of it, the USS *Liberty* story has attracted the attention of many authors in terms of complete books, and short references to the events in many more books and articles, including television documentary videos.

Judge Cristol's book, *The Liberty Incident* published in 2002 would breathe new life into the story of the attack, and galvanize the surviving crew members, families and friends to a new breath of life to deal with what would be called the "Cristol Travesty".

The *Liberty* saga continues to this day and perhaps will never fade from memory or history because the plight caused by two governments and their representatives is certainly without a doubt tragic, unprecedented in history, and calls for a full and complete investigation to clear the air.

To understand the *Liberty* story is to understand our Middle East foreign policy, the strange relationship with the State of Israel, the infiltration of the United States government by individuals who do not have America's interest at the forefront. The story is complicated by the unique place in history of the State of Israel and the very real interests of the Jewish people to be free from discrimination, hate, and fear of another Holocaust.

Unfortunately, the desire for peace and security in a dangerous land can lead to many complications for those countries and peoples of good will and concern. If not furthered under a sound Rule of Law regimen, the efforts to attain illusive security will degenerate into continuing war and cycle of violence as has in fact been evidenced for almost six decades of continuing strife, with no foreseeable relief in sight.

The story of the *Liberty* is rife with many elements including nuclear blackmail, political corruption, and the question of treason and crimes. It includes manipulation, super-power ultimatums and bluffs, and covert plans still secret today. The survivors, family and friends will never have peace and justice until the United States Congress faces up to its responsibility to represent the citizens of this country and not protect certain special interests no matter what the consequences may be.

It should be noted that the crew achieved several awards for their efforts in saving the ship and crew; nevertheless, these honors while not to be diminished in terms of what they represent were subsequently tarnished by the manner in which they were awarded. In recognition of their effort in this single action, they were ultimately awarded, collectively, one Medal of Honor, two Navy Crosses, eleven Silver Stars, twenty Bronze Stars (with "V" device), nine Navy Commendation Medals, and two hundred and four Purple Hearts. In addition, the ship was awarded the Presidential Unit Citation.[725] Captain William L. McGonagle's Medal of Honor was awarded not at the White House but at a ceremony at the Washington Naval Yard.

Jim Ennes reports he received a letter from Captain McGonagle notifying him and inviting him to attend a ceremony in the Naval Yard where he would receive the Medal of Honor from the Secretary of Navy, not the President of the United States, who in fact actually awarded the medal. Ennes noted the short notice of the invitation and the fact that usually the MOH is awarded at the White House by the President with "great fanfare and elaborate ceremony"—"McGonagle's medal should have been awarded with no less pomp." Further, Ennes claims that the State Department asked the Israeli ambassador if

541

his government had any objection to the award and was advised no.[726] Because of the administration's sensitivity to Israeli interests, the ceremony was low keyed. What a slap in the face and degradation. The Captain was to assume command of a newly constructed ammunition ship, the USS *Kilauea*.

Citation awards did not make any mention of the attack as being conducted by the government and military forces of Israel.

Like the *Flying Dutchman,* the failure of ultimate justice will doom the legend of the ship to forever sail through time as a significant sign of disrespect for our honorable servicemen and servicewomen knowing that politicians will in the end sacrifice them for their own political careers and self interests. If a nation expects its service men and women to be ready to provide the ultimate sacrifice for their country and the common good, then the politicians and leaders have to acknowledge they have a covenant not to allow those lives to be wasted and turned into meaningless fodder.

Epilogue

It has been some 44 years since the attack on the *Liberty*. There has been no Congressional investigation into the circumstances of the attack itself, or the subsequent cover-up by the Johnson Administration and subsequent administrations, notwithstanding new evidence. With the passage of time and the death of many key participants it is unlikely that such a "new look" will occur. President Johnson did not run for reelection, and is deceased; and Israeli Chief of Staff Rabin was assassinated. Perhaps too much embarrassment is likely to attach to the involved individuals and governments. Generally, covert operations are to remain covered-up in secrecy. Nevertheless, USS *Liberty* survivors, family members and supporters still hope for justice.

One should not be shocked to know that our government has a propensity and "MO" of using denial and cover-up by ordering the destruction of evidence. The most recent example of that has to do with the George Washington University National Security Archive Project release of the "Zelikow Memo" dealing with an internal critique of Bush torture memos declassified, that sheds light on disputes over the treatment of detainees. Allegedly, Bush ordered the destruction of the Zelikow Memo because it took exception with Bush's position on the issue. A copy had been found at the State Department and produced pursuant to a FOIA request. Refer to the GWU-NSAP website at:

.

When we started this *Liberty* saga we posed a number of questions, whether any of them have been satisfactorily answered is up to the reader and subsequent researchers. As the author, I can be reasonably certain that my research provided me with several answers, as follows:

1. Contrary to the claims of Mr. A. Jay Cristol, there has been no forensic investigation of the attack. The FBI investigation into the attack on the USS *Cole* is the benchmark.

2. Key leaders in both the U.S. and Israeli governments, early on, agreed to cast the attack as a case of mistaken identity, even though questions were unanswered—in essence, a political cover-up and insult to American service personnel.

3. Evidence of an "intended attack" has allegedly been lost or destroyed on orders of certain key persons in the Johnson administration, perhaps even by the President himself—not an uncommon action in the political context.

4. Notwithstanding CIA Director Helms' claim, there was a nuclear element to the Six-Day War; and the Soviets were a major player. A potential nuclear catastrophe was averted and the three governments wanted this information withheld from the public. The United States government has acquiesced in Israel's nuclear weapons program.

5. There was a contention between the Johnson administration and the military over whether the attack was an accident or intended; and whether for political reasons President Johnson put the interests of Israel before our national interests.

6. The failure of subsequent presidents and congresses to call for an investigation has been and is a political decision, not one based on evidence or the record. The evidence and record has never been established and most likely will not be.

7. The U.S. government effort to remove Nasser failed. The Israelis out maneuvered both the United States and Soviets and cemented certain land gains as was their original objective—land gains that are still a contention in terms of Middle East peace.

The Six-Day War was one of those major events that occur when people and governments are not ready to rectify an injustice. The failure to provide for a Palestinian state—something that should have been resolved in the context of acknowledging the State of Israel. After all that is the supposed objective of the Middle East peace process. Resulting from that war were new borders favoring Israel from a military advantage, and land development process. The Sinai was handed back to Egypt but the land gains in the Golan Heights remains along with portions of Old Jerusalem and the West Bank. Additionally, the Gaza strip remains a human concentration camp and breeding grounds for potential radicals and terrorists, and a sore public relations trap for Israel. Israel has become more isolated and continues in a state of war with its Arab neighbors, some who continue to deny Israel's existence as a sovereign state.

Since that War the United States has become the major arms supplier to Israel and the guarantor of its security, as well as being Israel's prime veto agent in the UN. One of the major offerings of the United States to any friendly country is to put it under the nuclear umbrella of the U.S. Israel, in fact, does not need that cover, as it is a major nuclear power onto itself with missiles, aircraft, and submarines able to serve as nuclear delivery vehicles on an extended regional basis. The problem is keeping that force in check—a responsibility of the United States as part of its Middle East foreign policy—though not publically acknowledged.

Obviously, the area is vital to the U.S. interests because of oil, and is yet very unstable as evidenced by the "Arab Spring". Our ability to be the honest broker is compromised by our unyielding support for Israel at a time when it has become more internationally isolated; and because of our support for entrenched dictators in area counties. As those dictators fall, we are confronted with a dilemma to support democracy trends versus the propensity for stability, which causes us to support other area dictators.

While the true story of the *Liberty* and the Six-Day War may not be fully known, or understood, it is clear that there were broad ramifications evidenced by the fact that CIA Director Richard Helms advised President Johnson that there were no nukes in the area according to his knowledge; yet, General Wheeler was unsure of that. Consequently, the *Liberty* was dispatched to monitor the combatants in a duplicitous war where our objective was to get rid of Nasser, and Israel was more interested in doing its own thing to make it more secure with certain land grabs. We were the Israeli's insurance policy in case of intervention by the Soviets. Most likely, there was a

546

joint CIA/Mossad covert operation to accomplish mutual objectives—still undisclosed. While this compromises the U.S. position in terms of disclosing information dealing with those events, it boils down to us being blackmailed to keep quiet on the *Liberty* matter— shoveled under the rug of national security. The *Liberty* tragedy evidenced a disconnect between our political establishment and the military, almost as significant as the President Truman and General MacArthur contention over the Korean War and MacArthur's desire to nuke airbases in Manchuria and Shantung, precipitating a constitutional crisis between the President and the military. Truman prevailed and fired MacArthur.

One final comment: Middle East peace is so precarious that the U.S. must be ready to act as a check-and-balance on events in the area. While Israel has said it will not be the first to introduce nuclear weapons in the area, we must continue to monitor regional events to make sure that does not happen, as it would be fatal to our national interest of protecting the oil resources of the area. We have *defacto* become the guarantor of the global economy. This very issue is now before us as the Israeli Prime Minister is calling for a preemptive strike on Iranian nuclear facilities—history will be unfolding before our very eyes—with ancient enmity. While we, as a nation, are not associated with the ancient enmity found in the Middle East, we are in the most recent context because of CIA intervention in Iranian affairs over the past decades.

While the *Liberty* never fully implemented its mission, today's technology provides a broad-spectrum capability to monitor activities and events in the area. Relying on Israel to provide HUMINT is a flawed intelligence policy.

A support flotilla of ships recently attempted to break the Israeli blockage of Gaza wherein *Liberty* survivor Joe Meadors was on one of the ships and was temporarily arrested—kind of a spite of Israel. The nation of Turkey, a U.S. ally, suffered several civilian deaths on that flotilla and has diminished its relationship with the Israeli government. Will Israel attack Iran's nuclear facilities and will the U.S. support or block that threat? A recent, January 14, 2012, Wall Street Journal online article notes: *U.S. Warns Israel on Strike: Officials Lobby Against Attack on Iran as Military Leaders Bolster Defenses.* The U.S. wants time for sanctions to take hold, warns Iran against provocative actions in the Straits of Hormuz, and needs to safeguard U.S facilities in the region. Israel has been reported to say it will not tell the U.S. in advance of any attack she may make against Iran. The point is that Israel will do its own thing as a sovereign nation. Of course, we have the ability to monitor any war-like-action. The full story has yet to play out! Are we a victim and captive of our own Middle East foreign policy—just as was the *Liberty*?

ENDNOTES

1 Johnson, Bridget, *Gadhafi, Son Charged with Crimes Against Humanity*, June 27, 2011,

http://worldnews.about.com/b/2011/06/27/gadhafi-son-charged-with-crimes-against-humanity.htm

2 Kelly, Martin, *Lyndon B. Johnson – Thirty-Sixth President of the United States,*

http://americanhistory.about.com/od/lyndonbjohnson/p/plbjohnso n.htm.

3 Memmott, Mark, *WikiLeaks' Assange May Be 'Talking Himself' Into Espionage Act Charge* , http://www.npr.org/blogs/thetwo-way/2010/11/30/131690619/wikileaks-assange-may-be-talking-himself-into-espionage-act-charges

4 WikiLeaks website: http://wikileaks.org/

5 Memmott, Mark, *40 Years Later, Pentagon Papers Being Declassified; Go Online Today*, June 13, 2011, http://www.npr.org/blogs/thetwo-way/2011/06/13/137148143/40-years-later-pentagon-papers-being-declassified-go-online-today

6 This arose as a quotation by John Emerich Edward Dalberg Acton, first Baron Acton (1834–1902). The historian and moralist, who was otherwise known simply as Lord Acton, expressed this opinion in a letter to Bishop Mandell Creighton in 1887,

http://www.phrases.org.uk/meanings/absolute-power-corrupts-absolutely.html

7 de la Vega, Elizabeth, *United States v. George W. Bush et al.*, Seven Stories Press, 2006.

8 Bugliosi, Vincent, *The Prosecution of George W. Bush for Murder*, May 19, 2008, http://www.huffingtonpost.com/vincent-bugliosi/the-prosecution-of-george_b_102427.html

9 Human Rights Watch, *United States: Investigate Bush, Other Top Officials for Torture*, July 11, 2011,

http://www.hrw.org/en/node/100390
10 Wikipedia, *Extraordinary rendition by the United States*,

http://en.wikipedia.org/wiki/Extraordinary_rendition_by_the_United _States
11 Findlaw, United States v. Nixon, 418 U.S. 683 (1974),

http://caselaw.lp.findlaw.com/scripts/getcase.pl?court=us&vol=418& invol=683
12 Ennes, James M. Jr., *Assault on the Liberty: The True Story of the Israeli Attack on an American Intelligence Ship*, Raintree Press, 1979. The ship was official designated AGTR-5, with the letters referring to her as an Auxiliary General Technical Research ship. Foreign governments would find this designation less uncomfortable than referring to her as "spy ship", or intelligence gathering ship when visiting their ports.
13 Letter to the Honorable Rob Simmons, House of Representatives, dated March 16, 2005, from Department of Navy, Office of the Judge Advocate General, signed by Jane G. Dalton, Captain, JAGC, U.S. Navy, Assistant Judge Advocate General.
14 Admiral Staring letter to Secretary of the Navy, dated 7/27/2005:

http://www.ussliberty.org/staringhilllettertosecnav.htm
15 Wikipedia, *Khobar Towers bombing*,

http://en.wikipedia.org/wiki/Khobar_Towers_bombing
16 Letter to the Honorable Rob Simmons, Loc. cit., Office of the Judge Advocate General letter of March 16, 2005.
17 FBI, *USS Cole bombing*, http://www.fbi.gov/about-us/history/famous-cases/uss-cole
18 Wikipedia, *Thomas Hinman Moorer*,

http://en.wikipedia.org/wiki/Thomas_Hinman_Moorer

19 B-29s Over Korea, *Why Truman Fired MacArthur*, http://b-29s-over-korea.com/Why-Truman-Fired-General-MacArthur/Why-Truman-Fired-General-MacArthur.html
20 CTKA, *Citizens For Truth About the Kennedy Assassination*,

http://www.ctka.net/home.html
21 USSLibertyinquiry.com, *Findings of Moorer Independent Commission*,

http://www.usslibertyinquiry.com/evidence/usreports/moorer.html
22 Thorn, Victor, quoting Liberty survivor, Phil Tourney,

http://www.whale.to/c/exclusive_interview.html The quote is attributed to Captain Joseph Tully of the USS *Saratoga*.

23 Jewish Virtual Library, The Entebbe Rescue Mission

http://www.jewishvirtuallibrary.org/jsource/Terrorism/entebbe.html.

24 9/11 Commission Report can be found here:

http://www.911commission.gov/report/911Report.pdf.

25 Thomas, Gordon, *Secret Wars,* page 8, Thomas Dunn Books, 2009.

26 Wikipedia, *Operation Mockingbird*,

http://en.wikipedia.org/wiki/Operation_Mockingbird
27 Office of Historian U.S. Department of State: Use search function for

topics: Six-Day War and USS Liberty, http://history.state.gov/
28 Cristol, A. Jay, *The Liberty Incident: the 1967 Israeli Attack on the U.S.*

Navy Spy Ship, Brassey's Inc., 2002.

29 Libertyincident.com, http://www.thelibertyincident.com/
30 USSLiberty.org, *Boston Declaration*, January 8, 2004,

http://www.ussliberty.org/bostondeclaration.pdf
31 U.S. State Department, Office of the Historian, Document No. 256.

Diplomatic Note From Secretary of State Rusk to the Israeli Ambassador

(Harman), June 10, 1967,

http://history.state.gov/historicaldocuments/frus1964-68v19/d256
32 Geneva Convention: Article 51 Grave breaches to which the preceding

Article relates shall be those involving any of the following acts, if committed against persons or property protected by the Convention: willful killing, torture or inhuman treatment, including biological experiments, willfully causing great suffering or serious injury to body or health, and extensive destruction and appropriation of property, not justified by military necessity and carried out unlawfully and wantonly. Article 52 No High Contracting Party shall be allowed to absolve itself or any other High Contracting Party of any liability incurred by itself or by another High Contracting Party in respect of breaches referred to in the preceding Article. Check this website:

http://www.usslibertyinquiry.com/arguments/american/usposition.html
33 Wikipedia, *Michael Oren*

http://en.wikipedia.org/wiki/Michael_Oren
34 Crewdson, John, Chicago Tribune Online, Special Report, *New revelations in attack on American spy ship*, October 2, 2007,

http://www.chicagotribune.com/services/newspaper/eedition/chi-liberty_tuesoct02,0,43090.story
35 The National Security Archive Project, George Washington University,

http://www.gwu.edu/~nsarchiv/
36 Ennes, page 143.
37 Tourney, Phillip F. and Glenn, Mark, *What I Saw That Day: Israel's June 8th, 1967 Holocaust of US Servicemen Aboard the USS Liberty and its Aftermath*, Liberty Publications, Idaho, Copyright not stated, believed to be 2011, page 62 et seq.
38 Usslibertyinquiry.com, *IDF History Report, June 1967*,

http://www.usslibertyinquiry.com/evidence/israel/idfhr.html
39 Ennes, pages 7, 8.
40 Bamford, James, *The Puzzle Palace: Inside the National Security Agency*, Penguin Books, 1983, page 273.

41 Gerhard, William D, *Attack on a Sigint Collector, the U.S.S. Liberty, Special Series Crisis Collection* Volume 1, William D. Gerhard, Henry W. Millington, NSA/CSS, 1981. Declassified with redactions. See page 2 illustration. Hereafter referred to as the "Gerhard Report".

42 Ennes, page 8.

43 Crewdson, John, *New revelations in attack on American spy ship*. loc. cit.

44 Gerhard Report, Chapter 1, page 1.

45 Ibid.

46 NSA/CSS Declassification and Transparency website:

http://www.nsa.gov/public_info/declass/index.shtml˙
47 Gerhard Report, page 3.

48 Gerhard Report, Chapter II, page 5.

49 Gerhard Report, page 12.

50 Gerhard Report, page 15.

51 Ennes, page 20, footnote No. 1: The first such system was put on the USS *Oxford* (AGTR-1) in February of 1964. It was the brain child of Navy Commander William C. White who would receive a Navy Commendation Medal for his work. When Technical Research Ships like the *Liberty* were taken out of service in 1969, the system was allowed to die. It was calculated that costs were five dollars per word.

52 Wikipedia, *John S. McCain, Jr.*,

http://en.wikipedia.org/wiki/John_S._McCain,_Jr˙
53 Ennes, page 29.

54 Ennes, page 33, footnote No. 2: Vice Admiral William Inman Martin: naval aviator; born 1910; U.S. Naval Academy, class of 1934; promoted to rear admiral July 1, 1959, vice admiral, April 10, 1967. His is a dual command: Commander Sixth Fleet, and Commander, Naval Striking and Support Forces, Southern Europe.

55 Ennes, page 34, footnote No. 3: The issue of when Liberty "chopped" (or changed operational commander) is important as Ennes notes because the Navy explains COMSIXTHFLT's failure to keep Liberty away from the war-zone by telling us that the ship was under control of USCINCEUR until June 7th, and that Admiral Martin, therefore, lacked authority to move her before that date. Liberty officers considered the "chop" date to be June 2nd.

56 Oren, Michael B., *Six Days of War: June 1967 and the Making of the Modern Middle East*, Ballantine Books, 2002, 2003, page 273.

57 Gerhard Report, page 21.

58 Jacobsen, Walter L., Lieutenant Commander JA, GC, USN, *A Juridical Examination of the Israeli Attack on the USS Liberty*, Naval Law Review, Vol. 36, Winter 1986, page 74.

59 Ennes, page 13.

60 Ennes, page 17, footnote No. 5: Comservron Eight message 240020Z May 1967.

61 The official time source for the military: http://tycho.usno.navy.mil/

62 Wikipedia, *El Arish can also be referred to Al Arish.*

http://en.wikipedia.org/wiki/Arish

63 Ennes, page 49.

64 Zulu Time, http://wwp.greenwichmeantime.com/info/zulu.htm

65 Green, Stephen, *Taking Sides: America's Secret Relations with a Militant Israel*, Amana Books, 1988, page 225, 226. Ship's "research dept." detected and ID planes that were directing "fire control radar" at *Liberty*.

66 National Museum of the Air Force: In the early 1960s, the USAF recognized the need for more tactical reconnaissance aircraft to reinforce the RF-101s then in service. The USAF chose a modification of the F-4C fighter. The RF-4C development program began in 1962, and the first production aircraft made its initial flight on May 18, 1964. The Air Force

officially accepted a total of 499 RF-4Cs:

http://www.nationalmuseum.af.mil/factsheets/factsheet.asp?id=414ˈ
67 U.S. State Department, Office of the Historian, *Document 262. Editorial Note,* http://history.state.gov/historicaldocuments/frus1964-68v19/d262ˈ
68 Program on Information Resources Policy, Harvard University, Seminar on Intelligence, command and control:

http://www.pirp.harvard.edu/pubs_pdf/stenbit/stenbit-i03-1.pdf The
Stenbit paper is dated July 2003.

69 Green, page 226.

70 Ennes, see Appendix A for a summary of messages.

71 Rabin, Yitzhak, *Yitzhak Rabin: The Rabin Memoirs,* University of California Press, First Paper Back Edition, 1996, page 110.

72 USSLibertyinquiry.com, *Yerushalmi Preliminary Inquiry Court Report,* page 3. This flight took off at 0410. Ship ID as US Naval supply ship.

http://www.usslibertyinquiry.com/evidence/israel/yerushalmi.pdfˈ
73 Second report from the Nord 2501was received. Ship identified as US Navy supply-type ship. [IDF History Department/Navy HQ War Log.], Cristol Timeline, .pdf file, page 14. Refer to Cristol's timeline at:

http://www.thelibertyincident.com/timeline.htmlˈ
74 Ennes, page 53.

75 Ibid.

76 Ennes, page 53, 54.

77 Yerushalmi Preliminary Inquiry Court Report, page 3. Pilot at first reported being fired on when attempted to ID ship—later discounted when debriefed. Israeli Navy Chief, Admiral Erell, is advised of the "Skunk-C" 0603 identification during a break in action with a suspected Egyptian submarine west of Atlit. He orders it marked green (neutral.) [IDF History

Department.] Per Cristol Time Line. [IDF History Department.] IAF Regional Control 501 receives a pilot's report that a ship spotted some 20 miles north of El Arish had fired on him as he was returning from the Sinai. As a result Israeli destroyers INS Jaffa (D-42) and Eilat (D-40) were ordered south to investigate. [IDF History Department.] Note: The Israeli Navy HQ War Log differs from the IDF History Report. The HQ War Log shows that two destroyers were ordered south at 0606 or 0608. This appears to be an error in either the original text or in translation.

78 Globalsecurity.org: The Israeli underground national military command center, "the Bor," is located beneath the Defense Ministry complex -- the Kirya, Israel's equivalent of the Pentagon -- in the Hakirya district. This facility is within a few hundred feet of the former Prime Minister's office in Tel Aviv:

http://www.globalsecurity.org/wmd/world/israel/tel_aviv.htm

79 Cristol, A. Jay, *The Liberty Incident: the 1967 Israeli Attack on the U.S. Navy Spy Ship*, Brassey's Inc., 2002, page 126: Pennink's notes of the Mintz interview contain a number of assertions made by Mintz that certainly raise questions about his credibility. Mintz told Pennink that "there were three attempts to contact the U.S. Embassy about the ship. He also remembers a phone call that Beni Moti made to the Military Attaché at 9:00 A.M. in the morning." While there is some dispute about whether the IDF ever contacted the U.S. Embassy to inquire about U.S. ships in the area, the call at 9:00 A.M. was just a few minutes after the Liberty arrived at Point Alfa. The air attack began just before 2:00 P.M.

80 Oren, page 264, see endnote 12.

81 Ennes, page 54. Gerhard Report page 33.

82 Ennes, page 55.

83 Oren, page 264.

84 Discovery Channel, *Attack on the Liberty*, Thames TV PLC, London, Transmission: Tuesday, 27th January, 1987, 1030 PM. Refer to written script transcript, page 28, 29.

85 Oren, page 259.

86 Bamford, James, *Body of Secrets: Anatomy of the Ultra-Secret National Security Agency*, Doubleday, 2001, pages 219 and 235.

87 Oren, page 259.

88 Ibid, page 260.

89 Van Creveld, Martin, *The Sword and the Olive: A Critical History of the Israeli Defense Force*, Public Affairs, 1998, page 192. Kindle, e-book version.

90 Hounam, Peter, *Operation Cyanide: Why the Bombing of the USS Liberty Nearly Caused World War III*, Vision, 2003.pages 7 to 13. See last paragraph of book. Why were planes placed on alert that day? The alert was between 2 and 4 AM California time.

91 USSLibertyinquiry.com, *Ram Ron Inquiry Report*, page 2. An English transcript of the Israeli report that is in .pdf format can be found at:

http://www.usslibertyinquiry.com/evidence/israel/ramron.html`
92 IDF GHQ Tel Aviv receives report from Southern Command that a ship is shelling El Arish.

[IDF History Department; US Naval Court of Inquiry/Document 1 of Exhibit 48: DTG 181030Z

June 1967, USDAO Tel Aviv 0928 to White House and others.] Per Cristol Time Line .pdf file. It is also noted that shelling report aroused attention of Supreme Command. Southern Command said shells did not reach coast. Head of Operations wanted report verified and to see if Israeli Naval ships in area. IDF History Report, page 10.

93 Ennes, page 55, 56.

94 IDF History Report, page 10.

95 USSLiberty.org, Naval Court of Inquiry Report, *Lt. George H. Golden Testimony before Naval Court of Inquiry*, page 63: "I have a lounge chair, most of us do have; while laying on my back sunbathing, I noticed a plane flying over. I dozed off, and approximately 25 minutes or so later on, I woke up and saw a plane circling again coming from the port beam, crossing the ship." Here is link to a copy of the NCI report:

http://www.ussliberty.org/nci.htm
96 Gerhard Report, page 23. See note 41 on page 24.

97 Ran Ron Report, page 2. Conflict with IDF History, page 10. Division commander not told about shelling or what to look for.

98 IDF History Report: In fact, the decision to send both aircraft and the torpedo boats was made at 1205 hrs in a joint decision of the air force and naval representative. This information is found in the Yerushalmi Report (the foundation of the IDF History Report) and is referred to (without time reference).

99 Oren, page 264. See endnote 13.

100 Ibid.

101 Ibid.

102 Stefanov, Sergey, Pravda.Ru, *Hot summer of 1967: The Israeli attack on America and the 'Soviet destroyer*, 14.09.2002 Source: Pravda.Ru, English version of Pravda, Russia; http://english.pravda.ru/news/russia/14-09-2002/17971-0/ Note: This reference was formerly posted as: http://english.pravda.ru/main/2002/09/14/36639_.html#, translated by Maria Gousseva.

103 Ginor, Dr. Isabella, *The Russians Were Coming: The Soviet Military Threat in the 1967 Six-Day War*, page 49. See endnote No. 41. Middle East Review of International Affairs, Vol. 4, No. 4 (December 2000).

http://meria.idc.ac.il/journal/2000/issue4/jv4n4a5.html
104 Ibid.

105 Ibid., page 50. See endnote N. 47.

106 Oren, page 91

107 Van Creveld, p. 175. See endnote 84 reference to 3 days later is to after May 11th.

108 Ibid.

109 Ynetnews.com, *Eiland to investigate Ashkenazi over flotilla*: Commission examining chain of flaws leading up to flotilla raid is slated to look into conduct of chief of staff himself, other senior officers during IDF takeover of Marmara: http://www.ynetnews.com/articles/0,7340,L-3904245,00.html

110 Ennes, page 59.

111 IDF History Department Report: Div. Commander told to listen to air-sea-liaison channel (86 and 186) and that planes would be dispatch after detected ship, page 10.

112 Ram Ron Report, page 3. See also: MTB Division 914 detected Liberty as a target on their Kelvin-Hughes war surplus radar at extreme range. [IDF History Department/MTB Division War Log.] Per Cristol TimeLine, .pdf file.

113 Ennes, loc. cit..

114 Ennes, page 60.

115 Painter's testimony before the Naval Court of Inquiry, starting at page 55.

116 Ennes, page 59.

117 Wikipedia, *Communication with Submarines*,

http://en.wikipedia.org/wiki/Communication_with_submarines

118 Ennes, page 38. See also the Captain's testimony before the Naval Court of Inquiry starting on page 31.

119 Wikipedia, *Mirage IIICJ, a French built jet*:

http://en.wikipedia.org/wiki/Dassault_Mirage_III

120 Ennes, page 62.

121 O'Sullivan, Arieh, *Pilot who bombed 'Liberty' talks to Post*, Jerusalem Post, 10/10/2003. See also: Forty-four years later, Liberty attack provokes passions By ARIEH O'SULLIVAN / THE MEDIA LINE 06/08/2011 08:30. http://www.jpost.com/Features/InThespotlight/Article.aspx?id=2241 11

122 Ennes, page 61.

123 Scott, James (2009-05-15). *The Attack on the Liberty*. Simon & Schuster. Kindle Edition. Even though my father had long ago packed up his memories of the Liberty and moved on with his life, I know how much Spector's apology meant to him. A burden had been lifted. My father reached out and took Spector's hand and said: "Thank you."

124 Cristol, page 42 and 45.

125 Cristol, page 45.

126 Flightlevel350.com, *MirageIII Aircraft Facts*, http://www.flightlevel350.com/Mirage-III_aircraft_facts.html. Note, the website was not found as of 12/26/11; however, the same information was found at: http://en.wikipedia.org/wiki/Dassault_Mirage_III

127 Wikipedia, *R550 Magic Missile*, http://en.wikipedia.org/wiki/R.550_Magic

128 U.S. State Department, Office of the Historian: *Doc. 211. Memorandum From the Joint Chiefs of Staff to Secretary of Defense McNamara*, May 6, 1965. Subject: Impact on Area Arms Balance of Military Sales to Israel. http://history.state.gov/historicaldocuments/frus1964-68v18/d211 See also, Doc. 99. Memorandum of Conversation, May 30, 1967, http://history.state.gov/historicaldocuments/frus1964-68v19/d99

129 Israeli Air Force, *The Jewel in the Crown*, http://www.iaf.org.il/1478-23715-en/IAF.aspx. Operation "Diamond" was one of the most complex and sensitive operations ever conducted by

Israel. An exceptional cooperation between the air force, and the
'Intelligence and special tasks organization' (the Mossad) brought to the
landing of an Iraqi Mig-21 at an Israeli air force base, Yael Bar and Lior
Estline, Nikolai Avrutov.

130 Wikipedia, *AIM-9 Sidewinder*, http://en.wikipedia.org/wiki/AIM-9_Sidewinder

131 Novia.net, *Grumman F-14 Tomcat*, http://novia.net/~tomcat/AIM-9.html. There is a note "Information from U.S. Navy Fact File" at the bottom of the page.

132 Polmar, Norman, *The Naval Institute guide to the ships and aircraft of the U.S. fleet*, Naval Institute Press, 2001.

133 Odlum, Sean, *The U.S.-Israeli arms trade - It always takes two to tango*, Berlin Information-center for Transatlantic Security (BITS), November 2002. http://www.bits.de/public/pdf/bn02-3.pdf

134 U.S. Air Force, *AIM-9 Sidewinder*, http://www.af.mil/information/factsheets/factsheet.asp?id=78

135 Oren, page 265.

136 Wikipedia, *Operation Opera*, http://en.wikipedia.org/wiki/Operation_Opera

137 Jerusalem Post, *Pilot who bombed 'Liberty' talks to Post*, By ARIEH O'SULLIVAN, Oct. 10, 2003.

138 Cristol, page 153. Also, Oren, Six Days of War, page 165.

139 Oren, page 165.

140 Cristol, supra, page 17. After Israeli MTBs are identified on water surface. Kursa makes three runs and Royal flight follows 20-22 seconds later. See Also: Both Kursa Flight and T-203 ask each other if they can identify the target. Kursa reports "I can't identify it but in any case it's a military ship." and "Its with one mast and one smokestack." Royal Flight, a pair of Super-Mystères armed with napalm canisters and already airborne, is

561

diverted towards this target from its assigned mission in the Sinai. [IAF audio tapes.] Per Cristol TimeLine, .pdf file.

141 MTB Division 914 reports target at 17 miles, speed 28 knots. Division requests air. Aircraft are

dispatched. Division told to tune to air frequencies. [IDF Navy HQ War Log.] Kursa Flight is to be vectored towards the target's reported position with instructions: "If it's a warship, then blast it." [IAF audio tapes.] Per Cristol TimeLine, .pdf file.

142 Ennes, page 68.

143 Ennes, page 80.

144 Ennes, page 72.

145 Pearson, Anthony, *Conspiracy of Silence*, Quartet, New York, 1978, page 125.

146 Anthony Pearson, pages 121-126.

147 WRMEA, *The Assault on the USS Liberty Still Covered Up After 26 Years*, http://www.wrmea.com/backissues/0693/9306019.htm

148 USSliberty.org, *Interview with Ambassador Dwight Porter*,

http://ussliberty.org/dwightporter.htm
149 Ennes, page 63, 64.

150 Ennes, pages 74, 75. See also, page 95 Naval Court of Inquiry record re original and smooth radio logs as exhibits 23 and 24.

151 US Naval Court of Inquiry, Exhibit 27, page 128.

152Wikipedia, *Hatzor Airbase*,

http://en.wikipedia.org/wiki/Hatzor_Airbase
153 Oren, page 266.

154 Cristol, page 46.

155 Ostrovsky, Victor, Hoy, Claire, *By Way of Deception: Making of a MOSSAD Officer*, Wilshire Press, 1990, pages 141, 142.

562

156 Ostrovsky, Victor, *The Other Side of Deception: A Rogue Agent Exposes the Mossad's Secret Agenda*, Harper Collins, 1994, pages 278-282.

157 Weir, Alison, *Israeli Assassinations and American Presidents*, January 25, 2012, http://original.antiwar.com/alison-weir/2012/01/24/israeli-assassinations-and-american-presidents/˙

158 Johnson, Chalmers, *Blowback*, The Nation, 10/15/2001, http://www.thenation.com/article/blowback˙

159 Rashid, Ahmed, *Taliban: Militant Islam, Oil & Fundamentalism in Central Asia*, Yale Nota Bene, Yale University Press, 2001.

160 Question re markings: Kislev to Thames TV why thought "American" and threw down headset. See quote page 46 and 47 of Cristol's book *The Liberty Incident*.

161 Refer to *Review of Department of Defense Worldwide Communication*, Committee on Armed Services, House of Representatives, Ninety-second Congress, May 10, 1971.

162 Naval Court of Inquiry, pages 36, 37.

163 Ennes page 74.

164 [LOG:] SOUNDED GENERAL ALARM - LARGE FIRE IN VICINITY OF FRAME 85, 01 LEVEL WHERE FUEL FOR MOTOR DRIVEN FIRE PUMPS ARE LOCATED. See also: Liberty sounds General Quarters. Large fire near frame 85-01. All ahead flank (maximum speed) ordered. [US Naval Court of Inquiry/Exhibit 27: Chronology of Events; USS Liberty Deck Log, 8 June 1967.] Saratoga changed course to 80° True and speed to 20 knots. [USS Saratoga Deck Log, 8 June 1967.] IAF HQ attempts to determine if the target had fired on the attacking planes. [IAF audio tapes.] Per Cristol TimeLine, .pdf file.

165 Wikipedia, *Knowingly*, http://en.wikipedia.org/wiki/Knowingly˙

166 See Ram Ron Report. Also see: IAF reports men jumping over side of ship and sending rescue helicopters. MTB Division 914 told not to attack,

possible mis-identification. Might need to give help. [IDF Navy HQ War Log.] Per Cristol TimeLine, .pdf file.

167 Captain McGonagle's testimony before Naval Court of Inquiry, beginning at page 31, et seq.

168 Ennes, *Assault on the Liberty*, Addendum to 2002 Edition, September 2002, page 6.

169 Lloyd Painter's testimony to Naval Court of Inquiry, page 57.

170 Ennes, page 82.

171 Cristol, page 55.

172 Ennes, page 85.

173 Ennes, page 86.

174 Ennes, page 94.

175 Ennes, page 96.

176 Tourney, *What I Saw that Day*, page 82.

177 Ennes, page 96.

178 Wikipedia, *Super Frelon*,

http://en.wikipedia.org/wiki/A%C3%A9rospatiale_Super_Frelon#Israel

179 Ennes, page 77, Note No. 8, see Appendix C, page 236.

180 Crewdson, John, Chicago Tribune Online, Special Report, *New revelations in attack on American spy ship*, October 2, 2007,

http://www.chicagotribune.com/services/newspaper/eedition/chi-liberty_tuesoct02,0,43090.story

181 Ibid.

182 U.S. State Department, Office of Historian: Doc. 207. Telegram From the Commander of the Sixth Fleet (Martin) to the Commander in Chief, European Command (Lemnitzer),

http://history.state.gov/historicaldocuments/frus1964-68v19/d207

183 Naval History and Heritage Command, Sinking of USS Maine, 15 February 1898,

http://www.history.navy.mil/photos/events/spanam/events/maineskg.htm'
184 Paper transcript of Tully speech to LVA.

http://www.gtr5.com/Witnesses/tully.pdf'
185 Moorer Independent Commission Findings, footnote No. 2,

http://www.usslibertyinquiry.com/evidence/usreports/moorer.html'
186 These tapes were initially released to a select few. They were released to the producer and director of the TV documentary, *Attack on the Liberty*, Thames TV PLC and Rex Bloomstein. Transmission date was January 27th 1987 at 1030PM.

187 Bregman, Ahron, *A History of Israel*, Palgrave Macmillan, 2002, page 121.

188 Cristol, A. Jay, The Liberty Incident, Brassey's Inc., 2002. See Appendix 2.

189 Cristol, page 39.

190 Michael Oren, page 266: Rabin in Pit and concerned about Soviets. Page 264 re shelling of El Arish.

191 Bregman, page 121.

192 Ibid.

193 [LOG:] LOUD EXPLOSION - PORT SIDE AMIDSHIPS. See also: MTB Division records smoking coming from target. [MTB Division 914 War Log.] Per Cristol TimeLine, .pdf file. Cristol's timeline can be found on his website. For information on USS Liberty Deck Log, see:

http://www.ussliberty.org/lib-logs.htm'
194 Cristol, page 45: Kursa flight of two planes made three strafing runs each.

195 MTB Division 914 reports range to target 11 miles, requests aircraft leave area. [IDF Navy HQ War Log.] Per Cristol TimeLine, .pdf file.

565

196 [Chief Smith:] We called at 1208Z schematic and repeated three times that we were under attack. Immediately after 1208Z, still in the same minute, they rogered for the message. (Com) HF (High Frequency) voice net, and authenticated who was transmitting. [US Naval Court of Inquiry/Document 78 of Exhibit 48: DTG 081358Z June 1967, Saratoga to COMSIXTHFLT.] Liberty radio logs reflect that she had been transmitting repeatedly since 1358: "We are under attack." [US Naval Court of Inquiry: Exhibits 23 and 24.] Per Cristol TimeLine, .pdf file.

197 Per Cristol TimeLine, .pdf file.

198 Oren, page 266.

199 Per Cristol, TimeLine, .pdf file. See IDF History Report, page 15.

200 Bregman, page 122.

201 Wikipedia, *Teyman Airport*,

http://en.wikipedia.org/wiki/Beer_Sheva_(Teyman)_Airport
202 Airports-Worldwide.com, http://www.airports-
worldwide.com/israel/teyman_israel.htm
203 Beer-Sheba (Commonly called "Sde Teyman") ICAO code: LLBS. Location coordinates: N31 17.3 E034 43.4, elevation: 656 ft (200 m). One runway 14/32 degrees of 3412 ft (1040 m) length. Located west of Beer Sheba. Opened when? Civil airport, not currently used by the IDF/AF. Up until 1966 was the main liaison airfield for the Southern Command HQ nearby.

204 It is also noted that shelling report aroused attention of Supreme Command. Southern Command said shells did not reach coast. Head of Operations wanted report verified and to see if Israeli Naval ships in area. IDF History, page 10.

205 Cristol notes that Kislev was sitting two chairs from Hod the commander of the air force in the "Pit" at the Kirya. He refers to Royal flight two Super-Mystère B2 jets armed with 30 mm guns and two canisters

of napalm and two 216 US gallon drop tanks. Mystères attacked ship broadside. Cristol, page 42.

206 Rabin, page 109.

207 Michael Oren, page 266.

208 IDF GHQ Tel Aviv receives report from Southern Command that a ship is shelling El Arish. IDF History Report, page 10.

209 Cristol, page 170.

210 Joseph Graziano, posted to the forum section of USSLibertyinquiry.com: http://www.ussLibertyinquiry.com, 3:27 PM November 5th 2004. The forum is no longer active. Graziano's involvement with the USS Liberty can be Googled. The excerpt shows the type of analysis directed toward the attack by Liberty supporters on the forum.

211 Check the comments of "Top Gun", Bruce Charles, December 2, 2003: Remember, the Israeli's first flew by the ship, then having POSITIVELY IDENTIFIED their assigned target turned back to the attack from a very low altitude. Rocket hits on the forward gun tubs show a "level" trajectory and thus, a "level" attack which is what the crew described as the initial attack flight path the Israelis used. Very "up close and personal." NOT the fighter aircraft attack profile depicted by Cristol. Cristol tried to deceive...

http://www.usslibertyinquiry.com/essays/airattack.html`
212 1435: [LOG:] TORPEDO HIT STARBOARD SIDE AMIDSHIPS. TWENTY SIX MEN DIED AS A RESULT OF THE TORPEDO HIT AND MTB STRAFING FIRE. See Also: Liberty hit by a torpedo and loses electrical power. [US Naval Court of Inquiry/Exhibit 27: Chronology of Events; USS Liberty Deck Log, 8 June 1967.] The Israeli Navy records the attack as taking place at approximate 1440.

213 Howard Films, *Loss of the Liberty*. 2002, video documentary produced by Tito Howard.

214 1516: CTF60, Admiral Geis, transmitted text of Admiral Martin's 1450 message to America and Saratoga adding "ASAP" and "Defense of Liberty means exactly that." [Naval Historical Center: DTG 081316Z June 1967, CTF60 to America and Saratoga.] IAF HQ orders the two helicopters to depart the American ship. [IAF audio tapes.]. At 1316Z the Commander, Task Force 60, reiterated the order to the America and the Saratoga, adding, "Defense of USS Liberty means exactly that. Destroy or drive off any attackers who are clearly making attacks on Liberty. Remain over international waters. Defend yourself if attacked." (Telegram 081316Z from CTF 60 to USS America and USS Saratoga, June 8; ibid.) At 9:11 a.m. (1311Z), the Commander in Chief, European Command, notified the National Military Command Center by telephone that the Liberty was under attack, had been hit by a torpedo, and was listing to starboard. (See State Department, Office Historian, Document 219.) See Gerhard Report page 39. The National Security Agency is notified of the attack by telephone from the NMCC. [NSA: "Attack on a Sigint Collector, the USS Liberty (S-CCC)", p. 32.] The Army Communication Center, Pentagon, transmits the first standoff message, 072230Z, to Liberty as information. (See 1455 and 2335 entries.) This message is mis-routed to the Pacific. [House Armed Services Committee Report, May 10, 1971.].

215 Van Creveld, page, 195.

216 IDF History Department Report, see pages 15 through 18 dealing with the torpedo attack.

217 IDF History Department/Navy HQ War Log.

218 US Naval Court of Inquiry/Document 87 of Exhibit 48: DTG 081235Z June 1967, Saratoga to CINCUSNAVEUR.

219 [JCS Fact Finding Team Report, June 1967: DTG 081250Z June 1967, COMSIXTHFLT to America and Saratoga.] [Naval Historical Center: DTG 091306Z June 1967, CTF60 to TF60.] (Telegram 081250Z from

COMSIXTHFLT to USS Saratoga and USS America, June 8; ibid.). See page 39 Gerhard Report. Sixth Fleet was 450 miles from Liberty in area of Crete.

220 US Naval Court of Inquiry/Document 82 of Exhibit 48: DTG 081254Z June 1967, Saratoga to CINCUSNAVEUR and copied to Sixth Fleet units.] [USS Liberty Deck Log, 8 June 1967.] 1455: State Dept., XIX, Doc. 218: Photos of aircraft and boats taken. After attack completed two Israeli helicopters orbited ship at about 081255Z range 500 yards. Israeli insignia clearly visible. Photos taken. Several projectiles have been recovered from topside areas. Number dead is estimated at 10, number seriously wounded at 15. Total wounded 75, number missing currently undetermined. Helos at 500 yards appears incorrect.

221 NMCC Memorandum for the Record 1530 EDT, 8 June 1967. U.S. State Department Office of the Historian, Document 219,

http://history.state.gov/historicaldocuments/frus1964-68v19/d219‘

222 Ennes, page 97.

223 Ennes, page 98.

224 Gerhard Report, page 32.

225 [Naval Historical Center: DTG 081316Z June 1967, CTF60 to America and Saratoga.] (Telegram 081316Z from CTF 60 to USS America and USS Saratoga, June 8; ibid.).

226 At 9:11 a.m. (1311Z), (See State Department Document 219.) See Gerhard Report page 39. [Note: Ennes, page 100, WH thought act of local commander and not Israeli government. Clark Clifford assignment. Accepts "feasible" error of war theory.]

227 IDF History Report pages 15 to 18: Division Commander Oren orders torpedo attack at 1418 which is delayed. At 1420 the MTBs are ordered not to attack because of ID issues. Attack is again ordered at 1437, and open with firing and torpedoes at 1443.

228 IDF History Report, page 17.

229 A. Jay Cristol, Appendix 2, Israeli Air Force Audio Tapes, page 209.

230 Gerhard Report, page 11.

231 Bamford, *Body of Secrets*, page 205: 3 NSA civilian Hebrew linguists assigned to Athens 512J processing center.

232 Audio of Charles B. Tiffany interview posted:

http://www.gtr5.com/witnesses.htm
233 This topic is contained in a 7 page DOD Military Command Center Message Center report from US Naval Attaché, Commander Castle detailing what he found out about the attack after talking with Israeli IDF Lt. Colonel Michael Bloch. The 7 page document is in .pdf format and seems to be two separate documents with redactions. Four other documents dealing with reports from Castle can be found on the State Department, Office of Historian website. They are docs., 211, 233, 276 and 289. It appears that the 7 page DMCCMC message was fragmented into the Office of Historian documents 233, 276, 289. It is believed this is so because paragraphs from larger document were directed to various parties.

234 US State Department, Office of the Historian, *Document 276*,

http://history.state.gov/historicaldocuments/frus1964-68v19/d276
235 Wikipedia, *Libyan Arab Airlines Flight 114*,

http://en.wikipedia.org/wiki/Libyan_Arab_Airlines_Flight_114
236 Scott, James M., *The Attack on the Liberty*, Simon & Schuster, 2009, page 81through 83, E-Book version.

237 Wikipedia, *EC-121 Shoot down*, http://en.wikipedia.org/wiki/EC-121_shootdown_incident
238 Bamford, *Body of Secrets*, page 195. See page 213.

239 Bamford, *Body of Secrets*, page 205, 206.

240 Scott, page. 83.

241 Bamford, *Body of Secrets*, page 213.

570

242 Bamford, *Body of Secrets*, page 216.

243 Scott, James, E-Book version.

244 A copy of the Nowicki letter can be found online at:

http://www.thelibertyincident.com/nowicki-email.html'
245 See FOIA Complaint filed by one Ahron Jay Cristol:

http://www.fas.org/sgp/foia/cristol.html. The Nowicki letter to Bamford is included.

246 Cristol on his website IDs Hickman as linguist No.3 with his oral history. http://www.libertyincident.com/hebrewlinguist3.html.

247 Chicago Tribune Digital Edition, *New revelations in attack on American spy ship*, John Crewdson, October 2, 2007:

http://www.chicagotribune.com/services/newspaper/eedition/chi-liberty_tuesoct02,0,43090.story'
248 Hebrew Linguist No. 3,

http://www.thelibertyincident.com/hebrewlinguist3.html'
249 Rabin, page 110.

250 Ennes, page 98.

251 The reader can check out the NSA disclosure site:

http://www.nsa.gov/public_info/declass/uss_liberty/index.shtml'
252 Gotcher Declaration. Dated: September 2, 2003,

http://www.gtr5.com/Witnesses/gotcher.pdf'
253 Steve Forslund Declaration,

http://www.gtr5.com/Witnesses/forslund.pdf'
254 Cobbs Statement Letter:

http://www.usslibertyinquiry.com/evidence/witness/cobbs.jpg'
http://www.gtr5.com/Witnesses/cobbs.pdf'
255 [IDF History Department/Navy HQ War Log.], per Cristol's .pdf timeline file available on his website.

256 U.S.State Department, Office of the Historian: *Document 284. Intelligence Memorandum Prepared in the Central Intelligence Agency*, see

Note 1. http://history.state.gov/historicaldocuments/frus1964-68v19/d284
257 Refer to the Dr. Bregman interpretation of the pilot dialogue tapes challenging Judge Cristol's interpretation.

http://www.usslibertyinquiry.com/commentary/travesty/whoiscristol.html. The word "antenna" rather than "masts" is reported in the Thames video, Attack on the Liberty, Discovery Channel, 1987. The Israelis had released a tape of pilot/controller dialogue.

258 Clark Clifford's report to the President is available at the LBJ Library. See also:

http://www.ussliberty.org/cliffor2.htm
259 U.S. State Department Office of the Historian, : *Document 236, Notes of a Meeting of the Special Committee of the National Security Council.*

http://history.state.gov/historicaldocuments/frus1964-68v19/d236
260 U.S. State Department Office of the Historian:

http://history.state.gov/historicaldocuments/frus1964-68v19/d258
261 U.S. State Department, Office of the Historian, *Document: 258. Memorandum From the President's Special Assistant (Rostow) to President Johnson*, see Note 2.

http://history.state.gov/historicaldocuments/frus1964-68v19/d258
262 U.S. State Department Office of the Historian,

http://history.state.gov/historicaldocuments/frus1964-68v19/d284
263 Wikipedia, *Sukhoi Su 7*, http://en.wikipedia.org/wiki/Sukhoi_Su-7
264 Ginor, Isabella, with Gideon Remez, *Foxbats over Dimona: The Soviets' Nuclear Gamble in the Six-Day War*, Yale University Press, 2007.

265 Priluki is also known for the largest airfield in Ukraine being main base of Soviet strategic bombers during Cold War:
http://ukrainetrek.com/priluki-city. See also, Ginor at page 136.

266 Ginor, 146.

572

267 Ginor, pages 146, 147.

268 Six-Day War: See the following link for list of Egyptian planes destroyed, http://www.zionism-israel.com/dic/6daywar.htm

269 Hounam, page 7.

270 *A Juridical Examination of the Israeli Attack on the USS Liberty*, Naval Law Review, Vol. 36 Winter 1986, Lt. Commander Walter L. Jacobsen, JA GC, USN., footnote No. 44.

271 Bamford, *Puzzle Palace*, page 280.

272 Alan Moore, e-mail to author.

273 Bamford, *Puzzle Palace* ,280.

274 Bamford, Puzzle Palace ,281.

275 Submarine Collisions,

http://everything2.com/title/Submarine+Collisions

276 Bamford, Body of Secrets, 188, 198, 190.

277 Bamford, Body of Secrets, page 194: Collected on the early hours of war but no translator for the processing center UJSA-512J so designated by NSA. In the mean time Hebrew linguists flown to Athens. Used designation "Special Arabic" to hide fact that eavesdropping on Israel.

278 Bamford, Body of Secrets, page 208.

279 Sheck Oral History.

280 NSA website with list of oral histories:

http://www.nsa.gov/public_info/declass/uss_liberty/interviews.shtml

281 Scott, page. 176.

282 Dr. Tordella became the deputy director of NSA in 1958, and remained in that post until his retirement in 1974. He thus became the longest serving deputy director in NSA's history. Dr. Tordella passed away on 10 January 1996.

283 On May 25, the New York Times revealed that U.S. submarines, specially equipped with electronic spying gear and operating under the code

name Holystone, had been monitoring Soviet missile activities for 15 years, sometimes within Russian territorial waters. http://www.time.com/time/magazine/article/0,9171,913370,00.html.

284 Ennis, page 64 and Note No. 1.

285 Rabin, page 110.

286 Hounam, page 123, see endnote No. 18 to Chapter 5, *Contact X*.

287 In the past, the formal responsibility was assumed by a small group of top intelligence, defense and foreign affairs officials known as the "40 Committee" and headed by Henry Kissinger. Presidents have almost always given their direct authorization for covert operations abroad (although their roles in the agency's various alleged schemes for assassinations are still far from clear), but they could always avoid personal blame if a secret operation was "blown" by disclosure.

http://www.time.com/time/magazine/article/0,9171,913370-2,00.html
288 Alan Moore e-mail exchange.

289 Global Security, *ELF*,

http://www.globalsecurity.org/wmd/systems/elf.htm
290 Fas.org, *ELF*, http:// www.fas.org/nuke/guide/usa/c3i/elf.htm. See United States Navy Fact File.

291 Obama, Netanyahu discuss Iran, Spokesman Review, March 6, 2012, page A3.

292 Deacon, Richard, *The Israeli Secret Service*, self published, no date shown, however appears after 1976.

293 Pearson, Anthony, *Conspiracy of Silence: The Attack on the U.S.S. Liberty*, Quartet Books, London, 1978.

294 Deacon, page 181.

295 Pearson, page 30.

296 Ennes, page 44 and 45.

297 Bamford, Body of Secrets, 190.

298 Ennes, page 39.

299 Ennes, page 42. Note: O'Connor's oral history.

300 Ennes, page 130, see footnote No. 6, Goulding, page 124, and wire-service stories.

301 Ennes, page 132.

302 Ennes, page 133.

303 Bamford, Body of Secrets, page 186.

304 Deacon, page 179.

305 GWU-NSAP, *Israel,*

http://www.gwu.edu/~nsarchiv/israel/index.htm˙
306 For more information: Cohen, Israel and the Bomb, pages 273-276.

307 Source: United States National Archive. For more information: Cohen, Israel and the Bomb, pages, 185-186.

308 Ibid.

309 Former IDF chief reveals new details of Israel's nuclear program, Haaretz.com, 9/16/11,

http://www.haaretz.com/weekend/magazine/former-idf-chief-reveals-new-details-of-israel-s-nuclear-program-1.384889˙
310 State Department, Office of the Historian, *Doc. No. 387*

http://history.state.gov/historicaldocuments/frus1964-68v18/d387˙
311 Cohen, Avner, Israel and the Bomb, Columbia University Press, 1998, page 273.

312 Cohen, page 309.

313 Even more significant are the views Allon expressed about the issues of nuclear weapons and ballistic missile. Not only that Allon made efforts to reassure Rusk categorically that Israel was not going to introduce such new and advanced weaponry, but the opinions he expressed implied that he personally minimized the importance of these projects and would oppose to such deployment. Allon told Rusk that Israel had no nuclear weapons and he reiterated Eshkol's pledge that Israel would not be the first to introduce

nuclear weapons. By linking the two issues Allon appeared equating non-introduction with non-possession of nuclear weapons. On the matter of the NPT, while Allon gave no formal promises to Rusk he expressed his own view "that sooner or later" Israel would sign the treaty. On the matter of the French missiles (MD-620), Allon described the Israeli-French project as dead and denied that Israel was making them in Israel itself. Both assertions were misleading, at least, perhaps more self-deception than deliberate deception. Source: United States National Archives.

For more details: Cohen, Israel and the Bomb, pages 303-310.

314 Israel's quest for a missile capability began at the same time as its quest for nuclear weapons. In April 1963--several months before the Dimona reactor began operating--Israel signed an agreement with the French company Dassault to produce a surface-to-surface ballistic missile. Israeli specifications called for a two-stage missile capable of delivering a 750-kilogram warhead to 235--500 kilometers with a circular error probable of less than 1 kilometer. The missile system, known as the Jericho (or MD-620), was designed to take less than two hours to prepare, be launchable from fixed or mobile bases, and be capable of firing at a rate of four to eight missiles per hour. In early 1966, the New York Times reported that Israel had bought a first installment of 30 missiles. After the 1967 war, France imposed an embargo on new military equipment, and Israel began producing the Jericho missile independently. In 1974, the CIA cited the Jericho as evidence that Israel had nuclear weapons, stating that the Jericho made little sense as a conventional missile and was "designed to accommodate nuclear warheads." See: http://www.skeptically.org/onwars/id14.html. See also: http://www.dassault-aviation.com/en/passion/aircraft/military-dassault-aircraft/md-620-jericho.html?L=1

315 Cohen, page 282.

316 21st Century Socialism, *Israel and the West: a nuclear romance*, by Noah Tucker, October 27th 2009

http://21stcenturysocialism.com/article/israel_and_the_west_a_nucle
ar_romance_01922.html

317 Howe, Russell Warren, Weapons: *The International Game of Arms
Money and Diplomacy,* Doubleday & Company, Inc., 1980, page 525.

318 Ennes, page 15.

319 Cohen, page 83.

320 *CHARACTER AND MOTIVE IN EVIDENCE LAW,* David P. Leonard,
Professor of Law and William M. Rains Fellow, Loyola Law School.

321 Newsweek, June 19, 1967.

322 Ennes, page 141.

323 Oren, Six Days of War, page 91.

324 Green, Stephen, *Taking Sides: America's Secret Relations with a
Militant Israel,* Amana Books, 1988, page 215.

325 Ennes, page 207.

326 A Conversation with the Assistant Secretary of Defense for C3I, The
Program on Information Resources Policy is jointly sponsored by Harvard
University and the Center for Information Policy Research. John P. Stenbit,
March 13, 2003.

327 Michael Oren reports the document can be found at
http://www.halcyon.com/jim/ussliberty/liberty.htm. See Oren, page 402 end
note no. 11.

328 Judge Yeshayahu Yerushalmi, a lieutenant colonel in the IDF, began a
procedure as examining judge. Yerushalmi was born in Poland in 1920 and
came to Israel in 1935. He graduated from Balfour College in Tel Aviv and
went on to study law at the University of Jerusalem. He joined the Haganah
and worked as a law clerk and lawyer from March 1942 to 1947, when he
joined the army as a private. He was soon transferred to the Military
Advocate General and became JAG to the air force and then JAG to the
navy. In 1957 he was appointed as a judge on the Court of Military Appeals,

a position he had held for ten years when he was appointed as examining judge in the Liberty matter.

329 Deacon, page 182.

330 Deacon, page 183.

331 Cristol, page 115, citing Finley in his footnote No. 47. It is believed the CIA Tel Aviv station chief was most likely John Hadden.

332 A petition filed with the UN Commission on Human Rights involving Haidar Bitar and Wurud Abboud against the State of Israel Pursuant to ECOSCO Resolution 1503 (XLVIII), 48 UN ESCOR (No. 1A) p. 8, U.N. Doc. E/4832/Add.1 (1970) Dealing with certain killings in the Southern Lebanon village of Qana.

333 Chomsky, Noam, *Rogue States: The Rule of Force in World Affairs*, South End Press, 2000, page 19, 20, 21, 28.

334 Wikipedia, *USS Stark*,

http://en.wikipedia.org/wiki/USS_Stark_%28FFG-31%29˙

335 Wikipedia, *Dilip Hiro*, http://en.wikipedia.org/wiki/Dilip_Hiro˙

336 Chomsky, page 28, citing Dilip Hiro and his book about the Iran-Iraq War.

337 Amnesty International release: Canada urged to arrest and prosecute George W. Bush, 10/12/2011. http://www.amnesty.org/en/news-and-updates/report/canada-urged-arrest-and-prosecute-george-w-bush-2011-10-12˙

338 Bamford, Body of Secrets, pages 201-203. Some 1000 killed in Sinai and around El Arish. Ariel Sharon was in this area. On page 203 he alleges Rabin, Dayan and top army leadership knew this and did nothing.

339 The memoires of Moshe Sharett (foreign minister at the time of Qibya) mince no words in accusing the Israeli military establishment of "manipulating facts, withholding information, and falsifying reports" in order to justify retaliatory operations. He was deeply shocked by the cover-

up of the Qibya massacre. See Yoman Ishi (Personal Diary) by Moshe Sharett, ed. Yaakov Sharett (Tel Aviv: Ma'ariv, 1978.)

340 Bamford, Body of Secrets, Page 203: Bamford alleges the whole Israeli war plan was based on lies that needed covering up.

341 Wikiquote, Charles de Gaulle,

http://en.wikiquote.org/wiki/Charles_de_Gaulle'
342 Howe, page 525 and 526.

343 Deacon, page 180.

344Deacon, page 181.

345 Pearson, page 31.

346 Pearson, page 31.

347 Pearson, page 32.

348 Tourney, page 154.

349 The Liberty Veterans Association, Inc., a California Non-Profit corporation, Plaintiff, Versus Tito Howard, et al, Defendants: Superior Court of the State of California in and for Los Angeles County Upper Division, Case Number LC068620.

350 Case Number: CV 04-6537-JFW (CTx).

351 Hounam, page 196.

352 Howe, page 525.

353 Ennes, page 143.

354 Ennes, page 130 citing Goulding, page 125; Norfolk Virginia-Pilot, June 11, 1967, page A6; and wire-service stories.

355 *John M. Hrankowski, 1946-2011 - Remembering a Hero*: Liberty News, the Newsletter of the USS Liberty, Vol. 42, December, 2001, page 3, article by Delinda C. Hanley.

356 Hot summer of 1967: The Israeli attack on America and the 'Soviet destroyer'. Sergey Stefanov PRAVDA.Ru. Translated by Maria Gousseva.

http://english.pravda.ru/news/russia/14-09-2002/17971-0/' ^{Read the}

579

original in Russian: http://pravda.ru/main/2002/09/13/47015.html. Note: The author has found that Internet URLs are subject to change for one reason or another.

357 WRMEA, *Dick Thompson: A Real American Patriot* (1929-2007), By Delinda C. Hanley

http://www.wrmea.com/archives/August_2007/0708023.html.

358 Arapahoe Library District,

http://arapahoelibraries.org/ald/aldsearch?author=Daichman%2C+Io sif

359 This is a Russian website with a picture showing the date of birth as 1948, http://bvi.rusf.ru/fanta/fwho098.htm. Searching this website is a tedious process.

360 During 1967 Six-Day War, a Mirage type fighter jet accidentally entered the airspace of the Dimona reactor, after suffering been damaged in an attack raid in Egypt. Having failed to respond to radio calls, the plane was subsequently shot down by nearby anti-aircraft: Haaretz.com, By Zohar Blumenkrantz and Anshel Pfeffer, 6/10/09,

http://www.haaretz.com/news/iaf-jets-scramble-as-plane-flies-over-dimona-nuclear-facility-1.6591

361 This "threat" was reported in a seven page cable from Commander Castle to the DOD National Military Command Center, Message Center, dated 1967 June 25.

362 Howe, pages xv to xvii.

363 Wikipedia, *Yom Kipper War*,

http://en.wikipedia.org/wiki/Yom_Kippur_War#cite_note-261

364 Nuclear Cleanup Stopped In Parks Township, Pittsburg Tribune,

http://www.pittsburghlive.com/x/valleynewsdispatch/lifestyles/s_762 465.html

365 Hersh, Seymour, The Sampson Option. Refer to Chapter 18, Injustice, dealing with NUMEC.

366 Americans Pay Dearly to Maintain Israel's Nuclear Secrets, CIA

endangers NUMEC toxic waste cleanup,

by Grant Smith, October 20, 2011,

http://original.antiwar.com/smith-grant/2011/10/19/americans-pay-dearly-to-maintain-israels-nuclear-secrets/
367 Script transcript, *Attack on the Liberty*, Thames TV PLC, London, for

transmission: 27th January, 1987, producer Rex Bloomstein. Master Tape:

No. 0380959.

368 Global Politician, *Israel is a net asset to U.S.*, Ted Belman, 4/24/2010:

http://www.globalpolitician.com/26372-israel-united-states-foreign-policy
369 *Western Intelligence and the Collapse of the Soviet Union, 1980-1990:*

Ten Years That Did Not Shake the World. Contributors: David Arbel -

author, Ran Edelist - author. Publisher: Frank Cass. Place of Publication:

London. Publication Year: 2003. Page Number: 149.

370 Janney, Peter (2012-04-02). Mary's Mosaic: The CIA Conspiracy to

Murder John F. Kennedy, Mary Pinchot Meyer, and Their Vision for World

Peace (Kindle Locations 5091-5100). Skyhorse Publishing. Kindle Edition.

371 The Central Intelligence Agency was created by Congress with the

passage of the National Security Act of 1947, signed into law by President

Harry S. Truman. It is the descendant of the Office of Strategic Services

(OSS) of World War II, which was dissolved in October 1945 and its

functions transferred to the State and War Departments.

http://en.wikipedia.org/wiki/Central_Intelligence_Agency
372 Hounam, page 229.

373 Meir Amit Intelligence and Terrorism Information Center,

http://www.terrorism-info.org.il/site/content/T1.asp?Sid=18&pid=121
374 Ibid.

375 Waller, Douglas (2011). *Wild Bill Donovan* (p. 296). Free Press. Kindle Edition.

376 George Washington University National Security Archive Project, *CIA History of DCI William Colby*, October 28, 2011,

http://www.gwu.edu/~nsarchiv/NSAEBB/NSAEBB362/index.htm
See Chapter 7 page 101 re Angleton's involvement with the CIA's domestic spying efforts.

377 Mangold, Tom, *Cold Warrior James Jesus Angleton*, Simon and Schuster, 1991.

378 Cohen, page 84.

379 Mangold, page 28.

380 Mangold, page 285, 290, 291.

381 GWU NSA, *Uncovering the Architect of the Holocaust: The CIA Names File On Adolf Eichmann*, March 24, 2005,

http://www.gwu.edu/~nsarchiv/NSAEBB/NSAEBB150/index.htm. Note 1: For further reading on the role of the CIA's Counterintelligence (CI) staff in locating documents and their relations with Israeli intelligence, see Timothy Naftali's essay "CIA and Eichmann's Associates," in U.S. Intelligence and the Nazis, (Washington, DC: National Archive Trust Fund Board, 2004), 339.

382 Cohen, page 48.

383 Cohen, pages 87, 88, 89.

384 GWU- NSA, Israel and the Bomb, News and Findings,

http://www.gwu.edu/~nsarchiv/israel/findings.htm
385 Cohen, page 85.

386 Cohen, page 102, 104, 108.

387 The Wall Street Journal, April 21, 2010, page A13.

388 Helen Kennedy, New York Daily News, *Ex-Mossad boss, Meir Dagan...*, http://www.nydailynews.com/news/ex-mossad-boss-meir-dagan-israeli-attack-iran-stupidist-article-1.1037219' March 11, 2012.

389 Ranelagh, John, *The Agency: The Rise and Decline of the CIA*, Simon and Schuster, New York, 1986, page 285 re NK speech.

390 Eveland, Wilbur Crane, *Ropes of Sand: America's Failure in the Middle East*, W.W. Norton & Company, London, New York, 1980, page 95.

391 Eveland, page 157.

392 Eveland, page 227.

393 Eveland, page 160, page footnote.

394 Eveland, page 309.

395 Eveland, page 310.

396 Eveland, page 323.

397 Kyle, Keith, *Suez: Britain's End of Empire in the Middle East*, I.B. Tauris Publishers, London, New York, 2003, Protocol of Sevres, page 327.

398 Eveland, page 323.

399 Eveland, page 324.

400 Eveland, page 324-325.

401 Ginor and Remez, page 30.

402 Deacon, page 168.

403 Deacon, page 169.

404 Wikipedia, *Lavon Affair*, http://en.wikipedia.org/wiki/Lavon_Affair

405 Thomas, Gordon, *Seeds of Fire: China and the story behind the attack on America*, Dandelion Books Publication, Arizona, 2001, page 24.

406 Thomas, page 23.

407 U.S. State Department Office of the Historian, *Document No. 96. Memorandum From the President's Special Assistant (Rostow) to President*

Johnson, May 23rd, 1967.

http://history.state.gov/historicaldocuments/frus1964-68v21/d96
408 Deacon, page 170.

409 Deacon 173-174.

410 Deacon page 176.

411 Deacon, page 177.

412 Janney, Peter (2012-04-02). *Mary's Mosaic: The CIA Conspiracy to Murder John F. Kennedy, Mary Pinchot Meyer, and Their Vision for World Peace* (Kindle Locations 4955-4960). Skyhorse Publishing. Kindle Edition.

413 Nelson, Phillip F. (2011-10-20). *LBJ: The Mastermind of The JFK Assassination*. Skyhorse Publishing. Kindle Edition.

414 Citizens for Truth About the Kennedy Assassination,

http://www.ctka.net/home.html
415 GWU-NSA website dealing with the Bay of Pigs information,

http://www.gwu.edu/~nsarchiv/NSAEBB/NSAEBB355/index.htm
416 List of CIA covert operations,

http://pw1.netcom.com/~ncoic/cia_info.htm#Plausible%20Deniabilit
y
417 Deacon, page 178.

418 Deacon, page178.

419 Ostrovsky, page 321.

420 Wikipedia, *1983 Beirut Barracks Bombing*,

http://en.wikipedia.org/wiki/1983_Beirut_barracks_bombing . Search
for Ostrovksy and Israel.

421 Ranelagh, see footnote to page 580. Only a footnote reference to the Mossad and whether CIA helped Israel with nuclear program. See Seymour Hersh's *The Sampson Option*.

422 Pearson, page 15.

423 *Russia says Syria's Assad too slow on reforms, warns of spreading conflict,* Washington Post,

http://www.washingtonpost.com/world/middle_east/un-diplomat-syria-responds-to-annan-on-his-proposals-to-end-the-bloodshed/2012/03/13/gIQAOTXDAS_story.html, by AP Press, March 13, 2012 updated March 14.

424 Ibid.

425 Pearson, page 17.

426 Pearson, page 19.

427 Pearson, page 24.

428 Pearson, page 22.

429 Deacon, page 181.

430 Eveland, pages 324-325.

431 Parker, Richard, *The Six-Day War: A Retrospective.* Contributors: Richard B. Parker - editor. Publisher: University Press of Florida. Place of Publication: Gainesville, FL. Publication Year: 1996. Page Number: 257.

432 Ibid. See endnote No. 359 above.

433 Copeland, Miles, *Without Cloak or Dagger*, Simon and Schuster, New York, 1974.

434 Parker, page 246. See Eveland, page 323.

435 Cockburn, Andrew and Leslie, *Dangerous Liaison The Inside Story of the US-Israeli Covert Relationship*, Harper Collins, 1991. See pages 146 and 147.

436 Parker, page 239.

437 Ibid.

438 Parker, page 136.

439 *Eveland v. Director CIA*, U.S. Court of Appeals, First Circuit, 843 F.2nd 46, April 4, 1988.

http://law.justia.com/cases/federal/appellate-courts/F2/843/46/33946/

585

440 Washington Report on Middle East Affairs, *In Memoriam A Respectful Dissenter: CIA's Wilbur Crane Eveland*, by Mary Barrett, March 1990, http://washreport.net/component/content/article/125/1077-in-memoriam-wilbur-crane-eveland.html

441 Ibid.

442 Helms, with William Hood, page 300-301.

443 GWU- NSAP, Israel and the Bomb, News and Findings,

http://www.gwu.edu/~nsarchiv/israel/findings.htm

444 Hounam, pages 250, 251.

445 Hounam, page 267.

446 Piper, Michael Collins, USS Liberty – Government Propaganda, American Free Press, http://www.government-propaganda.com/US-liberety-ship.html. Tracing to the original article is problematic. Piper's website is: http://mikepiperreport.com/.

447 GWU- NSAP, Pentagon Proposed Pretexts for Cuba Invasion in 1962, http://www.gwu.edu/~nsarchiv/news/20010430/. Describes Operation Northwoods during the Cuban crisis.

448 Raviv, Dan, and Melman, Yossi, *Every Spy A Prince: The Complete History of Israel's Intelligence Community*, Houghton Mifflin Company, Boston, 1990, Page 198: Angleton help protect Israel's nuclear secret.

449 Hersh, pages 144 to 147.

450 Ranelagh, Page 253 re Liberty. See endnote 44 for the chapter.

451 Hounam, page 189.

452 Ennes, Supplement, 2002 Adendum, page 5. Ennes citing Rowley.

453 Hounam, Peter, Operation Cyanide: Why the Bombing of the USS Liberty Nearly Caused World War III, Vision, 2003.

454 Vanunu appears in court against Yedioth-Ahronoth, http://www.haaretz.com/news/vanunu-appears-at-court-in-case-against-yedioth-ahronoth-1.123316

455 Telegraph.co.uk, *"How I escaped Mossad's clutches"*, Peter Hounam, Published: 7:00AM GMT 20 Feb 2010.

456 Victor Ostrovsky, *The Other Side of Deception*, Harper Collins, copyright 1994, page 208-210.

457 Wikipedia, Robert Maxwell,

http://en.wikipedia.org/wiki/Robert_Maxwell˙

458 Gordon Thomas and Martin Dillon, *Robert Maxwell, Israel's Superspy*, Carroll and Graf Publishers, 2002.

459 Wikipedia, Dolphin Class Submarine,

http://en.wikipedia.org/wiki/Dolphin_class_submarine˙

460 Hounam, page 196.

461 Hounam, page 198.

462 Hounam, page 199.

463 Hounam, page 200, and 201.

464 Hounam, page 201.

465 Hounam, page 251.

466 Hounam, page 214.

467 Hounam, page 229.

468 Hounam, page 229.

469 State Department, Office of the Historian, *Document: No. 124*,

http://history.state.gov/historicaldocuments/frus1964-68v19/d124˙

470 Howe, page 524.

471 Deacon, page 169. The author claims Evron was Israel's most powerful person in Washington, more highly regarded than the Israeli ambassador.

472 Hounam, page 267. Evron's revelations occurred at a 1992 conference in Washington on the 25th anniversary of the Six-Day War.

473 Ibid.

474 British Pathe, Russian Ship Attack by U.S. Planes,

http://www.britishpathe.com/record.php?id=71404˙

475 Usslibertyinquiry.com, *The Air Attack: Errors in the Attack Profile*, Bruce Charles, December 2, 2003,

http://www.usslibertyinquiry.com/essays/airattack.html

476 Hounam, page 268.

477 Hersh, page 186, 187.

478 Hounam, page 279, endnote No. 22.

479 Hounam, page 125.

480 Hounam, page 125, chapter endnote 22.

481 Hersh, page 309, 310.

482 Ben-Menasche, "Profits of War", page 112.

483 World Sea Fishing,

http://www.worldseafishing.com/forums/showthread.php?t=103444&page=3

484 Hounam, page 125.

485 Howe, page 526-527.

486 Howe, page 527.

487 Ennes Book Review, Ussliberty.org,

http://www.ussliberty.org/secret.htm

488 Timesonline, David Holden,

http://www.timesonline.co.uk/tol/news/uk/crime/article6823299.ece
The reader will find references to this website but it is difficult to access.

489 Isabella Ginor and Gideon Remez, *Foxbats Over Dimona*, Yale University Press, 2007, page 142-143.

490 Van Creveld, page 192.

491 Hounam, pages 7 to 13. See last paragraph of book. Why were planes placed on alert that day. See his conclusion. Alert was between 2 and 4 AM California time.

492 IDF GHQ Tel Aviv receives report from Southern Command that a ship is shelling El Arish. [IDF History Department; US Naval Court of Inquiry/Document 1 of Exhibit 48: DTG 181030Z June 1967, USDAO Tel

Aviv 0928 to White House and others.] Per Cristol Time Line .pdf file. It is also noted that shelling report aroused attention of Supreme Command. Southern Command said shells did not reach coast. Head of Operations wanted report verified and to see if Israeli Naval ships in area. IDF History, page 13.

493 Refer to Hounam page 268.

494Van Creveld, Sword and Olive.

495 Cristol, *Liberty Incident*, Chapter "Did Dayan Do It".

496 Hounam, page 268.

497 Hounam, page 269.

498 U.S. State Department Office of the Historian, Document 257. Telegram From the Department of State to the Embassy in Israel,

http://history.state.gov/historicaldocuments/frus1964-68v19/d257'

499 Ennes, page 74.

500 Ennes, page 74, footnote No. 3.

501 Chief Wayne Smith, testimony before NCOI, page 94.

502 Ennes, page 75, footnote No. 6.

503 Ennes, page 77, footnote No. 8.

504 *McNamara: From the Tokyo Firestorm to the World Bank*, Alexander Cockburn, July 07, 2009:

http://www.counterpunch.org/2009/07/07/mcnamara-from-the-tokyo-firestorm-to-the-world-bank/'

505 *Lyndon B. Johnson: Portrait of a President*. Contributors: Robert Dallek - author. Publisher: Oxford University Press. Place of Publication: New York. Publication Year: 2004. Page Number: 284.

506 Ibid.

507 State Department Office of the Historian, Doc. No. 277. Memorandum by President Johnson, http://history.state.gov/historicaldocuments/frus1964-68v33/d277.

508 U.S. State Department, Office of Historian: Doc. 219. Memorandum for the Record, June 8, 1967, 3:30 p.m. SUBJECT: The USSLiberty (AGTR–5) Struck by Torpedo.

http://history.state.gov/historicaldocuments/frus1964-68v19/d219
See also, documents 211 and 215.

509 Hounam, page 270.

510 Hounam, 270.

511 Hounam, page 270.

512 GWU-NSAP, *Pentagon Proposed Pretexts for Cuban Invasion in 1962*,

http://www.gwu.edu/~nsarchiv/news/20010430/
513 Hounam, page 270,

514 Transcript, *McGeorge Bundy Oral History Interview III*, 3/19/69, by Paige E. Mulhollan, Internet Copy, LBJ Library. See page 21.

515 Ibid.

516 Hounam, page 271.

517 Transcript, *McGeorge Bundy Oral History Interview III*, 3/19/69, by Paige E. Mulhollan, Internet Copy, LBJ Library. See page 23.

518 Hounam, page 271.

519 Alan Moore, Valdez CT, e-mail to this author, 8/16/2009.

520 Hounam, page 272, see endnote 14: Memo to Bundy dated 10 March 1965, LBJ Library.

521 Admiral Martin retransmitted his 1539 message to CNO and CINCUSNAVEUR. [JCS Fact Finding Team Report, June 1967: DTG 081349Z June 1967.] National Security Advisor W. W. Rostow advises President Johnson by telephone that Liberty has been attacked. [LBJ Library: White House Daily Diary, 8 June 1967; NSA: "Attack on a

Sigint Collector, the USS Liberty (S-CCC)." Confirmed by personal interview with W. W.

Rostow at Austin, Texas, March 7, 1990.]

COMSIXTHFLT transmits to NSA a CRITIC message. (A message containing information

indicating a situation or pertaining to a situation which affects the security or interests of the U.S.

to such an extent that it may require the immediate attention of the President.) It repeats the first

paragraph of his 1520 message (i.e., current known situation.) See also 1617 entry. [Naval

Historical Center: "Naval Security Group File on U.S.S. Liberty": DTG 081349Z June 1967

(sanitized); NSA: "USS Liberty, Chronology of Events, 23 May-8 June 1967."].

522 Rostow memo to President. [NSA: "Attack on a Sigint Collector, the USS Liberty (S-CCC)";

LBJ Library.]

State Department advised Soviet Charge' in Washington by phone of attack on Liberty and

dispatch of aircraft to scene. [LBJ Library: DTG 081536Z June 1967, SECSTATE WASHDC

209218 to AMEMBASSY MOSCOW.]

Liberty records two unidentified jet aircraft observed. [US Naval Court of Inquiry/Exhibit 27:

Chronology of Events; USS Liberty Deck Log, 8 June 1967.] State Dept. XIX, Doc.210.

523 Ennes, page 99.

524 [DTG 081416Z June 67, JCS to USCINCEUR.] JCS transmitted that use of force was authorized.

525 Liberty received, via HF voice, message from COMSIXTHFLT: "Assistance is on the way." [US Naval Court of Inquiry/Exhibit 24: Radio Log; USS Liberty Deck Log, 8 June 1967.]

526 President arrived at White House Situation Room meeting which had been in session for some

time. Present were:

Secretary of Defense Robert McNamara,

Secretary of State Dean Rusk,

Chairman, Foreign Intel Adv Bd Clark Clifford,

Under Secretary of State Nicholas Katzenbach,

Ambassador to Russia Llewellen Thompson,

Special Consultant McGeorge Bundy,

National Security Advisor W. W. Rostow

[LBJ Library: White House Daily Diary, 8 June 1967.]

Fifth standoff message, 080917Z from COMSIXTHFLT to Liberty, received back from NCS

Greece by Army Relay Station DCS Asmara for relay to NCS Asmara after having been

mistakenly sent to NCS Greece at 1415. [JCS Fact Finding Team Report, June 1967.] State Dept. XIX, Doc. 213. Washington, June 8, 1967, 12:01 p.m. /1/Source: Johnson Library, National Security File, NSC Histories, Middle East Crisis, May 12-June 19, 1967, Vol. 7. No classification marking. A typed notation on the message indicates it was approved by the President at 11:35 a.m.; transmitted by U.S. Molink at 12:01 p.m.; and received by Soviet Molink at 12:05 p.m. According to the President's Daily Diary, he met with McNamara, Rusk, Clifford, Katzenbach, Thompson,

Bundy, and Walt Rostow, from 11:06 to 11:45 a.m. in the White House Situation Room. (Ibid.).

527 Tourney, What I Saw that Day.

528 The byline read: "SAN'A, Yemen (CNN) -- A Yemeni court has handed down death sentences to two men -- one currently in U.S. custody -- for their roles in the bombing of the USS Cole, an official source in San'a said. The court Wednesday also sentenced four others to prison terms ranging from five to 10 years for their involvement in the attack, which killed 17 U.S. sailors."

In the case of the terrorist attack on the USS Cole the FBI was immediately assigned to the investigation as if he matter were a criminal case to eventually be prosecuted. It was as noted in a Yemeni court. Unfortunately, the matter of the attack on the USS Liberty was not to be handled that way for a variety of reasons.

529 List published by Liberty supporters on the Internet.

http://www.gtr5.com/quotes.htm
530 See State Dept. release [Clark Clifford report].

531 Moorer Commission Findings,

http://www.ussliberty.com/findings.htm
532 [transcript from NBC's Liberty Story, aired on national television 1/27/92].

533 Reference to Tony Hart:

http://www.usslibertyinquiry.com/evidence/usreports/moorer.html
534 Transcript, *Robert S. McNamara Oral History Interview I*, 1/8/75, by Walt W. Rostow, Internet Copy, LBJ Library. See page 35.

535 Transcript, *Robert S. McNamara Oral History, Special Interview I*, 3/26/93, by Robert Dallek, Internet Copy, LBJ Library. See page 17.

536 Wikipedia, *Robert McNamara*,

http://en.wikipedia.org/wiki/Robert_McNamara

537 Helms, pages 300-301.

538 Sunday, October 10, 2004 10:20 AM.

539 Meaning, if we sink the Liberty, then you will counter the Russian threat if we move against Syria since you will believe that the Russians were responsible. However, if you posit this to a greater depth, then factor in Angleton and his excessive compulsion with the Russian cold war threat, which would set the stage for a nuclear show down and we would undermine the Russian intrusion into the Middle East.

540 FAS, *Mediterranean Eskadra*,

http://www.fas.org/nuke/guide/russia/agency/mf-med.htm
541 Soviet Official's comments on Soviet Policy on the Middle Eastern War. Document addressed "To White House Situation Room" dated June 67, copy released from LBJ Library.

542 The Pravda link is not active, however, note: http://www.ussliberty.com/pravdura.htm. Try this link: http://pravda.ru/main/2002/09/13/47015.html.

543 For example, in http://www.nsa.gov/liberty/51665/3106024.pdf two entire sections are excised before section 3 begins "Comment: The Nikolaj Podvojskij was in the area of the USS Liberty immediately after the attack..." (spelling as in original documents).

544 The 6-Day War: *A Soviet Initiative*, http://www.3maj.hr/en/products/delivered.pdf. Gideon Remez and Isabella Ginor, Phd., 10/12/2008, Global Politician. This is an abstract follow-up to their book and criticisms over whether Russian started the war with the intent to eliminate Israel's nuclear program.

545 *Moscow's Still Holding*, Webster Stone, The New York Times online magazine, 9/18/1988, http://www.nytimes.com/1988/09/18/magazine/moscow-s-still-holding.html?pagewanted=all&src=pm

594

546 White House, *Memorandum of Conversations*. Subject: The Hot Line Exchanges. Participants: Ambassador Llewellyn E. Thompson, Mr. Nathaniel Davis, November 4, 1968. Source is the LBJ Library.

http://history.state.gov/historicaldocuments/frus1964-68v19/d245
547 Refer to the White House, President Lyndon Johnson Daily Diary for June 8, 1967, available at the LBJ Library.

548 U.S. State Department Office of the Historian, *Document 244, Memorandum for the Record. Subject: Hot Line Meeting June 10th 1967*,

http://history.state.gov/historicaldocuments/frus1964-68v19/d244
549 Sergey Stefanov PRAVDA.Ru Translated by Maria Gousseva Read the original in Russian: The English version is on the web: http://pravda.ru/main/2002/09/13/47015.html.

550 Wikipedia, *Antikythera*, http://en.wikipedia.org/wiki/Antikythera
551 Middle East Review of International Affairs, Vol. 4, No. 4 (December 2000).

552 Middle East Review of International Affairs, Vol. 7, No. 3 (September 2003).

553 Isabella Ginor and Gideon Remez, *Foxbats over Dimona: The Soviets' Nuclear Gamble in the Six-day War*, Yale University Press, 2007.

554 Ginor and Remez, page 2.

555 Ginor, Remez Abstract, section on Archival Documents.

556 *Forty years ago, the Soviet Union wanted to bomb Israel*, 5/20/2007, Victor Baranets, http://www.kp.ru/daily/23904.5/67480 Needs translation from Russian to English.

557 Ginor and Remez, page 10.

558 Ginor/Remez Abstract: See Note: [39] Soviet Policy and the 1967 Arab-Israeli War (Reference Title: CAESAR XXXVIII), March 16, 1970, p. 20,

http://www.foia.cia.gov/docs/DOC_0001408643/0001408643_0028.gif The quotes follow two still-sanitized paragraphs, which judging by their context appear to elaborate how "on June 9 and 10... the Soviets began to threaten some (undefined) action if Israel did not stop" its advance into Syria. Why this should be censored, while Kosygin's Hot Line message containing this threat has long since been released, is unclear--perhaps indicating that a more concrete threat was conveyed through other channels.

559 Hounam, pages 7 to 13. See last paragraph of book. Why were planes placed on alert that day. See his conclusion. Alert was between 2 and 4 AM California time.

560 Ginor and Remez, page 16, 17.

561 Ginor and Remez, page 18.

562 *Egypt rejects US Nuclear Umbrella*, Fareed Mahdy, 8/20/2009, http://original.antiwar.com/fareed-mahdy/2009/08/20/egypt-rejects-us-nuclear-umbrella/

563 *Nasser Nationalizes Suez Canal 1956*, Jewish Virtual Library, http://www.jewishvirtuallibrary.org/jsource/Peace/nasser1.html

564 Ginor and Remez, pages 20-21.

565 Cohen, *Israel And The Bomb*.

566 Michael Oren, *Six Days of War*.

567 Russia concerned about missiles and nukes at its borders. German-Israeli discussions. As example of trade off effect, for pulling weapons from Cuba, US pulled from Turkey. Page 33, citing Seymour Hersh, Israel did intend to buffer nuclear threat from Russian, more so that Egyptians. Page 33, 1955 in conjunction with Czech arms deal, Russia agreed to provide Egypt with a small experimental nuclear reactor. US made similar deal with Israel. Note page 31, reference to Dimona and research reactor at Nahal Sorek.

568 Ginor, Remez, page 31, chapter notes 14, 15, 16 and 17.

569 Ginor and Remez Page 36, Russian document relates Israel's desire to build own bomb. This person was Isser Harel, founder of Israeli intelligence. Page 40, Harel, Sneh, Eshkol issue and release of info by

596

Harel. Did Eshkol make an overture toward Russian? Harel's book appeared in 1987, the year after Mordechi Vanunu revealed the Dimona operations to the world (see Hounam). Page 41, 42, Ben-Gurion dismissed Harel.

570 6-Day War: A Soviet Initiative.

http://www.globalpolitician.com/25223-ussr-soviet-union-israel-six-day-war

571 Ginor and Remez, page 54.

572 Ginor and Remez, page 55.

573 Ginor and Remez, page 30.

574 Hersh, *The Sampson Option.*

575 Ginor and Remez, Page 58, 2/23/66, Syria coup in which Baath party took control...General Hafez al-Assad became defense minister.

576 Ginor and Remez, page 68.

577 Ginor and Remez, page 56-57.

578 *A Tale of Two Fleets*: http://www.dtic.mil/cgi-bin/GetTRDoc?Location=U2&doc=GetTRDoc.pdf&AD=ADA422490

579 Ginor and Remez, pages 68, 69.

580 Ginor Remez, Page 72, 73.

581 Ginor and Remez, Israel tested a nuclear device in February 1967, page 74. Refer to footnote 30 for chapter 8, a reference to Cohen.. See quote from Nasser on bottom of page 75.

582 Ginor and Remez, page 78, Also, know on page 79 more about demand that Sixth Fleet be moved.

583 Alexander Rozin, his e-mail is: alerozin@yandex.ru. Website is:

http://alerozin.narod.ru/1967.htm

584 Ginor and Remez, page 87.

585 Ibid., page 141, see chapter notes 8 and 9.

586 Ginor and Remez, page 80, Sub K-125. , 82 , 83.

597

587 *Montreux Convention,*

http://en.wikipedia.org/wiki/Montreux_Convention_Regarding_the_ Regime_of_the_Turkish_Straits

588 Ginor and Remez, page 82.

589 Ibid.

590 The Soviet Navy information, Alexander Rozin e-mail, alerozin@yandex.ru. Website: http://alerozin.narod.ru/1967.htm

591 Ginor and Remez, Note comments on page 85.

592 Ginor and Remez, Page 86, 92.

593 Six-Day War, http://www.zionism-israel.com/dic/6daywar.htm

594 Ginor/Remez Abstract, Note: [38] "R," "Tu-16s to Haifa!" February 5, 2007,

http://www.avia.ru/cgi/discshow.cgi?id=6179038139283193386491068805255&page=9 ; "Vesny," "Forty years have gone by," part I, June 5, 2007 http://www.botinok.co.il/node/31505, part II, June 6, 2007, and additional posting on June 10, 2007,

http://www.botinok.co.il/node/31548. This Jewish writer, now in Israel, was in 1967 an air force lieutenant in a technical role in Reshetnikov's corps.

595 Ginor and Remez, page 96, Referring to CIA Memo, Page 96. See page 103.Page 104.

596 Ginor and Remez, page 107.

597 Ginor and Remez, Foxbat, page 107, 108.

598 Ginor and Remez, page 112.

599 Ginor and Remez, page 124-125. Map insert.

600 Ginor and Remez, pages 130, 131. See also Michael Oren, Six Days of War, page 99.

601 June 5, 1967 In an unusual incident an Israeli MIM-23A shot down a damaged Israeli Dassault MD.450 Ouragan that was in danger of crashing into the Negev Nuclear Research Center near Dimona, the first combat firing

of the Hawk, the first combat kill attributed to the Hawk system [3].

http://en.wikipedia.org/wiki/MIM-23_Hawk
602 Ginor and Remez, pages 134, 135.

603 Ginor and Remez, pages 138,139, Chapter endnotes 2 and 3.

604 Ginor and Remez, page 140.

605 Ginor and Remez, page 145.

606 *Prozorlivyy*, Russian-ship.info, http://russian-ships.info/eng/warships/project_56m.htm
607 NATO Code Names, http://www.ais.org/~schnars/aero/nato-shp.htm
608 Ginor and Remez, pages 170, 174, 175.

609 Ginor and Remez, pages 176, 178.

610 Ginor and Remez, page 178, Note: Another attack without ID. This could have been Zakharov's sub off Haifa near Atlit.

611 Ginor and Remez, page 180.

612 Ginor and Remez, page 182, and page 190.

613 Ginor and Remez, page 190.

614 Wikipedia, *Nastoychivy, DD 610*,

http://en.wikipedia.org/wiki/File:RFS_NASTOYCHIVY.JPG
615 Ginor and Remez, Page 202 and 203.

616 Ginor and Remez, page 204.

617 Ginor and Remez, page 204-205.

618 Ostrovsky, Victor, The *Other Side of Deception: A Rogue Agent Exposes the Mossad's Secret Agenda*, Harper Collins, 1994, page 27, footnote No. 7.

619 The readers can Google the word *Sayanim*.

620 VT, Veterans Today,

http://www.veteranstoday.com/2011/12/26/sayanim-israeli-operatives-in-the-u-s-2/

621 Tenet, George, *At the Center of Storm: My Years at the CIA*, Harper Collins Publishers, 2007, pages 66-72.

622 Perry, Mark, *False Flag*, Foreign Policy.com, January 13, 2012:

http://www.foreignpolicy.com/articles/2012/01/13/false_flag

623 Haaretz.com, *Mossad Agents Posing as CIA Spies*,

http://www.haaretz.com/news/diplomacy-defense/israeli-official-report-of-mossad-agents-posing-as-cia-spies-absolute-nonsense-1.407285

624 Ostrovsky, *The Other Side of Deception*, page 32.

625 Cristol, A. Jay, *The Liberty Incident: The 1967 Israeli Attack on the U.S. Navy Spy Ship*, Brassey's, Inc., 2002.

626 In September 1998, the University of Miami announced the creation of the Sue and Leonard Miller Center for Contemporary Judaic Studies and appointed Dr. Haim Shaked as its Founding Director. Dr. Shaked has also served, since 1986, as the Director of the Middle East Studies Institute and is the incumbent of the Dr. M. Lee Pearce Chair in Middle East Peace Studies. Since 1995, Dr. Shaked has been involved in the creation of the first private (not-for-profit) university in Israel: The Interdisciplinary Center, Herzliyya.

http://www6.miami.edu/miller-center/pages/faculty.html

627 Cristol, page xix.

628 Hounam, page 162.

629 Hounam, page 223.

630 For a literal translation see: http://en.wikipedia.org/wiki/Mossad

631 Thomas, Gordon, *Gideon's Spies: The Secret History of the Mossad*, Thomas Dunne Books, 1991, pages 361-362.

632 Ostrovsky ,*The Other Side of Deception*, page 261-264.

633 IDF History Report.

634 Tourney, pages 81 – 82.

635 Cristol, pages 92–93. Citing Ennes, Assault on the Liberty, page 206, footnote 5.

636 Presidential Positions,

http://www.thelibertyincident.com/presidents.html.

637 Injured Crew List,

http://www.thelibertyincident.com/docs/InjuredPersonnel.pdf

638 Access to Medical Records, http://www.archives.gov/st-
louis/military-personnel/public/active-duty-medical-records.html

639 Cristol, page 97.

640 Jerusalem Post, *Judge Cristol tells Post how he set record straight on USS Liberty*, Joel Lyden, July 10, 2003,

http://www.mefacts.com/cached.asp?x_id=10058

641 Witnessed by Phillip Tourney who was present at the forum. See his book at page 168.

642 Captain Ward Boston Declaration,

http://www.ussliberty.org/bostondeclaration.pdf

643 Cristol comments on Boston,

http://www.thelibertyincident.com/boston-comments.html

644 Document 204, Editorial Note,

http://history.state.gov/historicaldocuments/frus1964-68v19/d204

645 Cristol, page 141.

646 Helms, page 300-301.

647 Helms, page 301.

648 Dayan, page 347.

649 Van Creveld, e-book location,3822-28.

650 Dayan, page 380.

651 Cristol, pages 143 – 144.

652 Michael Oren, Six Days of War.

653 IDF History Report: However, before midnight 7-8 June, the Minister of Defense informed the Chief of Staff that action on the Syrian Front would be permitted up to the international boundary only.85 The Chief of Staff

opposed a limited operation, which would not be worthwhile and might be interpreted as a failure.86 The GOC Northern Command was of the same opinion. However, despite the Defense Minister's instructions, battle procedure continued in the Northern Command in the hope that perhaps after all the restrictions might be lifted.

654 Van Creveld, page 192.

655 IDF History Departments Working at Cross Purposes, http://www.jpost.com/Defense/Article.aspx?id=220972. By YAAKOV KATZ,05/17/2011 16:25.

656 The author of the cited e-mail provides enough identifying information to reference his identity and others referred to therein. The actual code-name of the person providing the radar-gap information is being withheld because it adds nothing to this report.

657 Robert the Bruce, http://www.scottishweb.net/articles/6/1/Robert-the-Bruce---King-of-Scotland/Page1.html

658 Liberty News Letter, Volume 41, September 2011.

659 Crewdson, John, *New revelations in attack on American spy ship*, Chicagotribune.com, October 2, 2007.

660 Letter was signed by Jane G. Dalton, Captain, JAGC, U.S. Navy. Further, the letter notes that a copy of the Court of Inquiry's record of proceedings is available to the public and can be obtained from the Office of the Judge Advocate General (Code 15), 1322 Patterson Ave., SE, Suite 3000, Washington Naval Yard, DC 20374-5066. Requester is required to pay the reproduction costs.

661 Refer to Chapter 12 of Cristol's book, America Investigates.

662 Smith, Jeffrey R., Washington Post Staff Writer, *War Crimes Act Changes Would Reduce Threat Of Prosecution*, Wednesday, August 9, 2006; A01.

663 Neff, Donald, *U.S. Vetoes of U.N. Resolutions on behalf of Israel, If Americans Knew*, http://www.ifamericansknew.org/us_ints/p-neff-veto.html˙

664 For a discussion of International War Crimes see:

http://www.nesl.edu/userfiles/file/wcmemos/hendersn.htm˙

665 American Society of International Law, http://www.asil.org/.

666 Presidential Immunity,

http://www.law.cornell.edu/supct/html/historics/USSC_CR_0457_0731_ZO.html. Immunity of President of US.

667 War Power – the Constitution,

http://www.americanforeignrelations.com/A-D/The-Constitution-The-war-power.html˙

668 *The Imperial Presidency* by Arthur M. Schlesinger, Jr. was written in 1973.

669 Wikipedia, http://en.wikipedia.org/wiki/War_Powers_Resolution: The War Powers Resolution of 1973 (50 U.S.C. 1541-1548)[1] is a federal law intended to check the power of the President in committing the United States to an armed conflict without the consent of Congress. The resolution was adopted in the form of a United States Congress joint resolution; this provides that the President can send U.S. armed forces into action abroad only by authorization of Congress or in case of "a national emergency created by attack upon the United States, its territories or possessions, or its armed forces."

The War Powers Resolution requires the President to notify Congress within 48 hours of committing armed forces to military action and forbids armed forces from remaining for more than 60 days, with a further 30 day withdrawal period, without an authorization of the use of military force or a declaration of war. The resolution was passed by two-thirds of Congress, overriding a presidential veto.

603

The War Powers Resolution was disregarded by President Clinton in 1999, during the bombing campaign in Kosovo, and again by President Obama in 2011, when he did not seek congressional approval for attack on Libya, arguing that the Resolution did not apply to that action.[2] Some presidents have declared their belief that the act is unconstitutional. [3][4]

670 Van Creveld, Sword and Olive.

671 Colonel Ram Ron report to the Israeli Chief of Staff dated 6/16/67.

672 LVA War Crime Complaint, page 11.

673 These charges of the indictment can be found in the 1981 NSA History, Attack on A Sigint Collector, the U.S.S. Liberty, page. 38-40.

674 See page 2 of the report.

675 Command Responsibility, http://www.crimesofwar.org/a-z-guide/command-responsibility/

676 Pointer Oliphant, and Tourney.

677 http://www.usslibertyinquiry.com. Note: You will be redirected to: http://www.gtr5.com/, the USS Liberty Memorial site. The original Liberty website, http://www.ussliberty.org will also route you to the "gtr5" memorial site. Over the past several years formatting for these Liberty sites have been changed, however, much of the original content remains.

678 CRS Report for Congress, In Re Terrorist Attacks on September 11, 2001, Dismissals of Claims Against Saudi Defendants Under the Foreign Sovereign Immunities Act (FSIA), October 29, 2008, Anna C. Henning Legislative Attorney American Law Division.

679 CRS Report for Congress, October 29, 2008,

http://fpc.state.gov/documents/organization/112480.pdf

680 Hounam, page 272.

681 McPhearson Oral History, mcpher03.pdf. BIOGRAPHIC INFORMATION: HARRY MCPHERSON

604

Lawyer; b. Tyler, Tex., Aug. 22, 1929; B.A., U. South, 1949; D.C.I. (hon), 1965; student Columbia, 1949-50; LL.B., U. Tex., 1956; admitted to Texas bar, 1955; asst. gen. counsel Democratic policy com., U.S. Senate, 1956-59; asso. counsel, 1959-61; gen. counsel, 1961-63; dep. under sec. internal. affairs Dept. Army, 1963-64; asst. sec. state ednl. and cultural affairs, 1964-65; spl. asst. and counsel to Pres. Johnson, 1965-66; spl. counsel to Pres. Johnson, 1966-69; private practice law, Washington, 1969-

682 Jacobsen, Walter L., Lt. Commander, *A Juridical Examination of the Israeli Attack on the USS Liberty*, Naval Law Review, Vol. 36, Winter 1986.

683 Ibid, pages 93 to 97.

684 Ibid, 108.

685 Preface to 911 Commission Report.

686 Bamford, James, A Pretext For War: 9/11, Iraq, and the Abuse of America's Intelligence Agencies, Doubleday, 2004. Bamford is a literary expert on the NSA and signals intelligence gathering. He was formerly the investigative reporter for ABC's World News Tonight with Peter Jennings, and the author to two books dealing with intelligence agencies, "Body of Secrets" and the "Puzzle Palace".

687

688 *New counterterrorism guidelines permit data on U.S. citizens to be held longer*, Washington Post World, By Sari Horwitz and Ellen Nakashima, Published: March 22, http://www.washingtonpost.com/world/national-security/new-counterterrorism-guidelines-would-permit-data-on-us-citizens-to-be-held-longer/2012/03/21/gIQAFLm7TS_story.html?wprss

689 *NSA Chief Seeks Bigger Cybersecurity Role*, Siobhan Gorman, Wall Street Journal, February 27, 2012, page A5.

690 *National Security Court? We Already Have One*, by Bill West, IPT News, January 26, 2009,

605

http://www.investigativeproject.org/984/national-security-court-we-already-have-one

691 http://www.msnbc.msn.com/id/6986647/.

692 CIA memo to White House Situation Room approved for released August of 2000 with redactions. The memo was dated June 1967 with the day's date redacted. The Soviet sources was a "medium level soviet official". It is also marked "Copy LBJ Library" which is its source.

693 James Bamford, *The Puzzle Palace*, page 218.

694 Cold War Museum website:

http://www.coldwar.org/museum/PressReleases/PressReleaseVintHil l.asp

695 Cold War Veterans, http://www.coldwarveterans.com

696 RB-29, http://www.rb-29.net/html/84.rb-29.1727/84.02.01part2.htm

697 Defense Prisoner of War/Missing Personnel Office,

http://www.dtic.mil/dpmo/

698 http://www.rb-29.net/HTML/06CWMConn/LinksPgs/02.Hist91stSRS.htm

699 *Fighting her battle decades after a war*, The Spokesman Review, Sunday, October 2, 20011:

http://m.spokesman.com/stories/2011/oct/02/fighting-her-battle-decades-after-a-war/

700 Wikipedia, 91st Network Warfare Squadron,

http://en.wikipedia.org/wiki/91st_Network_Warfare_Squadron

701 The Abbreviated Life of the Ill-fated RB-29 #44-61727, "So Tired", Part 1 http://www.rb-29.net/html/84.rb-29.1727/84.01.01part1.htm.

702 Sakhalin or Saghalien, is a large island in the North Pacific, lying between 45°50' and 54°24' N. It is part of Russia, and is Russia's largest island.

606

703 The Abbreviated Life of the Ill-fated RB-29 #44-61727, "So Tired", Part 2

http://www.rb-29.net/html/84.rb-29.1727/84.02.01part2.htm

704 Over flight surveillance of the Soviet Union by the first U-2 flights would show dramatically that the Soviets were not nearly advanced in conventional arms as the Pentagon had assumed. There was no "bomber gap" or "missile gap". Hersh, "The Samson Option", page 50.

705 Bamford, *The Puzzle Palace*, page 243. In July 1955, just eighteen months after the contract with Lockheed was signed, the "Black Lady" became operational and a fleet of twenty-two was deployed at a cost of $3 million below the original cost estimate.

706 Hersh, page 47.

707 *Operation Overflight: A Memoir of the U-2 Incident*, Francis Gary Powers with Curt Gentry, Brassey's Inc, 2004, page ix.

708 Ibid.

709 "Blow-back" involves a catastrophic failure in intelligence follow through and just plain failure of the program. An example would be the CIA failure to follow-up after the Russian defeat in Afghanistan that allowed the Taliban to come into power.

710 Ibid, page 323.

711 Ibid, page 324: Francis Gary Powers died on August 1, 1977, while conducting a traffic report over Los Angles for KNBC News Channel 4, when his helicopter crashed killing him and his cameraman George Spears.

712 Bamford, *The Puzzle Palace*, page 189.

713 Nelson, Phillip F. (2011-10-20). LBJ: The Mastermind of The JFK Assassination (Kindle Locations 8208-8210). Skyhorse Publishing. Kindle Edition.

714 Hersh, pages 52 and 53. The sensitive of reporting on Israeli activity is also noted by Hersh. No paper work was involved and no notes taken. "Ike didn't want any notes—period," recalled Lundahl.

715 Hersh, page 54.

716 Ibid.

717 Bamford, *The Puzzle Palace*, page 241.

718 Bamford, *A Pretext For War*.

719 Bamford, *The Puzzle Palace*, page 624: Acronyms and Abbreviations. Refer to Senate Bill S.2525, National Intelligence Reorganization and Reform Act of 1978.

720 The following is a brief excerpt from a technical abstract on SIGINT by an outfit called Alpha Alpha-ES GmbH, taken from their Internet site: Adequate equipment can yield easy detection of radar positions within broadcast area. Also, direction finding (DF) antennas and corresponding receivers can easily determine the broadcasting direction of stations in the HF, VHF and UHF frequency bands, as location is established through the intersection of DF's from at least two DF stations. In summary, Signal Intelligence provides useful information without high risk for personnel. In more limited capacity, Signal Intelligence indicates the intentions of radio broadcasters and radar installations, either within the country or at remote locations.

721 Zelikow Memo Release,

http://www.gwu.edu/~nsarchiv/news/20120403/
722 Bamford, *The Puzzle Palace*, page 274.

723 Bamford, *The Puzzle Palace*, page 273.

724 LBJ's Silver Star: The Mission that Never was, By Barrett Tillman and Henry Sakaida,http://www.b-26mhs.org/archives/manuscripts/lbj_fake_silverstar.html.

725 War Crimes Complaint, page 7.

726 Ennes, page 194.

Bibliography

- Arbel, David and Ran Edelist, *Western Intelligence and the Collapse of the Soviet Union, 1980-1990: Ten Years That Did Not Shake the World*. Publisher: Frank Cass. Place of Publication: London. Publication Year: 2003.
- Bamford, James, *The Puzzle Palace: Inside the National Security Agency*, Penguin Books, 1983.
- Bamford, James, *Body of Secrets: Anatomy of the Ultra-Secret National Security Agency*, Doubleday, 2001.
- Bamford, James, *The Shadow Factory: The Ultra-Secret NSA from 9/11 to the Eavesdropping on America*, Double Day, 2008, E-Book Edition.
- Ben-Gurion, David, *Memoirs*, The World Publishing Company, 1970.
- Bransten, Thomas R., *Memoirs: David Ben-Gurion*, Compiled by Thomas R. Bransten, The World Publishing Company, 1970.
- Bregman, Ahron, *A History of Israel*, Palgrave Macmillan, 2002.
- Bugliosi, Vincent, *The Prosecution of George W. Bush For Murder*, Vanguard Press, 2008, E-Book Edition.
- Cockburn, Andrew and Leslie, *Dangerous Liaison The Inside Story of the US-Israeli Covert Relationship*, Harper Collins, 1991.

- Cohen, Avner, *Israel and the Bomb*, Columbia University Press, 1998.
- Chomsky, Noam, *Middle East Illusions*, Rowman &Littlefield Publishers, 2003.
- Copeland, Miles, *Without Cloak or Dagger: The truth about the new espionage*, Miles Simon and Schuster, New York, 1974.
- Cristol, A. Jay, *The Liberty Incident: the 1967 Israeli Attack on the U.S. Navy Spy Ship*, Brassey's Inc., 2002.
- Dallek, Robert, *Lyndon B. Johnson: Portrait of a President*, Oxford University Press, New York, 2004.
- Dayan, Moshe, *Moshe Dayan: Story of My Life*, Morrow, 1976.
- Deacon, Richard, *The Israeli Secret Service*, self published, no date shown, however appears after 1976.
- De la Vega, Elizabeth, *U.S. v. Bush*, Seven Stories Press, 2006.
- Ennes, James M. Jr., *Assault on the Liberty: The True Story of the Israeli Attack on an American Intelligence Ship*, Raintree Press, 1979.
- Eveland, Wilbur Crane, *Ropes of Sand: America's Failure in the Middle East*, W-W-W-Norton & Company, 1980.
- Findley, Paul, *They Dare to Speak Out: People and Institutions Confront Israel's Lobby*, Lawrence Hill Books, 2003.

611

- Friedman, Thomas L., *From Beirut to Jerusalem*, Anchor Books, Doubleday, 1989.
- Ginor, Isabella and Remez, Gideon, *Foxbats Over Dimona: The Soviet's Nuclear Gamble in the Six-Day War*, Yale University Press, 2007.
- Goldschmidt, Arthur Jr., *A Concise History of the Middle East*, 7th Ed., Westview Press, 2002.
- Green, Stephen, *Taking Sides: America's Secret Relations with a Militant Israel*, Amana Books, 1988.
- Halevy, Efraim, *Man in the Shadows: Inside the Middle East Crisis with a Man Who Lead the Mossad*, St. Martin's Press, 2006.
- Helms, Richard with William Hood, *A Look over My Shoulder: A Life in the Central Intelligence Agency*, Ballantine Books, 2003.
- Hersh, Seymour M., *The Sampson Option: Israel's Nuclear Arsenal and American Foreign Policy*, Random House, 1991.
- Herzog, Chaim, *The Arab-Israeli Wars: War and Peace in the Middle East from the War of Independence through Lebanon*, Vintage Books, 1982.
- Hounam, Peter, *The Woman from Mossad: The Story of Mordechi Vanunu & The Israeli Nuclear Program*, Frog, Ltd., 1999.
- Hounam, Peter, *Operation Cyanide: Why the Bombing of the USS Liberty Nearly Caused World War III*, Vision, 2003.

- Howe, Russell Warren, *Weapons: The International Game of Arms Money and Diplomacy*, Doubleday & Company, Inc., 1980.
- Jacobsen, Walter L., Lt. Commander, *A Juridical Examination of the Israeli Attack on the USS Liberty*, Naval Law Review, Vol. 36, Winter 1986.
- Janney, Peter (2012-04-02). Mary's Mosaic: The CIA Conspiracy to Murder John F. Kennedy, Mary Pinchot Meyer, and Their Vision for World Peace. Skyhorse Publishing. Kindle Edition.
- Kyle, Keith, *Suez: Britain's End of Empire in the Middle East*, I. B. Tauris Publishers, London and New York, 1991.
- Loftus, John and Mark Aarons, *The Secret War Against the Jews: How Western Espionage Betrayed the Jewish People*, St. Martin's Griffin, 1994.
- Mangold, Tom, *Cold Warrior James Jesus Angleton: The CIA's Master Spy Hunter*, Simon & Schuster, 1991.
- McGarvey, Patrick J., *C.I.A. The Myth and the Madness*, Penguin Books, 1972.
- Nelson, Phillip F. (2011-10-20). *LBJ: The Mastermind of The JFK Assassination*. Skyhorse Publishing. Kindle Edition.
- Oren, Michael B., *Six Days of War: June 1967 and the Making of the Modern Middle East*, Ballantine Books, 2002, 2003.

- Ostrovsky, Victor, Hoy, Claire, *By Way of Deception: Making of a MOSSAD Officer*, Wilshire Press, 1990.
- Ostrovsky, Victor, *Other Side of Deception: A Rogue Agent Exposes the Mossad's Secret Agenda*, Harper Collins, 1994.
- Parker, Richard, *The Six-Day War: A Retrospective*. Contributors: Richard B. Parker – editor. Publisher: University Press of Florida. Place of Publication: Gainesville, FL. Publication Year, 1996.
- Pearson, Anthony, *Conspiracy of Silence: The Attack on the U.S.S. Liberty*, Quartet Books, London, 1978.
- Perlmutter, Amos, *Military & Politics In Israel: Nation-Building and Role Expansion*, Frederick A. Praeger, 1969.
- Piper, Michael Collins, *Final Judgment*, American Free Press, 6th Edition, 2004.
- Powers, Francis Gary, and Gentry, Curt, *Operation Overflight: A Memoir of the U-2 Incident*, Brassey's Inc., 2004.
- Rabin, Yitzhak, *Yitzhak Rabin: The Rabin Memoirs*, University of California Press, First Paper Back Edition, 1996.
- Ranelagh, John, *The Agency: The Rise and Decline of the CIA from Wild Bill Donovan to William Casey*, Simon and Schuster, 1986.

- Raviv, Dan, and Melman, Yossi, *Every Spy A Prince: The Complete History of Israel's Intelligence Community*, Houghton Mifflin Company, Boston, 1990.
- Raviv, Dan, and Melman, Yossi, *Friends in Deed: Inside the U.S. – Israel Alliance*, Hyperion, 1994.
- Sasgen, Peter, *Stalking the Red Bear: The True Story of a U.S. Gold War Submarine's Covert Operations Against the Soviet Union*, St. Martin's Press, 2009, E-Book Edition.
- Segev, Tom, *One Palestine Complete: Jews and Arabs Under The British Mandate*, Henry Holt and Company, 2000.
- Scott, James, *Attack on the Liberty: The Untold Story of Israel's Deadly 1967 Assault on a U.S. Spy Ship*, Simon & Schuster, 2009, E-Book Edition. E-Book Edition.
- Tenet, George, with Harlow, Bill, *At the Center of the Storm: My years at the CIA*, Harper Collins Publishers, 2007.
- Thomas, Gordon, *Gideon's Spies: The Secret History of the Mossad*, Thomas Dunne Books, St. Martin's Griffin, 1999.
- Thomas, Gordon, *Seeds of Fire: China and the story behind the attack on America*, Dandelion Books Publication, Arizona, 2001.
- Thomas, Gordon, *Secret Wars: One Hundred Years of British Intelligence Inside MI5 and MI-6*, Thomas Dunn Books, 2009.

- Tourney, Phillip F. and Glenn, Mark, *What I Saw That Day: Israel's June 8th, 1967 Holocaust of US Servicemen Aboard the USS Liberty and its Aftermath*, Liberty Publications, Idaho, Copyright not stated, believed to be 2011.
- Van Creveld, Martin, *The Sword and the Olive: A Critical History of the Israeli Defense Force*, Public Affairs member Perseus Books, 1998, 2002. E-Book Edition.
- Video: *Attack on the Liberty*, Discovery Channel, Thames Television, 1987
- Video: History Undercover, Cover Up: Attack on the USS *Liberty*, 8-9-2001.
- Video: Loss of the Liberty, Howard Films.
- Video: USS *Liberty: Dead in the Water*, BBC London, two parts. 6/2002; DVD: A Source Films Production, USS Liberty Friends, Satellite Beach, FL 32937.

About the Author

Robert J. Allen has an under-graduate degree with a major in Political Science, and a Juris Doctorate of Laws degree. He was a member of the Washington State Bar Association for thirty years and is now retired. His present focus is in the area of electronic publishing. He is also a retired Police Captain formerly in charge of the department's investigative division at the time of retirement. He joined the U.S. Marine Corps as an enlistee out of high school.

About the Cover

The cover depicts the USS *Liberty* the day after the Israeli attack on the ship. Hovering over the bow is a helicopter participating in the removal of the dead and injured as well has transporting personnel to assist with the crew's damage control efforts. In the background is either the USS *Davis* or USS *Massey*, destroyers that were the first United States military units to arrive in aid of the ship and crew.

INDEX

620

621

623

624

625

626

629

633